Representations on the Margins of Europe

Eigene und fremde Welten

Representations of Patterns of Social Order

The series »Eigene und fremde Welten« is edited by Jörg Baberowski, Vincent Houben, Hartmut Kaelble and Jürgen Schriewer, in connection with the Collaborative Research Center no. 640 (SFB 640) »Changing Representations of Patterns of Social Order. Cross-Cultural and Cross-Temporal Comparisons« based at Humboldt University, Berlin (Germany).

Volume 3

Tsypylma Darieva is a postdoctoral research fellow at Humboldt University, Berlin. Her research focuses on the anthropology of migration, memory and postsocialism. *Wolfgang Kaschuba* is Professor of European Ethnology and Director of the Institute for European Ethnology at Humboldt University, Berlin.

Tsypylma Darieva, Wolfgang Kaschuba (eds.)

Representations on the Margins of Europe

Politics and Identities in the Baltic and
South Caucasian States

Campus Verlag
Frankfurt/New York

Distribution throughout the world except Germany, Austria and Switzerland by

The University of Chicago Press
1427 East 60th Street
Chicago, IL 60637

A Note on the Cover Image:
Archi Galentz was born in 1971 in Moscow to a family of Armenian artists. He studied at the University of the Arts (Universität der Künste) in Berlin, Germany, where he still lives. His painting »The Orange Rider« (»Der Orangene Reiter«), 2003, is a response to the work »The New Hero« by Serbian artist Marina Abramovich and a powerful image of the crossroads at which postsocialist countries stand in their processes of transformation.

Galentz's work can be described as a present-day reaction to the imaginary boundaries of the rapprochement between East and West. Unlike the white flag depicted by »The New Hero«, the wind blowing the red-orange flag in »The Orange Rider« represents the new ideological struggles and the permeability of symbolic boundaries in a new Europe.

Bibliographic Information published by the Deutsche Nationalbibliothek.
Die Deutsche Nationalbibliothek lists this publication in the Deutsche Nationalbibliografie; detailed bibliographic data are available in the Internet at http://dnb.d-nb.de.
ISBN 978-3-593-38241-8

For further information:
www.campus.de
www.press.uchicago.edu

Contents

Narratives

Rites

Acknowledgements

The volume grew out of a workshop entitled »Identity Politics in Armenia: Doing Research in Ethnological and Historical Perspectives« held in April 2005 in Yerevan. The essays by Levon Abrahamian, Hrach Bayadyan, Tsypylma Darieva, Wolfgang Kaschuba, Maike Lehmann, Harutyun Marutyan, Artur Mrktychian and Ashot Voskanian were given there as papers. Out of this, we widened the geographical span of our perspective by including additional scholars who work in different countries in the region, and thus the structure of this volume differs from that of the workshop. This volume aims to offer a variety of local responses to the growing European rhetoric in the Baltic and South Caucasian societies. A slight majority of the authors come from the field of anthropology and this gives us an opportunity to approach the task ethnographically. Our aim is to combine a deeper critical analysis of transformation processes in these regions with an understanding of the context from an insider perspective. Moreover, a significant number of the contributors have personally experienced the Soviet past and post-Soviet reality in one or another way and in pursuing their careers have crossed the real and symbolic boundaries between East and West.

Two English spelling rules – British and the US American – are adopted by the authors in this volume. The transliteration of Russian and local words follows generally accepted Western spellings such as Karabakh, rather than Gharabagh. Special signs from the local languages in the Baltic and the South Caucasian States are recognized respectively.

We are grateful to all contributors for their cooperation and especially to those whose papers have been added. Jörg Baberowski, Olga Brednikova, Karsten Brüggemann, Dace Dzenoska, David Feest, Florian Mühlfried, Bahodir Sidikov and Asta Vonderau have written chapters for this collection that significantly enhance its value. We are grateful to Ab Imperio for the permission to translate the essay by Olga Brednikova in an updated form. All essays have been significantly expanded and refocused for this collection. The editors are deeply grateful to the sponsors (German Research Society) and to the Brusov University for the opportunity to hold the workshop in Yerevan, and especially to the rector Suren Zolyan. Special thanks to Maike Lehmann for her efficient support at different stages of this project and to Gertrud Hüwelmeier and Ekaterina Gvozdeva for their critical reviews of earlier drafts of this book. Our thanks go to Karsten Schoellner, Anja Gottschalk, Helena Kühlmann, Victoria Bishop Kendzi and Deborah Johnson for English editing, to Martina Klausner, Alexander Formosov and Dmitri Mikhalitzyn, student assistants at the Humboldt University, for their generous help in preparing the final typescript, in particular, to Felix Herrmann for his patience and huge support in the formatting and indexing of the text. As editors, at Campus Verlag we also want to thank Paul Knowlton for proof reading and Petra Zimlich, our editing officer for her careful coordination.

Introduction: Politics and Identities on the »Margins« of New Europe

Tsypylma Darieva and Wolfgang Kaschuba

One of the central features of the current transformation on the Eurasian continent after socialism relates to the notion of »experiencing Europe«[1]. The tectonic shifts in West European boundaries and the geographic fragmentation have raised many questions about the ways of social and cultural remaking of collective identities and belonging to »remote« regions of the »New Europe«. Since the Baltic nations joined the European Union, debates about reorganizing post-Soviet republics have grown increasingly heated. »Representations on the Margins of Europe« presents case studies in the post socialist South Caucasian and Baltic states, those regions which since 2004 have joined, or are expected to join, the European Union. The fact is that the previous relative stability of identities, social categories, and national narratives of this region that had served well until the recent past, have become problematic as representations for the present and future. The euphoria of national liberation movements in the Baltic States and South Caucasian republics at the end of the 80s have 15 years later been replaced by the desire of »to-be-a-part-of-Europe«. Though not exhaustive, the range of contributions collected here cover three South Caucasian and three Baltic countries, each with their different modes of symbolic redefinition of geographical and political belonging, cultural division and unity. Focusing mostly on the contemporary post-Soviet period, the chapters demonstrate the specifics of the interplay between local representations of national identities and the larger political affiliation to New Europe. The question is: how do the citizens in the Baltic and South Caucasian states cope with EU expansion and the feeling of existing simultaneously »inside« and »outside« Europe?

In endeavouring to understand post socialist transformation anthropologists have done significant contribution, and posed key questions about such issues as the creation of markets, new property relations, and the construction of democ-

---

1   See Bellier, Irene & Thomas Wilson, »Building, Imagining and Experiencing Europe: Institutions and Identities in the European Union«, in: *The Anthropology of European Union* ed. by Bellier & Wilson (Oxford: Berg 2000), pp. 1–30; John Bornemann & Nick Fowler »Europeanization«, in: *Annual Review of Anthropology* 2 (1997), pp. 487–514; Karl Schlögel, *Die Mitte liegt ostwärts. Europa im Übergang* (Munich: Hanser 2002).

racy.[2] Katherine Verdery is right in arguing that »the post socialist change is much bigger«[3], and this idea helps to throw light on the intersecting facets of the contributions collected here. After socialism, the tectonic shifts of European boundaries and in the hierarchy of the relationships of center and periphery led to new challenges that small nation-states had to face in a very short time after gaining independence: symbolically remarking territories, reordering their »worlds of meaning«, and giving new contours to national histories and memories not only as »local« but also as »European«. And this is an uneasy balancing act, as the contemporary logic of local identity politics, the regeneration of nationalism, fits with some difficulty into the basic format of European self-representation. Moreover, it occurs in those societies where the notion of belonging to political or cultural »Europe« was always contested. As some chapters of this book show, whereas the Western core of the European project has long promoted a culturally integrative, more inclusive ideology of a new European unit, national narratives in these states (re-) form their identity in terms of difference from their neighbors by establishing new linguistic, cultural, or religious boundaries. Apparently, »Europeanization« faces a serious conflict here between the integrative political center and the particularistic »periphery«. This distinction makes the contrast between the »old« and »new« Europe visible not only in a demonstrative presentation of political values close to the US policies but also in an unstable redefinition of local collective identities. Alongside the recognition of the EU as a powerful political institution where a new »promised world« is being designed, often influenced by post-national ambitions, the radical change in the small countries includes the creation of nation-states and the marking of territories as »ours« by introducing completely new calendars, by establishing holidays to punctuate time in opposition to Moscow and differently from the rest of the world. The clearest example of the particularization of identities and the sense of dividedness can be seen in the (re-)emergence of new local terms and names for geographical places and locations. The results of inter-ethnic conflicts and dramatic wars found their expression in radically »returning« old names and symbolically »renaming« places with specific pronunciations. In the South Caucasus, for example, two separate terms have been established for the single geographical place and administrative unit Nagorny Karabakh: the Ar-

---

2   See Chris Hann, Caroline Humphrey, Katherine Verdery, »Introduction: Postsocialism as a Topic of Anthropological Investigation«, in: *Postsocialism. Ideas, Ideologies and Practices in Eurasia* ed. by Chris Hann (London: Routledge 2002), pp. 1–15; Caroline Humphrey, *The Unmaking of Soviet Life. Everyday Economies After Socialism* (Ithaca & London: Cornell University Press, 2002); Ruth Mandel & Caroline Humphrey, *Markets and Moralities. Ethnographies of Postsocialism* (Oxford: Berg 2002).

3   Katherine Verdery, *The Political Life of Dead Bodies. Reburial and Postsocialist Change* (New York: Columbia University Press, 1999), in particular p. 35.

menian Arts'akh and the Azerbaijani Qarabakh.[4] The same place can be called differently by the local population and by academics, as, for example, is the case with the Estonian city Tartu / Dorpat. In this regard, one of the striking points in the reconfiguration of local identities in this region is the growing particularization of geographical names for a single place. Moreover, the competing names for a single region, town, or city are obvious indicators of the contested nature of the rapid transformation. The aim of this anthology is to reflect on these changes and reveal how different identity strategies; arguments of history, and figurative signs of collective remembering are constructed and represented in smaller nations such as Armenia or Estonia. In the geographical span between Riga and Baku anthropologists and historians look at different sites of cultural inclusion and exclusion from the Russian and / or Soviet past and how they are (re-) turned to a European present and future. This volume describes and analyzes the politics of the remaking of cultural and historical identities that have been diversely affected by the encounter with an idealized picture of the West and the »values of European civilization«. We try to look critically at the new political rhetoric by emphasizing not Europe itself but the permeability of boundaries and its involvement in a larger Eurasian context. Addressing the problem of semantic redefinition of »meaningful worlds«[5], the chapters include practices, expectations, and beliefs that serve, like landmarks, to differentiate and change the face of a new landscape. If we talk about the reorganization of »meaningful worlds«, then this pertains to the semantics of the ambivalent transformation of group identities and how this process is communicated on the level of (everyday) representations in increasingly globalized places – particularly in places undergoing rapid transformation of social and economic orders, in places that are considered peripheral to the centers of European power[6] and which are marked by a new creativity in the ritualistic dimension. The authors look at how old and new images of national identifications in the South Caucasian and Baltic states are reconfigured by local elites and ordinary people in order to represent themselves as a part of, or beyond, the imagined Europe and to give new contours to their »past«. The issue of such a »politics of representations« – the way meaning is struggled over, contested, and transformed – informs the whole collection of essays.

Inclusion, separateness, and the »margins« are celebrated in speeches, rites, and advertising and present themselves in different domains of social and symbolic life, such as the coming to terms with the past and identifying a new image for future solidarity. Therefore, the essays written by anthropologists and his-

---

4   See the paper by Ashot Voskanian in this volume.
5   Verdery, Katherine 1999 (note 3).
6   Jon Mitchell, *Ambivalent Europeans. Ritual, Memory, and the Public Sphere in Malta* (London: Routledge, 2002).

torians focus on images and practices of performative identity politics in those societies which ideologically and morally have to negotiate the interplay between »post-colonial« nationalism, New Europe, and Russia.

»Re-united« on the Margins?

In this book we have restricted our discussion of the transformation of national representations for a variety of reasons to the southern and western periphery of the former Soviet Union. Following the »singing« and »colored« revolutions and the accession of the Baltic republics to the EU, questions about meaningful reorganization of small post socialist societies situated between Russia and Europe have become increasingly pressing and dramatic. Over 25 million people in the Baltic and South Caucasian states have garnered international interest where high-level politics and geo-strategic issues are concerned and put the South Caucasus and the Baltic States into the global geopolitical spotlight by becoming the new »insiders« of an imagined Europe, not only in a political and economic sense but also in a historical and cultural one. But like other countries in Central and Eastern Europe, the societies are still considered »terra incognita« and are usually seen in Western Europe as unknown and questionable newcomers. The question is how the symbols of old and new boundaries are perceived and contested in the shaping of new alliances, how they compete and coexist in the liminal area which, having once formed the northern and southern edges of the Soviet Empire, today forms the new margins of imagined Europe?

The research presented in the three parts of this volume does not intend to reveal new »gray spots« of periphery, exotic »backward« sides of Eastern Europe and other »Europeanness«. Based on ethnographical and archival work, the authors try to provide answers to the question of how both the local ordinary people and the elite cope with the particular changes in the course of EU expansion so as to offer deeper insights into the transformation of collective self-representations in relation to symbolic proximity to and distance from Europe. The South Caucasus, being situated between Iran and Russia, has never before been as »close« to Europe as it is today. In June 2006 the foreign minister of Azerbaijan, invited by the German Friedrich Ebert Foundation to Berlin, characterized the new relationship between Europe and Azerbaijan in the following terms: »As a strategic partner in terms of oil supply it might be the time to talk about ›Europe on the way to Azerbaijan‹ and not the other way around.« Armenia and Georgia, on the other hand, geographically located behind the eastern border of Turkey, the most contested candidate for accession to Europe, present themselves as more European than their »Asian« neighbor, and mostly in cultural terms as Christian nations. On the other hand, looking back to the late period of the Soviet past, one should not forget that the Baltic and South Caucasian republics were associated with avant-garde non-conformist political and cultural movements: The Baltic states, in Russian *Pribaltika*, as well as Yerevan and Baku had a reputation as economically prosperous and »advanced« places in the Soviet world. Moreover, many individuals saw these fringes of the Soviet territory, in particular the Baltic states, as a unique place for intellectual freedom, presenting its »own West« and »own Europe« with their prominent *samizdat* history and emotional freedom, their numerous islands of public civic life in small cafes, and the relatively minimal presence of socialist architecture. The Southern Caucasus, besides its industrial significance, attracted ordinary Soviet citizens with a well »developed« tourist infrastructure and a unique mosaic of historical and cultural peculiarities. The social phenomenon of Radio Yerevan, a series of political anecdotes, was prominent beyond the Soviet borders for its creatively critical and non-conformist attitude to Soviet power.

Further, the elites and ordinary people in the former Soviet republics had developed their specific symbolic hierarchies interconnected with Europe and »Western civilization« before the EU accession occurred. For example, these regions were recognized by the early Soviet rulers as the most »advanced« in the classification of the people's images. The early Soviet nationality policy divided its population into two broad categories: eastern and western nationalities; but the dichotomy was not so much geographic as ideological and developmental.[7] In contrast to the vast majority of Soviet nationalities, which were judged as »culturally backward«, Georgians and Armenians were deemed »advanced« alongside Russians, Jews, and Germans and were grouped together as Western nationalities. The same thing occurred with Latvians, Lithuanians, and Estonians after their incorporation into the Soviet Union. Today they make up the unknown eastern fringes of the European Union and in the new political imagination defined by the European neighborhood policy.

Thus, in this introduction we place the »margins« of Europe in inverted commas since the notion of »Europe« as a political and cultural construct has never had fixed borders and has always been characterized by shifting and moving boundaries and, therefore, always requires reinvention and redefinition. With the inverted commas we criticize the new European hegemony and an emerging symbolic marginalization of Eastern Europe. Moreover, we intend, in contrast to this, to bring the »margins« into the light of contemporary discussion. It is evident that »Europe«, like other symbolic ideas, does not exist without its

---

7   Terry Martin, *The Affirmative Action Empire. Nations and Nationalism in the Soviet Union, 1923–1939* (Ithaca: Cornell University Press, 2001), in particular p. 23.

»Other«. What we want to emphasize here, though, is the centrality of the meaning of boundaries and »margins« in studies of global complexities and the ambivalence of self-representations that shape the notions of »them« and »us«. Anthropologists have pointed out for some time that identities are never better perceived than in places and times of encounter with their »others« within real and metaphorical frontiers[8] beyond the bounded container ideology. By paying attention to real and symbolic entanglements between center and periphery, we are not simply dealing with the »clash« between West and East, the alien and contested old past and the new future, but with a much more complex encounter of a set of local and global technologies of representations. We should think beyond the usual dichotomy between center and periphery relationships and rather emphasize its ambiguity, an ambiguity experienced in many other places once defined as margins of »Old Europe«.

With this perspective in mind, the essays deal with the symbolic reorganization of national identities that are »in between«, having already departed from the »Soviet block« past and not yet arrived at the imperative »European« future. The moment of splitting into small nation-states is subject to the dramatic process of »un-making« Soviet identity, such as in the geographical term *Pribaltika*, and at the same time brought moments of a contested »making« of images of their own Europe. As is pointed out in this volume, »every country re-invented its ›national‹ Europe: in extreme cases in times of war, but most often within the context of culture. For culture delivered an abundance of motifs in the form of history and literature, art and popular humor upon which a state could measure itself at the cost of the other.«[9]

In these processes, old ideologies and infrastructures are torn down but some elements still overlap with new ones, producing varied and extremely contested forms of symbolic articulations and cultural practices which are not only the lenses of people's understanding of social order but also the means of social and political mobilization.

Staged Identities

Recently, the term »representation« has become widely popular in the jargon of the social sciences and the humanities. By »representations« authors stress the

---

8 Frederik Barth, *Ethnic Groups and Boundaries.* (Boston: Little Brown, 1969); Thomas, Wilson & Hasting Donnan, (eds.) *Border Identities: Nation and State at International Frontiers* (Cambridge: Cambridge University Press, 1998).
9 See the essay by Wolfgang Kaschuba in this volume.

growing significance of symbolic semantics in the studies of global »markets« of identities that are characterized by complex processes of redesigning and re-definition.[10] In general, representation means presenting again, a presenting of something not present which may take a linguistic as well as a visual form. Jack Goody emphasizes that re-presentations are basic to human communication and human culture and that the word »representation« has a plurality of meanings.[11] In this collection we focus on representations not only as manifestations of norms and orders in a simplified division into verbal statements and actions but rather in the broader meaning of the term, namely as praxis. Under practices of rep-resentations we mean embodying concepts, ideas, emotions, and moralities in a symbolic form that can be publicly transmitted and meaningfully interpreted. Representations are the set of actions and performances comprised of actors and audience. In this way representations should be understood as »powerful« acts of communication, rhetoric, and transmission. Referring to a broader concept of representations, some authors demonstrate in their essays that beliefs and prac-tices not only reflect and communicate social orders and realities but also pro-duce them. Thus, representations are seen as going beyond the simplified level of symbolizing the world and as broader than Durkheim's mechanistic conception of collective representations. Looking at visual, figurative, and linguistic repre-sentations of social ruptures, the authors reveal the power of representations as a communicative reality which, by presenting an absence, actively produces, con-trols, modifies, and finally changes the social order and identities. In that sense, representations function less like the model of a one-way transmitter and more like the model of dialogue. Finally, authors question the established representa-tional politics through a critical genealogy of practices.

In all of the essays »identities« are used in their constructivist sense and can be seen as creative and destructively innovative. In the encounters between groups, collective identities are (de-) constructed and there is a wide set of encounters related to a concrete place and time. Seen in this perspective, identities are not things, but relations that are given content according to their ceaseless historical construction.[12] As relations in the processes of public negotiation they can be reinterpreted and mobilized by individuals and political movements that exploit common identifications so as to build new ethnic, national, or regional solidar-

10   For further works on the theory and praxis of the term »representation« see the website of the Humboldt Collaborative Research Center »Changing Representations of Social Order. Intercultural and Intertemporal Comparisons« at www.repraesentationen.de.

11   Jack Goody, *Representations and Contradictions. Ambivalence towards Images, Theatre, Fiction, Relics and Sexuality* (Oxford: Blackwell Publishers, 1997), in particular p. 31.

12   John Comaroff, »Ethnicity, Nationalism, and the Politics of Difference«, in: *The Politics of Difference: Ethnic Premises in the World of Power*, ed. by E. Wilmsen & P. McAllister (Chicago: University of Chicago Press, 1996), pp. 163–205.

ities and seek support. To legitimize the national order of things, arguments for shared origins, descent, and culture have to be plausibly established.[13] In these processes, culture or the »world of meanings« appears as the raw material for the politics of identity and can be either taken up for use or disregarded.[14] The concept of ›markets of identities‹ is helpful for understanding the mechanisms of production or overproduction of culture used in (re-) building the »sovereign state« and new political affiliations. But identity has to be »sold« as a product on the global market and for this purpose one needs to present it in a proper »localized« way, manifesting it in speeches, labels, and rituals associated with this specific region. In this way one has to refer to a set of materials for identification of cultural and historical sources out of which particular new ideologies and orders arise. Following independence, governments and people in the Baltic and South Caucasian states have been actively engaged in the processes of »post-colonial« nation-building and of designing their specific »national character« as represented in public events, monuments, museums, advertisements, school books, etc. The essays collected in this volume show that in spite of the introduction of a new political order and in spite of now being »inside« supranational Europe, nationalism has not lost its powerful effect on people's imaginations in this region. But nevertheless, the interesting point in this development is the growing significance of existing and emerging ties to transnational or regional affiliations as well as the growing production of reinterpretations of national histories and identities within and beyond the European context. Despite the general commonality in these regions that once shared a single socio-economic and political system, they have increasingly diverged in their interconnectedness to global networks, to Europe, to the US, or to Asia. The size of the population on the »margins of Europe« has significantly changed and this is one of the obvious dynamic features of these societies. The growing role of migration and mobility results in the establishment of an actually existing transnational mode of life. Every seventh citizen of Lithuania is living and working somewhere between Klaipeda and Dublin. In Armenia, towards to the end of the 90s, an anecdote was circulating about the paradoxical act of »repatriating« dead bodies of some famous Armenians from the diaspora to the homeland, in contrast to the mass exodus of living Armenian souls to Russia and the US. The globalized migration of ordinary people in search of work and survival brought new experiences of

---

13   See in Beate Binde, Peter Niedermüller, Wolfgang Kaschuba, »Inszenierungen des Nationalen – einige einleitende Bemerkungen« in: *Inszenierungen des Nationalen. Geschichte, Kultur und die Politik der Identitäten am Ende des 20. Jahrhunderts (Cologne: Boehlau, 2001), pp. 7–18.*

14   Guenther Schlee, »Introduction. Approaches to ›Identity‹ and ›Hatred‹: Some Somali and Other Perspectives«, in: G. Schlee (ed.) *Imagined Differences. Hatred and the Construction of Identity* (Münster: LIT Verlag, 2002), pp. 3–32, in particular p. 8.

neo-liberalism and new life styles, thus bringing the Baltic and South Caucasian states closer not only to Western Europe, but also to the USA.

Europe's New Orient?

Given these ambivalent encounters, our contributors offer some »open« answers to the following questions: What are the dominant symbols and agents of the dramatic transformation and the restructuring of belonging, and how are they articulated and negotiated in small nations? How are they performed on the public stages of nation-state projects and how does this relate to local everyday life?

One phenomenon that emerges from these case studies presented here is a common »mood« of being and belonging to the »margins« of cultural domination of the Soviet and now the European era, in spite of their geopolitical significance on the Eurasian continent. The new political and economic frames challenge the people's competing emerging self-representations and reorientation strategies which are experienced not as a purely ideological, legal, or economic phenomenon, but rather present themselves as a cultural struggle over past and future, manifested in figurative creations such as nation branding, monuments, banquets, or schoolbooks, as well as painful daily discourses about growing inequality and being the »backward« and uncivilized part on the periphery of New Europe. In spite of the desired expansion of the European Union into the Baltic states and in spite of officially being »inside« Europe, local everyday discourses produce the sense of being »outside« European economic prosperity and »civilization«, as it is discussed in the chapter by Vonderau.

The chapters show that the remapping of this part of the Eurasian continent has brought a new variety of social disconnections and experiences of »othering« or »orientalization« of Eastern Europe based on cultured hierarchical distinctions developed by locals in the course of coming to terms with the West. Recently, Michal Buchowsky raised the question of »the spectre of Orientalism« in Central Europe.[15] By transferring the classical Saidian[16] dialectical definition of Orient and Occident into capitalism and socialism, civility and primitivism forming a class distinction between elites and plebs, Buchowsky reveals a whole spectre

---

15   Michal Buchowski, *The Spectre of Orientalism in Europe: From Exotic to Stigmatized Brother.* Unpublished manuscript. Paper presented at the Institute colloquium, Department for European Ethnology, Humboldt University Berlin, January 2006, in particular p. 5.

16   Edward W. Said, *Orientalism. Western Conceptions of the Orient* (London: Penguin Books, 1995).

of neo-orientalism in Central Europe. Thereby the postmodern, postindustrial, and post socialist meaning of Orientalism [is] understood as ... »a way of thinking about and practices of making the other«, as well as a mindset that creates »social distinctions«, which stretches beyond Said's and his followers' definition of it.

Such encounters are ambivalently expressed in local terms, as has already been mentioned, in the sense of being inside European »civilization« in opposition to Moscow, and simultaneously outside Western »culture« and »morality« in comparison to Brussels. This process of ambivalent »marginalization« reminds us of the growing trend to compare socialism with colonialism and post socialism with post-colonial studies.[17] For example, Alexei Yurchak[18], inspired by critics of Charkrabarty,[19] calls for a »language that would de-center and ›provincialize‹ the ›master narrative‹ of Europe, defining more precisely that the ›object of provincializing‹ is not just ›Europe‹, but ›Western Europe‹, thereby creating a post-Soviet ›master narrative‹ in the history of socialism that implicitly and explicitly reproduces the binary categories of the Cold War and of the opposition between the ›first‹ and ›second world‹«. Chris Hann has also argued for a greater focus on the significance of the long-term similarities and contacts between East and West, since »there is an implicit danger in the phrase ›anthropology of Europe‹. It risks imputing some sort of cultural and civilizing unity to this place called Europe and some anthropological rationale for specifying boundaries of this type. The practical difficulties in reaching agreement over these boundaries highlight their deeply problematical character«.[20]

The most visible global challenge facing these small nations, namely the departure from the Soviet past, can be experienced variously as either liberation or loss, or both. The positive side of a new order is often articulated as liberation from the Soviet past and totalitarian state control, combined with the successful passage to the source of wealth, »modernity«, and prestige presided over by a small group of winners. The negative mode of »experiencing Europe« is characterized by the well-known threat of the loss of strong national traditions and local morality and the creation of more »losers« in the process of the neo-liberal transition, comprising a majority of the population in these regions.

Interestingly, in many cases the geographical »extension« of Europe not only generates hierarchical differences in the »New Europe«, but also stimulates the

---

17   Chris Hann, Caroline Humphrey, Katherine Verdery, »Introduction«, op. cit. (note 2).
18   Alexei Yurchak, *Everything Was Forever, Until it Was No More. The Last Soviet Generation* (Princeton & Oxford: Princeton University Press, 2006), in particular p. 9.
19   Dipesh Charkrabarty, *Provincializing Europe: Postcolonial Thought and Historical Difference* (Princeton, NY: Princeton University Press, 2000).
20   Chris Hann, »*Not the Horse We Wanted!« Postsocialism, Neoliberalism, and Eurasia* (Münster: LIT Verlag, 2006), in particular p. 245.

cultural »essential« moment once promoted in the Soviet past. In fact, the contemporary political potential of ritualized representations in Eastern Europe is greatly influenced by former socialist practice.[21] There are, of course, important differences between the societies discussed here. But prior to 1991, these societies shared a common past and common regime by being inside of the socialist Soviet Eurasia. They were ruled by the Communist Party of the Soviet Union, which administrated production and distribution not only of goods but also of cultural texts, including historical ones. This aspect, which is still much present in »folk« models of national identity, should not be forgotten in exploring the material and symbolic dimensions of the politics of representations in the former Soviet block. The visual and oral presence of political and cultural icons and posters has profoundly impacted the ways people »preserve« or »lose« their national identity.[22] The systematic »production« of the cultural technologies of Soviet rule, in combination with ethnographic knowledge communicated in museums, censuses, and maps, has shaped the ways national and regional identity projects deal with modern »representations«. This specific aspect of the display of social and political orders is still relevant in the ways small nation-states present themselves today and this perspective is critically examined in this volume.

Within the process of reinterpreting the Soviet past, we observe a growing self-orientalization and emerging discourses about Europe's new Orient. Two years after joining the EU, Lithuania now sees itself as an important member of the union, bringing political, economic, and cultural ideas and innovations to Europe. Vonderau's essay discusses the collective feeling that can be observed there, of living in »yet another Europe«, of being different in the sense of »backwardness«.

But there is a fundamental difference between the Baltic and the South Caucasian states. Whereas Baltic nations conceive their past as backwards and uncivilized through the images and memory of violence and Stalinist despotism, in the South Caucasus the dominant local discourse is based on the return of Orientalism following the collapse of the Soviet Empire. The Soviet past is seen, in contrast to the Baltic States, as a period of modernization, Europeanization, and the suppression of traditionalism. Bayadian examines dimensions of Soviet-Armenian identity and argues that Soviet policy towards the nationalities and

---

21   Gerald Creed, »Economic Crises and Ritual Decline in Eastern Europe«, in: *Postsocialism*, op.cit. (note 2) pp. 57–73, in particular p. 69.

22   Ronald Gregor Suny & Terry Martin »Introduction«, in: *A State of Nations. Empire and Nation-Making in the Age of Lenin and Stalin*, ed. by Suny & Martin (Oxford: Oxford University Press, 2001), pp. 3–20; Rogers Brubaker, *Ethnicity without Groups* (Cambridge: Harvard University Press, 2004); Francine Hirsch, *Empire of Nations: Ethnographic Knowledge and the Making of the Soviet Union* (Ithaca: Cornell University Press, 2005); Victoria Bonnell, *Iconography of Power. Soviet Political Posters under Lenin and Stalin* (Los Angeles: University of California Press, 1997).

the process of maintaining power over Soviet republics can be characterized as Russian-Soviet Orientalism. He shows that in the Soviet Union the availability of some means of cultural representation (for example cinema), which made possible modern forms or »styles« of imagination, were restricted for the ethnic cultures.

As the case studies show, today the relations between social change, ideological transition, and tectonic shifting of European boundaries are expressed explicitly in the domains of symbolic life such as meaningful icons and sacred objects, collective narratives, ceremonies, and everyday rites. They not only help to maintain a specific image of national identity, but also offer a »software« or instrument for the redefinition of the »we« group and the exploitation of a marketable image. Some »materialized« symbols and icons that are overcharged with imaginative and social sacred qualities appear as key themes in a number of chapters. National representations are here not simply »symbolic and manifesting realities« but also enter the imagination as a source of power and new interpretation. Socially constructed representations such as museum objects can be a vehicle of influence on contemporary life. Material icons bear a heavy semantic and symbolic burden in the negotiation of new borderland identities between Russia and Europe, in this case represented by Estonia. In her paper Brednikova discusses the centrality of the »material evidence of history« that plays an important role in the representation of a »divided« history in Narva. It is built around key sites: monuments in central parts of the city, tourist zones, and city museums.

Dzenovka focuses on the practice of nation branding in Latvia as a way of improving the national image and suggests that nation-branding is a set of government practices that aims to animate the nation's image for outside consumers. In the Latvian context nation-branding is articulated with a particular form of ethnic nationalism grounded in claims of historical injustice and the need to protect and cultivate the nation which, according to the Latvian self-narrative, had been pushed towards extinction during the Soviet period. The resulting historical formation – »the land that sings« – is one of hostility towards difference, as seen in the case of the Gay and Lesbian Pride Parade in July of 2005. Consequently, European presence in Latvia is also characterized by the increasing visibility of voices criticizing the narrow conception of the nation and promoting recognition of, and tolerance towards, difference.

One central feature of the transformation analyzed here is signaled by the rediscovery of repressed history, violent pasts, and the creation of new victimized identities. In her study, Darieva looks at the shifting meaning of the remembrance of loss in post-Soviet Armenia. One of the crucial points in creating a new moral universe is the re-establishing of memory and justice towards the Armenian *yeghern* (grief and mourning) not only in terms of the post-Soviet »return of the repressed«, but within a broader framework of recognition of a silenced and »forgotten« local loss in terms of a global morality. She analyzes the transformation from »silenced to voiced« in public remembrance politics, focusing on the urban area immediately sorrounding the Armenian genocide memorial in Yerevan. Marutyan's chapter, by contrast, shifts our ethnographic focus from the present time to the previous periods between perestroika and the collapse of the Soviet Union. Making use of his experience inside the social Karabakh movement at the end of the 80s and beginning of the 90s, Marutyan presents an account« of protest slogans and posters in Armenia as the memory of the deportation and death in 1915 whereby was strongly and successfully mobilized among ordinary Armenians.

The relationship between narrative and issues of national identity provides significant means for representations of the contested reorganizing of a »meaningful world«. The explicit engagement with history is a striking point in the identity politics in the former Soviet republics. Following the collapse of the socialist orientation towards the future, they have been at the forefront of exploring traumatic memories and recovering »secret histories« in studies of post socialist historiography and iconography.[23] Individual and collective narratives, then, circle around a specific event to determine the »historical truth« – we call these relations the »politics of dates (time)« as in the focus of the Second World War in Feest's paper or attention on 1965 as the turning point in Lehmann's contribution on »bargaining« over the Soviet Armenian national identity. Nowhere is this more so than in school books where the narration of the national time and space receives a fixed treatment – Mkrtychian takes this approach in developing a critical understanding of the Armenian pattern of »self-narration«. Similarly, contrasting ideologies and cultural geographies form the basis of Brüggemann's study of Estonia's »escape« from Russia. Estonia, after being largely conceived as part of the East in Western Europe and as »our West« within the Soviet Union, at the end of the 1990s tried discursively to become a part of the Scandinavian »North«. The paper argues that the first year of being politically a part of the »West« has again brought to the Estonian agenda the need to differentiate itself from the East. This need was underscored particularly by the festivities for the 60th anniversary of the end of World War II in May 2005 the Russian president Putin tried to exploit history for Russia's political purposes, expecting that everybody would exclusively follow the Russian interpretation of history concerning

---

23   See in Rubie S. Watson, »Introduction«, in: *Memory, History and Opposition under State Socialism* ed. by R. Watson (Santa Fe: School of American Research Press, 1994), pp. 1–20; Peter Niedermüller, »History, Past, and the Post-socialist Nation«, in: *Ethnologia Europaea* 28 (1998), pp. 169–82; Pierre Vitebsky, »Withdrawing from the Land: Social and Spiritual Crisis in the Indigenous Russian Arctic«, in: *Postsocialism,* op. cit. (note 2), pp. 180–195.

the »liberation« of the Baltic States in 1944. Thus, the »escape from the East« is not yet concluded and history, as was to be expected, did not end with EU and NATO enlargement.

A more dramatic effect of »experiencing« Europe is discussed in the last part of the book. We use the term ›rites‹ in its broader sense to explore the ways in which different groups (ethnic and sub-cultural) articulate their identity in the public sphere and resist the external pressure of capitalism and Western values. The four essays focus on the question of how the imposition of new European »values« and neo-liberalism undermines local cohesion and old norms which in socialist times had been supported and institutionalized. Paradoxically, democratic elections and the politics of new European membership seem to intensify the ritual dimension and to stimulate the essentializing of local »cultures«. This part of the volume discusses the force of representations which seem to disintegrate individuals and groups into the pluralistic spectre of unstable societies and destabilize old symbolic norms in the face of political and social change. The growing folklorization and ritualization of grand politics is the central feature of Voskanian's characterization of the current configuration of political subjectivities in Armenia.

Mühlfried's study reflects the overlapping of local and global bonds manifested in the changing meaning of the traditional Georgian banquet. The arrival of European and Western NGOs has brought an unexpected change in local understandings of social phenomena that were traditional and taken for granted. Here Mühlfried shows the growing pluralization in the values of the iconic marker of national identity, the Georgian wine-consuming culture *supra*, through encounters with Western donors and diasporic experiences. In the diaspora, sipping wine is not a deadly sin, and some of the people gathered take pleasure in having escaped the rigidity of the banquet tradition in Georgia. Consequently, it is possible to toast and to remember, to evoke and to dream of home – but it is not obligatory: the *supra* becomes an option, and the procedure becomes more virtual.

Again Abrahamian's essay looks at the transformation of local social orders and begins with the political aspect, showing how the terms »European«, »Western«, and »democratic« are often used in the margins of New Europe in quite different contexts than in Old Europe. In Armenia, under the *evroremont*, the popular »Westernization« of interior design in offices and private apartments, one can see a less visible »Asian« mode of life and values. The symbolism of repair is not just a metaphor: home is one of the main symbols of Armenian national identity. Abrahamians's essay shows from an anthropological perspective how the notions of family and home essentialize the Armenian collective identity, especially during the critical periods following the collapse of the Soviet Union.

Finally, Sidikov's research on emerging new clan elites in Azerbaijan after the violent conflicts stresses again the power of »diacritical features« in reconfiguring group identities. These features include the moments of exploiting tragic history, remembering cultural geography, and revitalizing genealogical knowledge in order to legitimate proper belonging and an access to local economic capital.

At the end of this review more questions have arisen about the politics of representations and symbolic fragmentation on the enormous Eurasian continent. The authors have described and analyzed a set of local responses to the growing hegemony of a new European rhetoric and in doing so have opened new fields of investigation. Moreover, the cooperation between anthropologists and historians seems to bring a fuller examination of politics of identities, memories, and belongings through the combination of archival research and field work. They have questioned the representational politics through a critical genealogy of practices and provided deeper insights into the choreography of staged and contested identities on the »margins« of New Europe.

Old and New Europe: Representations, Imaginations, Stagings

Wolfgang Kaschuba

At present, Europe is (again) proving itself to be an extraordinarily varied and dramatically embattled political field. The current symptoms for this state of affairs can be seen in almost any random selection of details: the debates regarding EU membership as a strategic discourse for national position and international resources, the jockeying for the position of opinion leader after the Iraq war, the formation of a European »right-wing« in the Eastern European societies, the conflicts surrounding the practices of fundamentalist religions within and outside of Europe, or the extraordinary problematic border regimes on the Mediterranean and in Eastern Europe in light of human rights issues.

All these themes are situated on thoroughly different levels of politics and discourse. Nonetheless, they all belong to a passionately and fundamentally »European«-led debate over national legitimation and the ethic principles of politics. Moreover, they are all of one cloth in so far as the mode and subject of the negotiations in these political fields are presented primarily as »cultural«. This is the impression one necessarily gains upon closer examination of the individual areas. Decisive questions regarding the interrelationship between the individual interests of nations and European visions of community are negotiated specifically in the context of national and European identity discourses. Furthermore, cultural self-presentations and symbolic semantics play a decisive role in these discourses: for example, as references to history and ancestry, to language and religion, and to aspects of civilization and mentality.

The debates of the last few years concerning the eastern expansion of the EU and Euro-Islam are two exemplary demonstrations of how intensive and how ideologically entrenched the discussion of identity politics is. This is not without reason, since precisely those cultural representations are being fought over that will ultimately define »Project Europe« and then literally embody it. On the one hand – and from a historical perspective – this concerns the shaping of a new European »collective memory«. Yet at the same time, in this act of self-Europeanization, the particular, »local« historical traits of Europe are once more to be distinctly inscribed into the increasingly globalized and thus anonymous horizons of economics, society and culture. However, it is still under contentious debate which traits are to be emphasized, how many different traditions and references are to be included, and how many of the eastern and the western traits are to be integrated. On the other hand, the current European spaces and borders play an essential role in this, as it is in relation to these spatial markings that symbolic accentuations are placed and new affiliations and demarcations are possible. However, affiliations and demarcations always generate altered pictures of »us« and »them«, and thus produce new social and cultural differences both within and to the outside.

Of course, this concept of cultural difference has been utilized in the past as a tried and tested means for national as well as European identity politics and it will undoubtedly continue to be used in the future. Yet here the talk of »old« and »new« Europe takes on its special significance, since a strategic position of difference can be derived from it that operates within Europe and probably carries far-reaching consequences; since the concern will be with a Europe whose form is determined not only from the center outwards, but also decisively from its edges inwards. And it is these open, European edges which are located – from a historical, cultural and geopolitical viewpoint – in an East in many ways not yet identified with Europe which is still seeking its affiliations and loyalties in the interstitial space between Europe and Asia. The following deals with several historical and current facets of European identity politics.

Historical Self-conceptions

Even a cursory glance back into history will confirm: Europe never stood solely for a geographical or political space. Rather it always and primarily described a symbolic figure, an idea, an invention, that had lasting consequences. The Renaissance had already »thought« this Europe as a myth and a topology, that is, as a grand »narrative« and as the central »site« of history, society, and culture – as the *Gesamtkunstwerk* of a civilization. Europe thus ultimately framed itself as a vision of a bourgeois civilization of travel and reading, of curiosity and knowledge, of discussion and comparison, of transfer and transgression of frontiers. And it was these ideas and ideals of the first European-educated elite that conjoined trade, science, and art across the borders of regimes and whose multifarious traces we still encounter in libraries today in the legions of volumes of European travel literature. This travel literature furthermore comprises a unique historical document of European neighbor-relations. For it was here that the »European« view observed, noted, and compared whatever seemed noteworthy at home as well as abroad: from agriculture to architecture, from medicine to geography, from piety to festivals.

This gesture of observation and its empirical consequences set in motion an extraordinary dissemination and fluidity of knowledge concerning the self as well as the others. The question that continually arose as a central concern was that of the cultural self-conceptions of each and their reciprocal relations. Who are we? Who and how are the others? What do they think of us? This led to the construction of reciprocal and thoroughly dense pictures of social identities: stereotypical prejudices as well as positive knowledge of people and landscapes, of mentalities and nationalities. Yet in each case, imaginations of a European diversity emerged from this – usually lightly romanticized and (too) often in abstraction from the so thoroughly »European« reality of religiously motivated struggles and continental wars.

From this centuries-long cultural »contact work« of migrating craftsmen and bourgeois authors the specific features of the European worldview developed all the way into modernity: a characteristic and remarkably dense form of the perception of self and others. Thus a strategic project of »identity« arose, in which constant intellectual exchange, by means of literature and images as well as through dialogue and the discourse of difference, played an essential role. This exchange was then once more programmatically entrenched during the European Enlightenment, when Rousseau reflected on nature and civilization, when Herder developed his ideas of peoples and cultures, or when neo-humanist thoughts came into circulation on the relations between freedom and compulsion, between individuality and society.

It was here at this time that the arts and sciences intervened actively and insistently in the process of creating social meaning and identity, a position they have never retreated from since. The concern was on the one hand with »inner«, national conceptions of identity; and, on the other hand, with the framing of a European civilization that from that point in time saw itself as the center of the world – with all the familiar consequences of European imperial and colonial politics. Yet it is significant here that no other civilization has developed this intensive form and this dense, and above all, popular tradition of constant observation of self and others – also in the sense of an increasingly reflexive and often critical gesture towards »one's own« and a specific form of acquiring knowledge about the »others«. This »European« knowledge that we still have at our disposal today is built upon the historical formats and media of bourgeois travel and educational culture. Thus, within the history of Europe, cultural diversity, social contact, and intellectual reflexivity reciprocally pre-suppose and fertilize each other.

Of course this concept of identity also brought a burden with it from the very beginning. The European nationalism of the 18th century and the European colonialism of the 19th soon one-sidedly declared difference to be the most important source of identity. Now cultural differences were a greater concern than European commonalities – except perhaps in the common colonial gesture of dominance of the »white man«; while differences were »genetic«, national-cultural ones. What was sought for was the internal cohesion of the nation on the one hand and, on the other hand, whatever marked this off externally from neighbors and enemies. This in a lasting way changed the ideological semantics of the concept of Europe, reducing it to a concept of the construction of differences in which each nation tried to identify itself as an independent »people« and thus to distinguish itself as a »community of common descent« from the others. This ethnic and national affiliation was in turn supposed to offer the citizen a putatively secure anchor through the torrent of European upheavals leading up to the nation state and industrial capitalism. For this, one needed an external difference, and conceptions of an enemy that could be mobilized. Thus the German wanted to be the non-Frenchman, the Norwegian the non-Swede, the Pole the non-German.

Identity no longer implied a bridge but a trench, and Europe came to describe a space in which many nations played the role of center and main actor and tended to merely assign supporting roles to others. Every country re-invented its »national« Europe: in extreme cases in war, but in every case within culture. For culture delivered an abundance of motifs in the form of history and literature, art and popular humor, upon which a state could measure itself at the cost of the others.

These constructions of difference led to the national conceptions and semantics in our collective memories that have more permanently molded our common »cultural memory«. At the same time, they supplanted many other conceptions of the European tradition describing Europe as a society of exchange, transfer, communication, and commingling. Then an »iconic turn« in European identity discourse took place, which only today we are beginning to fully reconstruct in our academic disciplines. This is why the cultural motifs of this memory are so familiar and prevalent to this day: they arose in a specific bourgeois public sphere that thought in national terms and yet constituted itself as a truly »European« public sphere transcending institutions, media and audience. Thus, across all national boundaries, we recognize our own historical pre-judgments in these received conceptions and images, which for that reason still seem so thoroughly plausible to us after generations.

This thinking in terms of difference is today in many respects still very close to us and uninterrupted, precisely in Europe of all places. Just how close, was demonstrated quite plainly by the fall of Yugoslavia after 1990, when at the end of the socialist era social and political tensions were rapidly carried over into aggressive discourses about ethnic descent and cultural difference; resulting in the murderous »ethnic cleansings«, which had begun above all with Milosevic's chauvinist dream of a Greater Serbia and took their justification from these discourses. Such mobilizations of the »healthy common sense of the people« were possible and clearly still are even after German National Socialism as long as it is possible to shut the eyes of a nation and ethnocentrically veil the horizons of societies, whereby the collective memory is so immersed in monolithic nationalist or racist colors that the putatively threatened »us« of the culture can be contrasted with a dangerous »other«.

Admittedly, Europe has certainly learned something about dealing with military and international conflicts from the conflict in Yugoslavia. Nonetheless, it still sees itself confronted once again with problematic situations with opposed fronts of »us« and »them«. This time fundamentalist Islam and, thereby, sectors of European migration act as both catalysts and targets of a new discourse of the Other, in which both aggressive, old stereotypes and new constructions of difference get articulated alongside substantiated concerns.

On the other hand, it is precisely the post-WW II European history which has demonstrated that this continual preoccupation with »the others« was also capable of a sustained dismantling of traumatic war experiences and conceptions of the enemy. Otherness and diversity are thus experienced not only as a threat, but also as an opportunity. An example of this in more recent history is seen in the new and truly neighborly relationship between Germany and France. Another present and future example may be the changing mutual perceptions of Germans and Poles, who seem to be gradually losing their national »formatting«. Furthermore this can be seen conversely in the discourse about contrasting conceptions of society and social politics being carried out in contemporary Europe, which in many aspects involves a demarcation over and against the USA. For the rejection of the socially disintegrative and politico-economically neo-liberal social politics over there is bound up here with an avowal of a European »social charter« that refers explicitly to common European traditions and values spanning national differences. These traditions also play an essential role in answering the question of where »old« and »new« Europe would like to agree on certain commonalities.

Old and New: The West Against the East?

The perceptions and conceptions of Europe are changing markedly both within and outside of the continent. They are moving away from the classical geo-political conception of a European landscape made up of separate nation states and national characters toward a conception of a largely common European cultural identity – an identity conceived in both the singular and the plural, ranging from religion to art and bound up with visions and myths. In this question of turning »European« into a »community«, those political, structural, and statistical models of planning and control, ranging from economic statutes to construction ordinances and producing in their sum an extraordinarily normative and thus »Europeanizing« effect, play a not inessential role. They simultaneously produce both European formats of knowledge, administration, and politics, and European viewpoints of observation, perception, and exchange. These formats and views, in return, increasingly organize essential components of our world and everyday life into a »European« mosaic, in our own eyes as well.

Thus even more interesting than the superficial question of the geographical space of Europe and its political order seems to me to be the question of this imaginary space of a European identity and of a progressive factual and symbolic »Europeanization« of the societies within it. This concerns, on the one hand, a transfer of common forms of knowledge and practice, which impregnate our everyday life in terms of a European lifestyle; and, on the other hand, the conceptions and symbols that are supposed to outwardly convey the corresponding forms of European life on its way towards becoming a society and a community. In both cases, these efforts result in active representations of »European-ness«, that is, in integrative elements of being European that combine what is new with what is already familiar to us.

In spite of these clear trends, such representations do not in any way produce a standard European culture or even a unified culture. Rather, a look at history shows that the historical contact and the social exchange between European societies has in no way led to cultural uniformity, be it in music or cuisine, lifestyles or value-systems. And this prospect holds equally for the future. Even the contemporary Europeanization of constitutions, law, and politics will not supplant the diversity of their application in local, regional, and national variations. The cultural traditions in European societies are obviously much too resilient and the contexts of their living environments too differently composed. Europeanization, in deepening knowledge about others and contact with others, necessitates creating new openings in the societies, for it creates new supranational connections and alignments. At the same time, however, it enables new distances and differences, because these processes of alignment and understanding are then more consciously perceived and more critically reflected upon.

This reflexivity in turn results in individual paths of development – be they regional, national, or supranational – that produce unofficial »Euro-regions« independently of any planning from Brussels. At least this is what one could call these cultural spaces, which – in contrast to the official Euro-regions – are simultaneously generated »from below«. This has occurred above all since 1990, motivated by new regional constellations in economics and transport, in tourism and ecology. More than a few of these regions simply cross the old borders and territories, in some cases already overstepping the old »Iron Curtain«. As a result, Europe without a doubt becomes larger and more diverse as a cultural landscape – not only in spite of, but also precisely because of such Europeanization processes.

In addition, there is of course an external view from which Europeanness as a common political label as well as a common attribution of cultural identity is perceived with increasing clarity. The European Union and the constitution as well as the European lifestyle and cuisine, European pop music and European soccer are increasingly registered in the USA or in Japan as phenomena in which one purports to recognize a growing European collective identity – even in the wake of the differences of opinion within Europe regarding the Iraq war or the failed constitutional referenda.

Conversely, there is also an extraordinarily skeptical viewpoint according to which Europeanness appears as a threatening horizon toward which all local worlds have to orient themselves – at the cost of their »original« cultural substance and their particular form of life. The incursions of legal and political regulations are increasingly perceived by many to be so intrusive and dominant at the level of everyday life that they see Europeanization as a kind of »miniature« globalization; that is, as an economically and legally coercive path towards »Brussels« regulated living conditions. From this standpoint, the EU and its bureaucratic center in Brussels embody more of an undesired generator of norms and institutions.

However, there is also currently an interesting fault line seen running through all these discussions in and about Europe, which cuts across the direction of argument discussed above. This line is visible as soon as talk turns to »old« and »new« Europe and as soon as one attempts to take stock of societies under these headings. Of course the conceptions of »old« and »new« are to some extent based on the old borders between East and West. Yet by no means do they simply take up the map of post-war Europe; rather they incorporate the individual dynamic that arose out of the changed opportunities for development following the collapse of the Soviet Union, above all for the societies and states in the East of Europe. And these development opportunities seem to have a thoroughly ambivalent nature.

On the one hand, the »new« is representing a Europe with greater flexibility and new social forms, far from the norms of Brussels. Immediately after 1989, new national and ethnic identities were confidently developed in Eastern Europe, which to some certain extent released the built-up potential for conflicts, and to some extent created a new potential for conflict. It is thus not only during the Iraq war and in reaction to Rumsfeld's speeches that some East European states have, in the meantime, built up new international roles as middlemen and coalitions – roles that were unavailable to their Western neighbors for historical or geopolitical reasons. At the same time, right after 1990, in view of the internal opportunities for restructuring economic and in social politics, there was quite open talk to the effect that after the demise of the socialist state and economy everything pointed favorably in the direction of a development of neo-liberal economic and social relations – going even further than in the West. Late-industrial capitalism sought to open a new field for maneuvering to provide Eastern Europe with a proper »leap forward« and, conversely, to place pressure on Western Europe. This calculation seems partially to be coming true, even if at the same time some aspects of East European economies recall visions of early rather than late capitalism.

On the other hand, upon a second glance it becomes apparent that the political and cultural power relations in Europe have in no sense fundamentally changed as a result. Rather, in the course of European unification it is clear, time and again, how much all essential forms of representation of Europeanness – now as then – can be attributed to the core of »old« Europe. All large European projects – from conceptions of history, of constitution and of civil society to the arenas of high culture and pop culture all the way to the social spaces of lifestyle and consumption practices – carry the unmistakable stamp of the West. In contrast, the East – the putatively »new« Europe – is clearly ascribed almost no political competence, social substance, or cultural resources – or at least not any that ultimately have to be preserved and integrated into the European center. In this regard, the historically negative connotation of the European »East« has not changed at all. Even now the discussion seems exclusively to be one of its suitability to »connect« to, that is, whether the East European societies as well as East European biographies can be fitted into the canon of the West European cultural model. The recent debates on the draft of the constitution have shown this quite clearly.

And it is here, in turn – with the question of the admissibility of the »others« – that Brussels‹ norms and formats are apparently very much desired. For here there is no demand for any more European diversity or for any social and cultural experiment, and least of all for mediation of the »post-socialist« experience. For socialism and its consequences embody precisely that European »Other« in the eyes of the old Europeans, that is, the abandonment of the central, cultural roots of Europe in its traditions of Christianity and the Enlightenment. And here Europe's capacity for integration is simply overtaxed – so the prevailing argument goes.

»Europe's Orient«?

This argument of cultural »overstress« resounds louder, the further East one looks – that is, the further we pass beyond the imaginary cultural border at which the »occident« and its putative religious-civilizing unity seems finally left behind: beyond the Ural River and the Dardanelles. Up to now, for those who argue on behalf of the »occidental« concept of Europe, the Caucasus and Asia Minor lie unequivocally beyond the conceivable borders of their »cultural« continent. In the meantime this has changed very little ideologically, as the old fear of a »dissolution« of Europe by the East, as well as a »displacement« of Europe towards the East, remains. Nonetheless, even hardliners are gradually awakening to the fact that »European« world politics can no longer be carried out solely by referring back to their traditional world view. Thus, the borders of Europe appear to be gradually shifting due to the compulsion to remove the restrictive borders of thought.

For it is only natural that the contemporary discussion regarding »old and new Europe« offers, in contrast, sufficient basis and reason to discuss European ideas in terms of a new, reflexive relationship between Western and Eastern Europe. On the one hand, this includes coming to terms historically with that symbolic geography of Europe that has, over the previous three centuries, increasingly positioned the West as the center and pushed the East to the sidelines. In light of the protracted construction process of a »European« world view, the individual historical preconditions and motives for this tendency are extremely informative and also instructive for the present. On the other hand, this symbolic construction of the East – naturally reinforced by the effects of the division of Europe after 1945 – led to the fact that the social spaces and horizons in the East and the West have developed differently. The division created, in each case, new proximities and new distances – and not only within Europe, but also in relation to the »rest of the world«, as was expressed in the divergent experiences and world views. This holds not only for the period after the division, but also for today: whereby these differences are in no sense restricted to political visions and coalitions, but are above all to be found in the everyday lives of citizens, who in many cases still live in a cultural style colored by the East or the West. Societies often tend to change in their conditions and habits rather slowly in dealing with travel or literature, with foreign languages or fashion. Thus, picking the people up where they are, in »their« particular worlds, while at the same time overcoming this old cultural division, is certainly one of the most pressing tasks in old as well as new Europe.

This need is emphatically underscored by the example of the young East Europeans now unreservedly clamoring for positions in the West European labor markets and universities. For these people, this Europe still appears largely as a blank slate where the old markers are no longer valid. Thus in planning and conceiving their lives they develop their own map of Europe, with signs that point in many aspects unequivocally toward the »old«, that is, to the West. The historical circumstances and experiences of their parents are apparently already quite distant to them. For them the post-socialist space seems not so much to present an opportunity for something »new« as to embody the burdens of the »old«. Thus they make their way towards »their« Europe, which they themselves, as East-West migrants, help to shape in its symbolic geography. Often it is only from this position, from the vantage point of the migration country, that they in turn perceive their native country as a part of Eastern Europe, as »their« Eastern Europe. Along with their new language they also learn a new concept and a new perspective. In this way they literally re-construct their native identity, and thus themselves, anew: as a former »East European«, which, at home, they never were.

Then as now the catch-all term »East Europe« embodies a thoroughly West European concept that never served the East as a geo-political conception or was used as a point of reference. Not without reason is it said that as early as the 18th century Europe's West, with its increasingly alienating perspective on the East, ultimately created its own »Orient« – a view which is naturally close to Edward Said's criticism of Orientalism and all the images this includes.

However, these semantics seem to be changing at present, as the concept has since come to play a new role in European politics. Alongside the derogatory symbolic connotation of »East Europe« a bureaucratic meaning has also emerged marking an official European area for accession and development. Thus, it has become not only politically but also financially relevant, and many countries find it very convenient to gradually come to embrace this undesirable term. After all, it can be used to signal willingness for European integration and ultimately perhaps to attain access to the EU or at least to European funds.

Thus the concept of »East Europe« marks both an old and at the same time a new ideological project, that once again excludes a real symmetry in European politics and culture. Again, the »new« East Europe appears as the weaker, inauthentic counterpart to the »old« European core, which represents the whole. Ultimately »new« has a chimerical meaning. It is a synonym for the not truly authentic, for a precarious, unstable, »second-class« Europe. Thus the path still seems long to the European project aimed at conceiving itself anew, no longer only from its old center outwards, but also from its new borders inwards.

In fact, the scales are still too unbalanced for this, especially in the cultural arena and also with regard to the internal structure of the societies. For in the majority of the East European countries and, furthermore, in almost all the former member states of the Soviet Union, questions of a new, often clearly nationally – and ethnically – based politics of history and identity play a particular role. Often these regions have to attempt to transfer the most varied experiences with the old government and the most varied desires for a new independence onto common conceptions of an »us«. These conceptions are meant to moderate the new social reconfiguration and to mark it as a symbolic transition into the postsocialist times. Often rediscoveries and new discoveries of national history and ethnic culture are the central vehicles of identity politics, often the only ones, which frequently become an »invention of tradition«: that is, an almost artificial staging of cultural descent and heritage. Furthermore, many of the restored and newly founded nation-states of the East prove in addition to be socially quite heterogeneous in their ethnic as well as linguistic make-up and in their political dispositions. This diversity, often in combination with the inability to find their way out of the »ghettos of memory« of either ethnic victim-mentalities or the Soviet victor-mentality, makes it tremendously difficult to develop real »shared identities« in such heterogeneous societies.

Thus it is no wonder that in this precarious situation of transition, there is often particular recourse to symbolic politics and dramatic self-staging as the most effective stylistic means for forming identity. In this way, the »society« is supposed to be sworn-in in a sweeping emotional and aesthetic manner as a »community«. In symbolism and in drama, ideas of heritage, fate, community, and authenticity seem to present themselves as the most efficacious means for generating identification and movement: that is, as an intensive form of representation. This explains the strong affinity of such »transitional« societies to representative acts and dramatic self-presentations: to national celebrations, days of remembrance, and anniversaries, which create an aura of national feeling and are meant to convey a conception of a national public.

European Biographies?

If the images and conceptions of Europeanness prove themselves to be as change-able and malleable, in history and in the present, as outlined here, then European ethnology needs to deal with them intensively in its research and in particular with the question of how these conceptions gain an immediate influence – in the form of »soft« media and discourses and as »hard« institutions and laws – on *Lebenswelten* and local everyday lives. And it must further ask how collec-tive memories and individual life conceptions are formed by this. Europe, as an idea, an imagination, an experience, has also always indicated a specific bi-ographical space – the space of a life story, in which the individual shaping of one's life has long included both dimensions: on the one hand, the social and cultural framing conditions, influenced by the European norms, patterns, politi-cians, and lifestyles, and, on the other hand, the course of one's life, connected through media, tourist, professional, and social interactions with a European world beyond the smaller regional or national horizon. Thus every utterance of »we Europeans«, beyond its lofty and dramatic effusiveness and its propa-gandistic implication of times now gone, often has today a truly inconspicuous and thus all the more effective quotidian meaning. It describes the desirable and undesirable traits of a European »we« composed of individuals, in no sense imag-inary. In conclusion, I would like to discuss a few examples of this biographical »Europeanization«.

Most conspicuous is the incursion of European law and European politics upon our individual as well as collective mobility in the last decade. This con-cerns holidays and studies abroad, traffic and passport issues, and the circum-stances of immigration and emigration. It must be said that most internal bor-ders have since fallen, at least within Western and Southwestern Europe. And although the new external borders are subject to a common regime of borders, the practice varies highly from place to place and is unreliably configured.

At any rate, the consequences this kind of politics has a correspondingly deep impact on European societies: migration and the presence of »foreigners« has long become normal everywhere. Yet this normalcy has proven to be fragile, especially when fears of foreign infiltration arise and aggressive assertions regard-ing what is »our own« ensue. This is taking place at present in more than a few European countries.

In many cases such fears resonate with those false conceptions of homogene-ity which national societies, in 19th century terms were understood as »pure« communities of descent and common culture. In contrast, the newer concep-tion – that nationality and ethnicity are not genetic facts but rather a cultural construction – has apparently found little footing in Europe and in Germany, in particular. Thus, the opening of borders within Europe and to Europe, especially in the 1980s and 90s, seemed to many not to be a path toward greater permissiveness and freedom, but rather to be the gateway for foreigners and foreignness.

Of course the altered forms of migration in and to Europe play a central role in these fears. For, in contrast to the decades following WW II, it was not just Polish and Turkish immigrants who moved to Germany or Algerians to France – that is, groups who for the most part moved along the established, historically familiar lines of European migration. Rather the European societies are confronted with global migration routes and with globally active migrant groups from Africa and Asia – that is, with people of whom they are historically ignorant and about whom they know very little culturally. Furthermore, European countries are often no longer the destinations, but now just the stopping-off points in a migration that proceeds in stages and indeed often across continents. A European space that ends up being this open seems to further fuel this »foreign infiltration«.

This is especially true when these »other« migrants also have a »foreign« religious background – when there is talk about only one »true« religion in a fundamentalist sense and about the struggle against the influence of the Islam on Europe. European societies are no longer used to such fundamentalist discourses about religious identity, and thus they respond helplessly to them – at least this is so for the Westerners. For this reason the increased presence of these tendencies within Islam must seem to them an especially grave threat to their own culture; as a threat, namely, to their own Christian and enlightened nature, which now – in the face of its endangerment – appears all the more valuable.

There is no question that this fundamentalist project is being discussed and promoted amongst migrant groups. The terrorist bombings in European cities speak for themselves in this regard. It is equally beyond doubt that the groups which sympathize with this position represent a miniscule portion of European Muslims. And it also seems undeniable that, upon rational reflection and in the long run, there is no reason to fear a strong influence of Islam on Europe, a Europeanization of Islam is much more to be expected. For the lifestyles of the migrants in European societies alone will ensure in the medium-term future that the notions of Sharia as a binding canon of values cannot even become a common guiding theme in Muslim migrant communities. They themselves are far too heterogeneous and have long been too deeply involved in their own development of »European« culture. Informed observers of both Islamic and non-Islamic backgrounds have long agreed upon this.

Against this, more awareness needs to be raised of the fact that, historically seen, migration is nothing new, and that Europe is not threatened by such long-distance immigration, rather it itself only came about historically through internal and external migration. The relatively new and static picture of a Europe of nations must be more strongly contrasted with both historical and contemporary images of the older Europe of mobility and cultural diversity: a Europe of interaction and blending, of which we ourselves today are the result. For, we are all cultural products of a historical European migration – genetic and cultural »hybrids«. Even affiliation with the Muslim religion has long been normal in European biography.

Such a level of self-awareness can naturally only be achieved when we consistently refuse to chime the tone of »guiding national values« in the collective memory – not only in politics, but in culture as well. For even Goethe was, in his time, known as more of a Hessian and a European than as a German. And the question as to whether the Islamic religion and Turkey could »somehow« be part of a new Europe should be discussed neither with warped geographical arguments nor with Old Frankish, occidental ones. For both geopolitics and history could allow for an almost endless number of arguments both for and against. In reality, in contrast, Moslems and Turkish people by the millions are already Europeans – be they simple migrants, Turkish participants in the Eurovision Song Contest, soccer players in the European Champions League, or even religious zealots. But whatever they are, most of them became so here, in Europe. Thus, the decision as to what is »European« (insofar as it needs to be answered) can only be a political one, and it has to be founded in a cultural perspective.

This demonstrates our own, in many ways truly »European« biography. It is built upon literature and music, travel and television, migration networks and Internet contacts, films and sports – constantly, daily, anew. It will be a biography with ever more European know-how: one knows where Porto and Bruges are through tourist visits, feature articles, or from the topography of the Champions League. Whoever visits a European city instinctively seeks a market place or a similar historical center – usually with success and rightfully so, for here, in contrast to American and Asian cities, the historical model of the »European city« is of one with a fixed center. And the education coming-of-age as well as the lifestyles, above all of the younger generations, take on an increasingly European form.

Characteristic European landscapes of vacations, history, lifestyles and cuisine have long since been a component of the biographical experience and memory. The Euro-landscape of the common currency is perhaps boring, but also reassuring. To this extent, we already possess various European »world views«, which often merely need to be more strongly raised into consciousness from the unconscious. For the irony is that these similarities often take precisely the form of differences, seemingly grave differences at first. Thus, on the one hand the political history of Europe in the last 60 years has meant in many respects a history of »divided« biographies in Western and, above all, in Eastern Europe: divided at first by the political division and the ensuing divergence in world views and conceptions of life; then divided once more by the devaluation of the »socialist years« after 1990, which for many in retrospect have become empty. Just as many East European countries attempted to erase the socialist period from their history, so too did many people from their own life stories. In order to preserve an employment position, the family, or even the social esteem of others, the »socialist« components of biographies were often faded out. It is only today that we are gradually learning that this chapter of (East) European history should by no means be erased from our collective memory as a putative »aberration« – and furthermore, that this biographical »schizophrenia« is a collective one, having arisen out of mutual confusions, that, in turn, also bind us together.

Finally, Europeanization also means, above all, cultural exchange and social encounter. It means adopting the models and fashions of others, such that at the end we can no longer recognize the starting point and can no longer seriously ask what is »ours« and what is »foreign«. Cultural traits are often completely unconsciously adopted, and the ensuing connections and mixtures of a linguistic, intellectual, aesthetic, legal, and political nature have long been a part »of us«. This naturally also holds for the connections between people. As co-workers, friends, partners, or family, one rarely asks to see a passport.

But such connections and mixtures do not occur by accident and without preconditions. Instead, they build upon the foundation of historical knowledge gathered in the »old village of Europe«: that is, in the first »global village« of the traveling bourgeoisie of the 17th and 18th centuries. This village and its surroundings have since then been continually extended and broadened. How far – that has been and is debatable!

Translated by Karsten Schoellner

Icons

»Windows« Project Ad Marginem or a »Divided History« of Divided Cities? A Case Study of the Russian-Estonian Borderland[1]

Olga Brednikova

The modernist project of building nation-states proved to be entirely successful, and the notion of the world as a multicoloured mosaic has been perfectly internalized. For modern men, the world is a map made up of bright colour-logotypes, and it is a piece of cake for a schoolchild to decorate a skeleton map, having coloured in the empty spaces which are separated from each other by uneven lines. In fact, coloring in the vast patches of the Soviet Union in a soft salmon-pink was a difficult and quite boring task. Although this space has now been compressed and has become variegated with other colours around its borders, more fractured skeleton borders have appeared. These »curved lines« and »other colours« do not only embody separation and isolation, but also the peculiarity and difference of another state. The state border acts as a break line, a fracturing of space that is not continuous but discreet, torn apart by the borders of nation states. Such »break points« will become the only basis for social research, a testing ground for various theoretical constructs operating so well at the heart of the »centripetally organized« nation states[2] but which are frequently questionable at the periphery.

The new post-Soviet borderland presents itself as a unique site for social research, where it is possible to observe simultaneous processes. Although they may differ in terms of meaning, significance and social effects, some of these include the process of »divergence« of those formerly »one's own«, that is border reinforcement and the formulation of »the other« in relation to active nation building. Also, the processes of eroding borders owing to the inexorable progress of globalization, the eroding »Westphalian cartography« as well as the erosion of state boundaries are present. The phenomenon of the »compression of time and space« in the globalized world significantly accelerates the pace of life and brings distant territories into closer proximity. State borders are already being interpreted as a symbol of the past, of a rigidly fixed world or »space of place«, which is now being restructured and transformed into a dynamic world or »space

---

1　This is a translated and slightly edited version of »Istoricheskii tekst Ad Marginem ili razde-lennaya pamyat razdelennykh gorodov?« In: *Ab Imperio 4* (2004), pp. 289–312.

2　As a famous Soviet poet Vladimir Majakovskij has written: »it's a well-known fact that the Earth begins with the Kremlin«.

of flow«.[3] Significant cross-border flows of people, information, goods etc. overcomes and ignores borders, and the borders themselves become unstable or are an element of the modern world that is on its way out.

The current essay will only look at an aspect of mutual relations between the two towns located on different sides of the recently erected state borders between Russia and Estonia. Namely, this paper will examine the process of writing »new history«, i.e. the appearance and functioning of new historical narratives that are reflected in the popular (or perhaps even »pop«) artefacts of history.

Researching Borderlands

From the 1990s onwards, thanks to the considerable »tectonic shift« that reshaped the geopolitical map of the world, research into borders and border territories will enjoy unprecedented popularity in the social sciences. »It is a paradox, but the border theme is attracting more attention than previously, during the time of the iron curtain«.[4] The popularity of the theme is not just linked to the appearance of new borders and the disappearance or transformation of the meanings or values of old borders. It is also related to the opening up of borders, the relatively free circulation of goods, capital, people, and information etc. A border is now »not so much a limitation, but a meeting point, the site of cooperation, a neighbourhood«.[5] Moreover, the formerly static dichotomy of East-West is disappearing or being re-territorialized. West and East as well as the state are associated with these blocks; they lost and then reacquired the image of the »other«. In this connection, research interests in territory, borders and identities are being brought up to date. The study of border territories can help us to find answers for some fundamental research questions, such as how the »other« is constructed, how this is reflected in social actions and practices, how it is represented and how the »other« constitutes »us«.[6]

Practically all those researching borders and border territories observe the

---

3   Manuel Castells, *The Power of Identity* (Oxford: Blackwell, 1997).

4   Josef Langer, »Towards a Conceptualisation of Border: The Central European Experience«, in: *Curtains of Iron and Gold. Reconstructing Borders and Scales of Interaction,* ed. by Heiki Eskelinen, Ilkka Liikanen & Jukka Oksa (Aldershot: Ashgate Publishers, 1999), pp. 25–42, in particular p. 25.

5   Sergey Medvedev, »Across the Line«, in: *Curtains of Iron and Gold. Reconstructing Borders and Scales of Interaction,* ed. by Heiki Eskelinen, Ilkka Liikanen & Jukka Oksa (Aldershot: Ashgate Publishers, 1999), pp. 43–56, in particular p. 54.

6   Anssi Paasi, »The Finnish-Russia Border in the World of De-territorialization« in: *Working Papers of NUPI on North European and Baltic Sea Integration* (Oslo: NUPI, 1999).

special status of borderlands, setting them apart from the rest of the space of the nation state and endowing it with special values. The uniqueness of border-lands is linked first of all with the proximity of the neighbouring state, which, in turn, gives rise to interaction and the mutual exertion of influence. Social activity in borderlands is largely organized thanks to the presence of »neighbours«.[7] All border spaces are heavily marked by national symbolism. On top of that, the meeting of borders brings national identity up to date, constantly calling for »documentary evidence« of national identity, in particular the passport. In this connection, researchers believe that the proximity of the »other« should provoke and recall national identities and thus constantly recall and exacerbate differences: »Border regions are a privileged site for articulating national differences [...]. It is Freudian narcissism«.[8]

In current research, however, borders are not seen as isolated spaces, where national differences are accentuated, but as a creative cross-border space.[9] E. Zerybavel considers border zones to be situated in »several mental spaces at once«. Such a temporary situation implies that border space is essentially ambivalent, which presents a serious threat to today's rigid structure of classification.[10] So borderlands are not just zones where »rigid classificatory structures« like nation states are challenged, but must also be considered »not as an analytically empty transit zone, but as a site of creative cultural production«.[11] Border territories are seen as the centres of globalization, fulfilling not only an integration function, but also producing transborder social groups, particular lifestyles and identities. In this way, current research views border zones as an attempt to move away from the binary opposition of borders. New concepts of border space present new possibilities for the theorisation and conceptualisation of social space. For example, borderlands could be viewed and analyzed as a metaphor. The work of Gloria Anzaldua can be considered an example of such conceptualization of borderlands.[12] Her research focuses on the experience of life in the Mexican-American border territory and sets out the specific history of

---

7   Cf. in particular Daphna Berdahl, *Where the World Ended. Re-unification and Identity in the German Borderland* (Berkley, Los Angeles & London: University of California Press, 1997).

8   Peter Sahlins, *Boundaries: The Making of France and Spain in the Pyrenees* (Berkley, Los Angeles & Oxford: University of California Press, 1989), pp. 270–271.

9   Olivier Ruiz, »Visiting the Mother Country: Border-Crossing as a Cultural Practice«, in: *The U.S. – Mexico Border. Transcending Divisions, Contesting Identities*, ed. by. David Spener & Karl Staudt (Boulder, CO: Lynne Rienner Publishers, 1998), pp. 105–120.

10   Yael Zerubavel, *The Fine Line. Making Distinctions in Everyday Life* (New York, Toronto, Oxford & Sydney: Free Press NY, 1991), p. 35.

11   Renato Rosaldo, *Culture and Truth. The Remaking of Social Analysis* (Boston: Beacon Press, 1989), p. 208.

12   Gloria Anzaldua, *Borderlands / La Frontera. The New Mestiza* (San-Francisco: Aunt Lute Books, 1999).

the Mexican Chicanos, Mexicans who have lived in the border zone for a long period of time and who the author believes have a particular border culture and »intermediate identity«, linked to the uniqueness of the practices of constant border crossings. According to Anzaldua, in borderlands »the lifeblood of two worlds merg[e] to form a third country – a border culture. [...] A border is a dividing line, a narrow strip along a steep edge«[13] of the states themselves, and the Chicanos themselves are »faceless, nameless, invisible«[14], but could easily become small change in political games. Borderland inhabitants »constantly walk out of one culture and into another«[15], and it does not seem so important to »stick« to one culture or another, which is precisely why a border culture with an ambivalent identity comes into being, which tolerates difference and divided, or perhaps undefined, loyalty, i.e. it is possible to talk of a particularly instrumental, but unemotional attitude to citizenship.

Thus, we can identify two central theses around which the current debate on borderland is formulated:

Borderlands are »Freudian narcissism«; the situation of the proximity of the border provokes a search, formulation and accentuation of the difference of the inhabitants of neighbouring states. In this way, a defined (formulated) social border between »them« and »us« is formulated, coinciding with the limits of the nation state. Borderlands have a mirror effect. There is a constant convergence of images, models of behaviour and lifestyles. The social border in border territories is eroded and some kind of unified cross-border space results that are »temporary« in the context of nation states.

Divided Cities

This paper addresses precisely this »problematic« marginal space with the so-called divided cities Ivangorod and Narva which are situated on the Russian-Estonian border. In Soviet times Ivangorod and Narva shared a territorial and administrative border with the status of a border of Union republics. Thus Ivangorod and Narva created a single labour market and a single infrastructure, and even until 1999 a unified water collection and purification system was in place. Moreover they constituted a single space of daily life, that is, a common space where daily routines were carried out. People worked, lived, went shopping, took their children to school, had gardens, and buried their dead and so on in

---

13 Anzaldua, *Borderlands*, op.cit. (note 11), p. 25.
14 Anzaldua, *Borderlands*, op.cit. (note 11), p. 33.
15 Anzaldua, *Borderlands*, op.cit. (note 11), p. 99.

Figure 1.1: The Border between Narva and Ivangorod demarcating Russia and new Europe in July 2000. Photo: O. Brednikova.

both towns. For example the huge firm »*Krengolmskaya Manufaktura*«, situated in Narva, built houses for its workers in Ivangorod. The differences between the towns defined a different administrative outfit, which in turn decided on sources of financing, supply, infrastructure, and the general conditions of these towns. It could be said that the towns had different statuses. Ivangorod was a small peripheral town of the Russian Federation, whilst Narva was the third largest in Estonia.

Although during Soviet times the formal administrative borders of territories often played no role at all in everyday life, there was nonetheless a symbolic hierarchy constructed through prestige. In the case of Ivangorod and Narva, it was more prestigious to live in Narva, for Estonia was considered to be the »near abroad« by Soviets. The »reality« of the administrative border constantly reproduced itself both through the myth about differences in everyday culture between Russia and Estonia. In spite of the lack of significant differences in the lives of the population on both sides of the border river, some kind of cultural border existed in people's minds, bringing it into correlation with the administrative border.

Without taking the reproduction of the cultural border between the towns into account, Narva and Ivangorod are currently exposing the problem within the social debate as divided cities, as »a formally divided but inseparable pair« (from an interview with a female inhabitant of Narva aged 47). A simple experiment may be done in terms of their »inseparability«. In an online journal database for 2003, there are nearly as many publications in the mass media containing the word »Ivangorod« as those containing the combination of »Ivangorod and Narva«.[16] Incidentally it is worth noting that »Narva« appears as an independent entity and is not necessarily connected with Ivangorod, whereas Ivangorod is almost always »accompanied« by Narva. However, if a text is talking about the two cities at the same time, they are nearly always presented and the problem is exposed in the discourse of the Russian mass media as something joint. To this end the most frequently employed category is »divided city«, that is, a space which was once united but which is now a divided urban space. Researchers categorizing Narva and Ivangorod as a double town and a bi-national town make a significant contribution to reinforcing notions of »unity« or at least the dubious links and interdependency of these towns.

Artefacts of History: The Creation of the »Popular« Narrative

During the last century, Russian and Soviet history has already been rewritten several times. When this occurs, a reinterpretation of events takes place, the same facts are subject to differing moral evaluations, and in addition »new«, previously neglected facts are enlisted. At the same time, those facts previously deemed current and fundamentally important are effaced. The post-Soviet generation socializes itself with the help of new textbooks. And although for adults history lessons remain in the distant past, everyone is in one way or another involved in, or observant of, such a new interpretation process. This work will only consider some of the artefacts which play a role in the representation of history: memorials, museum exhibits and souvenirs. Of course, these artefacts are not all of equal significance, they are varied and present new historical narratives of various kinds. In addition, they address different audiences – who goes to museums and buys souvenirs these days? Nonetheless, these artefacts – as »material evidence of history« which bears a heavy semantic and symbolic burden – play an active part in the representation of various histories. They are like pieces of a puzzle, which fit into the general picture; they have some general meaning, they historicize and make space a subject of discussion.

　　Accordingly, the museum exhibits, memorials and souvenirs on display in

---

16　　The source www.public.ru (accessed on May 12th, 2004).

Narva and Ivangorod will be analyzed. Here the task of the current research is not so much to answer the question as to »how history is made« but to understand the reasons and aims behind its richly varied versions and forms.

Museum Composition in Narva

A museum composition can be looked at as the most concentrated and conceptual form for representing various versions of history. Together, the various thematic exhibits create concepts, or »complete images«, of history, bringing a certain »message« from the depths of the centuries to today. Of course, such messages are not always so obvious. But we can say with certainty that even museum expositions that have remained unchanged for decades will provide us with different messages and will be integrated according to various political conditions and in varied cultural contexts. We will try here to »read« the modern version of history that is presented in the Narva museum.

The Narva museum is situated inside the old medieval fortress and the architectural peculiarities of the museum – the tall, narrow tower with a thematically different hall on each floor – allows one to create individual, self-contained, and logically complete historical images that are often unconnected to one another. We can focus here on two of the historical concepts that stand out the most, the two dominating historical narratives that pertain to various periods – Swedish Narva and Narva at the beginning of the last century.

The largest and most impressive exhibit in the Narva museum is called »The Swedish city of Narva«. This exhibit came about in 2000, and was presented to Narva by the Swedish government. Narva's Swedish period lasted for about 120 years, and is now known as Narva's »Golden Century«, due to the quick pace at which trade, craftsmanship, and science developed. The main theme or key idea in the exposition is connected with the success and prosperity of Narva in that period. The exhibit employs modern museum technology – music, lights, interactive models, etc. – and attracts a lot of visitors.

The other image of the city is »Narva at the beginning of the last century«. First and foremost, this is a city of culture, with a fertile cultural life in which the artistic and poetic intelligentsia of St. Petersburg actively took part when visiting Narva-Joesuu on vacation. The photographs of familiar and widely known personalities of the Silver Age are placed against the peaceful seascapes of Ust-Narva, of views of old Narva, etc. The exhibit is done in the yellow and beige tones of old photographs, and, in accordance with the concept, should evoke the impression of »gentle nostalgia« – of the peaceful, beautiful, stylish, culturally rich, and poeticized life of Narva in the beginning of the previous century.

Of course there are other exhibits that produce varied images of the city. We see the image of medieval, chivalric Narva, or the image of mercantile Narva.

And nearly all the compositions emphasize the special, transitory role of Narva in both the geopolitical and the cultural sense. Besides these, the museum also holds many temporary, often changing, or transitional exhibits that take up the upper floors of the fortress or the »empty« space in the corridors connecting the main exhibits. For example, an exhibit called »Narva and the Tatars« is located between the first and second floor of the museum. However, these images are located on the periphery of the exhibition halls – they are not as accented or noticeable as Swedish Narva or Narva in the Silver Age.

We should note here that, as a rule, the exhibits are not connected. The only connecting factor is the sequence of the epochs – the simple chronological flow of time. We cannot really say that there is continuity between these epochs, or that they are connected and flow logically from one to another, or that there is »evolutionary development«. The images of Narva are more autonomous and self-referential. For example, »Cultural Narva in the beginning of the last century« in no way »carries anything over« from the Swedish period. There are even some inconsistent and contradictory valuations when integrating the same events. For instance, in the »Chivalric Narva« hall, one of the last written comments says, »Then the Swedish troops laid siege to and destroyed Narva«, then the next hall introduces the visitor to the »Golden age of Swedish Narva«.

One interesting fact is that as of now the image of Soviet Narva has practically disappeared: nobody denies it, nobody argues about it, and nobody remembers »the horrors of the totalitarian regime«. It simply does not exist. D. Khapaeva noted this phenomenon when she wrote that today there is not just a decline in the interest in Soviet history (interest in which grew during the period of Perestroika), but rather complete silence, a »removal of part of the past from history«.[17]

The presence of a neighbouring city is almost absent from the exhibitions. Only the model of the two fortresses reflects exactly how near Narva's neighbour is, because the closeness of the two fortresses is an important factor in the uniqueness of the area: »The Narva fortress and the Ivangorod fortress are the two closest enemy fortresses in the world.« In Soviet times, both fortresses together made up a single tourist complex, and most tourists went to see them both, thus having the opportunity to compare and contrast.[18] The image of the two fortresses together was firmly established and widely recognized. For example, no one today is much bothered by the fact that both fortresses appear on the Estonian 5-kroon bill; apparently, there is even some symbolic border expan-

---

17   Dina Khapaeva, *The Era of Cosmopolitanism* (St. Petersburg: Zvezda Publishing House, 2002), p. 135.

18   Right up until Estonia's break away from the Soviet Union, excursions ended on the Friendship Bridge, from which there is a beautiful panoramic view of both fortresses, and on which there is now located an international border.

sion going on. Ivangorod is mentioned in the history of Narva in connection with the »battle between Narva and Ivangorod for primacy in the region«. Here, emphasis is placed on the fact that Ivangorod was founded more than 200 years after Narva.

The fact that Russia is such a close neighbour is not stressed at all. The Russian ethnicity (or nationality) is only mentioned once throughout the entire museum. One of the commentaries to the »Narva – a Swedish« exhibit states: »After the capture of Narva by the Swedish army, there were 24 hours allotted for the pillage of the city, in which were killed both Russians and peaceful citizens.« Of course, such a statement can be interpreted as either a misstatement or a conscious opposition of »Russians« and »peaceful citizens«. This statement is practically the only reference to their neighbour's ethnicity as it is also its only classification. Also interesting is that in the exhibit dedicated to the Narva of the Silver Age, there are no »Russian« poets or artists. These important and famous figures do not have an ethnicity; the only important thing is their cultural status.

However, although Estonia's neighbour is for the most part missing from the exhibition, the notion of a border resonates within the exhibits. In the last four years the museum has been host to at least two exhibits that were intimately connected with the existence of the border. One of these focused on the border with Soviet Russia from the 20s to the 40s, and the other was devoted to alcohol smuggling. The exhibits display a relatively cheerful image of the border, not one connected with any kind of drama. They are more akin to an »attraction«: interactive displays are used, and it is »fun« to walk past the guard at the checkpoint who puts a nice little stamp on your hand, or to wonder at the inventiveness of the smugglers.

Monuments

Monuments are meaningful artefacts that contribute to the representations of the city. Their meaning is even more significant in the Post-Soviet era as they play an important role in nation building according to Benedict Anderson.[19] In Narva, there have appeared two monuments in the last decade. The first one is a monument to Alexander Pushkin, erected on one of the main streets close to the main city square. According to town history, a monument stood on the exact same spot before the revolution, and was erected with money from Narva's inhabitants to honour the one-hundredth birthday of the poet. It was later destroyed and, a hundred years later, restored. In such a case, the monument takes on the meaning of »restoring what was lost«, and »returning to the

---

19   Benedict Anderson, *Imagined Communities* (Moskva: Kanon-Press, Kuchkovo Pole, 2001), p. 288.

past«. And Pushkin, of course, (being »our everything«) is undoubtedly, incontestably, a »hero«. Moreover, just like the personalities of the Silver Age that were mentioned above, he is »outside of ethnicity«. He, one might say, »belongs to the whole world«. However, in the nation-building situation in the Estonian Republic, the reference to a »Russian poet« takes on another meaning, related to the problem of preserving »Russian culture«. Currently, in Estonia in general and in »Russian-speaking« Narva in particular, there is active discussion concerning this very topic.

The second monument was erected in the year 2000, and is dedicated to the memory of the Swedish period of Narva; it is known as the »Swedish Lion«. It was erected on the initiative and with funding from the Swedish government. It, however, is located somewhat further away from the main streets of the city – in a park – and thus is not as noticeable as the Pushkin monument. Only one in four passers by can tell you where it is located. There is no explanatory text nearby, and its »message« may be lost to the uninformed.

Figure 1.2: Lenin monument inside of the museum's court in Narva 2000, Photo: O. Brednikova.

There is an interesting history surrounding the Lenin monument that once stood in the city's central square. A few years ago, the owner of a restaurant located within the fortress decided to purchase the statue and place it near the restaurant, in the courtyard of the fortress. The fact that it is now located near the city museum undoubtedly »museumifies« the sculpture, making it an exhibit as well. According to a legend that was thought up and actively spread by the restaurant's proprietor, anyone to whom Lenin points is destined for bankruptcy, which already happened to Krengolm's factory and restaurant. The statue is now turned toward the city of Ivangorod, and »there, things are *really* bad«.

Souvenirs

Souvenirs represent and propagate images of the city as a material incarnation of the symbols and signs that form the uniqueness of the area and as such they also contribute to the writing of history, or at least of its various versions. They are, of course, directed »outward«. Being something »exotic«, they are intended for tourists visiting the city, who, in turn, will propagate these symbols in various directions. Being first the »spoils« of the tourist, and then collecting dust on some shelf in someone's house, souvenirs tell a story. They remind the tourist of the place where he or she procured the artefact.

We should note the variety of souvenirs that can be obtained in Narva that refer to different spaces. At any of the multitude of souvenir stands near the central square and in the fortress stores, one can find Easter eggs painted with the image of Nicholas II, religious icons, Soviet tin soldiers and busts of Lenin, nesting dolls and balalaikas, mittens and sweaters with Estonian patterns, alarm clocks with views of Narva, and the like. This variety, along with what might seem like incongruity, reflects and represents modern Narva. One can read the history of the city through these souvenirs, a history that is being distributed to the tourists. Various images of the city are for sale: »Pre-revolutionary Narva« and »The Soviet Period«, as well as »Estonian Narva« and »Russian Narva«. »Pre-revolutionary Narva« is represented mostly by antiques whose origin is not quite clear, but just the fact that they are being sold in Narva allows one to connect, for example, an antique chair with Narva at the beginning of the twentieth century.

There are an overwhelmingly large number of Soviet souvenirs available. They have become universal markers of the entire post-Soviet region. Their popularity among foreign tourists is more or less understandable, and connected with their exotic quality. What is interesting is that they are becoming popular among the inhabitants of the post-Soviet areas themselves. As one young woman buying a horn used by the Pioneers (a Soviet youth organization) for someone as a birthday present noted, »This is hilarious!« This kind of irony is connected with having a feeling of power over time, with taming your past and distancing yourself from it. It is an indication that that particular historical period has ended, has been assigned a meaning, and its symbols are already becoming souvenirs to be sold. Narva, just like the entire post-Soviet region, is included in this process. On the one hand, this type of attitude towards everything »Soviet«

creates a distance from it, and on the other hand it unites it with everything »post-Soviet«.

The sale of Soviet souvenirs in Narva is completely understandable – it is a past that is too close; it is still »alive« in people's memories. Nevertheless, some of the souvenirs for sale have an exclusively »Russian« feel about them – icons, nesting dolls, balalaikas, fur hats, and the like. Of course, the sale of these souvenirs is connected with the high demand for them. You can surely find these things almost anywhere, but the Orthodox icon brought home from Narva by a Scandinavian tourist will give the impression that Narva is Eastern Orthodox, a »Russian city«. This is how the presence of such souvenirs in Narva's tourist shops characterizes the area – they participate in creating the idea that Narva is »Russian orthodox territory« and »Russian territory«.

»Estonian« souvenirs are, for the most part, things with symbols of the state on them – lighters, pens, business card holders, and the like, all imprinted with emblems of the Estonian flag, crest, and other symbols of the Estonian Republic. Besides the state symbols, »Estonianness« can be seen in the hand-made items: the sweaters, the hats, and the mittens made using »national« patterns. This type of souvenir is sold all over Estonia; they »cover« the whole territory. Their presence in Narva is in no way connected with any local tradition specific to the city. Rather, it confirms the fact that Narva is an »Estonian city«, which also attests to the city's ethnicity.

Museum Composition in Ivangorod

Being now located near an international border, the museum of the city of Ivangorod has moved more than once due to the appearance of these new borders and the general restructuring of the state. It now takes up half of a small building not far from a border checkpoint and a bus station. The Ivangorod fortress doesn't contain a museum, and is simply a »protected historical site«. You can tell that the museum employees have tried to include the already existing exhibitions into the new museum space, thus giving the impression that the Ivangorod museum does not have a holistic concept of how to represent the images of the city and its history. Neither are there separate but »logically isolated«, self-contained, and autonomous images. The exhibitions look eclectic: the same hall, the same exhibition space, can encompass the most varied epochs and historical events. For example, the stands on the history of the Ivangorod flax-jute factory are right next to the mineral display and the exposition dedicated to the daily life of Russian peasants. The space is not divided, and there are no »invisible boundaries« that form logical and conceptual nooks, or that allow one to recreate and envision various historical events and facts. In fact, the most accentuated and detailed hall is the one devoted to the courage of Peter the First's army and the

Figure 1.3: Souvenir shop by the city museum in Narva 2000,
        Photo: O. Brednikova.

ship building industry during his reign. There is practically no notable social history; there is nothing of the sort in any hall. However, as opposed to the Narva museum, it is there – chronologically tied into other themes and exhibits. And so within the history of the flax-jute factory the Soviet period is present. It should also be noted that the museum also includes a small and de-emphasized, but thematically separate, exhibit on World War II.

The museum's composition gives you the sense of the unity of Russian history throughout the entirety of Russia. For example, in the exhibit on peasant life of the 18th century, there is a model of a house that a peasant of the Tver' region might have lived in. And there is no basis or explanation for this... nothing explaining what a peasant house from such a faraway place as Tver' is doing in an Ivangorod museum. There is no text concerning the differences between a peasant home in Tver' and one in Ivangorod. The fact that there is only a house, without explanation, leads one to infer that peasant houses were all identical, regardless of location.

Despite the seemingly eclectic nature of the entire composition, in the Ivangorod museum there is a unifying idea, one that connects the entire route travelled when going through the museum. According to the exhibit, throughout Ivangorod's entire history, the town has served it's only – although exceptionally important – purpose: safeguarding the western border of the Russian empire. And the accent here is not on the fact that Ivangorod is some kind of »gateway to another world«, but rather that it is above all an outpost and fortress, that it fulfils a key role in the defence of the nation.

A strategy completely different from the one used in the Narva museum was chosen in creating the plan for exhibits in the Ivangorod museum. The exposition is not based on recreating or conceptualizing a particular historical period, giving it specific, individual characteristics. Instead, museum planners looked for a »suitable personality« around whom could be built a definite historical narrative. And of course, this »personality« must be somehow connected to Ivangorod. In speaking about the plans for the formation of the new exhibition, the museum director concentrated on a number of famous people who were born in, spent time in, rode by, or noted the beauty of Ivangorod. Their accomplishments, service, and glory are only important in regard to their involvement with Ivangorod. For example, it is important that Georg Ots'[20] uncle lived in Ivangorod and sang in the city choir, and that his nephew visited him a number of times here. It's important that Baron Shtiglits (founder of the Russian Bank and the Art Academy in St. Petersburg), who for the most part worked in St. Petersburg, is buried in his family's vault in Ivangorod. And thus the local details, the

---

20   Georg Ots is a famous Estonian singer at Soviet times.

uniqueness of the area, are explained based on its »relation to greatness«, its role in »big history«.

Monuments

In the last decade in Ivangorod, just as in Narva, two monuments have been erected. Both of these refer to the same period of Russian history – the era connected with Peter the Great. Here is a very illustrative and revealing quote from an interview with the director of the Ivangorod museum:

> Recently in Ivangorod, in the year 2000 to be more exact, we opened to the public a memorial to the fallen soldiers of Peter the Great. It was actually erected before that, but it was opened on November 19th, 2000. There is an inscription there on a marble slab that says something to the effect that here lie the soldiers of Peter the First, who died during an unsuccessful storming of the Ivangorod fortress in August of 1714. Even before that, we erected a memorial cross where the headquarters of Peter the First were located.

> [In Ivangorod] there really should be many more monuments... I myself have raised the question of erecting a monument to Peter the Great. I went personally to the governor of Leningradskaya Oblast when he was here on a visit. I said, ›Valeriy Pavlovich, it would be nice to have a memorial in honour of the capture of Narva‹. He thought about it and answered, ›But Narva's not ours anymore, is it now?‹ So there you go – no monument. But it seems to me that we still need some kind of monument. I mean, he [Peter the First] was only in Petrozavodsk one day, and they have a monument. Just one day! He had two battles here; he was here a lot!

Peter the Great is the exceptional, unparalleled hero. He is fought over, as you can see by the reference to Petrozavodsk. What is important is that he is undoubtedly a hero, acknowledged by everyone, and has become a powerful symbol of Russian history. This is the reason why Peter is somewhat of a »wild card«, and is such a prized resource in Ivangorod. Other »monument candidates« are the artist Bilibin – a native of Ivangorod, and Baron Shtiglits, who is buried in Ivangorod. It seems to me that this strategy of monument building is only worthwhile when it concerns famous personalities and figures. It is not the actual historical facts that are important – Ivangorod needs a hero.

Interestingly enough, in both Narva and Ivangorod, the same historical period is in the forefront – the era connected with the Great Northern War. Obviously, one could even speak about a »dialog«, or a contraposition, carried on through the medium of these monuments. There is a project drawn up for a joint monument between Narva and Ivangorod. This would consist of statues of Peter I and Charles XII, standing on opposite sides, each holding a double-edged sword. From the commentary on the project that has been published in both Narva and Ivangorod local newspapers, the project is meant to express the interdependency and close ties between the two cities which, according to the author, needs to be »read« not as enmity, but as the inseparability and indestructibility of this relationship. And thus, near the border on the Estonian side, a joint memorial (re)creating a unified history is already in the works. The sculptor is from Ivangorod, and the statue is to be located in Narva. However, this is all still just an idea, and the financial backing needed to fund the project has yet to be found.

In closing, I would like to give another quote that illustrates how legends, and also monuments, are born:

And among the most recent historical acquisitions is the imperial oak tree in the park of Baron Shtiglits. They say that it was planted by Peter the First. Why? Because it is exactly this location that saw the death of 1000 horsemen in the year 1700 while crossing the river. Most likely that is why. Because Peter the First was here and planted it. It looks massive too, just about 300 years old. It's a huge, thick oak. There are hen houses, cowsheds, and the like there now. There it is, though – obviously the imperial oak of Peter the Great (laughs). There's also another oak there in Parusinka in Ivangorod. It has a fence around it. They say that it was planted by Alexander III in 1890. But that one's a rather sickly oak. The other one is obviously an imperial oak.[21]

Souvenirs

Ivangorod and its history are not really present in souvenirs. And this is despite the fact that the Ivangorod fortress and museum is visited by tourists, even if not as many as those who visit the museum in Narva. At the modest souvenir counter in the museum, you see only religious »icon« and »folk« painted Easter eggs and nesting dolls which carry with them more of a national feel, and lack any expression of the specific locality. No Soviet souvenirs are sold.

Different Histories for Different Projects?

History, being an academic or even more widely, a social construct, is written everyday. It is always created in the »here and now«. It is not, however, a collection box. History is not just the pile of certain sequential, chronologically arranged, and non-contradictory facts that is filled with »new events«. It is always a project, a project of the present time. We write history as it corresponds to our »today«, to our current strategic goals and long-term projects. That is why history, for the most part, tells us more about the present than it does about the past.

---

21   We can also note another important detail in this dialogue – the »hierarchy« of Russian tsars.

History, in the end, is basically just a text illustrating various »material evidence of the past«. Writing history, then, is mostly an editor's job: rewriting and perfecting, skipping one chapter and inserting another, changing parentheses to quotes, changing capital letters to lower-case and vice versa, etc. In this work, having only touched on the problem of which means and methods are used in creating history, we are trying to reflect upon why one particular version of history is called for and not another, and also which larger-scale and global projects this version fits into.

The History Written in Narva

The reconstructed historical narratives of Narva, in my opinion, are somewhat of a variegated, patchwork mosaic of facts, references, important figures, and the »necessary« time periods. Thanks to this variety and hodgepodge, the flow of historical time in Narva is neither linear nor evolutionary. Its historic images are almost unconnected to one another: they are autonomous and self-sufficient. Moreover, either the images are self-referring and self-sufficient, or there is no »common denominator« – when, for example, a common moral appraisal (what is good and what is bad) unites all possible images. »Education in Narva in the 20th century«, »Mercantile Narva«, and »Chivalric Narva« are all »right« and »good«. It seems that the various epochs in Narva's history are equally important, and that the various historical images of Narva do not compete with each other for dominance; they are not arranged in any kind of hierarchy according to events. They all have an equal right to coexist peacefully. A cemetery in which German soldiers from WW II are buried was recently restored in order to restore »justice« and »balance«. What is important is that the Soviet soldiers« cemetery has not been destroyed or forgotten. This symbolic act illustrates the changing accent on, and rewriting, the history of the »Great Patriotic War« (the Eastern European Theatre of WW II) into the history of the Second World War. Even the Soviet period, which has been virtually removed from the museum exhibitions, still remains in the souvenirs. It seems that every image can be made to be »exotic«, obviously to increase its sales and to take into consideration a varied consumer base.

It is both interesting and important that in an environment of active nation building, the national history of Narva takes a role nowhere near as dominant. It is just »one of…«, and has the same right to exist as the »Swedish« or »Tatar«: history of Narva. You get the impression that the local history in Narva is more import and in greater demand than a unified national history. And it is this local history, alongside the others, that includes the »national component«.

In the modern version of Narva's history, there is no hero image, and in particular no war hero image, or image of a defender of the motherland. Currently, there is no »Military Narva«. The historic images of the town are not created using any outstanding heroes around which a narrative is built. Historic periods are either defined anonymously or »populated« with important – but in no way central – figures. In other words, there is no »heroization« of history like in the Soviet era.

Almost no »other« is required for the creation of historical images in Narva for constructing a »self«. The close proximity of a neighbouring state in general and Ivangorod in particular, is of little significance. An impression is formed of the ignorance of neighbours, and adopting the metaphor of Erhard Stoelting,[22] it could be said that Narva »looks away from the border«, ignoring its neighbours. Common history is only important in the context of general Soviet history, but it is unified for the entire post-Soviet space and is not defined specifically by proximity to Ivangorod. To be fair, it should be pointed out that, contrary to the accepted version of history, everyday discourse deals with the presence of Ivangorod as well as that of »the Russian neighbours«. Thus the curator in the Narva museum comments, »Look here, Russia catapulted such cannon-balls!« What matters here is not so much the evaluative utterance but the fact of naming, accentuating and categorising, the isolation of the »other«. And it should be noted that this comment was made in Russian for exclusively Russian-speaking visitors of the museum.

I believe it is appropriate to view such a strategy for writing history as an identity policy. Attention to the local makes it possible to overcome a number of limitations and a narrowly oriented national approach and create a wide spectrum of all possible historical versions. In Narva, what is being brought up to date is not a policy of difference and opposition, that is, the actual creation of new and different social borders but rather a policy of identity in connection with the relevance of the most diverse forms and images. Evidently, the policy of difference would not have allowed for the creation of such a variegated mosaic of versions, and would have limited the possibilities presented by a policy of identity. Various groups in different situations and contexts can call for a more appropriate and adequate alternative for the situation, and the more proposed versions there are, the wider the possibilities of identification. And it is also possible to construct locality, exclusivity and uniqueness of a place through the diversity exhibited and communicated to the outside. I consider that such a strategy is built into the more global project of »creating a part of Europe« within which there are no longer borders, but where there is most likely still a demand for punctuated, local and at the same time very diverse identities and, accord-

---

22   Erhard Stoelting, »The Social Meanings of Borders«, in: *Nomadic Borders, Working Papers of CISR 7*, ed. by Olga Brednikova & Viktor Voronkov (St. Petersburg: Centre for Independent Social Research, 1999), pp. 87–90, in particular p. 88.

ingly, diverse versions of history. It appears that Narva is in some sense already »more a part« of Europe than the rest of Estonia, for it goes beyond the national level (recall, for example, its identification with Sweden), and is inscribed in a different »European project« which has better prospects and seems more alluring.

I would like to give two current examples in favour of the »European project« of Narva. On the announcement board of a building in Narva hangs an advert for language courses, and it reads: »Estonian – guaranteed success in citizenship exams! English – most recent communication methods!« Emphasis and priorities are clear from this announcement – English is for communicating, whereas Estonian is exclusively for official procedures. Knowledge of various languages is required to solve all sorts of problems, so for universal communication English is the language of choice, whilst Estonian is intended for a unique, authorised task, but certainly not for long-term prospects. Setting out to become part of Europe also means taking on its risks and problems. A teacher from a Narva high school talked about the fact that straight after the accession to the EU, the principal ran through the new professional tasks at the teachers' in-service: »We must all be prepared for the fact that in the new academic year we will have pupils from other countries, for example from Turkey.« The problem had not yet appeared and was hypothetical, but being European and sharing common duties and responsibilities, they were prepared to take it on and to start finding ways to solve it.

The History Written in Ivangorod

The history of Ivangorod is written slightly differently. Its aims and challenges are different; it points to a different project. Above all, its orderliness, consistency, logic should be noted. It is a consistent and orderly history of solidity, a history of an outpost on the western border. It is also an unconditional and accentuated military history in which basic moral values are linked to »prowess« and »the fatherland«. In history and what was created in Ivangorod, the form of the enemy can change constantly, but what remains constant is the overall purpose of the town. In this version, Ivangorod acquires an important and exclusive status as the »defender of the Fatherland«.

This historical narrative is created by formulating a form of hero, around which history evolves. Therefore, we are dealing first and foremost with the hero-soldier. He must be free from doubt and exclusive, irrefutable. Thus, Peter I becomes a hero, his image is already formulated, his moral values and interpretations are indisputable and they are not subject to revision or re-evaluation even during a period of radical reassessment. There is even some competition for him, and exploitation of the form is legitimised by the fact that Peter I »was often near Ivangorod«. In this connection, I think the relation to the Soviet pe-

riod is interesting here. Its displacement is perhaps linked not so much to the
»disagreement« but to some »lack of absolutism« or »lack of certainty«. A quick
and fundamental revision and re-interpretation of what went on casts doubt on
the value of the Soviet period. From the whole of Soviet history, only the period
of the Great War is relevant, because it fits in well with general military history.
Moreover, the military period makes it possible to find »heroes free from doubt«
and use a strategy for writing history using well-known figures.

The history of the town is inscribed in national Russian history, common to
the whole of Russian territory. This is precisely why it is not so important that
the museum should display a model of a peasant house of Tverskaya province
(are they the same all over Russia?), whilst in the souvenir shop you can buy
uniform, faceless »Russian« souvenirs. What is important is their »Russianness«,
their belonging to Russia. The production of locality in Ivangorod is not linked
to the creation of uniqueness, but rather with the claim of a special status and a
special mission for the town whose history is inscribed in the common, unified
history of Russia. In this connection, a policy of »participation« in the »great«
and »integral« was chosen, inscribing city's history into the history of the state.
There is a reason why increasing the significance and status of the town is often
formed by exploiting the »greats«, for example through the fact that famous
figures had been to Ivangorod:

Just think, there are few towns in Russia, especially such tiny ones as Ivangorod! Yet
Yeltsin and Sobchak flew over here in a helicopter, and Zhirinovsky was here. And Putin
himself, when he was still working together with Sobchak, came here (Female citizen of
Ivangorod, aged 34).

As in Narva, in Ivangorod the »other« is neither required nor formulated. Incidentally, the close proximity of neighbours, whilst not accentuated, is nevertheless considered. In the promotional brochure of the Ivangorod fortress it
says: »Nowadays, together with our Estonian neighbours and Narva, Ivangorod
is by its very history called towards mutual cultural enrichment and the strengthening of good relations with neighbouring countries.« These words on the one
hand demonstrate some kind of complicity and solidarity with Narva by forming
common goals – »together with our Estonian neighbours« – and on the other, a
recognition of their otherness through the designation of the »ethnicity« of the
neighbours. It is therefore important that »neighbouring countries« which are
anonymous follow the mention of Narva and Ivangorod, as they have no different characteristics or qualities except that they »are neighbours«. The »other« is
not so relevant; the history of Ivangorod is merged with the history of Russia,
although the absence of the »other« is not as unimportant as in Narva. It appears
that Ivangorod is more oriented towards Russia, and that for its history it is much
more important to be »complicit«. In my view, the strategy for the creation of a

version of Ivangorod history is its inscription in Russian national history. In this way, Ivangorod is more included in the project of nation-building than Narva.

So in Narva and Ivangorod there is a need for various histories, the writing of those histories serves different purposes and they are inscribed in different projects. It is significant that the histories of »divided cities« practically do not enter into the dialogue, they do not compete or solidify in the interpretation of joint historical events. Moreover, in these histories there is even a need for »close neighbours« to play the role of the »other«, some locating axes in order to find their position in terms of one another. For Narva and Ivangorod other references are important and significantly »shattered« in the space. It could be said that Narva and Ivangorod are looking in opposite directions, and if Narva is turning towards Europe, leaving aside its national level, then Ivangorod is looking towards Russia, taking part in the internal national project.

In Search of Adequate Explanatory Patterns... In Place of a Conclusion

The social transformations in post-Soviet space are generally conceptualised on the basis of the prospects of nation building, in particular the creation of a national history proper, and »native« national heroes. Moreover, the prospect of colonial/postcolonial and imperial/post-imperial research requires the active use of metaphors of change in relation to the Soviet Union. In accordance with this approach, identity in post-imperial conditions is confirmed »differentially« through a game of comparisons and contrasts, and the whole post-colonial theory is to a large extent built around the understanding and conceptualisation of the »other«.[23] Clearly, these concepts have an explanatory power and heuristic potential. Undoubtedly, in Tallinn or Tartu other histories are being written, and in Petersburg or Moscow other strategies are used for building forms which differ from those in Narva or Ivangorod. And these »other histories« fit perfectly with the explanatory pattern suggested by concepts of nation state building or post-imperialism. I think that a good example of this could be found in the fragment of an observation mission to Tartu, in which the »national hero« of Colonel Dudaev, who in 1991 refused to withdraw his troops from among the local population, certainly figures. And this evaluation beautifully illustrates the situation of »mirroring«, although with different interpretations. In Russia and Estonia the same figure is endowed with contradictory assessments.

---

23   Cf. in particular Homi Bhabha, *Nation and Narration* (New York: Routledge, 1990).

As is well-known, the weakness of »global« theories lies above all in their high degree of generalisation. And contrary to general trends, there are certainly marginal cases which perhaps are not fundamentally opposed, but nevertheless require their own conceptualisation. And these marginal cases are often *ad marginem* spaces. As demonstrated above, researchers link the particularity of borderlands exclusively with the proximity of neighbours, when social life is largely predetermined not so much by the context of one's own state as of that located close by. However, it remains that in the strategies for writing one's own histories and, more broadly, in identity policies, Narva and Ivangorod do not need each other at all. Until now, they have rather been important as a single region of everyday life or as a space for concentrated cross-border links and networks. In this connection, the use of approaches and concepts of borderlands cannot present an adequate explanatory pattern.

To grasp the social transformations in this new (post-soviet) borderland, it is necessary to take into account some significant local particularities in connection to the nation states involved. In relations between Narva and Ivangorod, the latter's status as a rather small town and its position within the social space of Russia is problematic as is the complex situation regarding citizenship in Narva, being some kind of a problem zone for Estonia. Both parties deem a resolution of their problems possible only via the »third court« – the EU. Thus, a three-tiered approach, taking into account the global/transnational, the national and the local is adequate.

I think in order to understand the interaction of the two towns and some processes »reshaping identities« the use of metaphors is heuristic. The current border is not a mirror when there is an interdependency, when there is a need for the »other«, and relations are practically mirrored, they reflect one another, even though perhaps with different »signs«. Neither is the border »shop window« when the aim of interaction is to present, to exhibit something outside. I believe that in the researched situation the metaphor of the window is more appropriate. The border becomes a window beyond which life itself carries on. One can look into this window, but those looking will remain external observers, since there is no participation in observation. This »peeping« will not change life on either side of the window, for on both sides each active person is involved in his own project.

From Silenced to Voiced: Changing Politics of Memory of Loss in Armenia[1]

Tsypylma Darieva

Recent work on social and cultural politics of memory in Europe has been dominated by certain phenomena such as the trauma of displacement and grievous loss. Not only most obvious instances such as the Holocaust, but also other violent catastrophic events in different parts of the world receive more and more attention from scholars and politicians. The shift of European borders has given rise to questions about the moral demarcation of the landscape of a »New Europe«, such as reconsideration and reorganization of the boundaries of a moral community of remembrance and the construction of a new »shared memory« in Europe. This process includes the struggle over »symbolic properties« and competing political views on space and the boundaries of a new »community«. A good example of this process is the debate between Germany and Poland over contested representations of a »shared« European victim identity, a violent past and, in particular, about the proper location of the future European Centre against Expulsion *(Europäisches Zentrum gegen Vertreibung)*. The interesting point about the vision of the recent European victimization history relates to the inclusion of Armenian loss and suffering during the large-scale massacres in the Ottoman Empire at the beginning of the 20th century. On the chronological scale, the Armenian expulsion and suffering are classified as the genealogical beginning of a »shared memory« of European death.

The act of revealing genocide and expulsion in »ethnic«, »regional« or »national« histories involved more than the emergence of a single »shared memory«. Following perestroika, the reemergence of the »suppressed« in socialist societies

1   I wish to thank to Levon Abrahamian for his useful comments during my field work in Yerevan. A part of the paper was presented under the title »Memorizing after Violent Loss in Armenia« at the German Society of Anthropology (DGV) Conference held in Halle (Saale) in September 2005, and another part under the title »Changing politics of memory of loss in Armenia« at the 11th ASN Convention in March 2006, at the Harriman Institute Columbia University, USA. I am most grateful to Stephan Feuchtwang (London School of Economics and Political Science, UK) who made an inspiring comment about the concept of this paper and Elsa-Bair Guchinova (Institute for Ethnology and Anthropology, Russian Academy of Sciences, Moscow, Yerevan) for discussion of the draft of this paper.

also produced new »disjunctive moments«[2] and counter-memories[3], which supplemented the reordering of meaningful universes and the emergence of new polities. In the course of the major transformation in post-socialist Eastern Europe, reviving the issue of genocide in Serbia in 1990 comprised such a »disjunctive moment« in the reordering of the history of former Yugoslavia.[4] The memory of mass executions in the Serbian-Croatian conflict produced reciprocal accusations of genocide and acts of revenge that represented a powerful emotional trigger for Serbian violence at the beginning of the 1990s, which ultimately has been successfully incorporated into the victimization myth of a separate national rebirth of Serbia. One could compare this with the movement among Armenians during the violent Karabakh conflict between Armenia and Azerbaijan at the beginning of the 1990s when the memory of the Armenian trauma of 1915 was transferred to the present and was emphasized during the Karabakh development.[5]

In her study on the politics of dead bodies Katherine Verdery made a useful suggestion to broaden the perspective on post-socialist changes. It is not only a problem of creating markets, making private property and constructing democracy, but also »a problem of reorganization on a cosmic scale, and it involves the redefinition of virtually everything, including morality, social relations, and basic meanings«[6]. More precisely, the process of moral purification includes claims for assessing blame and demanding accountability for example in defining »historical truth and justice«[7], which occurs at many different sites of memory. The post-Soviet revival of memory of the violent past goes hand in hand with establishing a new arena of moral »purification« in the sense of re-

2   David Apter, *Rethinking Development* (Newbury Park: Sage, 1987).

3   Peter Homans (ed.), *Symbolic Loss. The Ambiguity of Mourning and Memory at Century's End* (Charlottesville & London: University of Virginia Press, 2000), pp. 1–40.

4   Bette Denich, »Dismembering Yugoslavia: Nationalist Ideologists and the Symbolic Revival of Genocide«, in: *American Ethnologist* 21 (1994), 2, pp. 367–390.

5   Stephanie Platz, »The Shape of National Time: Daily Life, History and Identity during Armenia's Transition to Independence, 1991–1994«, in: *Altering States: Ethnographies of Transition in Eastern Europe and the Former Soviet Union,* ed. by Daphne Berdahl, Matti Bunzl & Martha Lampland (Ann Arbor: University of Michigan Press, 2000), pp. 114–139, in particular p. 134. In April 2005 according to the results of a sociological survey conducted by the Armenian Centre for Military and National Research over 80% of the respondents listed »Armenian massacres in Azerbaijan 1988–1990, Sumgait, Baku, Kirovabad« for the question of »which events have endangered the Armenian life in terms of genocide?« See in *Hayots ceghaspanutyun 90 tar'va sahmanagtsin* [The Armenian Genocide on the edge of 90 years], (Yerevan: Razmavar'akan yev azgain hetazotutyunner'i haykakan kentr'on, 2005). The answers of 1900 respondents from Yerevan and all other Armenian administrative units have been calculated in that survey.

6   Katherine Verdery, *The Political Life of Dead Bodies. Reburial and Postsocialist Change* (New York: Columbia University Press, 1999), p. 35.

7   Verdery, *The Political Life of Dead Bodies,* op.cit. (note 6).

trieving and remaking the memory of the Armenian massacre as a new »cosmic« order of the Armenian nation, once suppressed by the Communist government. In this paper, I am going to draw attention to the postsocialist change on the »cosmic scale« of remembrance of loss and death among post-Soviet Armenians. One of the crucial points in creating a new moral universe in Armenia is the re-establishment of memory and justice regarding the Armenian *yeghern* (grief and mourning) not only in terms of the post-Soviet »return of the repressed«[8], but in a broader framework of recognition of a silenced and »forgotten« human loss in terms of global morality.[9] To illustrate this change, I will focus on the area surrounding the Yerevan's memorial on Armenian Genocide, which occupies a clear-cut piece of urban territory but did not always present a »fixed space« in the memory of its inhabitants or is the collective Yerevan memory more gener-ally. The idea of periodical shifts in the meaning of places and monuments of commemoration as they are contested by different interest groups[10] is involved in understanding the recent remaking of identity in Armenia. My concern is how the memory of catastrophic loss in 1915, having once been a political and social taboo in the Soviet past, has today become a crucial moral code in the formation of national and personal identities in the Armenian Republic, pro-ducing different sets of ritualized practices of public commemorations. I will show how the issue of memory of trauma and loss, which earlier was uneasily localized in the urban landscape of Soviet Yerevan around the monument, fol-lowing independence became the driving force in establishing and expanding the central national-timeless-sacredness across borders. Using my ethnographic observations from spring 2005 in Yerevan, I will analyze the urban practices of post-Soviet commemorations as an example of the politics of (trans)national grief that define the contemporary Armenian cosmic scale of death and rebirth.

---

8   Rubie S. Watson, »Introduction«, in: *Memory, History and Opposition under State Socialism* ed. by R. Watson (Santa Fe: School of American Research Press, 1994), pp. 1–20.

9   I use the term of global morality in the sense of moral universalization of local and national suffering and loss by involving of international organizations across borders. The idea of the global morality was discussed by Daniel Levy and Natan Sznaider in their work on the cosmopolitization of memory of Holocaust. One of the principles of global morality, as a result of universalization of the Holocaust, is related to the possibility of real or symbolic expecting of moral and economic compensation by former victims from the side of perpetrators. See Daniel Levy & Natan Sznaider, *Erinnerungen im globalen Zeitalter: Der Holocaust* (Suhrkamp-Verlag: Frankfurt am Main, 2001), p. 239.

10 Frances Pine, Deema Kaneff & Haldis Haukanes (eds), *Memory, Politics and Religion. The Past Meets the Present in Europe* (Münster: Lit Verlag, 2004), pp. 1–29. James Young, *At Memory's Edge: After-Images of the Holocaust in Contemporary Art and Architecture* (New Haven & London: Yale University Press, 2000). Andreas Huyssen, *Present Pasts: Urban Palimpsests and the Politics of Memory* (Stanford: Stanford University Press, 2003).

The Signposts of Remembering

In the spring of 2005, the street lanterns in central Yerevan were covered by red-and-black posters with an image of the mountain Ararat and the Sardarapad Memorial bell-tower headed by the English inscription ›1915–2005 Recognition‹ At the same time, at the central crossroads one could see a huge white poster like an advertising board announcing the international conference »The Armenian Genocide« in April 2005. Local TV programs broadcasted the weather report with an unusual geography extending far beyond the national borders, bringing information about the atmosphere and air temperature not only in the usual locations of Russian Krasnodar and St.Peterburg, but also in Kars and Erserum, located behind the closed border between Armenia and Turkey. In these days, the metaphors »warm« and »cold«, »sunny« and »cloudy« received a new rhetorical and moral dimension in Armenia.

Driving down Mashtotz Avenue (formerly Lenin Street) a taxi driver asked me where I came from and added that his grandparents originated from »Western Armenia«.[11] »My grandfather was five years old when he rescued himself from the Turks, do you know how? When the Turks came to kill his parents he managed to escape by creeping into the *tonir* – the oven for preparing the Armenian bread *lavash* – and the killers didn't find him. He stayed inside of this oven several days and then fled alone by foot to Echmiyatzin.« I asked him, where his grandfather came from exactly in Western Armenia. The taxi driver hesitated for a while and replied, »...I suppose from the region of Van.« Such dramatic family stories told in an everyday situation reminded me of a short verbal snapshot during a guided tour, were omnipresent in encounters in Armenia and they were the subjects of narrative and self-representations among Yerevantsi in April 2005. I want to emphasize the fact that the fragmented stories of loss and suffering were not always incorporated into daily conversations, but when they were brought up they were presented by ordinary people to a non-Armenian in an allegorical manner by using tropes and mythicized deeds. The loss was presented not as pain or knowledge of lost territories, but rather as a heroic deed of surviving ancestors.

»You know, our bread *lavash* has a specific history. Our bread is light and is easy for transportation. Do you know why the Armenian *lavash* is so thin? In order to dry it fast and take it with you after expulsion«, a 45–year-old boxing trainer told me while ordering traditional Armenian food in a restaurant.[12]

The identification with victimhood and the inscription of trauma into every-

---

11   Armenians call the territory of the present Turkish Anatolia »Western Armenia« which is similar to another tradition of calling Istanbul »Constantinople«.

12   The Armenian bread lavash (*hats*) has a much longer history. See Alla Ter-Sarkisyants, »Tra-

day life and material culture are not new in Armenian society. Nora Dudwick, an American anthropologist who conducted her fieldwork in Armenia between the end of the 1980s and the beginning of 1990s, during the period of the Karabakh movement and the war between Armenia and Aserbaidjan, observed social and economic life in Yerevan during perestroika. »Since coming to Armenia, I had based my understanding of Armenian culture on a set of Armenian self-representations that had been profoundly shaped by collective memories of the state-organized violence in the Ottoman Empire between 1915 and 1918. While the conflict with Azerbaijan escalated, self-representations of Armenians as an ancient, cultivated and Christian people increasingly dominated the movement discourse, and the image of victim became increasingly foregrounded«.[13]

Similarly, after the disintegration of the Soviet Union the hardship of economic survival and energy crises was symbolically associated by local people with a return of historical grievance, regression and rupture.[14] Even though they emerged victorious from the Karabakh war between Armenia and Azerbaijan, Armenians identify themselves mostly as the »victims«[15] of the war. Armenian civilians killed during pogroms in Baku or Sumgait and Karabakh soldiers are perceived and memorialized as recent saints and martyrs of the Armenian nation. In the spring of 2005, the remembering of Armenian pain among ordinary people was often expressed through the practices of mythicized self-representations. I argue, that these are not necessarily a particularly post-Soviet innovation; rather the increasing emotional force of victimhood in the period of transition has been much shaped by the previous Soviet ideological frame of interpretation of loss in terms of historical heroism and martyrial struggle in the cosmic world once divided into two political poles. In her recent work on the processes of the »unmaking« of the Soviet life Caroline Humphrey made the valuable observation that the current transition in Russia »is heavily ideologized or mythicized, no less so than the revolutionary transition to socialism«.[16]

ditional Food of Armenians«, in: *Traditional Food as Expression of Ethnic identity*, ed. by S. Arutyunov & T. Voronina (Moscow: Nauka, 2001), pp. 119–131.

13   Nora Dudwick, »Postsocialism and the Fieldwork of War«, in: *Fieldwork Dilemmas. Anthropology in Postsocialist States*, ed. by Hermine G. De Soto & Nora Dudwick (Madison, StateWis.: University of Wisconsin Press, 2000), pp. 13–30.

14   In her excellent ethnography of the Armenian daily life between 1991–1994, Stephanie Platz has described the level of catastrophic demodernization during the energy crisis in Armenia. See in Platz, *The Shape of National Time*, op.cit (note 5).

15   Thanks to Lale Yalcin-Heckmann (Max Planck Institute for Social Anthropology, Halle) who read the very first draft of this paper and for bringing this observation to my attention.

16   Caroline Humphrey, *The Unmaking of Soviet Life. Everyday Economies after Socialism* (Ithaca & London: Cornell University Press, 2002), p. 21.

Soviet Past and Tabooization of Loss

In countries with a totalitarian and communist past, violent loss and remembrance practices have been highly selective, partly forgotten and even erased like the missing faces in official state portraits during Stalinism.[17] Officially, in the former Soviet Union there was one dominant, powerful collective locus of memory of violent loss, which became the central symbol of Soviet collective memory and commemoration ceremonies: the victory and memory of victims of the Second World War, called the Great Patriotic War. A particular meaning of this site of memory lay in the fact that the remembering and representations of the violent loss have been turned into the glorification of fallen soldiers as heroes by the state propaganda. Memory of loss and death in the Soviet time was homogenized and perpetuated through numerous monuments, texts, memorializing practices and finally shifted to the notion of »the struggle«. The specific socialist notion of »struggle« and identity of a fighter was visualized in the pantheon of places of the Patriotic War throughout the territory of the Soviet Union. It was embodied in the dead »idealised personae of youthful war heroes« such as Gastello or Zoya Kosmodemianskaya[18] and in living cultivated personae of Soviet veterans of different ethnic and social backgrounds, who still play a significant role as »political grandfathers« in the genealogy of postsocialist visions of national solidarity and future. Even after the disintegration of the Soviet Union, each year in May in the former Soviet republics of South Caucasus and Central Asia (but not in the Baltic states) political »grandfathers« appear on the public arena around the Victory Memorials for traditional ceremonies celebrating the heroism of the Soviet people and its successors. On the 9th of May, the Day of Victory, Yerevan central newspapers printed the number and names of Armenian generals and heroes who belonged to the central pantheon in the Soviet eschatological order.[19]

The political theater of glorifying an anonymous fallen hero of the Soviet Union left little space for individual and local expressions of pain and loss. Even citizens with Jewish background who were soldiers in the Soviet Army and who lost relatives during the large-scale massacres of the Jewish population in Belorussia and Ukraine had not explicitly developed any »traumatic memory« of

---

17   David King, *The Commissar Vanishes: The Falsification of Photographs and Art in Stalin's Russia* (New York: Metropolitan Books, 1997). Pine, Kaneff, Haukanes, *Memory, Politics and Religion*, op.cit. (note 10).

18   Nina Tumarkin, *The Living and the Dead. The Rise and Fall of the Cult of World War II in Russia* (New York: Basic Books, 1994).

19   The memory of struggle and of fighters during the Second World War is today overlapping with the new national symbol of victory by Armenians in the Karabakh War, which is marked by commemoration of the day of conquest of the city of Shushi (May 9th) in 1994 by the Armenian Liberation Army.

the Holocaust, an explicitly victim identity; in contrast, many Soviet Jews perceive themselves as a part of the big nation-state that defeated fascist Germany. In the Soviet Union the Jewish genocide and suffering has not been particularized as the ultimate suffering of a specific group; it was forgotten, since for a long time the official discourse refused to memorialize Jewish Holocaust victims.[20]

During the Soviet period, the Armenian massacre of 1915 in the Ottoman Empire was not included in the official repertoire of national memory and commemoration. Many Yerevantsi emphasized that in the Soviet time there was very little verbal and visual information about the violence and expulsion of Armenians from Eastern Anatolia. Until the beginning of the 1980s it was scarcely communicated in school curricula, school-books including only some »unrememberable« lines with complicated numbers and dates«.[21] In Soviet Armenia the memory of the violent loss and expulsion of Armenians from Eastern Anatolia to Syria was a political taboo until at least 1965. Publicly, the knowledge about death and loss was restricted to a very limited space being hidden »between the lines« of city guide books or in exclusive departments of the National Academy of Sciences and state archives with highly restricted access. As a result, the art of remembering the Armenian genocide in Armenia took a fragmented and formulaic form in the production of a few academic books filled with dry official documents, which were far removed from popular and personal practices of remembering. A 70-year-old local ethnographer at the Armenian Academy of Sciences told me that as a descendent of Armenian survivors and of a *repartriant*[22] from Egypt she had long been prevented in her struggle to investigate the memories and testimonies of the few surviving victims. In the Soviet Republic of Armenia the group of Armenian *repatrianty* originally from Eastern Anatolia had been largely excluded from the officially glorified »national landscape« and

---

20 In my previous research project on post-Soviet Russian speakers in Berlin many Russian Jews in Germany, in contrast to the German government, did not associate with belonging to the victims of Holocaust. One interviewee revealed me to his »ignorance« of Jewish suffering during the World War II by telling me that he only understood the whole meaning of the word »ghetto« after his migration to Germany. Also see Tumarkin, *The Living and the Dead*, op.cit. (note 10), p. 221 who noticed that in »Khrushchev's cosmology, to admit the reality of the Holocaust – the Nazi genocide of the Jewish people – meant to deprive the larger Soviet polity of its status as super-victim, par excellence, which was touted as a major source of legitimacy«.

21 From the interview on 2.05.2005 with a local 35–year-old historian in Yerevan.

22 A group of Armenian re-settlers from the Middle East and other Western countries who survived after the expulsion and massacres and arrived in Soviet Armenia at Stalin's invitation towards the end of the 40s are called *repatrianty* in Armenia. Around 200,000 people were attracted by the Stalin campaign (see Nora Dudwick, *Memory, Identity and Politics in Armenia* (Ann Arbor: UMI, 1994) and Ronald Grigor Suny, *Looking Towards Ararat: Armenia in Modern History* (Bloomington: Indiana University Press, 1993)), but because of hard political and economic conditions a large number of repatriates left Soviet Armenia in the 70s and emigrated to Western countries.

been seen as an inappropriate academic source. »No local Armenians supported my idea of collecting data on testimonies. I think because they did not experience the loss personally and in their families, but me, I experienced it on my skin«- explained the ethnographer in her interview.[23] At the end of the 1950s a young woman was allowed to collect ethnographic data among survivors of Armenian massacres only within the framework of the official research ideology of the Academy of Sciences – to show the variety of Armenian folklore. Focusing on linguistic differences and forms of folklore texts, songs and poems among *repatrianty*, she looked at the same time for »secret histories« of the Armenian tragedy. But the results of these collections have been published only recently after 1991.[24]

This example shows us how strongly the official ideology and the authorities shaped the politics of remembering Armenian loss during the Soviet era. Not surprisingly, at the end of the 1940s the arrival of Armenian »returnees«, *repatrianty,* and the emergence of new city districts with demonstrative, evocative names such as Sebastia, Nor Kilikia or Zeytun (places in Eastern Turkey) resulted in restrictive and repressive controls by officials. The fear of punishment for having contact with taboo peoples and some visible cultural differences easily produced a hostile mode of relationships between the locals and newcomers. The ethnographer remembered in the interview that the local population in Yerevan started to call the newcomers *akhpar,* a word with a derogatory and abusive connotation. The term »akhpar« was used by newcomers to address brothers and unfamiliar male citizens on the streets (see the contribution by Abrahamian in this volume). It sounded phonetically different from the local term *yeghpayr.* Moreover, *akhpar* was close to the local pronunciation of the term *ahgb* which means »garbage«. The resettlers were hardly seen as deserving social solidarity, on the contrary they were condemned to the category of a hostile »diaspora« with a foreign bourgeois background and caste in the image of exotic and dangerous[25] foreigners possessing prestigious consumer goods, like French soap, rare in the Soviet Union.

In Soviet times, the Armenian loss and trauma were never publicly articulated in the language of victims, perpetrators and symbolic recognition. It seems that the memory of loss encapsulated in the socialist order has produced specific decontextualized and quite paradoxical forms of memories. If we look at exist-

---

23   The interview was conducted in Yerevan on the 2nd and 3rd of May 2005.

24   The part of the ethnographic materials (Cilicia. Oral tradition of Western Armenians) was first published in 1994 with the help of the Armenian *Catholicos* of Cilicia. See also Verjine Svazlian, *The Armenian Genocide. Testimonies of the Eyewitness-Survivors* (Yerevan: Gitutyun Publishing House NAS RA, 2000).

25   Many repatriates after their arrival in Soviet Armenia were arrested and deported to Siberia, mostly to the Altai region.

ing »silent disagreements«,[26] so-called small acts of private remembrance of loss in Armenia, they are mostly encoded through social practices of knowing about descent – origins in the territories far behind the Armenian-Turkish border in »Western Armenia«. For example in the talk with the taxi driver mentioned at the beginning of this essay. At the same time, the memory of loss, or at least the symbolic representation of Armenian loss, was present paradoxically on a much larger scale through acts of »symbolic possession« of lost landscape. This can be vividly seen in numerous pictures of the holy Mount Ararat in private and public spaces.[27] Moreover, Mount Ararat which is situated in Turkish territory and clearly is visible from the windows of many Yerevan residences. In the Soviet past, the image of Mount Ararat was successfully incorporated into official Armenian iconography such as the heraldic figure on the Soviet Armenian coat of arms, the name of the Soviet Armenian soccer team and the brand name of the most famous alcoholic drink »Armenian Cognac«, thus producing a sense of possession of Ararat as a symbolic cultural property. Through similar depictions of Mount Ararat in school-books, calendars and in cook books such as »The Armenian cuisine« published in 1960,[28] it has been symbolically (re)turned to the cultural landscape of Soviet Armenian identity. In that sense the memory of the traumatic past in both public and private spaces appears to be transmitted less from person to person than by formulaic evocative indications such as the image of the holy mountain. The social remembrance of descent, the acts of singing songs half in Armenian and half in Turkish, or the possession of a few household objects recalling the expulsion after 1915 existed in the Soviet past only in hidden spaces which were suppressed, decontextualized and dissolved into the Soviet cult of the »struggle« against fascism and the post-Soviet economic struggle for survival.[29]

---

26 Watson, *Memory, History and Opposition*, op.cit. (note 8), p. 11.

27 The term »symbolic possession« was mentioned by Nora Dudwick in analyzing the issue of the 1915 genocide in Armenian collective memory at the end of the 80s. See Dudwick, *Memory, Identity and Politics in Armenia*, op.cit. (note 22).

28 A. Piruzyan, *Armyanskaya kulinariya* (Moskva: Gostorgizdat, 1960).

29 During my interviews in a private house of a two-generation family, the 60-year-old mother told me about her husband's origin in Kars. He was living in Russia at the time of the interview. After she mentioned that the family actually possessed an engraving with a view of the Armenian church and the Kars city wall I asked her to show me this engraving. For a while she could not remember where she had put it in and suddenly she went out to the balcony and brought an old dusty broken engraving in her hands. »I found it outside near our generator we received from our relatives in the US. Do you remember the really hard time without energy and lighting in Yerevan, daughter?« – the mother reminded her daughter. The personal memory of the energy crisis at the beginning of the 90s dominated our conversation. The mother and daughter told me about the quality of the American generator and its role in saving their lives in a dark Yerevan.

The Uneasy Localization of Loss in Soviet Yerevan

In spite of its depersonalization and political tabooization, the memory of violent loss was a part of Armenian social identity, which found its first vocal articulation in Yerevan in the mid-1960s. In April 1965, half a century after the catastrophic event, a closed session of the Armenian Communist Party, dedicated to the 50th anniversary of the Armenian tragedy, was organized in the Opera House building. At that time, no public commemorations were arranged in Yerevan by the authorities. Thousands of city inhabitants gathered at the central Lenin Square in Yerevan and finally an unexpected public protest broke out around the Opera building. This anti-authoritarian demonstration is seen by local historians as the first public expression against forgetting the Armenian tragedy and the lost territories in Turkey. With the slogan »Lands, Lands!« the demonstrators demanded the recognition of the Armenian massacres by the central authorities in Moscow. At the same time it was an unveiling of a previously unarticulated desire to allow official mourning and grieving ceremonies for ordinary people in public places. In fact, subsequently and in a very short time, according to a Party decision. The Genocide Memorial was erected on the green hill of Tsitsernakaberd in 1967,[30] close to central Yerevan. From that point a public stage for a controlled mourning *yeghern* practice has been constructed in the Republic of Armenia. Since 1967, the hidden and disordered practices of mourning were appropriated by the officials and taken under control. At the same time, a new form of commemoration practice settled into the cyclical life of the city landscape, localized around the Genocide Memorial. Within the urban landscape the new monument is distinguished from other public commemorative places by its visible, but at the same time, isolated location on a green hill encircled by a natural barrier, the river Razdan, and in that sense by spatial separatedness from central streets. At this point the local authorities tried to take control over the memorialization of Armenian loss.

The establishment of an uneasy public mourning practice began in Yerevan in that period. Especially in the middle of the 1980s a mourning ceremony and procession became the major commemorative event in the city each year on April 24th. On that day, local inhabitants, like pilgrims, gather at the bottom of the hill and slowly move to the top towards the Genocide Memorial with red tulips, white carnations and small candles in their hands.

After 1965 the remembering of the catastrophic event in Armenia was officially allowed but turned into a commemorative ceremony of a very specific kind. It was well incorporated into the Soviet model of national remembrance and into the Soviet Union's foundation myth. The construction of the new

---

30   Some more details are presented in the contribution by Maike Lehmann in this volume.

monument brought a »sacred« space into the iconography of remembering and the urban memorial landscape, but this action did not signal any radical change in the »universe of meaning« and politics of memory. Thus, the Armenian collective desire to mark a particular historical consciousness and cultural belonging did not conflict with the socialist cosmology beginning only in 1917. After considering how to regulate and to control people's spontaneous movement at the city square, the Central Committee of the Communist Party of Armenia decided to operate within the framework of the celebration of the 20th anniversary of the victory in World War II, incorporating the atrocities of the Ottoman Turks towards Armenians into the abstract symbology of the antifascist struggle of the Soviet people against Hitler's aggression and expansion.

The design of the Genocide Memorial was very much influenced by the monumental architecture of Soviet war memorials, which was quickly spreading in the 1960s throughout Soviet territory.[31] At that time, the Memorial in Yerevan consisted of two objects – a tomb and an obelisk. The massive grey stone mausoleum with 12 slabs and the eternal flame inside the tomb took on the meaning of a collective grave, and a separate needle-thin stone obelisk located next to the tomb symbolized the rise of Armenian people from the dead and its regeneration within the Soviet space. The obelisk appears as a larger spire built over the top of and encapsulating a smaller spire. The museum for the Armenian genocide on the grounds of the memorial complex as well as other graves[32] constructed in a recognizable form of Armenian traditional stone crosses (*khachkar*) were erected much later, after gaining independence in 1991. At the end of the 1960s the remembering of the Armenian pain was a localized historical event, which was not supposed to challenge the ideals of the collective Soviet identity and Soviet power. The Armenian pain was represented in the same language and visual forms as the heroic symbols of the Second World War. The Yerevan monument corresponds to the later design of Soviet war memorials in many aspects: being situated on a grassy hill at a distance from the city center like the memorial and museum for the defenders of Moscow, in its typical monumental design including a triumphal obelisk, long huge mourning avenue and the memorial wall, as in the Soviet art of mourning and remembrance of dead through officials placing memorial garlands around the tomb, and in the minute of silence.[33] In this sense the »bad« unnatural and unrecognized deaths of the Armenian people

---

31 Harutyun Marutyain also mentions this aspect in his analysis of the Karabakh movement in this volume.

32 The graves in the form of traditional *khachkars* were dedicated to memory of Armenian victims in Sumgait, Karabakh and Baku.

33 See Tumarkin, *The Living and the Dead,* op.cit. (note 10). Ethnographical and historical work shows how state and party authorities stage-managed a national trauma into a heroic exploit that glorified the Communist Party.

were converted into a performed ritual of remembering the »hard past« and the martyr-like symbolism of a »good death«. Further, the absence of a visualized death or a killed body is conspicuous for visitors at the Memorial. Inside the mausoleum, which looks like a famous tomb of the Soviet Unknown Soldier, there are no visible signs of a victim or a dead body, only the eternal flame in a circle reminiscent of the Soviet star. The most striking point in the whole design of the monument is the absence of any »ethnic« Armenian signs or traditional inscriptions in the Armenian alphabet on the slabs and walls, such sign and inscriptions are omnipresent in the Soviet and post-Soviet architecture in Armenia.[34] Over the years political orthodoxy tried to pursue one historical interpretation of the Genocide Memorial to be accepted by all. Among Yerevantsi it was supposed to be associated with the holy place of generalized memory of victims of violence, related to the symbol of struggle against fascism; with the ability of Armenian life to regenerate under Soviet rule and with a commitment to Soviet-Armenian patriotism. The inclusive interpretation of the struggle against fascism easily combined Hitler's Germany with Turkey into a common image of the enemy since Germany built a political alliance with Turkey during the WW I.

In spite of the partial official recognition of Armenian suffering, until the end of the 80s the representation of the past and commemorations of Armenian loss continued to be a partly taboo memory. In March 2005 the newspaper »*Golos Armenii*« (Voice of Armenia) published documentary archive data revealing the way the decision was made by authorities as to how the massacres of 1915 should be publicly remembered in Soviet Armenia. In 1985 attempted Demirchian, the first secretary of Armenian Communist Party, to bring up the issue of memory on a political level by introducing an official Day of Remembrance in Armenia to be implemented by a national law (*ukaz*), but without success. The restrained proceedings of the day of mourning were supposed to remain within usual frameworks on the same »regional level« without being incorporated into the cultural and political repertoire of state ideology. In the newspaper one can read the extract from the decision of the Party session: »On the eve of the 24th of April to organize necessary mass political measures and actions for a mass explanation of the historical role of the Great October Socialist Revolution in rescuing the Armenian people from physical extermination, to reveal the achievements of the revived Armenian people under the Soviet power as a triumph of Lenin's national policy of the Communist Part of the Soviet Union.«[35]

---

34   The interesting contrast to that is the memorial ensemble in the Victory Park in the northern part of the city of Yerevan. The design of the wall of heroes is made in Armenian ethnic style. It is a row of Armenian red tufa *khachkars* – cross stones decorated with the fruit symbols of Armenian peasant culture like pomegranate, wine, trees.

35   Levon Mikaelyan, »Session of Politburo of the CC CPSU from 21.02.1985«, in: *Golos Armenii*, (March 17th, 2005), p. 6.

With the localization of Armenian loss, Soviet officials in Yerevan tried to restore the socialist order and to centralize the people's memory in one manner and one place. But the relationship between the dominant version of history and local engagements with it was more complex. German ethnographer Jürgen Gispert mentions in his analysis of the genocide monument, that for architects in the mid-60s the idea of the pillars was to shelter the entrance into the tomb and in that sense they carried a primarily technical significance.[36] In 2005, many locals and tourist guides interpreted the original idea of the slab in terms of an intimate relation to traditional Armenian stone crosses *khachkars*. The museum guide and the visitors to the Memorial used to say that the 12 pillars stand for 12 Armenian *villayets*[37] in Eastern Anatolia, symbolizing territories lost after the expulsion and killing of Armenians in 1915. Similar to the re-intepretation of the Memorial concept, other parts of the monument have also experienced alternative imaginings beyond the »monologic historical explanation«[38] and fixed spatial contours of the Soviet Armenian representation. Unlike the traditional narrative related to the symbol of regeneration of Armenian life within the Soviet space, the high obelisk spire generated a variety of alternative interpretations and associations among local people, which can be recognized as a »counter-mourning« response.[39] A friend of mine bringing me to the Memorial for the first time in 2004 explained that the obelisk symbolizes the memory of a divided Armenia, where the smaller part is modern Armenia, and the larger one represents the lost territory of historical Armenia. Another interpretation was framed in present political discourses of hierarchical relationships between Russia and Armenia, leaving aside the memory of loss. According to this interpretation the larger part stands for »big brother« Russia and the smaller one for the smaller Republic of Armenia. A decade earlier, after the Karabakh conflict, the spire was reinterpreted according to the current political order,[40] moving far away from usual explanations. The smaller spire, which symbolized the Republic of Armenia, was replaced by the image of a self-proclaimed Nagorny Karabakh Republic, whereas Armenia was upgraded to the bigger spire, pushing out the memory of the »big brother« Russia.

---

36 Jürgen Gispert, »The ethno-philosophical interpretation of the Memorial for Armenian Genocide in the Ottoman Empire in Yerevan«, in: *Researches of Contemporary Problems at the Universities. The conference papers, 25–26.11.1999* (Yerevan: Hayastan, 2000), pp. 66–89, in particular p. 73.

37 *Villayet* is the Turkish term for an administrative unit in the Ottoman Empire.

38 Gail Kligman, *The Wedding of the Dead; Ritual, Poetics, and Popular Culture in Transylvania* (Berkeley: University of California Press, 1988).

39 Homans, *Symbolic Loss*, op.cit. (note 3), pp. 1–40.

40 This specific interpretation, related to the Karabakh war, I have borrowed from Gispert, »The Ethno-philosophical Interpretation of the Memorial for Armenian Genocide in the Ottoman Empire in Yerevan«, op.cit. (note 36), pp. 66–89.

With reference to the above-mentioned examples it is obvious that the monument was implicitly producing a specific »hidden« meaning for the local people, a place of creative reinterpretations and of silenced protest against the suppressed memories of Armenian tragedy.[41] In 2005, ordinary participants of the mourning march told me that in the Soviet time not everybody attended the procession to the Tsitsernakaberd hill in April; it was a normal working day and was not supported by the authorities. »Before 1988, April 24th was not an official holiday, and people were penalized for leaving work to come to the memorial. People made the treck after working hours (or simply slipped away during work hours) with colleagues or family members.«[42] People like members of the intelligentsia, students and school children visited the memorial place on their own initiative. The Yerevan anthropologist Gayane Shagoyan told me that at the beginning of the 1980s in Gumri (Leninakan) in April many schoolgirls followed their own private silent mourning practice by wearing black collars and black cuffs instead of white over the brown school uniform dress. These examples of expressing »silent disagreement«[43] demonstrate the local attitude towards the official politics of representation of the past. The active construction of popular imaginations and disagreements have contributed to a new way of memorializing loss and of the post-Soviet representation of Armenian tragedy, which has undergone a deep transformation by reordering meaningful imaginations.

(Trans) Nationalization of Loss

After the collapse of the Soviet Union and the dramatic experiences of social and economic upheavals in Armenia one can identify the dynamic revival of memory of collective death on the official level and its transformation into a symbol of total ethnic tragedy incorporated into the nation-state ideology. In the mid-1990s in Armenia, the 24th of April was proclaimed as a Day of Remembrance and as a day off, »the black day of the calendar«. Having once been a taboo and an unauthorized representation of the past, today the symbol of loss and trauma is the collective property and the symbolic capital of the new nation state and different social groups. This capital provides these domains with the central power for constructing a new postsocialist (trans)-national community of loss and with

---

41 At the end of 70s and in the 80s according to local media sources around 250,000 people participated in the self-organized public »pilgrimage« to the memorial hill. See Mikaelyan, »Session of Politburo«, op.cit. (note 35), p. 6.

42 Dudwick, *Memory, Identity and Politics in Armenia*, op.cit. (note 22), p. 80.

43 Watson, *Memory, History and Opposition*, op.cit. (note 8).

Figure 2.1: The mourning procession to the Armenian Genocide Memorial, Yerevan 2005, Photo: T. Darieva.

a tool for establishing a new moral order in relationships with citizens and the whole world. The interesting point in the route that Armenia took in changing its morality after socialism is that unlike other postsocialist lands in Eastern Europe or the Baltic States there was only very weak critique and views opposed to the communist past and the Russian presence. The new rhetoric in the efforts to restore »justice« and to reveal the political dimension of Armenian pain was conceptualized less in terms of demanding recognition of the »suppressive« character of the communist past and the Russian-Soviet political domination since 1917. Rather, it is a demand for proper memorialization of forgotten loss in 1915, in which the determination of future politics concerning neighboring Turkey comes to the fore. The main vector in »restoring« this moral universe was reliance on an idenity of unrecognized suffering of Armenians as a Christian group before 1917. After 1991, the memory of death and suffering has taken on a new globalized dimension by assessing the notion of the »perpertrator«, »guilt« and »reparation« towards an outside »evil«.

Armenians have successfully »domesticated« and appropriated the Memorial from the Soviet period, turning it into one of the central holy places of ethnic history in a global sense. For example, popular views have immediately transformed the Soviet symbol of the eternal flame, which played a significant role in

the Soviet political culture as the memory of an »unknown hero«, into the traditional »sacred« symbol of Armenianness. The presence of the eternal flame today
will often be associated with the maintenance of the ancient religious tradition of
fire worship among Armenians. This tradition is based on the memory of pagan
Zoroastrian beliefs and comes from »time immemorial«, before Armenians were
baptized.[44]

The most visible transformation of post-Soviet Armenian memory politics
regarding the massacres occurred in 1995 with the construction of a new holy
place on the Memorial grounds – the museum of Armenian genocide. Dedicated
to the 80th anniversary of the execution of Armenian intellectuals in Istanbul,
the museum in Yerevan was built on the southern part of the memorial grounds
like a second tomb beneath ground level inside of the Tsitsernakaberd hill. It
looks at the holy Mount Ararat which rises up on the »other« side of the closed
border and which, like a monumental side scene, plays an enormously impress-
sive role in the whole Memorial panorama. Attached to the National Academy of
Sciences, the museum is today the leading center in coordinating the politics of
memory and its representation. In contrast to the mausoleum, the museum has
created an official visualized landscape of remembering with a specified topography of lost lands, ethnic suffering and of the sacredness of death. In April and
September the museum represents one of the most attractive sight-seeing places
in Yerevan both for tourists and locals; on the 24th of April many participants
of the mourning march include a visit to the museum into the dramaturgy of
the »pilgrimage«. In general, in this »hot« period between April and September,
Yerevan turns into a place of gatherings of the global Armenian diaspora, which
after the collapse of the Soviet Union worked out various kinds of connections
with the homeland. One of the central organizing points of the seasonal global
encounters relates to the Day of Remembrance in the form of visiting the Memorial on the hill. The post-Soviet politics of memory of loss and of the massacres
was actively shaped by the increasing significance of connections with the Armenian diaspora (*spiurk*) in the US which was beyond the scope of imaginations
during the Soviet period.[45]

Inside the museum one can observe the results of the ideological and material
involvement of the Armenian diaspora in the national project of the homeland
such as the museum's web site and leaflets, which were sponsored by the Ameri-

---

44   See Platz (note 5) where she describes the symbolic meaning of fire and light among Armenians
      in the period of economic and energy crises and how people linked fire with ethnic belonging
      in their mythicized story telling.

45   Armine Ishkanian, »Diaspora and Global Civil Society. The Impact of Transnational Di-
      asporic Activism on Armenia's post-Soviet Transition«, in: *Central Asia and the Caucasus.
      Transnationalism and Diaspora*, ed. by Touraj Atabaki & Sanjyot Mehendale (London & New
      York: Routledge, 2005), pp. 113–139.

can Armenians from Boston-Watertown. In 2002 a new visible sign of changed regimes of relationships between the Republic of Armenia and the Armenian diaspora was the erection of a new sculpture »Mother arising out of the ashes« on the grounds of the Memorial complex symbolising the Armenian victimhood *per se.* Set up in 2002 a little to the side of the museum and the monument, the sculpture is a copy of the original statue located in Los Angeles in the Ararat Eskijian Museum.[46]

The changed political order gave the old silenced mourning ceremonies a new meaning of »textualized« memorialization constructed to evoke deep emotion and the memory of the collective death of Armenians as a specific group. The exhibition shows a stone map of »historical Armenia« and oversized photographs of Armenian life in Ottoman *villayets* at the beginning of the 20th century. The images of Armenian churches, schools and local orchestras in different provinces express a sense of a lost paradise and a past Armenian »good life« in Western Armenia. The scenes of cultural renaissance are followed in the neighbouring hall of the museum by images of »ultimate death« and starvation shown in huge photographic[47] reproductions between bright narrow windows stylized in a form of a Christian cross. The emotional exhibition creates a new topography of Armenian death with a sacral religious connotation. And this is one of the crucial points in the reordering of the world of meaning and memorialization practices – the revealing of the sacredness of the martyr's death in the Christian tradition, which provides visitors with a new sense of memory and an emotive man-made representation of death. Death once constructed as an »unknown death« in common graves in terms of the good »Soviet struggle« has been reorganized into a new moral logic beyond melancholic silenced and localized mourning practices. The new iconography of death and loss introduces a way local people and global tourists should »share the memory« with the help of materialized images such as documents of Armenian suffering and photographs of starving bodies. In the museum we finally find the highlight of the visualized representations of the Armenian death – female bones and a skull inside a crystal vase covered by a transparent white lace cloth with an embroidered golden Christian cross. According to statements of the museum director, the bones and the skull have been transferred to Yerevan by the previous Armenian *Catholicos* Garegen II from the Der-Zor desert in Syria - the Armenian »Auschwitz«, the place of Armenian expulsion and death. The emphasis on the female gender of the bones that represent any and all bones of collective death brings about a

---

46   See in www.ararat-eskijian-museum.com (accessed on July 15th, 2006).
47   The pictures were taken by Armin Wegner, whose photographic collection documents conditions in Armenian deportation camps in 1915–1916 – he had been sent to the Middle East as a member of the German Sanitary Corps. See more in www.armenian-genocide.org (accessed on February 21st, 2006).

new identification of the Armenian massacre and loss with a symbol of a totally defenseless victim. The sacral dimension of representation of loss can be also seen in the exhibition of lost territories. In the room with the vase filled with the bones and skull visitors find six small transparent vessels containing sacred earth from the regions in Anatolia where Armenians lived.[48] »This homeland earth has been taken by survivors and guarded by them like relics. When they learned about the opening of the museum people from all over the world sent their relics here«, – explained a tourist guide in the museum. This import of relics and the travelling of earth across international borders signified the new political order and new poetics of memory of loss in post-Soviet Armenia.

The new narratives contrast with the Soviet model of commemoration, while the story of the »rebirth« of the Armenian nation under Soviet power is taken off from the »performative« stage of memory. Even the cultural vitality of ancient Armenian cultural history seems to disappear in the darkness of the death. Rather the visitor is confronted with the representation of the total suffering Armenian nation, thus emphasizing the notion of the point of departure of national history from a traumatic past at the end of the 19th century. In that sense, the post-Soviet Armenian collective self-representations of death, loss and suffering almost forget the dominant notion of the »struggle« and the value of »regeneration«. Instead, one can observe a process whereby the cult of death, intensified through religious connotations, is coming into the foreground by establishing a new politics of unrecognized »bad« death expressed in the language of global responsibility.

The Friends of the Armenian Nation or Transnational Reburials

By establishing a research institution with around 30 researchers, the museum became the central guardian of the registers of Armenian memory and the politics of recognition. Explaining the museum's central significance for post-Soviet Armenia, the museum director Lavrentiy Barsegian told me about the new results of museum activity in which some socialist names of Yerevan's streets were renamed and reconverted to fit the new moral order of memory of Armenian trauma.

We have now streets and schools named after friends of the Armenian people – Anatoly

---

48   Still this example very much recalls the tradition of the Soviet post-war monuments, such as the Tomb of the Unknown Soldier in Moscow, which is surrounded by marble blocks with sacred earth from each of six »hero cities«. See Tumarkin, *The Living and the Dead,* op.cit. (note 10) and Verdery, *The Political Life of Dead Bodies,* op.cit. (note 6).

France or James Bryce. Nobody in his hometown Edinburg in Scotland knows James Bryce, but here we remember him in Yerevan and each year on his birthday we put flowers on James Bryce Street. Not only streets but also Yerevan's schools have been renamed, one school has recently received its new name of Henri Morgentau, and another the name of Franz Werfel...[49]

The postsocialist political regime created a powerful instrument in making a new landscape of memory by transmitting the memory of loss into the body of the modern city, in particular by renaming streets and administrative institutions. An interesting point in this renaming process is that the restructuring of the places of the national memory is conceptualized on a much larger scale than before, namely it goes beyond regional and national boundaries. Here I would like to draw attention to an increase in global linkages with localized loss in Yerevan, linkages which shape the logic of the new politics of the memory of loss in Yerevan today. We are witnessing the shift to a new form of representation of Armenian loss and death going beyond ethnic, national and regional boundaries by the inclusion of famous international names into the Armenian pantheon.

Between the memorial and the museum there is another political »stage« in the reorganization of the Armenian loss – a 100-meter-long basalt mourning wall. On one side the visitor sees the engraved names of villages and towns where the Armenian population was killed. On the other side the wall includes eleven small containers with urns symbolizing miniature graves of dead prominent persons who contributed to the history of revealing the Armenian genocide. Their names are inscribed on the stone containers in Armenian and English. After the museum was established in 1995, handfuls of earth were taken by museum members from different graves in different places of the world and transferred to the Yerevan Museum of Genocide. Among the names of prominent »reburied« persons we find the Austrian Franz Werfel, the German Armin Wegner, the British James Bryce, the American Henry Morgenthau.[50]

Armin Wegner was in Yerevan in 1987. He said that after his death he wanted to be buried here on the hill. In 1997 his son Misha brought the urn with the earth from his grave. Have you seen our mourning wall? We buried the urn of Wegner inside of this

---

49   Henri Morgenthau (1891–1967) was the US ambassador in Constantinople during WWI and famous for his memoirs »Ambassador Morgenthau's Story« published as a book in 1918. The work was a damning indictment of Ottoman leaders for their entry into WWI and of the Armenian massacres; James Bryce (1838–1922) was a British historian, statesman and professor of law at Oxford. In 1876 he took an explorative trip to Ararat, found wood on Great Ararat and published a book about his adventure in Transcaucasia and Ararat in 1878; Franz Werfel (1890–1945) was an Austrian writer of Jewish origin. He is known for his famous novel »The Forty Days of Musa Dagh« about the drama of the Armenians published in 1933. The book was first translated into Russian at the beginning of the 60s.

50   Armin Wegner (1886–1978), see above the note 47.

wall... Similarly we took the earth from the graves of Johannes Lepsius, Anatole France, and Lord James Bryce and brought it here, because they belong to the eleven friends of the Armenian people. The last reburial was that of an Arab lawyer, who in 1916 wrote a book about the Armenian pogroms and in doing so helped the Armenian people to survive...

– the director of the museum explained to me.

This aspect of memorializing acts in post-Soviet Armenia has a different logic and meaning than in the case of »repatriated dead bodies« in Eastern Europe,[51] which was seen as a return of »cultural treasure« to its proper national homeland.[52] The practice of transferring earth from personal graves of non-Armenians with significant symbolic capital, as well as the above-mentioned practice of re-naming of streets, indicates the changing frame of Armenian politics and poetics of memory. This change does not necessarily produce strong emotional sentiments of personal or ethnic death, but by bestowing a new social status of »friend« to a foreigner it creates a new genealogy of Armenian suffering. Like displaced and lost ancestors, they are worshipped and »returned« to the localized site of remembering and in that sense we observe how Armenians convert an ethnic notion of loss and death into a global memory of forgotten human loss.

Among the friends of Armenian people we have an Estonian Mother Boel, who organized an orphanage in Aleppo for Armenian children expelled from Western Armenia. Once I visited Aleppo and met a person who introduced himself as a pupil of Mother Boel. For a long time we could not find her grave in Aleppo. Later we discovered that she was buried in Germany, so we sent our colleague to Germany and he brought the earth from her grave to Tsitsernakaberd.

At the same time, the process of converting the local and ethnic notion of tragedy into global loss through the transfer of earth from remote cemeteries in Europe, the US or the Middle East to Yerevan's holy place involves acts of »domestication« which marked the arrival of »ancestors« and the dramaturgy of each transaction. As the director of the Genocide Museum explained, the Armenian Church was invited to each reburial ceremony. During this ceremony the head of the Armenian Church (*Catholicos*) consecrated the newly arrived earth in the miniature graves inside the mourning wall according to traditional Armenian funeral rites. The Jewish, Catholic and even Moslem religious backgrounds of the dead persons play no role in the new displaced memorial life. The ability to

---

51 Verdery, *The Political Life of Dead Bodies,* op.cit. (note 6).

52 Levon Abrahamian has mentioned the case of the symbolic »return« of famous deceased diaspora Armenians from dead abroad, such as the ceremony of reburial of Andranik, the Armenian national hero during the first Armenian republic 1918–1920, who died in Paris. See Levon Abrahamian, »Borba s pamyatnikami i pamyatyu v postsovetskom prostranstve (na primere Armenii)«, in: *Acta Slavica Iaponica* XX (2003), pp. 25–49, in particular p. 46.

give non-Armenians the status of »Armenian treasures« is tied to the idea initiated by the state authorities that they represent bodies of the persons who have contributed something very significant to the national history and culture.

A Torch March

Ninety years after the expulsion and death we observe a dynamic turn in the act of memorializing Armenian loss in the modification of the public landscape. Numerous different objects and activities related to memory work are produced in the city – the revival of traditional Armenian stone monuments (*khachkars*), posters, texts, books, souvenirs, rituals at schools, universities and pre-schools, vivid museum exhibitions, internet websites, concerts, films, and the days of remembrance. At the beginning of the 21st century, the principle change in the politics of memory of loss in Armenia relates to the shift from silent abstract mourning to loud commodifying practices of representations of violence, which seem to reach a high level of standardization. The spectrum of standardization spans tropes used in academic conferences to aestheticized forms of material objects such as T-shirts, touristic products and the production of CDs with genocide music. It is not the intention of this essay to analyze the whole variety of »memory souvenirs«, but rather to focus on one of the central public events of the Memorial gatherings on the Day of Remembrance to show the changed framework of remembering.

The Day of Remembrance on *yeghern* on the 24th of April created a fixed point in time and space in the »cosmic order« of Yerevan and at the same time a base for the development of a new commemorative event. The traditionally silent march to the mausoleum *yeghern*, which can be called the mourning pilgrimage, contrasts with a new youth march developed in the few last years (since 1999) – a torch march, *djeherov yert*. Both events are public marches that share the same destination – the sacral place of the Genocide Memorial on Tsitsernakaberd hill – but the new version of commemoration suggests a reconsideration of the meaning of collective loss and its relationship to the world. By juxtaposing these two events we can see how memorialization takes a »voiced« form. With the youth pilgrimage a new performative power and sense of memory of violence appeared, whereby unspeakable localized mourning practices are replaced by a loud rhetoric of disagreement and politicized demands for recognition of the cataclysmic event and for a »restoration of justice« directed at global morality. The art of remembering during the torch march of young nationalists in Armenia is different from the mourning pilgrimage as the march has established a specific »public stage« in Yerevan. In order to understand the scope of changed meanings of collective remembrance of loss and the ways of assigning new values and political routes in the city Yerevan, I will briefly compare the youth torch march with traditional public pilgrimage according to specific symbolic components of gatherings: routes, attributes, participants and behavior.

In the late evening of April 23rd 2005, thousands of young people, mostly students and school children, gathered at the central Hanrapetutyan Republic Square, the former Lenin Square. On the place where once the Lenin statue was dramatically removed[53] a huge electronic billboard screened impressive video fragments of the famous film »Ararat« by Atom Egoyan.[54] Cracking roasted sunflower seeds, both, young men and women seemed to be relaxed waiting for friends and classmates. In contrast to the traditional mourning ceremony, which brings together highly heterogeneous participants of different ages and generations, the proclaimed *djeherov yert*, which was organized and mobilized by the Armenian Dashnaktsutiun youth confederation,[55] attracted mostly youth, students and older school children. The organizers emphasized that such meetings have taken place since 1999 and in this year they even received official support on the part of the city mayor, so the streets in central Yerevan were already blocked by early afternoon. Many young people were dressed in the uniform of a white T-shirt with recognizable images of the Genocide Memorial and the logo »I was there«, some wore shirts with the emblem of Armenian Revolutionary Federation, some with hand-made inscriptions »we do not forget«, some of the young students wrapped their bodies in the cloth of Armenian national flag. Besides age and dress code, the most striking performative moment was that instead of the usual tulips and small candles young participants carried torches in their hands. The leader of the local Dashnaktsutiun youth federation, whose father died during the Karabakh war, explained to me that the flames for the torches were going to be brought from Jerablur, the monument for Armenians who fell during the

---

53 For more detailed information about this act, see in Abrahamian, »Borba s pamyatnikami i pamyatyu«, op.cit (note 53). Today the beheaded statue of Lenin is laying on the earth inside the courtyard of the National Museum of History just opposite the place where it once stood.

54 The film »Ararat« made in 2001 plays an enormously important role in the politics and aesthetics of modern memory of Armenian pain and loss.

55 The Dashnaktsutiun Party is the political organ of the Armenian Revolutionary Federation (ARF) founded at the end of the 19th century in Tbilisi. After the Russian revolution of 1917 and the expulsion from the eastern Anatolia members of the party continued their political activity in »exile« amongst the diaspora. Dashnaks were always in opposition to Soviet power and therefore they were officially forbidden in the Soviet era. See Richard Hovannisian, »Genocide and Independence, 1914–21«, in: *The Armenians. Past and Present in the making of the national identity*, ed. by Edmund Herzig & Marina Kurkchiyan (StateNew York: RoutledgeCurzon, 2005), pp. 89–112.

Karabakh war.[56] Behind uniformed young cadets with drums at the front of the demonstration, were representatives of local Armenian and American Armenian Churches carrying a wooden cross on their shoulders. Between the representatives of the Armenian Church and a 20-meter Armenian national flag carried by school boys and girls, were people carrying the national flags of those states that officially recognized the Armenian massacre as genocide. Whereas participation in the mourning pilgrimage on the 24th of April is considered to be the civic act of individuals and families beyond any spatial order and formality, the torch march was organized by a political organization well networked with local universities and high schools along a fixed time schedule and fixed route. Departing from the former Lenin Square the demonstrators moved at an energetic pace along the main Mashtotz and Bagramian streets with the goal of passing by the American and other Western embassy buildings of those countries, which have not yet recognised the Armenian genocide. At these moments the participants stopped to whistle loudly and cry »Hay dat!«[57] and »Hayastan!« (Armenia). After the arrival at the Memorial one could hear the singing of the newly created »genocide song« *Adana* by the American Daniel Decker. According to mass media reports, the group of singers sang in eight different languages.[58]

Conclusion

The changes in meaning of commemorations of the dead point to the emergence of a new set of emotional and voiced rites that relate to moral compensation. The example of a new commemorative practice in Yerevan indicates the radical post-socialist change in the memorialization of violent loss in Armenia. Needless to say, today these performative practices, like rituals, provide powerful media of expression for the collective belonging to one specific moral community – the descendents of victims. We observe a process of transformation of a silenced melancholic mourning memory into a voiced politics of recognition, where the

---

56   Jerablur is the official state funded cemetery for those soldiers and civilians who were killed during the Karabakh war. It was erected in the middle of the 90s.

57   *Hay dat* – ›Armenian question‹ or ›Armenian cause‹ – raises issues of genocide recognition and the lost lands in Turkey and Nakhichevan mostly elaborated among diaspora Armenians. For more details see Razmik Panossian, »Homeland-Diaspora Relations and Identity Differences«, in: *The Armenians. Past and Present in the making of the national identity,* ed. by Edmund Herzig & Marina Kurkchiyan (StateNew York: RoutledgeCurzon, 2005), pp. 229–243.

58   The author of the song Daniel Decker, the German Kye Augaten, the Bulgarian Tsvetan Tsvetkov, the Finnish Inka and the Moldavian Vitali Dani sang the song »Adana« on 24th of April in Yerevan. The source: www.armeniandiaspora.com (accessed on April 26th, 2006).

traumatic past is performed with the help of vivid visual props and public actions; the mourning procession is transformed into a political demonstration that celebrates the collective vitality. Moreover the »young« voices of the torch march turn away from the past and instead focus on the future.

As outlined above, this description of new commemorative practices further outlines a political and symbolic shift in the territorial sense of memory of loss. The new political tradition is obviously linked not only to the rapid transformation of political and social order, but also to the rapid transnationalization of the politics of loss with the growing quantity and quality of the ways in which the Republic of Armenia is connected with diasporic Armenian communities in the US. New actors, the formerly forbidden Dashnaktsutiun party and religious leaders, visible »returnees« who visit the Armenian homeland in April and invisible supporters, enable the framing of Armenian loss in a global context. What I want to stress here is the changed space for acts of remembrance whereby the notion of a »shared memory« of collective death is articulated on a broader scale, resignifying transnational borders of memory. Memorialization now encompasses multiple a and diverse range of public activities, in which the past is radically modified, in particular the tabooed moments of the past, and re-described in order to shape the moral landscape of a common future for all Armenians both in homeland and diaspora. The shift from »forgotten« and »silenced« to »remembered« and »voiced« Armenian loss started in the mid of the 1960s with a spontaneous movement from below during Khrushchev's political thaw, and also with international pressure on the part of Armenian diaspora lobbies. It has been transformed at the beginning of the 21st century into a standartised global form of construction of memory of human trauma and loss. The animation of the past takes many forms and serves many purposes, ranging from conscious recall to an unreflected fragmented re-emergence, from nostalgic de-contextualized longing for what is lost to polemical use of the past to reshape the national present and future in the global age.

Iconography of Historical Memory and Armenian National Identity at the End of the 1980s

Harutyun Marutyan

Prior to its collapse, in diverse parts of the Soviet Union there were several national mass movements. Among these, the Karabagh Movement or the Armenian revolution (1988–1990) stands out as being particularly significant. Initially the aim of the Karabagh Movement was to defend the Armenian majority's wish for national self-determination in the Nagorno-Karabagh Autonomous Region of Azerbaijan and to support the Karabagh Armenians in their efforts to join Armenia.[1]

The two and a half years the Karabagh Movement lasted had a considerable impact on Armenian society. The Movement engendered revolutionary changes in the lives of Armenians and challenged views, perspectives and the image that had developed over decades of Soviet rule. In essence it brought about enormous changes in Armenian national identity as a whole.[2] Anthropological research conducted during the Movement, including the examination and analysis of various speeches, posters and banners, mass-media publications, as well as content analyses of the memoirs of participants form the basis for this paper.

On the basis of my research and findings, I discovered that the memory of

---

1   On Karabagh Movement see, for example: Ronald Grigor Suny, *Looking toward Ararat: Armenia in Modern History* (Bloomington and Indianapolis: Indiana University Press, 1993), pp. 231–246; Mark Malkasian, *»Gha-ra-bagh!«: The Emergence of the National-Democratic Movement in Armenia* (Detroit: Wayne State University Press, 1996). On ethnography of the Movement see, for example: Nora Dudwick, »The Karabagh Movement: An Old Scenario Gets Rewritten«, in: *The Armenian Review* 42 (1989), 3, pp. 63–70; Dudwick, *Memory, Identity, and Politics in Armenia* (Doctoral dissertation: University of Pensaylvania, unpublished manuscript, 1994); Levon Abrahamian, »Karabagh Movement as Viewed by an Anthropologist«, in: *The Armenian Review* 43 (1990), 2–3, pp. 67–80; Abrahamian, »Archaic Ritual and Theater: From the Ceremonial Glade to the Theater Square«, in: *Soviet Anthropology & Archeology* 29 (1990), 2, pp. 45–69; Abrahamian, »Chaos and Cosmos in the Structure of Mass Popular Demonstrations«, in: *Soviet Anthropology & Archeology* 29 (1990), 2, pp. 70–86; Abrahamian, »The Anthropologist as Shaman: Interpreting Recent Political Events in Armenia«, in: *Beyond Boundaries: Understanding, Translation and Anthropological Discourse* (Oxford, UK/Providence: Berg, 1993), pp. 100–116.

2   The transformation of Armenian identity was assisted also (even if indirectly) by the policies of *perestroika*, democratization and *glasnost*, declared by Soviet leadership: these policies only leveled a road for the originating of the democratic Karabagh Movement and afterwards exhausted, as happened in other parts of Soviet Union.

the Armenian Genocide of 1915 was still the most important part of Armenian historical memory. I also found that during the Movement this memory was in the process of transformation, in result of which the self-image of the grieving and pleading victim was replaced by the image of the warrior.

One of the most fundamental changes that occurred, and which was a reflection of the revolutionary nature of the Movement, was an increase in the understanding of constitutional rights. The Soviet citizen who had until then played a passive role within the system of power came to understand that the supreme political power is embedded in the will of the people and that their vote will determine the leaders and the future progress of the country.

My findings demonstrate the significance of Armenians' recognition of the value of their joint efforts and collective will. An unprecedented increase of confidence regarding the nation's strength and faith in the possibility of independent action led to the prospect of establishing an independent state. This was an idea, which emerged quite strongly and shifted from a position of a »dream held by dissidents« to an idea that was perceived by a large majority of the people as being feasible and attainable through conviction and action.

A process of reevaluating the past and present began during the Movement regarding the formation of national identity and its expression. This process was conditioned and influenced by actions of the Soviet leadership and Soviet Army. The long-standing belief in the Russian people to be the »savior« of Armenians was seriously undermined and challenged. The influential role of the Armenian language and Armenian schools in the fight against cultural assimilation and for the preservation of Armenian identity were recognized.

As a result of the above-mentioned and other radical changes, which took place during the years of the Movement, a new national-democratic identity was formed, which became free of totalitarian ideology and which initiated the process of a free way of thinking, shaped by the embracing of democratic-national independence.[3]

Considering the complex nature of the topic, I will endeavor to present the changes in the national identity of the Armenian people and the main trends of their manifestation from the perspective of historical memory.[4] The subject

---

3   For more details see Harutyun Marutyan, »Banners of the Karabagh Movement as Cultural Indicators and Signs of a Changing Society«, in: *Joghovrdavarutyan zargatsume Hayastanum. Seminari nyuter [Democracy Building in Armenia: Seminar Proceedings]* (Yerevan: »Tigran Mets« Publishing House, 1999), pp. 184–189; Marutyan, »The Main Directions of Changes of Armenian National Identity During the Years of the Gharabagh Movement«, in: *Hayagitutyan ardi vichake yev nra zargatsman herankarnere. Zekutsumneri druytner [Armenology Today and Prospects for It's Development. Absrtacts of Papers]* (Yerevan: Yerevan University Press, 2003), pp. 55–56.

4   On the role of historical memory in the Karabagh Movement see, for example: Harutyun Marutyan, »The Genocide of the Armenians. Historical Memory and Transformation of Eth-

being extensive, I will focus only on typical examples.[5] It is my objective to reveal the significance of this factor in the identity changes brought about by the Karabagh Movement.

The memory of the annihilation of more than 1,5 million Armenians in Ottoman Turkey during 1915–1916 has always remained in the people's consciousness, in spite of decades of silence on the part of Soviet authorities. The leadership of the Soviet Union maintained silence because it did not want to damage its relations with Turkey and at the same time feared the rise of Armenian nationalistic sentiments. In the mid 1960's, the silence was broken and the Genocide gradually became a topic in works of literature and art, forming a new aspect in the psychology of the Armenian nation. This theme was first of all interpreted in terms of Armenians as helpless victims of the Turkish *yataghan* (curved sword) and deportations. The stereotype of the grieving victim was affirmed – a victim capable of generating only compassion and pity, grief and sympathy. Thus, works of art and literature emphasized the loss of the historical homeland, dozens of flourishing towns, thousands of rich villages, fertile fields and so on. Although the subject of the Genocide was no longer a taboo, the state sought to confine it to the commemoration of a catastrophe. The main content of works of literature in the mid 1960's on the topic of the Genocide was best expressed by the appeal of Soviet Armenian poet Silva Kaputikyan »You must avenge by living only«.

In 1967 on the picturesque slope of Tsitsernakaberd hill in Yerevan a monument dedicated to the victims of Genocide was built in record time. On April 24th[6] 1968, the people moved up to the monument in orderly columns, bear-

---

nic Stereotypes«, in: *Synopsis 3, Armenia: Viewed from Inside and Outside* (1994), pp. 111–119; Marutyan, »Historical Memory: Opportunity or Obstacle?«, in: *Regional Dynamics of the Black and Caspian Sea Basins* (Odesa: IREX Alumni Conference, 2000); Marutyan, »To the Role of Historical Memory in National Movements«, in: *IV Congress ethnographov i anthropologov Rossiyi. Thesisi dokladov [IV Congress of Ethnographers and Anthropologists of Russia. Executive summaries of papers]* (Moscow: Association of Ethnographers and Anthropologists of Russia, 2001), p. 96; Marutyan, »Historical Memory in the Scope of Ethno-Cultural Unity and Southern Caucasian Variety«, in: *The South Caucasus Network for Civil Accord. The South Caucasus: Ethnic-Cultural Diversity and Regional Unity* (Tbilisi: Center for Development and Cooperation, Center for Pluralism, 2003), pp. 9–19 (in Russian), pp. 69–78 (in English); Marutyan, »The Factor of Historical Memory in the Context of the Armenian Revolution of 1988–1990«, in: *Mezhdunarodnaya nauchnaya konferentsiya »Arkheologiya, etnologiya, folkloristika Kavkaza«. [Archeology, Ethnology and Folklore of Caucasus. Materials of International Conference]* (Tbilisi: Academy of Sciences of Georgia, 2004), p. 215; Marutyan, »Historical Memory in the Dialogue Between Cultures: Opportunity or Obstacle«, in: *http://www.pogranicze.sejny.pl/download/ historical_memory_final.pdf* (accessed on: April 21st, 2005).

5 This theme is developed in: Harutyun Marutyan, *The Iconography of Armenian Identity: Part 1. Genocide in the Posters and Banners of the Karabagh Movement* (Yerevan: Institute of Archaeology and Ethnography, Academy of Sciences of Armenia, 2001, unpublished manuscript).

6 It was on that day, that in Constantinople (now Istanbul), mass arrests of the Armenian in-

ing flowers to pay tribute to the victims of the Genocide. This procession did not have official permission, but was actually led by the communist leaders of Armenia, who were the first to lay wreaths at the monument early that morning. Subsequent annual processions of homage, undertaken by several generations of Armenians had an important role in passing on the memory of the Genocide.

The situation began to change from February 1988, with the beginning of a series of mass public meetings that led to the foundation of the Karabagh Movement. The subject of the Armenian Genocide appeared on banners and posters just after the Sumgait events (February 27th through 29th, 1988), which Armenians compared to the Genocide of 1915. The collective memory of the Genocide, which had been dormant, reemerged.

While working on the paper, I have mainly kept to the study of the visual language of the Karabagh Movement – on posters and banners.[7] The Karabagh Movement produced banners and posters in abundance. The changing icons serve as an index of the collective understanding of the Movement by its participants; changes in icons directly echoed changes in the situation. By observing these banners and posters, one can easily outline not only the various stages of the Movement, but also the spheres of influence, the stages of transformation of ethno-psychological orientations, and the changing identity of the nation as a whole. Posters can be said to be pictures, which are telling a thousand words. These posters and banners can also be considered to be »images of identity«, spontaneous interpretations by individuals without intermediaries. These »images of identity« represent not only a visual language of popular folk art; they

telligentsia started, followed by their exile and assassination. April 24th was accepted as the Remembrance day for the Victims of the Genocide.

7   See, for example: Levon Abrahamian & Harutyun Marutyan, »The Banners and Posters as a Mirror of the Karabagh Movement«, in: *Vsesoyuznaya Nauchnaya Sessiya po itogam Polevych Etnograficheskikh i Antropologicheskikh Issledovaniy 1988–1989 godov. Tezisi dokladov [All Union Scientific Conference Devoted to the Results of Ethnographic and Anthropological Field Work Researches of 1988–1989. Executive summaries of papers]* (Alma-Ata: Institute of Ethnography of Academy of Sciences of USSR, 1990), pp. 122–123; Harutyun Marutyan, »Iconography of the Karabagh Movement and Transformation of the Armenian Identity«, in: *Voprosi Ethnologii Kavkaza. Pervaya mejdunarodnaya konferentsiya. Tezisi dokladov [Problems of Ethnology of the Caucasus. The First International Conference. Executive summaries of papers]* (Yerevan: Yerevan State University Press, 1999), pp. 27–31; Marutyan, »Iconography of Gharabagh Movement: An Index of the Transformation of Armenian Identity«, in: *Armenian Forum. Journal of Contemporary Affairs* 2/4 (2000), pp. 39–55; Marutyan, »The Memory of Genocide as a Moulder of New Identity (end of 1980s – beginning of 1990s)«, in: *Patma-banasirakan handes [Historical-Philological Journal]* (Yerevan: National Academy of Sciences of Armenia, 2005), pp. 55–66; Stephanie Platz, »The Kharabagh Demonstrations: Visual and Verbal Representations of Armenian Identity«, in: *The Annual of the Society for the Study of Caucasia* 3 (1991), pp. 19–30.

serve also as a medium for a simple and direct expression of ideas.[8] In my paper, I have used the texts of some of the most typical posters as titles.

»Recognize the Great Genocide of 1915«

Figure 3.1: April 24, 1990, Yerevan. Photo: H. Marutyan.

The first major theme relates to the Armenian Genocide of 1915–16. It includes four groups. The first group is typical in the way it displays historical memory. It combines wreaths that function as posters.[9] The wreaths were diverse. Apart

---

8   See also: Levon Abrahamian & Harutyun Marutyan, »To the Iconographic Language of Political Actions«, in: *Hay Arvestin Nvirvats Hanrapetakan VIII Gitakan Konferans. Zekutsumneri tezisner [The 8th Scientific Republican Conference, devoted to Armenian Art. Executive summaries of papers]* (Yerevan: »Gitutyun« Publishing House of National Academy of Sciences of Armenia, 1997), pp. 5–6; Harutyun Marutyan, »The Role of Posters and Banners in the Mobilization of Society«, in: *VI Congress ethnographov i anthropologov Rossiyi. Thesisi dokladov [VI Congress of Ethnologists and Anthropologists of Russia. Composition of abstracts]* (Saint-Petersburg: Museum of Anthropology and Ethnography of Russian Academy of Sciences, 2005), p. 386.

9   For more details see: Harutyun Marutyan, »Wreaths as Posters. The Genocide and Iconogra-

from their main memorial function they addressed various elements of Armenian national identity, including the factor of historical memory. I would like
to dwell on only one such wreath (Figure 3.1), which represented the miniature
model of the Monument to the Genocide victims, made out of flowers. It was
carried to the Monument on April 24th, 1990. The model was two meters high
and draped in black with the bronze inscriptions »75«, and »Genocide« – both in
Armenian and English. The part representing the Eternal Flame, almost one and
a half meters in height, was in red carnations, and over this background »1915«
was written with white carnations. The four front »slabs« of the model were
draped with black cloth, over which the years of massacres and mass evictions
of Armenians both in Turkey and the Soviet Union were emblazoned in bronze
– *1896, 1909* (dates of massacres of Western Armenians in Turkey), *1988* (the
massacre in Sumgait, eviction of Armenians in Azerbaijan) and *1990* (massacre
in Baku, the end of mass eviction of Armenians in Azerbaijan). This massive
two-part construction was mounted on a stretcher-like pedestal and was carried
by four young people. The model was similar to those carried by demonstrators
during the official parades of the Soviet period. Evidently, such a dedication of a
model to its original can be compared with dedication of symbols of divinity to
deities, in the same manner as icons were contributed to shrines, or crosses and
crucifixion symbols to Christian churches, or even the portraits of the Communist party leaders to their live, dead or symbolic images.

Another group of banners used quotations from literature related to the subject of the Armenian massacres: »If evil of this magnitude can be ignored, if our
children forget / then we deserve oblivion, and earn the world's scorn«.[10] These
are lines from a story (1899) by a renowned writer of the end of the 19th and the
beginning of the 20th century, Avetis Aharonian, who had also been the chairman of the Parliament of the First Republic of Armenia; a slogan »Martyrs Command« (meaning that the dead, the innocent victims of the Genocide, appeal to
the living, that they should not be forgotten) – based on the works of Paruyr
Sevak, a Soviet Armenian writer of the mid-twentieth century; »The Cause of
Armenians is the Cause of Humanity« – the words belong to the well-known
French writer, humanitarian and public figure, Anatole France; the formula »No
one is forgotten, nothing is forgotten«, a translation from Russian, that related
to the victims of the siege of Leningrad/Saint-Petersburg (1941–1944) during
the Great Patriotic War (World War II).

The next group of banners was appeals/claims to recognize the Genocide of
Armenians, with/without offers of certain solutions. These banner texts showed

---

phy of Armenian Identity«, in: *Handes amsorya [Monatsschrift fur Armenische Philologie]* Vol.
1–12 (2001), pp. 355–407.

10   For more details see: Harutyun Marutyan, »Armenian Poetry as a Reflection of Identity«, in:
Haigazian Hayagitakan Handes [Haigazian Armenological Review] 20 (2000), pp. 269–306.

the changes of the addressees, as well as an evolution in the conception of the means for achieving the purpose:

In the beginning, in 1988, some of them had no direct addressees, such as – »Recognize the Great Genocide of 1915«, »We demand that the 1915 Genocide be recognized«.

Yet on that very day some of the banners did state more definite addressees: »We Claim that the 1915 Genocide of Armenians Be Recognized by the Government« and »We Demand of our Soviet Government that the 1915 Genocide Be Officially Recognized«. With some reservations, one can say that here the addressees, the authorities of Armenia, could rather be read between the lines, or guessed at from the specific banner language. It is typical that slogans of this type never mentioned the Supreme Soviet/Parliament of the Armenian Republic. The low level of legal knowledge among the people could probably have conditioned this: since it was the Central Committee of the Communist Party of the Republic that was then regarded as the supreme authority.

A larger number of banners demanding recognition of Genocide appealed to the next rank in the Soviet hierarchy, the supreme bodies of Soviet government. Even in these cases the demonstrators displayed a rather vague knowledge of the structure of the said government. Thus, on a banner of April 24th, 1988, the appeal was directed to the USSR, generally: for example, »USSR, recognize the 1915 Genocide«, a year later the same was repeated in the standard form but was expressed more sharply: »USSR, enough is enough, do recognize the 1915 Genocide!«

A number of banners appealed to the government of the Soviet Union, which actually had no authority to solve the problem: for example, »The Government of the USSR must officially acknowledge the 1915 Genocide of Armenians in Turkey!« (April 24th, 1988). Only a year later did more competently composed banners appear: »We demand that the Supreme Soviet recognize the Genocide of the Armenians« and »Genocide of the Armenians in 1915 must be recognized by the Supreme Soviet of the USSR« (both of April 24th, 1989), which were proof of improvement of the level of political-legal awareness of the people.

Still, the leadership of the USSR did not respond to the claim of the Armenians. Therefore, it was to be expected that appeals to the supreme international authority, the United Nations should appear (April, 1989): »We appeal to United Nations to accept the Armenian Genocide«.

Another group of appeals did not address any authority. At first glance they seemed to be addressed to mankind in general, for example: »The Genocide of Armenians is a crime against Humanity!« and »The Genocide of Armenians is a tragedy of world civilization« of April 24th, 1988; or one seen on April 24th, 1989: »What's the matter, World? Give a helping hand to a small nation«.

Though the World at large stayed indifferent, it sometimes appeared as mourning over Genocide victims. This could as well refer to a man-size model of the Globe carried to Tsitsernakaberd on April 24th, 1990, where the continents and oceans were fashioned in flowers, with a flower cross rising from the North Pole. Still, this was more a case of presenting what people wanted to be brought into reality: the World remained indifferent to the sufferings of Armenians.

The students of the music Conservatory saw only the authority of God over and above the official authorities and mankind, and, both in Armenian and English, they appealed to Him: »Lord God. You punish us for our lack of commitment«.

»Sumgait is a Sequel to the Genocide«

The second major theme refers to the tragic events of Sumgait, in February 1988 and their association with the 1915 Genocide.[11] Let us briefly review the events in Sumgait.

In response to the mass demonstrations in the Opera Square in Yerevan, where hundreds of thousands of people expressed their solidarity with the people of Karabagh, who had risen in a struggle for self-determination, on February 26th, the General Secretary of the Communist Party of the USSR Mikhail Gorbachev sent a statement to the peoples of Azerbaijan and Armenia. He called upon them for calm and suggested that the people return to their routine and maintain public order. In Yerevan the decision was made to end the mass meetings and get back to everyday life. Meanwhile, in the town of Sumgait, only 25–30 kilometers away from the capital of the Azerbaijani Republic, Baku, events took quite a different course. For three days from February 27th, mass rioting took place in presence of the Soviet Army units, in which 26 citizens of Armenian nationality were massacred according to official information. This was done with unbelievable cruelty, with the same barbaric methods that had been used by Turks during the Genocide at the beginning of the 20th century. The Armenians were beaten, tortured, raped, and thrown out windows, killed using steel bars and knives, butchered with axes, beheaded and burnt in fire.

The massacres in Sumgait were the response of Baku officials to the people of Mountainous Karabagh and the Armenian SSR, who had peacefully and democratically expressed their will to be reunited. The purpose of this criminal action

---

11   For more details see: Harutyun Marutyan, »Sumgait Massacres: Reality, Assesment, and Historical Memory«, in: *Handes amsorya [Monatsschrift für Armenische Philologie]* Vol. 1–12 (2002), pp. 158–206.

was to block the possible solution of the problem, terrorize the Armenians and, above all, by threatening activists with the prospect of new bloody actions, to make them and the Soviet Union authorities give up any hope of a fair solution for the Karabagh problem.

The identification of Sumgait with the Genocide manifested itself in diverse ways. The first was in the form of a women's mourning procession, on March 8th, 1988. The procession started at the Opera Square and moved to the Genocide Memorial: »people instinctively felt that Sumgait was but a sequel to the 1915, April 24th Genocide...«[12].

Identifying the new victims with the old – i.e. the victims of Sumgait with those of the Genocide – the following kind of »banner identification« is worth mentioning, first observed on April 24th, 1988. Some people in the procession carried large photographs of Sumgait victims, framed with black ribbons; others carried photographs of the renowned Armenian intellectuals Siamanto, Daniel Varujan and Grigor Zohrap, who represented the victims of the 1915 Genocide. On that day, the pictures of the victims of both tragedies, one which had occurred at the beginning and the other, which had occurred at the end of the twentieth century, were laid among the mass of flowers around the eternal flame commemorating the Victims of the Genocide. This action in a way united the old and the new victims, creating a visual link between them.

Another proof of the identification of new and old victims was that on the very same day of April 24th, a new *khachkar* (a stone slab with an elaborate carved cross) commemorating the victims of the Sumgait tragedy was placed near the Genocide Memorial.

The banners and posters conveyed this identification through their own specific language.

An interesting illustration of this issue was a poster observed at the women's procession on March 8th where the picture of the Genocide Memorial with »1915« written over it was accompanied by another, smaller picture of the same Memorial, with the date »1988« written underneath. This implied that the new tragedy was a minor version of the previous one. Written above was: »We will not forget the bloody Sunday of Sumgait!« Written at the bottom was: »We will not allow another genocide«.

The banners of April 24th, 1988 often bore slogans that simply recorded the similarity of the Genocide and Sumgait, such as: »The events in Sumgait are a sequel to the 1915 Genocide«, »Sumgait is a sequel to the 1915 Genocide« or »Sumgait is a continuation of the Great Genocide«. Some were more laconic, for

---

12   Harutyun Marutyan, »Grieving Processions, Memory days of Innocent Victims as forms of Manifestation of People's Believes«, in: *Hai Joghovrdakan Mshakuyt. XII. Hanrapetakan Gitajoghovi Nyuter [Armenian Folk Culture. XII Republican Scientific Conference. Composition of Articles]* (Yerevan: »Mughni« Press, (2004), pp. 98–102.

Figure 3.2: November 7, 1988, Yerevan, Lenin Avenue, Photo: H. Marutyan.

example one, where the dates 1915 and 1988 stood below the silhouette of Mt. Ararat – one of the main symbols of Armenian identity.

Other banners of April 24th took the idea further, explaining the logic of the continuity of genocide: »The unwillingness to recognize the 1915 Genocide led to the genocide in 1988«, or even more to the point: »If the Soviet Government had recognized the 1915 Genocide, there would have been no Sumgait in 1988«; or the more general: »Humanity must recognize the fact of the 1915 genocide, so that no Sumgaits ever happen again«. These last two banners, as well as the one chosen for the title to this chapter, show that already in April 1988 the name Sumgait had become synonymous with »genocide«.

Furthermore, Sumgait and the year 1988 appear side by side with other genocides: »Der-Zor, Buchenwald, Sumgait« (April 24th, 1988). Der-Zor is a desert in the North of Syria that was chosen by the government of the »Young Turks« as the main destination for Armenians who were being evicted from Western Armenia and other regions of Turkey. The Armenians who reached this region died not only at the hands of the Turk assassins, but also of famine and epidemics. About 200.000 Armenians were murdered here during the years 1915–16. The deserts of Mesopotamia served the Ottoman government the same purpose as Maidanek, Oswiecim, Buchenwald and other concentration camps did the Nazis during World War II. Later, the name Der-Zor became synonymous with the Genocide. This was the reason why, when intending to refer to the Genocide by means of a geographical name or toponyms, the banners of Karabagh Movement often displayed the name Der-Zor.

This poster apparently implied that the Armenian people viewed the events in Sumgait in the same way as those in Turkey of 1915 and those carried out by the Nazis in their concentration camps, where millions of people of many nationalities were systematically eliminated.

One banner characteristic of the banners in this category classified as the »genocide series« was the one of April 24th, 1989, that said: »...1915...1988 ...How long?« This formula leaves a »gap« before 1915, as well as between 1915 and 1988, i.e., between the Great Genocide and Sumgait, thus recording the genocides of Armenians in the past and those possible in the future. Chronologically, the »gap« coincides with the years of the Soviet regime, which, as the continuation points imply, were not devoid of non-bloody or white genocides that were in a variety of ways described in other banners of the same category.

The idea of the »genocides series« was conveyed through illustrations combined with data, in two main manners: with sketches of genocide victims and through maps. For example, in June 1988 a poster displayed the silhouettes of two groups of people separated by a *yataghan*. The groups actually symbolized the whole Armenian population: one could recognize men and women of all ages, who were clothed in »1915« and »1988« fashion, with the dates written above them. At the bottom were the flags of Turkey and of the Azerbaijan SSR, corresponding to the dates. Above the groups of people the figure »1.500.000« (the number of victims of 1915) was displayed and a question mark hinted at the unidentified number of Sumgait victims.

Another poster attached to this one conveyed the same idea of continuing genocides, but unlike the first one, here the year 1937 appeared between 1915 and 1988, symbolizing the mass deportations and imprisonments under Stalinism.

The idea of a »genocide series« was also conveyed through posters displaying maps. Thus, a poster of June 1988 (Figure 3.3) displayed the map of Transcau-

Figure 3.3: June 10, 1988, Yerevan, Theatre Square. Photo: L. Abrahamian.

casia and adjacent territories. The coloring of the poster was symbolic: Armenia and Karabagh were painted red, symbolizing blood and suffering; Azerbaijan and Turkey were black, and the grim background was rather eloquently explained by a yellow skull and bones over each of these countries. The years 1915 and 1988 completed the drawing.

A classical example of banners of the »genocide series« category is one of June 15th, 1988 saying: ».. . A whole nation was beheaded by the Turks. Just one Armenian did they want to leave alive, and that. . . for the museum. . . « The text was in the form of a quotation from a poem by Paruyr Sevak, »The Unceasing Bell-Tower«. Apart from the text, the poster was supplemented with drawings and figures. This is why we qualify the poster as a classical example of the reviewed category. The space below the text was divided into three sections. One bore the years of Armenian massacres; the second had the drawing of a Turkish *yataghan* with the figure indicating the number of its victims; the third bore the names of the places where these massacres had taken place: »1895/96, 500.000 – 1915, 1.500.000 – 1918 (Baku), 30.000 – 1920 (Shushi), 35.000 – 1988 (Sumgait), 26 . . . ?«

The first two components of the two posters just described occur in a large number of the »genocides series« posters. For example: »Sumgait is a sequel to the 1915 Genocide, 1920 massacres in Baku and Shushi« (November 8th, 1988) and »Baku – 1918, Shushi – 1920, Sumgait – 1988« (November 18th, 1988, Fig. 3.4). They refer to the massacres of Armenians in September 1918, that happened after Baku had been taken by the Turkish army; and the massacres of 1920 in Shushi, the then main city of Nagorno-Karabagh.

Sometimes the year 1949 and the region Altai appears in the genocides series, e.g. »Der-Zor, Altai, Sumgait...« (the banner was brought to the Genocide Memorial on April 24th, 1989). The year 1949 is as tragic one for Armenians (as well as for millions of Soviet people of the Stalin era), as was 1937. According to unofficial data, about 100.000 Armenians were exiled in June of that year, most of them to Altai region of the USSR, which is nearby Siberia. This still remains a coded message, its meaning is more explicitly disclosed in the following banner:

Panturkism – Der-Zor
Stalinism – Altai
??? -ism – Sumgait

The poster presents each of the genocides in parallel with the official ideology backing it, with the omission of an explanation for Sumgait. In this case the anti-soviet nature of the poster is apparent. While the genocide sequence discussed so far could be classified as a manifestation of confrontation between Armenians and Turks/Azerbaijanis, this last instance dares to question official Soviet ideology: the question marks before Sumgait could be easily deciphered as »perestroika«.

»See, Vardapet, How Not to Go Insane!«

The third major theme referred to mourning and moral responsibilities. It is only after having dealt with the emotions of a tragedy that the people are able to perceive it in depth, to understand, find out and analyze the reasons that have caused it. This was also the case in Yerevan after the tragic events of Sumgait. This becomes clear when analyzing the emotional posters of the days to follow. Here, elements of mourning were characteristic of a number of them, e.g. a poster of March 1988 gave a direct challenge: »Let all of us go on a mourning march to commemorate the Armenians fallen in Karabagh, Sumgait and elsewhere«. In another poster of April 24th, 1988 a weeping woman was depicted with an accompanying text that read: »Yerevan suffers and mourns«.

Figure 3.4: November 18, 1988, Yerevan, Conservatory building. Photo. H.
Marutyan.

The theme of mourning was underlined by several posters and banners of 1988–89 with a quotation from Paruyr Sevak's poem, »The Unceasing Bell-Tower«: »See, Vardapet, how not to go insane!« The poem was devoted to the tragic fate of the great Armenian musician Komitas, who lost his sanity after having witnessed the atrocities of 1915.

Along with banners containing elements of sorrow, mourning and woe, some of the banners publicly shamed the guilty.

The course of events was perceived by many as extremely unfair, so the posters accuse mankind of indifference and injustice. The following quotation was quite common in the years of the Karabagh Movement: »O, human justice, let me spit upon your face«. The quotation belongs to a well-known Western Armenian poet Siamanto, who fell victim to the Genocide. It was taken from a poem called »The Dance«, written as a result of the 1909 massacres in Adana. The poem described how the Turks made Armenian women undress and dance, while they poured petrol upon their bare bodies to burn them alive.

The quotation from Siamanto circulated in several variations, which proves that it had acquired the status of folklore.

»Find the Organizers of Sumgait«

The fourth major theme refers to the initiators of the Sumgait atrocities. This theme can be sub-divided into four comparatively large topics/groups.

The first contained demands for an inquiry into the events in Sumgait: »Political assessment of Sumgait«.

A number of topics could be distinguished in banners referring to the investigation called for into the Sumgait events. First among these were banners that demanded true and complete information. The reason behind this was the fact that the Soviet mass media did its best to downplay the significance of what had happened, presenting it as spontaneous disorders perpetrated by a number of hooligans. The possibility of planned action was not even considered, the figures denoting the number of victims seemed to be significantly reduced, as compared to the stories told by refugee witnesses. No comments were made about the reasons why the intervention of the army troops had been delayed. All this had caused the appearance of banners like: »We demand the truth about Sumgait«, and others.

All along, the Movement participants required an inquiry into the events in Sumgait, a political assessment in particular. When this proved unsuccessful, people made an assessment themselves. This is an important development that underlines one of the objectives of the Movement, that is, the importance of solving the problem by political means. Starting from November 1988 the demand for a *political* assessment gained importance. It was the time when the Movement was stepping into a more radical phase of perceiving the importance of political changes in the social life. For example, in the last official Soviet demonstration on November 7th people demanded a »Political assessment of the Sumgait crime«, »Political assessment of Sumgait«, in a march on November 18th: »A political assessment of the slaughter in Sumgait«.

In the banners the demand for a political assessment was accompanied with the qualification of the Sumgait events as being genocide. I would like to note that such a qualification, though used infrequently, could already be seen in the 8th of March demonstration, and became more common on April 24th, 1988. Here are some of the banners that contain a demand to describe Sumgait as genocide and to assess it politically: »We demand that the genocide in Sumgait and our refugee rights be acknowledged!« (June 7th, 1988); »The Supreme Soviet must recognize the genocide in Sumgait« (October 13th, 1988): below were the photographs of the officially acknowledged 26 victims, in front of which the people lit candles, apparently in prayer for the salvation of their souls.

There were banners that simply recorded that »Sumgait was an organized genocide« (first half of 1988), and there were more radical political statements, such as »The Supreme Soviet of the Armenian SSR must recognize the genocide of Armenians in Azerbaijan SSR during 1920–1988« (November 7th & 18th, 1988).

In the very first banners of the post-Sumgait period of the Movement the name »Sumgait« began to appear as synonymous with atrocities towards Armenians massacres and genocide. This was implied in the banners of October 1988: »Stop ›Sumgait‹ in Karabagh« – which was in response to new cases of violence towards Armenians in Khojalu, a settlement in Karabagh.

However, no political assessment of the events was being made by the Soviet authorities. Being, or rather pretending to be, blind was another policy adopted by the Center, and this was raised during meetings and appeared in commentary in the papers. Such policy was immediately perceived and reverberated in banners, of which the following is an example: »An assessment of Sumgait by ostrich logic«. It is believed that when threatened, ostriches prefer to bury their heads in sand and not to face the danger rather than escaping or defending themselves. The ostrich on the poster, with »Criminal Code of the USSR« written over its body, was acting the same way in front of an image of a Turk who was holding a book titled »Pan-Turkism«, with a bloody *yataghan* in another hand, titled »Genocide«.

The next group of banners reflects the perceptions of people about those directly responsible for the organization and perpetration of the Sumgait atrocities: »Moscow + Baku = Sumgait«.

A rather wide scope of perceptions related to the issue underwent radical changes over time. This happened in the course of events that resulted in the rise of political awareness. Thus, a banner of April 24th, 1988 stated: »The organizers of Sumgait are the enemies of Perestroika«. Another poster of April 24th, 1988 pointed more at ideological enemies, but of a different nature and associated with Pan-Turkism: »The Sumgait genocide is a beloved tactic of Pan-Turkism«.

It was perhaps this mentality that led many Armenians to believe (especially apparent on February 28th and April 24th, the days of commemoration of the victims to Sumgait and the Genocide) that exactly this ideology and its Azerbaijani version caused the tragedies in Sumgait and later, in Baku: for example, »April 24, Sumgait, Baku – all in the same handwriting« (April 24th, 1990).

The theme of friendship underwent interesting metamorphoses. Expanding from an issue of Armenian/Azerbaijani relations, it gradually included other spheres – that of the relations of Armenia with the Center, in particular. Therefore, it included the Armenian-Russian relations that had been idealized for centuries, and recorded their present status as assessed by the people.

Of these posters, taken in chronological order, the first refers to mid October, 1988 saying: »Friendship and brotherhood between the peoples of the USSR« which was written in red, as if in blood (Figure 3.5). Below was a picture of a blond armed soviet soldier with typical Russian features, holding a young man with both hands, while another, darker person dressed in Turkish-Islamic clothes, had his *yataghan* thrust into the youth's breast. The knees of the latter were bent and the wound was bleeding. His face was contorted in pain. It is typical that the person with the *yataghan* was dressed in clothes worn by Turks in the late 19th and 20th centuries, rather than a contemporary Azerbaijani. By this, the author of the poster had tried to imply that modern Azerbaijanis were related to Turks, not only by origin, but by a code of behavior as well. The poster also implied that there was a complete accord between the Russian soldier (meaning: the Soviet authorities) and the Azerbaijanis, as to their methods for treating the Armenians.

A specific continuation of the theme of Armenian-Russian friendship was a poster accompanied with tricolor banners, which read: »›The enemies forever‹ are annihilating Armenians with the approval of the ›friends forever‹« (November 18th, 1988). What caused the appearance of posters with such content, and the use of such expressions?

During the period of over three centuries of Armenian orientation towards Russia, the Armenians had been made to believe that in Russia and the Russian

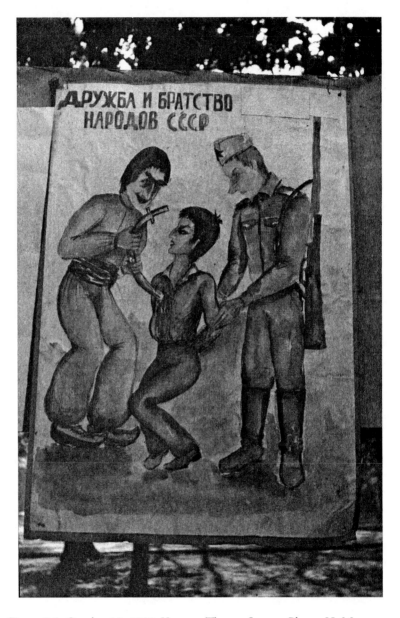

Figure 3.5: October 13, 1988, Yerevan, Theatre Square. Photo: H. Marutyan.

people Armenians had trustworthy friends who were their defenders and saviors, and that the Russians would always stand by them in the hour of need. Thus, a stereotype was created where Russia where personified in the image of an eternal friend. Another, radically different image of an eternal enemy was created, too, in the person of the Turk.

The above mentioned poster was not the only one to express this idea. Another poster of the same day read: »The genocide of Sumgait is the internationalism of the Kremlin«.

There were even more outspoken illustrations to comment on the role of Central Government as possibly guilty in the organization and perpetration of Sumgait events. These seldom depicted the Center alone, but more often it was in the context of close co-operation with Azerbaijan and Azerbaijanis. Thus, a poster recorded on October 13th, 1988, blamed the Center directly for the violence by Azerbaijanis against the Armenians. The poster depicted an arm with a red star on the black sleeve (probably symbolizing the »hand of Moscow«) that was winding a Turkish-Azerbaijani toy (ethnicity shown by the costume), its clothes stained with blood, holding a bloody *yataghan* and a pistol in his hand, standing by a pool of blood. On its right arm was written »Baku«, on the left arm – »Sumgait, Aghdam, Khojalu«, and around its neck the toy is wearing a round medal similar to those awarded to outstanding sportsmen, with »Shushi« written on it. Medals are usually given for certain achievements, and as the medal in the poster also stood out for its color, a conclusion could be made that the medal was an award for the 1920 massacre of Armenians in Mountainous Karabagh city of Shushi. The costume of the toy could be considered as another link between the past and the present, since such clothing was worn towards the end of 19th and the beginning of the 20th centuries.

Another peculiar manifestation of a change of attitude towards the Soviet and Russian soldier is seen in a quotation displayed in the following banner: »These are our children. Buchenwald – Oswiecim – Khatin – Experience exchange – Sumgait – Masis – Zvartnots – Shushi – Stepanakert. . . « (November 18th, 1988). Below the words »These are our children« a Nazi soldier and a Soviet internal forces soldier stand in a handshake with blood dripping from their hands.

The poster in question proceeded to express the change in the perception of the image of a Soviet/Russian soldier. But here, for the first time the actions of a Soviet soldier are compared with those of German fascists, who had inflicted the most vicious cruelties and caused the annihilation of millions of Soviet people. This was a blow to Soviet ideology and to the Soviet system in general. It was also a sign that the Karabagh Movement was on the verge of qualitative changes, gaining an anti-Soviet tendency.

Some of the banners seen on November 7th, 1988 were an extension of the same idea. One such banner at the Opera Square read: »Moscow protects the Azerbaijani/Turkish criminals«. The words were written in white over a black background, while the word »Turk« was written in red over »Azerbaijani«, as if to imply that these two ethnicities were perceived as one by Armenians, and that Moscow had been leading the same policy of protection towards both, in the past as well as in the present.

A number of posters carried by the people on that same day were about the role of Moscow/the Center. »Who is behind the Sumgait murderers???«; »Moscow is behind the Sumgait murderers«; »Look for the sources of Sumgait in Moscow«; »Moscow + Baku = Sumgait«; on November 18th: »Moscow, Baku, Sumgait«. The first three of the banners were in the form of questions and answers, a format that occurred in a number of instances during the Movement.

In another poster seen on April 24th, 1990, there is yet another reference to the parallels between Soviet and fascist behavior. The poster depicted a fascist swastika, the two »arms« of which curved to make bloody *yataghans*, the flag of Soviet Azerbaijan was attached to the third »arm«, with a crescent and star added to it, while another, crescent-shaped *yataghan* was added to the stem of the flag. The flag was dripping blood onto the flag of the Soviet Union attached to the fourth »arm« of the swastika. A text below this read, both in Armenian and Russian: »The inviolable alliance between [the] Kremlin and Azerbaijan. The red flag of the Empire will leave no trace of the blood of the massacred Armenians. This is worse than Fascism«. The word »Fascism« stood out for its larger lettering and was underscored in red, as if to symbolize blood.

I would now like to investigate only one poster pointing at the Soviet Army as being guilty for the initiation and perpetration of the events in Sumgait. The poster in question depicted a kind of a dialogue between two images personifying the Military Procurator and the Military Command. A rocket-like missile bearing the word »Initiator« stood between them, with a crescent and star, symbols of Islam, at the top. The poster was titled »The achievements in Home [our; Soviet] genocidonautics«. The last word was coined in the likeness of »astronautics«, a word that had always gone hand in hand with the word »achievements« in the Soviet Union. The expression made use of typical Soviet language. The person personifying »Justice« pointed at the rocket and addressed the one personifying »Command«: »What should we do with this Pogrom-missile? – It performed perfectly at the Sumgait launching site. We could keep it for multiple uses«. While directly accusing Azerbaijanis of being responsible for the violence in Sumgait, the poster implied that by not intervening for almost three days, the Soviet Army had actually assisted in the atrocities.

»We Should Fight, Not Weep...«

The fifth major theme refers to the process of re-evaluation of the past.[13] In the course of the Movement, each year on April 24th, and in 1989, on also February 28th (the first anniversary of Sumgait) a vast number of posters appeared. On these days alone, according to the data obtained through matching various sources, about 250 posters, as well as wreaths with a similar function were recorded. Of these around 200 referred to the subject of genocide. Even at first glance it becomes apparent that year after year the nature of the poster texts changed from pleading for justice, acknowledgement and fairness to uncompromising conclusions about the necessity of armed struggle, calls for independence and texts that record a development in the perception of the causes of genocide and those responsible for it. That is, the study of materials referring to genocide from these years indicates a continuous re-evaluation of the past and the present.

During the Movement ideas appeared that as a rule became accepted by wider masses of people only in the course of time. The following two notions expressed in the posters of April 24th, 1988 belong to this category, and at the time of their appearance suggested quite different solutions: »Armenians, let's rely upon ourselves« and »We are the sole protectors of ourselves«. For these suggestions to become mainstream months, even years, were required.

Two banners of April 24th, 1989 called on the people to be ready to fight: »No need to weep, neither to despair, / the struggle of Armenians will always be there...«; »April 24th, the day of remembrance and uniting for struggle!«

The January 1990 massacres of Armenians in Baku were succeeded by attacks by Azerbaijani troops at different parts along the border of Armenia and the Nakhichevan Autonomous Republic of Azerbaijan. The instinct for self-defense made many people rise up to fight. People armed themselves with hunting rifles and weapons confiscated from arsenals. Volunteer troops were being formed. The people called these fighters *fedayeens*, associating them with the partisans fighting for national liberation towards the end of the 19th and at the beginning of the 20th centuries, and treated them with great respect. It was after these events that the self-image of the people as martyrs eroded. The fact that the people no longer wished to be considered victims of genocide became immediately apparent in posters. Perhaps it was due to this, that all of about 60 posters of April 24th, 1990 completely lacked any pleading intonations.

Among the posters recorded on that day calling for people to fight and arm

---

13   For more details see: Harutyun Marutyan, »»We must fight and not weep...«: the Process of Revaluation of the Past and Present in the Context of Kharabagh Movement«, in: *Handes amsorya [Monatsschrift fur Armenische Philologie]* (Vienna: Mechitharisten-Congregation, 2003), pp. 411–468.

themselves, were six different posters with a text taken from a *fedayeen* song: »We should fight, not weep, but fight / to gain back the losses of the nation by the use of weapons«.

The fact that the text of an 80-year-old patriotic song was so often recalled is proof enough of a parallel between the events of the 1900's and those of the 1980's, and confirms a certain resemblance in the mentality of the Armenian people then and now.

I would like to stress once again that the main theme of the posters of April 24th, 1990 was that of a call to fight. The banners voiced the idea: »Armenian martyrs are calling for fight«. Note that while a poster »Martyrs command« in 1988 called for remembrance of the innocent victims of genocide, the posters of two years later already pointed at the necessity of struggle. The guiding ideas in the posters: »Only fighting peoples survive«; »The fight of a nation cannot be drowned in blood« sounded as irrefutable maxims.

Figure 3.6: April 24, 1990, Yerevan. Photo: H. Marutyan

Still, the formula that best described the spirit of April 24th, 1990 were the words of Movses Gorgisian, a member of the Armenian Party for Self-Determination, a devoted fighter for independence, who had fallen in a battle on the border of Nakhichevan: »Sorrow is forever, if there is no struggle« (Figure 3.6, posters both in Armenian and English).

»Der-Zor... Sumgait... Atomic Power Station... Nairit«

The sixth major theme was related to the extension of the notion of »genocide«. In the years of Movement following the massacres in Sumgait (which were un-equivocally identified with the Genocide of 1915), events that threatened the existence of the Armenian people, be they of a social ore political nature, were perceived from the perspective of genocide. Thus, the notion of »genocide«, as perceived by the people, included the expressions »white genocide« (bearing in mind the example of the ethnic cleansing of Nakhichevan and Nagorno-Karabagh of Armenians), »ecological genocide«, »biological, chemical genocide« (referring to the Armenian Atomic Power station and the giant »Nairit« chemical plant), »cultural, spiritual genocide« (reduced importance of the Armenian language, destruction of Armenian cultural heritage outside Armenia). Some political forces viewed the Soviet regime as yet another variety of genocide.[14]

»The Only Way to Avoid Genocide Is ... «

The seventh major theme includes the perceptions of the people related to the issue of avoiding genocide in the future.[15] There were several ways of avoiding genocide, as seen by the people, starting with various proposals to resolve the Karabagh problem, and up to a change in the general political orientation. Already in April 1988 the following suggestions appeared:

a) »By respecting the irrevocable rights of the people of Karabagh, we will prevent a new genocide, be it red or white«.

b) »Unwillingness to acknowledge the 1915 Genocide brought about the genocide of 1988«; »Had the Soviet government acknowledged the Genocide of 1915, there would have been no Sumgait«; »Mankind must acknowledge the fact of 1915, so that no more Sumgaits happen«.

c) »Impunity with organized pogroms gives birth to new pogroms« (May 1988).

---

14 For more details see: Harutyun Marutyan, »»Der-Zor... Sumgait... Atomic Power Station... Nairit«: Extension of the Notion of ›Genocide‹ During the Years of Karabagh Movement (1988–1990)«, in: *Nor Azgagrakan Handes: Gitakan ashkhatutyunner [New Ethnographic Journal: Scholarly Papers]* 1 (2005), pp. 78–88.

15 For more details see: Harutyun Marutyan, »The Strategy to Avoid Genocides According to Posters and Banners of the Karabagh Movement«, in: *Arkheologiya, etnologiya i folkloristika Kavkaza. Materiali mezhdunarodnoy konferentsii [Archeology, Ethnology and Folklore of Caucasus. Materials of International Conference]* (Echmiadzin: Institute of Archaeology and Ethnography National Academy of Sciences of Armenia, 2003), pp. 306–309.

d) Looking back on history, in order not to suffer yet another genocide, a further solution was offered in a poster of November 1988: »Der-Zor, Shushi and Sumgait / Where are you, Vardan and David? / We have had enough idle talk«.

The poster depicted a microphone similar to the one in Opera Square which orators used to appeal to the people (to symbolize a peaceful political struggle) and a catapult (probably to symbolize arms. Vardan Mamikonian was a national hero who had fought in a struggle for national independence against Persians in the 5th century. David of Sasoun is a character from the Armenian national epic poem who fought against Arab invaders. Both belong to mediaeval ages when for a long period the catapult was a typical weapon). A question mark stood beside the microphone and the catapult. The poster implied that a choice was to be made between political and armed struggle.

e) Another historical theme is evident in poster reminding people that: »»A nation that has forgotten its history is doomed to have it repeated...‹ G. Nezhdeh« (April 24th, 1990).

f) Both at the very beginning of the Movement as well as in 1990, one of the most frequently used slogans was a quotation from Yeghishe Charents, an outstanding Armenian poet of the 20th century, later a victim of Stalinism, where he addresses the Armenian people: »People of Armenia, your hope of salvation is in your collective strength«.

g) Certain stages in recent history of Armenia, when the country underwent radical changes, were also being considered as genocide: »The forced sovietization of Armenia is the peak of our genocide« (1989, April 24th); »The Great Armenian Genocide happened in 1920–1989« (October, 1989); »Genocide is continued in Soviet captivity«; »Being part of the Empire is a genocide in itself« (both of April 24th, 1990).

Independence was suggested as a solution: »Independence is the only way to avoid genocide«; »Armenia's independence is the answer to Sumgait« (both February 28th, 1989); »The only way to be spared from genocide is independence. Long live liberated and independent Armenia«; »Independence is the guarantee for preventing genocide« (both April 24th, 1989); »Genocide will cease with the re-establishment of a national State«.

Conclusion

A study of sources during the years of the Karabagh Movement reveals that the topic of Armenian genocide, due to the 1915 Genocide and the subsequent massacres of Armenians towards the end of the 20th century, remained the principal expression of historical memory amongst the Armenian people. At the same time, consideration of the posters of the Movement led to the conclusion that this memory was undergoing a process of change. Gradually the image of a victim pleading for mercy and justice was replaced with that of a warrior who had realized that national objectives could be only achieved through struggle.

A growth was observed in the political awareness of the masses while struggling for acknowledgement of the Genocide, for revelation of its initiators and perpetrators, and for them to be brought to justice. Seemingly fixed stereotypes that had formed in the course of decades and even centuries started to change. The past and the present were evaluated; there was realization of the need for radical political change. The people understood that in order to prevent genocide in the future, a complete change in the political structure of the state was required.

Thus, in the years of the Karabagh Movement the theme of genocide, transgressing the limits of pain and sorrow typical in its initial stages, drove people to activism which resulted in the formation of a new parliament, which was expected to choose a course of radical change.

Today, Armenia is leveling a road to democratic Europe. At the beginning of that road is the Karabagh Movement and the transformations it brought to the Armenian identity[16]. I would like to stress, that during the Movement the citizens of Armenia in a step by step manner came to realize that their fight for assistance in the struggle for the self determination of Nagorno Karabagh was not only one of national-liberation, but it also became a part of the dismantling process of the Soviet system. The first successes of the Movement prompted the Baltic republics to stand up for their rights, and afterwards brought on a wave of East European revolutions, which led to the destruction of the Berlin wall and the disintegration of world socialism. During the years of the Movement, citizens of Armenia really believed that »the truth must come and the truth must set us free«[17].

---

16   The awareness of being the first in the European and wider context thus destined to carry out a specific mission does not seem strange to Armenians. From his/her school years, the Armenian teenager knows that the Armenian people were the first in the world, to adopt Christianity as a state religion; that the ideas of the Tondrakian movement laid the basis for Reformation ideology; that the architectural achievements of the St. Amenaprkich (Our Savior) of Sanahin monastery and Cathedral of Ani are in the sources of Gothic architecture; that it was Armenian merchants, who opened the way for Europeans to develop trade with India and China etc, etc.

17   Lech Walesa, »In the Name of Human Dignity«, Speech at the international conference *Ultimate Crime, Ultimate Challenge: Human Rights and Genocide* (Yerevan, April 21st, 2005).

Neoliberal Imaginations, Subject Formation, and Other National Things in Latvia, the Land that Sings[1]

Dace Dzenovska

Nation- and Self-making: Introduction to Relational Articulations

In the context of discussing practices of nation-making in Papua New Guinea, Robert Foster[2] argues that nations by definition have an international dimension. Thus, »nation-making proceeds with heightened self-consciousness of how things are done in and by other nations, especially powerful ones – models to be emulated or rejected, but rarely ignored.«[3] However, the »other nations« do not constitute an outside in the process of nation-making, but are rather part of, and therefore inside, the nation in the making. As Doreen Massey suggests with regard to place identities, the specificity of the place is constituted through the particularity of the interrelations with the so-called outside.[4]

Moreover, the nation is not only a product of spatial, but also of, temporal relations. It takes shape in a historically sedimented hierarchical space organized along a number of axes such as north/south, east/west, developed/developing, old/new, advanced/backward, powerful/marginal and so forth. To put it another way, the contemporary international arena entails a hierarchy of nations arranged

---

1 I would like to thank Iván Arenas for a critical reading and rigorous commentary on this paper. I would also like to acknowledge the input of graduate students associated with the Berkeley Program of Soviet and Post-Soviet Studies at the University of California in Berkeley. A shorter version of this paper was presented at the 8th EASA (European Association of Social Anthropologists) Conference in Vienna, Austria, September 2004. Some parts of this paper have been published in the journal *Place Branding,* Henry Stewart Publications. (See Dace Dzenovska, »Remaking the Nation of Latvia: Anthropological Perspectives on Nation Branding«, in: *Place Branding* 1 (2005), 2, pp. 173–186.)

2 Robert J. Foster, *Materializing the Nation: Commodities, Consumption, and Media in Papua New Guinea* (Bloomington, IN: Indiana University Press, 2002).

3 Foster, *Materializing, op.cit.* (note 2), p. 11.

4 Doreen Massey argues that it is problematic to »characterize any place by counter-position to an other which is outside. If the global reality is, as has been argued above, part of the constitution of and therefore inside, the local, then the definition of the specificity of the local place cannot be made through counter-position against what lies outside; rather it must be made precisely through the particularity of the interrelations with the outside.« Doreen Massey, »Double Articulation: A Place in the World«, in: *Displacements: Cultural Identities in Question,* ed. A. Bammer (Bloomington, IN: Indiana University Press, 1994), p. 117.

according to the degree to which they approximate the model of market democracy. Nations which do not subscribe to this hegemonic frame of reference and try to contest it are often denied full membership in the international community or the legitimacy of their membership is questioned. Full and legitimate membership comes with a price. In order to belong, »rogue« or »new« nations are incited to recognize their immaturity, backwardness, and marginality and strive to remake themselves by emulating the development paths of Western nations. If post-colonial nations, or the so-called Third World, are marked as developing decades after the paradigm of development emerged through anti-colonial struggles, then the post-socialist space, the Second World, has been marked as »transitional« ever since the disintegration« of Soviet and Eastern European socialisms in the late 1980s. Both are marked as marginal, although degrees of marginality do exist between and within these »worlds«, and differentiation is much more intricate than I have so far depicted. The point, however, is that nation-making is always already entangled with practices of differentiation. While responses to these practices of differentiation vary widely, in this paper I focus on those through which the allegedly marginal nations and selves in Eastern Europe, more specifically Latvia, strive for belonging through remaking themselves. I attempt to unpack what kind of a nation and what kind of selves are being made in Latvia through practices and discourses of nation-branding (also referred to as national image-building) on the basis of interviews with nation-branding experts, advocates, and skeptics, as well as analysis of journalistic and academic publications on nation-branding.

In addition to recognizing the spatial and temporal relationality of nation-making, I endorse the notion that nation-making and self-making are mutually constitutive, for the nation does not exist above and beyond national subjects, but rather through them. As Doreen Massey argues, »if places are conceptualized in this way [as relational articulations] and also take account of the construction of the subjects within them, which help in turn to produce the place, then the identity of place is a double articulation.«[5]

An Authentic Peasant Nation on the Margins of Europe

Latvia is the last remaining genuine peasant nation in Europe. It has charming and genuine traditions and preserves an agrarian lifestyle across the continent. This idea needs to be presented as part of a wholesome, positive, earnest and friendly quality that Latvians possess. There are possible ways to expand this notion. Latvians, in addition to being

---

5   Massey, *Double Articulation*, op.cit. (note 4), p. 118.

well-educated, are also toiling, accomplishing people, driven by traditional values and work ethic. Latvians have an ability to maintain traditions while embracing modernity, to keep the old ways in mind while adopting progressive ones.[6]

Just as marginalized Papua New Guineans have attempted to transcend their marginal self and soil by turning to Christianity in order to ground a transnational identity that links them to the »superior white« community,[7] so too some Latvians on the margins of Europe have attempted to transcend their perceived marginality by turning to technologies of branding to remake the nation and self. Through the practices of branding, the nation and its subjects claim transnational belonging by embracing a particular world order and its associated conduct and technologies of self-representation. For example, Wally Olins, a prominent nation-branding expert, points out that »politicians everywhere in the world now realize that every nation has an identity – they can either seek to manage it or it will manage them«.[8] In other words, given this world order, or what nation-branding experts also refer to as the »reality of globalization«,[9] a country, especially a marginal one, has only two options: to brand and exercise control over its image and future economic development or not to brand, relinquish control of its image to others and risk remaining (or becoming) a global backwater.

In line with principles of strategic communication embraced by corporate consultants, nation-branding aims to turn a disadvantage – marginality – into an asset. Thus, for example, senior students of the Oxford Said Business School in London who were hired to prepare a report on how to brand the nation of Latvia to the »unaware«, »misinformed«, and »mistaken« Western audiences proposed that Latvia could market itself as »a natural place« or »an authentic peasant nation.«[10] In doing so, it could hope to increase its recognizability and desirability in the world market. Characterized as pristine, Latvia's landscape was thought of as marketable to Western landscapes implicitly depicted as oversaturated by complex technological advances and spoiled environments. Thus, the key message of the scenario entitled »a natural place« emphasized that »Latvia offers a uniquely unspoiled natural environment and nature is at the heart of Latvian

---

6   This was the key message underlying one of five brand scenarios for the nation of Latvia proposed by a team of consultants from the Oxford Said Business School in London. It was entitled »an authentic peasant nation«. The other four were: »the part of Europe with the best access to Russia«, »the keystone of the Baltics«, »a natural place«, and »a new dawn«. Spencer Frasher, Michael Hall, Jeremy Hildreth, & Mia Sorgi, *A Brand for the Nation of Latvia* (Oxford: Oxford Said Business School, 2003), pp. 43, 45. See in www.politika.lv.

7   Foster, *Materializing the Nation,* op.cit. (note 2), p. 132.

8   Wally Olins, *Trading Identities: Why Countries and Companies are Taking on Each Other's Roles* (London: The Foreign Policy Center, 1999), p. 26.

9   Frasher, et al. *A Brand for the Nation,* op.cit. (note 5), p. 5.

10   Frasher, et al. *A Brand for the Nation,* op.cit. (note 5).

people and their traditions«.[11] Peasant authenticity, in turn, was hoped to invoke an image of a vanishing and thus appealing European indigeneity – »Latvia is the last remaining genuine peasant nation in Europe«, as well as to speak to the ethnic Latvian self-perception as an agrarian nation rooted in the land.

At a first glance, the project of nation-branding is unsettling. The deployment of essentializing and exoticizing tropes in brand scenarios such as »an authentic peasant nation« and »a natural place« is unsettling from the perspective of a critical anthropology which aims to render visible power relations that enable some places to be marked as »traditional« and »natural« and others as »civilized« and »modern«. The project of rendering visible, so popular among critical anthropologists, is not quite appropriate for analyzing nation-branding, however, for nation-branding does not entail any pretense of equality or sameness. Rather, the project of nation-branding explicitly recognizes an unequal hierarchy of nations and attempts to capitalize on inequality to the advantage of the marginal. As Simon Anholt, another prominent nation-branding expert puts it,

All consumers, without even realizing it, see other countries according to an unspoken, but nonetheless very real hierarchy: some countries are perceived as having lower status (usually because they are poorer or less stable or less attractive in some way); some are equal and some are perceived as aspirational country brands, usually because they are richer, happier or more attractive.[12]

Consequently, the nation-branding project is unsettling on two accounts: it explicitly embraces seemingly problematic power relations and destabilizes familiar anthropological critiques. Yet this unease may itself be turned into an asset: if the project of rendering visible looses traction, what are appropriate analytical tools by which to make sense of the project of branding the Latvian nation?

Before beginning to answer this question, however, it is important to recognize that, rather than a fixed and limited entity, the nation is a discursive terrain within which competing notions of individual and collective selves are negotiated and within which various practices of government compete for legitimacy. Thus, while the Latvian nation has historically emerged as a dominant and highly valorized frame of reference for constituting and inhabiting individual and collective identities in Latvia, critiques of nation-branding as an offensive project of commodification did not surface in Latvia. Instead, one and the same individuals spoke about the Nation as a sacred entity and discussed the best ways to brand it for consumption in the global market. This seems to suggest that there is room for multiple, equally valid imaginations of the nation that collectively affirm its centrality. In other words, it is precisely *because of* rather than

11   Frasher, et al. *A Brand for the Nation*, op.cit. (note 5), p. 43.
12   Simon Anholt, *Brand New Justice: The Upside of Global Branding* (Oxford: Butterworth & Heinemann, 2003), p. 79.

in spite of the centrality of the nation that multiple and seemingly contradictory imaginations of the nation are possible, even necessary.[13]

Nation-branding, then, is one way of imagining, practicing, and thereby producing nationhood and selfhood. It is a set of productive practices of government that are animated by certain assumptions about the world-as-it-is and the world-as-it-should-be. Foucauldian analytics of governmentality seems especially conducive for unpacking the rationality inherent in the practices of nation-branding in Latvia.[14] Unpacking the rationality inherent in the practices of nation branding does not entail evaluating these practices against an ideal-typical model of rationality; the critical task is rather to discern the directionality that animates these practices and their contingent results.[15] Practices and discourses

---

13 Katherine Verdery, *National Ideology Under Socialism: Identity and Cultural Politics in Ceausescu's Romania* (Berkeley, CA: University of California Press, 1991), http://ark.cdlib.org/ark:/13030/ft8k4008hw/.

14 Lemke interprets Foucault's governmentality as follows: »the concept of governmentality demonstrates Foucault's working hypothesis on the reciprocal constitution of power techniques and forms of knowledge. The semantic linking of governing (›gouverner‹) and modes of thought (›mentalité‹) indicates that it is not possible to study the technologies of power without an analysis of the political rationality underlying them. In other words, there are two sides to govermentality. On the one hand, the term pin-points a specific form of *representation;* government defines a discursive field in which exercising power is ›rationalized‹. This occurs, among other things, by the delineation of concepts, the specification of objects and borders, the provision of arguments and justifications, etc. On the other hand, it also structures specific forms of *intervention.* For a political rationality is not pure, neutral knowledge which simply ›re-presents‹ the governing reality; instead, it itself constitutes the intellectual processing of the reality which political technologies can then tackle.« Thomas Lemke, »›The birth of biopolitics‹: Michel Foucault's lecture at the College de France on neo-liberal governmentality«, in: *Economy and Society* 30 (2001), 2, pp. 190–207, in particular p. 191; see also: Michel Foucault, »Governmentality«, in: *Power, Essential Works of Michel Foucault, 1954–1984, Vol. 3,* ed. by James Faubion (New York, NY: The New Press, 1994); Nikolas Rose, *Powers of Freedom: Reframing Political Thought* (Cambridge: Cambridge University Press, 1999); Wendy Brown, »Neoliberalism and the End of Liberal Democracy«, in: *Theory and Event* 7 (2003), 1; Pat O'Malley, Lorna Weir, & Clifford Shearing, »Governmentality, criticism, politics«, in: *Economy and Society* 26 (1997), 4.

15 I use Foucault's understanding of »rationality« not as an absolute value inherent in reason or an abstract entity, but rather as an instrumental and relative formation. Foucault argues that »one isn't assessing things in terms of an absolute against which they could be evaluated as constituting more or less perfect forms of rationality, but, rather, examining how forms of rationality inscribe themselves in practices of systems of practices, and what role they play within them – because it's true that »practices« don't exist without a certain regime of rationality. But, rather than measuring this regime against a value of reason, I would prefer to analyze it according to two axes: on the one hand, that of codification/prescription (how it forms an ensemble of rules, procedures, means to an end, and so on), and, on the other, that of true or false formulation (how it determines a domain of objects about which it is possible to articulate true or false propositions).« See in: Michel Foucault, »The Subject and Power«, in: *The Essential Foucault,* ed. by Paul Rabinow & Nikolas Rose (New York, NY: The New Press, 2003).

of nation branding make the nation into a particular object of reflection and target of intervention – it is not necessarily brought into existence« or represented anew, but constituted as a set of problems that require particular solutions, or, according to Paul Rabinow's interpretation of Foucault, it is problematized in a particular way:

Problematization... does not mean the representation of a preexistent object nor the creation through discourse of an object that did not exist. It is the ensemble of discursive and non-discursive practices that make something enter into the play of true and false and constitute it as an object of thought (whether in the form of moral reflection, scientific knowledge, political analysis, etc.).[16]

However, when working with the analytics of governmentality, it is important to remain attentive to the contingency of social relations and the effects of the articulation or joining together of multiple rationalities and technologies of rule. In order to analyze nation-branding as a project of nation and self-making in Latvia, then, I combine the Foucauldian analytics of governmentality with the analytics of articulation derived from Antonio Gramsci via Stuart Hall.[17] Whereas the former allows me to discern the logic that animates the practices of nation-branding, the latter, in emphasizing a non-necessary, yet also non-arbitrary joining together of multiple trajectories that produce specific effects, allows for a complex understanding of the relational intersection of particular spaces, subjects, and histories.

How Nation-branding Came to Latvia

Drawing on the combined analytical frame of governmentality and articulation, it can be concluded that the application of market principles to the nation does not debase an a priori existing and somehow authentic nation. Moreover, the historically informed understandings and practices of the nation present in Latvia do not simply appropriate technologies of branding for their own purposes. In other words, nation-branding in Latvia is neither the result of the impact of the global upon the local nor a simple appropriation of the global by the local. Fur-

16 Paul Rabinow, *Anthropos Today: Reflections on Modern Equipment* (Princeton, NJ: Princeton University Press, 2003), p. 18.
17 Stuart Hall, »Race, Articulation, and Societies Structured in Dominance«, in: *Race Critical Theories*, ed. by Philomena Essed & David Theo Goldberg (Malden, MA: Blackwell Publishers, 2002); Massey, *Double Articulation*, op.cit. (note 5); Tanya Murray Li, »Articulating Indigenous Identity in Indonesia: Resource Politics and the Tribal Slot«, in: *Society for Comparative Study of Society and History* (2002).

thermore, nation-branding is not a necessary outcome of the inevitable process of globalization. Rather, the report produced by the Oxford Said Business School[18] suggesting branding as the most appropriate mechanism for crafting a favorable image of Latvia in the international arena is itself a product of a contingent encounter between Ojārs Kalniņš, the Head of the Latvian Institute, an institution charged with the responsibility of providing information about Latvia to foreign tourists, journalists and business people, and Wally Olins, a prominent nation-branding expert who is also a faculty member at the Oxford Said Business School in London. Even though partially sponsored by the Latvian Institute, the report was not commissioned by it. As Ojārs Kalniņš put it, the government of Latvia was not ready to seriously consider a targeted and coordinated branding strategy for Latvia that would inevitably require substantial financial investment while the students of the Oxford Said Business School needed to undertake a pilot project as part of their study program.[19] The report, then, was a gift and an opportunity – a gift for the Latvian Institute and an opportunity for the students of the Oxford Said Business School. The cooperation resulted in the production of the aforementioned report (hereafter the Oxford report), a limited public discussion on the proposed brand scenarios and nation-branding more broadly, and the translation of Wally Olins' book into Latvian. While this particular initiative is a result of a mutually beneficial encounter between particular individuals, nonetheless it points to the existence of certain conditions within which it both makes sense, and continues to have resonance, in Latvian society. First, the establishment of the Latvian Institute in 1998 can itself be seen as the institutionalization of recognizing the importance of image-making in the international arena (though not necessarily yet in the market terms of branding) – recognizing thus the relational dimension of nationhood. Furthermore, there have been at least two conferences in Latvia dedicated to the issue of image-building that have included discussions on branding. There have also been previous attempts to come up with a logo that could popularize the image of Latvia; however none of them amounted to proper brands since they were not backed up by a coordinated communications strategy and a brand scenario. The only logo that has stuck and is currently used by the Latvian Tourism Development Agency – entitled »the land that sings« (Figure 4.1) – refers to land and folksongs, both of which are considered to be integral elements of the cultural heritage of ethnic Latvians. Inspired by the Herderian notions of folk culture, collection of folk songs played a significant role in cultivating national consciousness in the 19th century. Latvian song festivals became a site of resistance to the Baltic German hegemony in Rīga, later the capital of independent Latvia. The song festivals

18   Frasher, et al., *A Brand for the Nation*, op.cit. (note 5).
19   Author's interview, (July 2004).

continued throughout the Soviet period and once again became a site of civic mobilization and resistance to the Soviet power in the late 1980s. Yet, from the branding perspective, this logo has not grown into a brand for the nation of Latvia with a broad yet concrete message that could be appropriated by various sectors. As one international commentator recently put it, »we don't know much about Latvia, except that it is a land that sings«.[20]

Figure 4.1: Latvia, the land that sings. Latvia Tourism Development Agency 2004. (Published here with permission from the Latvian Tourism Development Agency.)

Last but not least, ongoing discussions in the public space about how Latvia is and should be perceived in the West also affirm the relational dimension of nation and self-making. Many events are evaluated not only from the perspective of their immediate effects for those involved, but also from the perspective of the image of Latvia they will create abroad. For example, recent homophobic practices of Latvia's politicians and the public at large around the first ever Gay and Lesbian Pride Parade in July 2005 were condemned by Latvian liberal elites not only for violation of human rights, but also for producing an image of Latvia as an intolerant and thus uncivilized place.[21] Emphasizing this point, one aca-

---

20 Personal communication (August 2004).

21 Prior to the parade, Latvian politicians came out with strong homophobic statements allegedly in defense of traditional family values. The parade itself was met by individuals who were throwing eggs and tomatoes, as well as shouting offensive statements. The parade was nearly forbidden by the Riga City Council, yet the organizers took the case to court and received permission at the last minute. Heated debates have continued ever since. In fact, in response to the increasing public visibility of homosexuality, one of the right wing parties proposed Constitutional amendments that would define marriage as a union between a man and a woman. During the debates on the proposed Constitutional amendments, one politician stated that to allow same-sex marriage would be the same as to grant human rights to monkeys

demic told me that on his recent visit to Britain, upon finding out that he was from Latvia, someone had commented, »ah, the place that hates gays«. So much for the land that sings.

The discourses and practices of nation-branding attempt to organize a disparate set of initiatives of image building into a coherent strategy aiming to remake the nation not only by altering representational practices, but, most importantly, by modifying the behavior of national subjects who constitute the nation. These practices and discourses of nation-branding bring into focus inflections in the conceptions of the nation and of individuals as national subjects.

Nation-branding – What Is It and Why Do It?

As argued by the authors of the Oxford report, the purpose of a national brand identity for Latvia would be to proactively and consistently communicate to the world that Latvia »exists«, is »normal«, and is »ready« to assert itself in a global market increasingly »cluttered« by nations competing for political influence and, more importantly, economic power and resources.[22] In the Oxford report, the national brand identity is defined as an umbrella identity that can incorporate and give meaning to sub-brands targeted at specific sectors, such as foreign direct investment, tourism, exports, and political influence.[23] The national brand is supposed to conjure up images that are both general and specific enough to attract the interest of the world that matters, and ultimately result in a »purchase decision«.

In the process, nation-branding aims to simultaneously discover and invent the truth about the nation that could form the basis of the nation's brand identity. The nation itself is assumed to exist a priori, with all its constitutive inclusions and exclusions, and to have an essence, what Slavoj Žižek calls »the Thing«, which is representable only through self-references.[24] »The Thing« is

---

(www.delfi.lv, October 13th, 2005). Another politician suggested that the Latvian normative (heterosexual) »us« is under attack from socialists who have already pushed through same-sex marriage in Spain. (http://www.saeima.lv/steno/2002_8/st_051026/st2610.htm).

22   Olins, *Trading Identities,* op.cit. (note 8), p. 3. It is clear that the word »world« in the Oxford report refers to a particularly situated perspective of the map, namely Estonia, Lithuania, Germany, Sweden, Finland, Denmark, Russia, key players in the EU (especially UK and Germany), and the USA. Frasher, et al., *A Brand for the Nation,* op.cit. (note 5), p. 37.

23   Frasher, et al., *A Brand for the Nation,* op.cit. (note 5).

24   »The element which holds together a given community cannot be reduced to the point of symbolic identification: the bond linking together its members always implies a shared relationship toward a Thing.... National identification is by definition sustained by a relationship toward the Nation qua Thing. This Nation-Thing is determined by a series of contradictory

real but elusive, more visceral than intelligible, yet it is taken to be the basis of the branding exercise and needs to be given concrete form through a series of statements and implementing strategies. Given the assumed existence of this national essence or »Thing«, the process is one of discovery. Given its near unrepresentability, the process is one of invention. The community conjured vis-à-vis the elusive »Thing« takes concrete form as the proactive owner of the brand:

> Ultimately, a brand is something that resides in the minds of the consumer, but its identity is synonymous with the associations that the owner of the brand wishes to build. A ›brand's identity‹ can be thought of as its charter, its manifesto, the identity card that describes its core values and associations.... Aaker suggests that brand identity ›represents the timeless essence of the brand. It is the centre that remains after you peel away the layers of an onion.‹ This process of »peeling away« is the foundation of our work in recommending a brand identity for Latvia. As such, creating a brand identity is as much an exercise of discovery as it is of invention.[25]

Substantiations of nation-branding draw their legitimacy from the rules of a particular economic order, also referred to by nation-branding experts as the »reality of globalization«.[26] These rules are not compiled in a single programmatic document or statement, but are discernable from the directionality or orientation of nation-branding practices towards specific ends, the logic of the technologies deployed, as well as the criteria used for evaluating the success of nation-branding efforts. The »reality of globalization« describes a particularly ubiquitous market mentality, where individuals and nations have to cultivate competitiveness and cannot afford to be passive. In this reality, there are no entitlements, only opportunities. While accepting the inevitability of this somewhat harsh reality, Simon Anholt nonetheless wants to find a way to use it for purposes of redistributive justice:

> My proposal is to take this sword called branding and place it in the hands of the people who actually need it and can make the best use of it. It's a good and a powerful sword, and *in the right hands* can continue to create the same miracles of prosperity for the South as it has done for the North.[27]

---

properties. It appears to us as ›our Thing‹ (perhaps we could say *cosa nostra*), as something accessible only to us, as something ›they‹, the others, cannot grasp; nonetheless it is something constantly menaced by ›them‹. It appears as what gives plenitude and vivacity to our life, and then the only way we can determine it is by resorting to different versions of the same empty tautology. All we can ultimately say about it is that the Thing is ›itself‹, ›the real Thing‹, ›what it really is about‹ etc. If we are asked how we can recognize the presence of this Thing, the only consistent answer is that the Thing is present in that elusive entity called ›our way of life‹.« Slavoj Žižek, *Tarrying with the Negative: Kant, Hegel, and the Critique of Ideology* (Durham, NC: Duke University Press, 1993), in particular p. 201.

25   Frasher, et al. *A Brand for the Nation*, op.cit. (note 5), p. 15.
26   Frasher, et al. *A Brand for the Nation*, op.cit. (note 5), p. 5.
27   Anholt, *Brand New Justice*, op.cit. (note 12), p. 1, emphasis added.

This statement suggests that using the tools of branding entails not only acknowledging the pervasiveness of a particular market – and marketable – reality and the associated understanding of a particular hierarchy of nations, but also its active construction. Most importantly, nation-branding is a set of practices that aim to align the way national subjects (and thus the nation) think of, and conduct themselves in accordance with the logic of, the »reality of globalization«. Consequently, the ability to recognize the usefulness of marketing tools for simultaneously increasing national prosperity and cultivating possibilities for self-realization is conditional upon seeing the world in a particular way, i.e. subscribing to a particular political rationality and conducting oneself accordingly. For example, some of the nation-branding proponents interviewed in Latvia seemed to think that the government and the public are indifferent or passively resistant to nation-branding for reasons such as ignorance with regard to the importance of proactive image-building and the benefits of market technologies outside the private sector, as well as due to historically acquired and inherited national character traits, such as modesty, pessimism, and short-term thinking. Such continuous commentary on advantageous and disadvantageous ways of thinking and acting within the discourse of nation-branding is indeed a technology of government – a pedagogical device for managing self-formation.

The efforts of nation-branding in Latvia are related to broader efforts to theorize and practice nation-branding. Various nation-branding initiatives with varying degrees of success have been launched in Britain, France, Spain, Croatia, and Estonia among others.[28] Instead of indifference, some of these have apparently encountered outright hostility. Wally Olins writes that »the concept of nation as a brand seems to excite visceral animosity«.[29] To illustrate this, Olins quotes the French political scientist Michele Girard:

In France, the idea of re-branding the country would be widely unacceptable, because the popular feeling is that France is something that has a nature and a substance other than a corporation... A country carries specific dignity unlike a marketed product... In France, it is unimaginable for Chirac to attempt to re-brand France.[30]

This critique exhibits traces of a rationality that posits the country and the market as distinct entities that operate according to different sets of rules. From

---

28 Stjepo Martinovic, »Branding Hrvatska – a mixed blessing that might succeed: The advantage of being unrecognizable«, in: *Journal of Brand Management* 9 (2002), 4–5, pp. 315–322; Fiona Gilmore, »A country – can it be repositioned? Spain – the success story of country branding«, in: *Journal of Brand Management* 9 (2002), 4–5, pp. 281–293; Bruce D. Keillor & G. Tomas M. Hult, »A five country study of national identity: Implications for international marketing research and practice«, in: *International Marketing Review* 16 (1999), 1, pp. 65–82.

29 Wally Olins, »Branding the nation – the historical context«, in: *Journal of Brand Management* 9 (2002), 4–5, pp. 241–248, in particular p. 241.

30 Olins, »Branding the nation«, (note 30), p. 241.

this perspective, nation-branding looks like commodification – a process that subjects the nation to the rules of the market, thus contaminating the essential French »Thingness«. Taking France as an example, Olins asserts that branding is ultimately the same as previous political efforts to change the image of the nation: »The Third Republic collapsed in the defeat of 1940 and was replaced by Petain's Vichy. Under Vichy, France was re-branded yet again; the Republican slogan, or as branding people would put it stripline, ›liberté, égalité, fraternité‹ was replaced with ›travail, famille, patrie‹«.[31] The only real difference is the rhetoric of branding and the use of marketing technologies.[32] It is implied here that image-making or branding technologies are generally neutral and can be separated from the logic from which they emanate. Thus, nation-branding is merely an improved version of an age-old practice that leaves the nation itself intact. The analytics of governmentality, however, counters such assumptions by positing that technologies of government necessarily exhibit the logic of the political rationality from which they emanate.[33] Thus, they cannot but (re)constitute the entity they target, rather than merely being tools that help an a priori existing entity along a particular trajectory of development. These differences are evident in the nation-branding discourse. For example, nation-branding experts use the concepts of nation, country, and market as synonyms, as exemplified by Anholt's frequent use of »emerging countries« and »emerging markets«,[34] whereas the aforementioned French political scientist seems to equate nation and country, while adamantly distinguishing between nation/country and market. The discursive collapse between nation/country and market points towards a distinct rationality that underlies nation-branding practices. This rationality resembles what Wendy Brown calls a neoliberal political rationality. From within this rationality, the collapse of spheres, such as the economic and the political, is not visible, i.e. does not make sense as a problem. Brown describes neoliberal political rationality as »*extending and disseminating market values to all institutions and social action,* even as the market itself remains a distinctive player«.[35] Brown explains why the notion of neoliberal political rationality introduces something new and cannot be merely thought of in terms of commodification. First, it is not a result of an inevitable historical development of capitalism; it is rather a contingent organization. Second, the notion of commodification posits a relative autonomy between the political, the economic, and moral rationale, whereas

31   Olins, »Branding the nation«, p. 243.
32   ibid., p. 241.
33   Lemke, »›The birth of bio-politics‹«, op.cit. (note 14), p. 191.
34   Anholt, *Brand New Justice*, op.cit. (note 12).
35   Brown, »Neoliberalism«, op.cit. (note 14), p. 2.

neoliberal political rationality reconfigures these spheres and integrates them, a relationship which is simultaneously productive and destructive.[36]

When asked to comment on the »visceral animosity« towards nation branding of the kind exhibited by the French political scientist, Simon Anholt responded as follows:

I get far more skepticism and negativity in rich countries, where people are often disturbed by moral and philosophical thoughts about whether it's *right* to brand a country, whether it's possible to »reduce a country down to the level of a brand«, etc. I hardly ever hear this kind of stuff in transition economies and LDCs [less developed countries], as people are generally united in their desire to improve the image of the country and try anything, which will increase their earning power and status in the world.[37]

In his response, resentment towards nation-branding on moral and ideological grounds is the luxury of the rich. Poorer nations, in other words, think more realistically about the economically differentiated world in which they operate and thus readily embrace nation-branding as a tool that can help foster their economic power. It is not that »transition economies and LDCs« are more inclined to sacrifice the dignity of the nation in order to secure economic gains. Rather, they recognize that their reality is largely shaped by a different, possibly neoliberal, rationality, and align their conduct accordingly. According to this rationality, nation-branding is a way of enhancing rather than sacrificing a nation's dignity and integrity.

The exercise of developing a pilot brand identity for Latvia was largely seen as an attempt to improve previous image-building efforts in Latvia and convince the government to back a fully blown branding campaign. Several of those interviewed, including the Director of the Latvian Institute, noted that the previous efforts have been fragmentary, have lacked vision, consistency, serious commitment, and have also suffered from lack of coordination. A representative of an advertising company in Rīga described the situation to me as follows:

Product brands are appealing due to their consistency and coordinated message. The current Latvian brand is schizophrenic; there is no consistency. Surfaces one group of people which says that we are a singing nation; others are talking about IT [information technologies]. ... A brand should be like a multi-series film – when you put the puzzle together, you get a clear picture – sexy and attractive for internal and external markets.[38]

However, branding is not only about the vision and the consistency of the message put forth by government agencies and politicians. More importantly, it is a matter of conduct that affects the whole population. What really makes

---

36   ibid., p. 4.
37   Author's interview (July 2004).
38   Author's interview (July 2004).

a brand successful is the fact that it is lived: »Country branding occurs when public speaks to public: when a substantial proportion of the population of the country – not just the civil servants and paid figureheads – gets behind the strategy and lives it out in their everyday dealings with the outside world.«[39] In the face of the impossibility of forcing the population to live the desired brand identity, nation-branding practices strive for an alignment of the nation's multiple »everyday dealings with the outside world« so that, while dispersed and diverse, these »dealings« would nevertheless be guided by the same rationality. Such an alignment can only be approximated, for the reality which nation-branding simultaneously presupposes and constructs takes as the subject of government a population consisting of free individuals with multiple and diverse affiliations and affinities.[40] Simon Anholt puts it as follows: »The ultimate aim towards which nation-branding should aspire is creating such a sense of pride and purpose that the entire population begins, almost by instinct, to perform such acts of conversion, every day of their lives: an impossible target to attain, of course, but the direction in which one should strive could not be clearer.«[41] Thus, in addition to a qualitatively different rationality that animates it, nation branding requires a specific set of technologies for prompting the desired conduct of the population, as well as that of the potential consumers of the brand identity.

The Technologies of Nation-branding and Self-making

Contrary to assumptions that the introduction of the free-market should erode national affinities, nation-branding practices and discourses affirm the importance of country of origin for both consumer choices and opportunities for individual and collective self-realization.[42] For example, a professor at the University of Latvia commented that in order to have success as an international consultant, a foreigner has to represent a country with political or economic authority.

39   Anholt, *Brand New Justice*, op.cit. (note 12), p. 123.
40   I leave the notion of »free individuals« uncontested, for I rely on Foucault's analysis which posits a relationship of power as »a mode of action that does not act directly and immediately on others. Instead, it acts upon their actions. … A power relationship … can only be articulated on the basis of two elements that are indispensable if it is really to be a power relationship: that »the other« (the one over whom power is exercised) is recognized and maintained to the very end as a subject who acts; and that, faced with a relationship of power, a whole field of responses, reactions, results, and possible inventions may open up«. See in: Foucault, »The Subject and Power«, op.cit. (note 15), pp. 137–138. Freedom, then, always already entails a limited but not wholly limiting discursive field within which individual actions are enabled.
41   Anholt, *Brand New Justice*, op.cit. (note 12), p. 124.
42   Anholt, *Brand New Justice*, op.cit. (note 12).

Thus, a foreigner's (for example, a nation-branding expert's) success is shaped in part by her national affiliation and the position of her perceived country of origin in the geopolitical hierarchy as understood by those she is advising. At the same time, the state's attempts to increase national prosperity, simultaneously understood as individual prosperity, through economic growth require that individuals conduct themselves in ways that communicate an attractive image of the country to potential tourists, investors, and consumers.[43] Individual self-realization takes place in relation to a collectivity (in this case the nation), and, similarly, the cultivation of the nation's prosperity depends on individuals who conceive of themselves as national subjects and constitute the nation through their conduct.

Nation-branding practices aim to govern or act upon the actions of individuals on three registers. First, it is necessary to align the activities of institutions and individuals in the position to govern so that they are animated by a compatible logic. Second, nation-branding entails acting upon the conduct of potential investors, tourists, and consumers in ways that result in a purchase decision. And, third, nation-branding practices aim to act upon the conduct of the individuals, who constitute the nation, so that »the entire population begins, almost by instinct« to »live the brand«.[44] The technologies of government appropriate for each of the three registers differ, yet are related in the sense that they all try to exercise what nation-branding experts call »soft power« – a reality partly determined by the predominant liberal notions of limited government and individual freedom and partly by the governor's positioning with regard to the governed. As Simon Anholt notes, »you can only wield hard power over countries which lie beneath you in the hierarchy of nations. For *emerging countries*, which lie beneath the rest, the only power they can hope to wield is soft«.[45]

On the first register (alignment of activities of the governing actors), the preferred technology of government is coordination. Nearly all those interviewed expressed concern with the lack of coordination that hinders nation-branding efforts in Latvia. The Oxford report differentiates between coordination and regulation, describing the proposed brand management process as follows: »While this process is to be supervised by the so called Brand Steward, the point is not for the Brand Steward to give directives to each of these groups; rather the point is to enable them, and give them tools that will ensure their efforts are harmonious with those of their counterparts in other arenas to guarantee a joint national vision«.[46] Within the framework of the European Union, this officially endorsed mode of governance is referred to as »the open method of coordination,« and

---

43   Anholt, *Brand New Justice*, op.cit., p. 13.
44   Anholt, *Brand New Justice*, op.cit. (note 12), p. 124.
45   Anholt, *Brand New Justice*, op.cit., p. 13, emphasis added.
46   Anholt, *Brand New Justice*, op.cit., p. 53.

is meant to replace or supplement the previous modes of governance dominant during the pre-accession period, namely regulation and harmonization.[47] Coordination is thought of as a flexible, voluntary approach to government, especially advantageous in spheres where full regulation is not possible for one reason or another, but is mainly promoted because member states want to maintain at least formal control over a particular policy area, thus asserting their sovereignty. Coordination is a practical scheme through which institutional and individual conduct can be aligned without impinging upon national, institutional, or the personal autonomy central to the (neo) liberal political rationality.[48]

Coordination is also conducive to the second register of government namely acting upon the conduct of the potential consumers of the national brand identity. Simon Anholt points out that »people are in any case somewhat skeptical of obviously pre-paid messages, and while image-building campaigns certainly have their place in a properly thought out brand strategy, just as much can often be achieved simply by aligning communications to a properly worked-out strategy, than by adding yet more new messages to the mix«.[49]

The third register – acting upon the conduct of individuals who constitute the nation – poses the biggest challenge to nation-branders. Alignment of conduct, so that each resident becomes a sales representative, as it were, is much more complicated in the case of nation-branding than in business. Anholt admits to serious limitations of know-how in this regard:

There is, in fact, little that is democratic in the way that most companies are run, and power brands are often the result of a very single-minded, even mildly deranged, »visionary« simply eliminating anybody who dares to deviate from the company line...

---

47   Burkard Eberlein & Dieter Kewer, »New Governance in the European Union: A Theoretical Perspective«, in: *JCMS: Journal of Common Market Studies* 1 (2004), p. 173–186; Jens Henrik Haahr, »Open Method of Coordination as Advanced Liberal Government«, in: *1st European Conference on European Union Politics* (ECPR, Bordeaux, France, September 26th – 28th, 2002); Sabrina Regent, »The Open Method of Coordination: A Supranational Form of Governance?« (ILO discussion paper DP/137/2002, 2002).

48   Graham Burchell puts it this way: »practical principles for effective conduct of government additionally will presuppose some way of conceiving how these individuals with diverse social and economic forms of existence, individuals who are members of particular groups and ›communities‹, who are living beings, parts of a biological population, and who have different particular interests, needs, aptitudes and abilities, are to be integrated within various sectors of ›society‹. The problem, then, that attempts to formulate practicable principles of government have to confront is to establish a scheme in which these different modes of integrating the individual within society and its englobing political order can be co-ordinated.« Graham Burchell, »Peculiar Interests: Civil Society and Governing ›The System of Natural Liberty‹«, in: *The Foucault Effect: Studies in Governmentality*, ed. by Graham Burchell, Colin Gordon, & Peter Miller (Chicago, IL: The University of Chicago Press, 1991), pp. 119–150, in particular p. 135.

49   Anholt, *Brand New Justice*, op.cit. (note 12), p. 123.

Countries are obviously different. A manager in a company may be ruthlessly single-minded and this can benefit the company enormously; the same approach by the leader of a country is called tyranny and seldom achieves positive results. And yet one knows from experience that getting many independent people and organizations (all with different interests, opinions and agendas) to speak with a single voice is a hard thing to achieve through consensus … But one thing is clear: unless a government can find a way of achieving in its committees the same single-minded sense of purpose and control which the crazy brand visionary achieves within a privately owned company, nothing will come of the national brand programme and it's doomed to fail.[50]

On this register, nation-branding straddles the boundaries between soft modes of exercising power and the necessity to assert authority vis-à-vis experts and visionaries. Both Anholt and Olins at different moments consider the possibility of keeping the national brand secret until it is ready to be launched, thus avoiding unnecessary obstacles. »The first rule of re-branding the country is to keep very quiet about your plans until you have real results to show, or the inevitable storm of invective will jeopardize the whole initiative.«[51]

Since there is no official branding program in Latvia as of yet, the current technologies that target individual conduct in the context of nation-branding mainly entail commentary on appropriate and inappropriate conduct. For example, one such instance is the already mentioned critique of Latvians as passive, short-term thinkers, ignorant of the benefits of proactive marketing strategies. Given that government as a practice is not limited to the state, but entails multiple actors who »shape the field of possibilities for individual conduct through a myriad of practices that aim to align individual conduct with the political goals of the state and the perceived needs of the population«,[52] multiple individuals not only govern themselves through their own conduct and commentary but also shape the field of possibilities of conduct and commentary for others.

Indeed, the rationality animating nation-branding and the associated technologies of government have strong affinities with the neoliberal form of governmentality as distinguished from earlier forms of liberalism by the following characteristics: (1) the market form serves as the organizational principle for the state and society; and (2) the social domain is encoded as a form of the economic domain, thus cost-benefit criteria can be applied to decision-making processes within the family, married life, professional life, and so forth.[53] Yet while a neoliberal political rationality can be discerned as animating nation-branding practices in Latvia, it does not form an iron cage that is imposed upon a population and determines forms of life thereafter. Rather, it is more enabling to think of

---

50   Anholt, *Brand New Justice*, op.cit, p. 135.
51   Frasher, et al., *A Brand for the Nation*, op.cit. (note 5), p. 51.
52   Burchell, »Peculiar Interests«,op.cit. (note 49) p. 19.
53   Lemke, »›The birth of bio-politics‹«, op.cit. (note 14), p. 200.

the neoliberal or any political rationality as subject to the contingencies of social relations as well as an articulation with other historically determined rationalities and technologies of rule that shape the conduct of individuals and institutions in Latvia.[54] If it is possible at any one point to argue that one rationality is dominant at a particular moment, this is not because of a decisive replacement of one rationality with another, but rather because of contingent articulations of multiple and entangled rationalities within a historically over-determined field of power relations. In Latvia, multiple and entangled rationalities and histories give shape to imaginations and practices of change and transformation, including the discourses and practices of nation-branding.

»Actually Existing Neoliberalism« or Neoliberal Nationalism

In her reflections on *Neoliberalism and the End of Liberal Democracy*, Wendy Brown argues that »neo-liberal rationality extended to the state itself indexes state success according to its ability to sustain and foster the market and ties state legitimacy to such success«.[55] Nation-branding practices and discourses do indeed exhibit the centrality of economic growth for state legitimacy indexed by such criteria as export volume, foreign direct investment, and tourism revenue. Ardent defenders of nation branding have set out to calculate the potential returns on government investment in branding in order to convince the government to back a branding campaign.

At the same time as the Latvian state's legitimacy hinges on an articulation of state practices and economic growth, in the post-Soviet historical terrain, state legitimacy is also tied to the state's ability to ensure the integrity of the ethnically Latvian nation. Fifteen years after the disintegration of the Soviet Union, Latvia is a place considered to be perpetually under siege – if not by the continuous danger of neighboring Russia and its fifth column – namely the Russian-speaking residents of Latvia, then by the immigrant, racial, or homosexual other. The wounds of the Soviet legacy have not healed, yet the European present has introduced the possibility of new troubling additions to the terrain of difference, such as Muslims, Africans, and sexual minorities. The sovereign Latvian present, understood as mastery over the self and future which could ensure the integrity of the ethnically Latvian nation, is a permanently deferred presence which incites

54   O'Malley, et al., »Governmentality, criticism, politics«, op.cit. (note 14).
55   Brown, »Neoliberalism«, op.cit. (note 14), p. 3.

new discourses of threat and justifies increasingly rigid and closed boundaries of the normative collective self.[56]

The explicit articulation of the political community in Latvia with the ethnically Latvian nation is the result of a historical legacy. It draws much of its legitimacy from claims of historical injury to the cultural integrity of the nation and national self-esteem produced throughout centuries of German, imperial Russian, and Soviet rule. Thus, in the late 1980s, the nation was the frame of reference in relation to which Latvian residents – at the time Latvians and Russians both – conceived their opposition to the Soviet Union. It is important to recognize, however, that this frame of reference did not congeal outside the Soviet socialist project, but rather through an intricate relationship with it.

It has been well documented how, from its inception, the Soviet state grappled with the relationship between national difference and the socialist project.[57] While some considered the assertion and cultivation of national difference as a temporary stage that would disappear along with class difference, others emphasized the importance of the national form for bringing socialist ideas and practices to the ethnically diverse Soviet peoples, resulting in the infamous formula »socialist in content, national in form«. Given the size and diversity of the Soviet Empire, the practices through which difference was constituted and managed diverged greatly. If in Central Asia and the Soviet North administrators and ethnographers labored to cultivate national consciousness, in the Baltic republics, national aspirations had to be kept in line since they threatened to exceed the form of, and impinge on, the socialist content. The result was that national difference in Latvia was both cultivated and disciplined throughout the Soviet period. With military and pioneer choirs performing alongside national folk dance ensembles, no party congress passed which did not celebrate and mark Latvia's socialist content and national form. In Latvia, being Soviet entailed being Latvian and not Belarusian, Georgian, Ukrainian or, most importantly, Russian.

---

56   In making this argument I build on Nikolai Ssorin-Chaikov's work on Subarctic Siberia during Soviet socialism where he argues that the socialist present was continuously deferred thus inciting practices of government which aimed to bring it about. Nikolai Ssorin-Chaikov, *The Social Life of the State in Subartic Siberia* (Stanford, CA: Stanford University Press, 2003).

57   Francine Hirsch, »Toward an Empire of Nations: Border-Making and the Formation of Soviet National Identities«, in: *Russian Review* 59 (2000), pp. 201–226; Francine Hirsch, »Soviet Union as Work-in-Progress: Ethnographers and the Category of Nationality in the 1926, 1937 and 1939 Censuses«, in: *Slavic Review* 59 (1997), 2, pp. 251–278; Bruce Grant, *In the Soviet House of Culture: A Century of Perestroikas* (Princeton, NJ: Princeton University Press, 1995); Nikolai Ssorin-Chaikov, *The Social Life of the State*, op.cit. (note 58); Yuri Slezkine, »Imperialism as the Highest State of Socialism«, in: *Russian Review* 59 (2000), pp. 227–234; Terry Martin, »Affirmative Action Empire«, in: *A State of Nations: Empire and Nation Making in the Age of Lenin and Stalin*, ed. by Ronald Grigor Suny & Terry Martin (Oxford: Oxford University Press, 2001).

Yet alongside the cultivation of particular forms of Latvianness, Latvians experienced the suppression of others, such as free access to former symbols of nationhood and other practices that fell outside the socialist frame. Most importantly, the Latvian nation suffered deportations of large numbers of Latvia's prewar residents and experienced an influx of residents from other Soviet republics. Thus, the Soviet period managed to cultivate both a strong sense of Latvianness and a strong resentment towards the Soviet regime, especially against its migration policies, which facilitated movement of large numbers of Russian speakers to the Latvian Republic, and thus contributed to the Latvian self-narrative as one of existential endangerment of Latvian national self in national soil.[58]

Despite political independence, the Latvian self-narrative continues to claim both historical and ongoing colonization. On the one hand, the narrative of colonization draws on the sedimented Soviet past and emphasizes the historical injustice of the Soviet occupation. In this form, it emphasizes Soviet traces evident in the Latvian landscape and the minds of its people, thus inciting continuous corrective action, including decolonization of the collective psyche. For example, several of the nation-branding proponents interviewed emphasized that traits they saw as characteristic of Latvians, such as modesty, passivity, fear, and short-term thinking, are products of oppression and need to be corrected in order to raise the national self-esteem that is necessary for successful nation-branding. One interviewee suggested that such individual conduct is a manifestation of collective pathologies and that Latvians might benefit from televised collective psychotherapy sessions. On the other hand, the European ›present‹ itself is often seen as colonizing, especially in moments when it demands a commitment to liberal modes of relating to difference which are seen as threatening to the integrity of the ethnically defined nation. In response, Latvians emphasize their suffering, and use it to justify protective measures for the ethnically defined nation. The following internal perceptions of Latvia, »Latvians believe they have suffered – and they want people to know it«, is quoted in the Oxford report. »We are such a tolerant society. Maybe that's why we have been occupied so many times«.[59]

Not surprisingly, the authors of the Oxford report interviewed only ethnic Latvians for the purposes of discerning the truth about the nation's identity, its »Thingness«, that could form the basis of the nation-state's brand identity. The interviews were arranged by the Latvian Institute and non-Latvians (the preferred label for all those who are not part of the ethnic nation) were simply not included. The efforts of nation-branding in Latvia, then, can be said to ex-

---

58   According to the Latvian Institute, the ethnic composition of Latvia changed as a result of the Soviet occupation as follows: in the pre-World War II period Latvians constituted at least 80% of the population and Russians less than 9%, yet in 1989 Latvians constituted 52% of the population and Russians 30%. (www.li.lv, accessed November 2005).

59   Frasher, et al., *A Brand for the Nation,* op.cit. (note 5), p. 9.

hibit traces of both a neoliberal political rationality and a rationality of corrective nationalism articulating a particular orientation of nation-branding practices in Latvia that I call *neoliberal nationalism*.

Contested Neoliberal Nationalism

In this paper I have suggested that nation-branding is a set of practices of government that aim to remake the nation in accordance with a neoliberal political rationality by shaping the conduct of individuals that constitute the nation. In keeping with my earlier assertion, that when working with the analytics of governmentality one should remain attentive to the contingency of social relations and the effects of articulation of multiple rationalities and technologies of rule, I want to reiterate here, that it is imperative not to treat practices animated by a neoliberal political rationality as fully determined by it and thus closed to critical interventions that might open possibilities for alternative ways of thinking and acting. Neoliberalism as a form of government not only constrains, but also enables subjects to act in a particular field of possibilities.[60] One should not easily dismiss the fact that Simon Anholt, while working from within the »reality of globalization«, is simultaneously concerned with the inequalities that it entails. This is to say that there are no privileged spaces of resistance, and while remaining attentive to the dire effects of neoliberal economic reforms, one could, perhaps, remain hopeful about the unintended effects of conduct influenced even by a neoliberal political rationality. What happens when marketing technologies are used to brand other visions of »the good life« that provide alternatives to neoliberal imaginaries? Simon Anholt seems to think that alternative ethics can indeed be cultivated through such undertakings. »And here lies the most exciting opportunity for brands from emerging markets. In purely branding terms, there are great gaps in the global palette of country-brands for countries which are ›about‹ qualities other than power, wealth and sophistication: perhaps creativity, philosophy, diversity, tolerance, trust, innocence, wisdom, challenge, risk, safety; and who knows what else besides.«[61] Thus, the neoliberal frame from within which Anholt operates not only constrains, but also enables him to act in a field of possibilities that has emerged as a result of an articulation of multiple spaces, subjects, and histories.

In the Latvian context, however, nation-branding is articulated with a particular form of nationalism that embraces an exclusive ethnic conception of the

---

60 Michel Foucault, »The Subject and Power«, op.cit (note 15).
61 Anholt, *Brand New Justice*, op.cit. (note 12), p. 151.

nation grounded in claims of historical injustice and the need to protect and cultivate the nation that, according to the Latvian self-narrative, has been pushed towards extinction during the Soviet period.[62] Alongside the strong sense of the need to cultivate and protect the ethnically Latvian nation and turn non-Latvians – former Soviet persons – into national minorities, the post-Soviet period also entailed rapid economic liberalization, which brought along modes of conduct widely referred to as neoliberal. Thus, the historical conjuncture that has enabled the formation I have called neoliberal nationalism congealed in the early post-Soviet period when market liberalization and national self-determination emerged as two definitive trajectories that shaped post-Soviet transformations in Latvia.

At the same time, the relational aspect of nation-making, and consequently nation-branding, brings into focus the fact that the articulation of market principles with ethnic nationalism is contested even at the moment it is enunciated. Such an articulation might actually hinder nation-branding efforts if the brand identity and the corresponding conduct of national subjects place too much emphasis on the integrity of the ethnically Latvian nation without incorporating elements of openness to difference. Some potential consumers, within Latvia and without, might not like the fact that the song heard in the »land that sings« is one of hostility towards difference, as in the case of the Gay and Lesbian Pride Parade in July of 2005. Consequently, the European ›present‹ in Latvia is also characterized by increasing visibility of voices critiquing the narrow conception of the nation and promoting recognition of, and tolerance towards, difference.[63]

Discourses and practices of recognition and tolerance are gaining influence not only in Latvia but also worldwide. However, they do not necessarily amount to resistance to hegemonic national or neoliberal narratives. For example, Charles Hale argues that the increasing recognition of cultural difference and indigenous rights in Guatemala is articulated with a hegemonic neoliberal framework, the result being that difference is tolerated or promoted in its ethnographic or folk aspects, but not in its potential politically transformative possibilities.[64] In other words, cultural difference is recognized in the public sphere as long as it does not

---

62   This narrative overlooks or perhaps consciously excludes the fact that Latvianness was also actively cultivated during the Soviet period. In fact, many argue that the current form of nationalism is largely shaped by the Soviet emphasis on national self-determination within ethnically designated territories.

63   For example, in 2004, the Government of Latvia launched a National Program for the Promotion of Tolerance substantiated by references to European Union anti-discrimination directives and United Nations conventions.

64   Charles R. Hale, »Does Multiculturalism Menace? Governance, Cultural Rights and the Politics of Identity in Guatemala«, in: *The Journal of Latin American Anthropology* 34 (2002), pp. 485–524.

threaten the foundations of the neoliberal project, thus resulting in a formation Hale terms »neoliberal multiculturalism«.[65]

Interestingly, similar trends can also be observed in Latvia. Struggles for recognition on the part of variously defined others have indeed resulted in the increased visibility of difference, yet, as in the case of Guatemala, this difference is also subject to policing. Those who inhabit it are incited to perform an enriching multicultural pageant of diversity rather than embrace transformative difference. Whereas Hale analyzes this remaking of difference into diversity through the prism of a critique of Neoliberalism, thus focusing on how cultural rights are privileged over socio-economic justice, the contemporary Latvian context lends itself better to the prism of a critique of political liberalism for there are, at this time, no significant socio-economic differences that overlap with ethnic, cultural or otherwise defined differences.

These resonant, yet different circumstances affirm the relevance of articulation as an analytical frame for making sense of the specificity of the spatial and temporal trajectories that shape contemporary politics of nationhood and difference in Latvia and for places such as Guatemala. In addition to being a set of practices of government, nation-branding – and thus nation-making – is also a terrain of struggle. While specific, these struggles are not marginal, for they have been shaped by processes that reach well beyond the bounds of contemporary Latvia both in time and space. Through an investigation of the particularity of the spatial and temporal interconnections through which Latvia is constituted as a place and Latvians as particular subjects and as a people, remaking selves in the alleged margins of Europe can tell us much about the contemporary historical conjuncture not only in Latvia, but also elsewhere within the »reality of globalization«.

---

65   Hale, »Does Multiculturalism Menace?«, op.cit., p. 487.

Narratives

Estonia and its Escape from the East: The Relevance of the Past in Russian-Estonian Relations[1]

Karsten Brüggemann

Introduction

In April 1988, some young Estonian academics introduced a program for more autonomy in economic matters for the then Soviet Republic under the title »Ise-majandav Eesti« (Self-managing Estonia). Its Estonian abbreviation is spelled IME – miracle.[2] What is nowadays seen as a kind of first step to political independence was too much even for Gorbachev's Perestroika. It was, nevertheless, one of the first official steps to differentiate Estonia administratively from the rest of the Soviet Union. The miracle became real after 1991. Skeptics may argue that the newly won independence did not last long in economic matters. In May 2004, Estonia became a member of the EU, thus losing much of its economic independence. However, the optimistic point of view says that in becoming a full member not only of the EU, but also of NATO, Estonia finally accomplished its »return to Europe« after the »dark period« under Soviet occupation during the second half of the 20th century. No doubt, in the end even Russia's foreign policy had to come to terms with the fact that the three former Baltic Soviet Republics, at least for the time being, could not be treated like any other part of the so-called »near abroad«. Still, becoming a member of the institutionalized »West« in military and economic terms did not loosen Estonia's dependency, at least informally, on its »Eastern neighbor« (*Idanaaber*), as Russia is euphemistically called today in the Estonian media.

So far, Estonia's political performance in the context of an enlarged West may seem a bit contradictory. Promoting itself during the accession process as a kind of mediator between the West and Russia, it had to realize that no one actually wanted it to fit into that role. On the other hand, in 2005, Estonia,

---

1   This paper was written in the framework of a research project funded by the Estonian Science Foundation ETF 6469. A part of this paper has been published in Karsten Brüggemann, »Leaving the ›Baltic‹ States and ›Welcome to Estonia‹: Regionalizing Estonian Identity«, in: *European Review of History* 10 (2003) (= Topical Issue: »Geschichtsregionen: Concept and Critique«, ed. by Stefan Troebst), pp. 343–360.
2   See David J. Smith, *Estonia: Independence and European Integration* (London: Routledge, 2001), p. 45.

together with its southern neighbors, again found itself in a situation of being opposed to Russia and surrounded by German-Russian gas-pipelines under the Baltic Sea. However, it was not so much the actual political situation that drew its shadows on Estonia's relations with its »Eastern Neighbor«, but rather the antagonistic view of 20th century history that divides the two countries. Instead of being a mediator itself, Estonia now seeks help from Brussels in the conflict over the border-treaty with Russia that had been already formulated in the 1990s, but only signed on May 18th 2005 in Moscow. However, this Russian-Estonian honeymoon did not last. The treaty was signed during the month of the 60th anniversary of Stalin's triumph over Hitler, when clearly no Russian official would dare offer a divergent interpretation of history. Thus it was only a question of time that Russia would withdraw its foreign minister's signature, after the Estonian parliament ratified the treaty on June 20th by adding a preamble that refers to the Soviet occupation. In fact, from an Estonian point of view, the preamble only tries to bring the now confirmed »Soviet« border of 1944 into accordance with Estonia's 1992 constitution, which refers to the border as it had been confirmed in the 1920 Tartu peace treaty.[3]

This article is concerned with neither Estonia's foreign policy alternatives, nor Russia's Baltic policy. Instead, it deals with the process of a small country of the so-called »New Europe« reorienting itself mentally and historically. This is a contested process due to the emergence of different strategies of identity politics in elite discourses, beginning in the 1990s. Interestingly, these controversial strategies also include an idiosyncratic form of playing with national symbols. These semantic games do not, however, have a chance of being welcomed by any majority. Furthermore, especially at the end of the 1990s, some political actors tried to make Estonia discursively a part of the Scandinavian »North«, in order to escape the connection with the former Soviet Union. However, the metaphorical meaning of the Baltic Sea as a bridge to Scandinavia and Western Europe is only one of Estonia's two main geographical determinants. The other is its location

---

3   Toomas Sildam, »Venemaa taganes piirilepetest«, in: *Postimees* (June 28th, 2005); Krister Paris, »Venemaa tahab põhja lasta allkirjastatud piirilepingud«, in: *Eesti Päevaleht* (June 28th, 2005); Hannes Krause, »Moskvaga piirilepingute tegemine tähendab pidevat köielkõndi«, in: *Eesti Päevaleht* (December 24th, 2005). Russian President Vladimir Putin gave the order to withdraw the signature eventually on September 1st, 2005, BNS reported the same day. The treaty can be found on the homepage of the Estonian Foreign Ministry: http://web-static.vm.ee /static/failid/146/Riigipiiri_leping_Venemaaga_est.pdf (accessed on December 14th, 2005). The preamble is reported in: http://www.riigikogu.ee/?id=32793 (accessed on December 14th, 2005); see for the full text *Riigi Teataja* 2005, II, 18, 59. See also the comment by Estonia's foreign minister, Urmas Paet, »Piiridega piiritus«, in: *Postimees*, (10.05.2005), and the overview on ten years of negotiating the Russian-Estonian border by Eiki Berg & Saima Oras, »Kümme aastat Eesti-Vene piiriläbirääkimisi / The Estonian-Russian Border: Ten Years of Negotiations«, in: Andres Kasekamp (ed.), *The Estonian Foreign Policy Yearbook 2003*, (Tallinn: The Estonian Foreign Policy Institute, 2003) pp. 45–75.

at the »border of civilization« next to Russia. In Estonian eyes, this means being entirely different from the »East«, and thus it was no surprise that Huntington's »Clash of Civilizations« was welcomed in order to pretend this strategic position and to defend Western values.[4] However, this last concept, which stems from the traditional »bulwark« idea directed against the enemies of Western Christendom, is contested by the Russian interpretation of geographical space and historical process. The way prominent 19th century Russian historians, such as Sergei Soloviev or Iurii Samarin, imagined the political and cultural meaning of geography is popular even in contemporary interpretations. According to this view, the Eastern Baltic rim, from St. Petersburg up to Kaliningrad/Königsberg, is seen as the westernmost part of the Great Russian plain, stretching from the Ural Mountains to the Baltic Sea. Thus, the historical logic of this interpretation, as determined by geographical facts, leaves no doubt that the Eastern Baltic rim »naturally« belongs to Russia.[5]

For most of the past 300 years, Estonia has been under the control of the »Russian Bear«, with not even 30 years of independence. This paper looks at Estonia's »escape from the East«, as I would metaphorically call the entire process of Estonia differentiating itself from Russia's past and present. It argues that Estonia and its southern neighbors are increasingly concerned about the fact that even NATO-membership may not secure their existence. Every time a Russian military airplane illegally crosses into Estonian air space, the media asks questions about national security. Although at least Finland is strengthening the Baltic's stance against Moscow, it seems to the Estonian public that Brussels is not working towards the same direction. According to the External Affairs Commissioner of the European Union, Benita Ferrero-Waldner, the Baltic States are to solve their problems with the Russian Federation mostly on their own.[6] Together with the reported attitude of Russian policy toward Baltic independence as a whole, this is why Estonians, as well as Latvians and Lithuanians,

---

4   For example Peeter Vihalemm, »Changing National Spaces in the Baltic Area«, in: *Return to the Western World. Cultural and Political Perspectives on the Estonian Post-Communist Transition,* ed. by Marju Lauristin & Peeter Vihalemm, (Tartu: Tartu Ülikooli Kirjastus, 1997), pp. 129–162, in particular pp. 131–132; Ott Kurs, »Eesti piirid Euroopa riikide taustal«, in: *Akadeemia* 5 (1993), pp. 451–468; Cf. Merje Feldman, »Does the EU offer Security? European Security in the Estonian Identity Discourse«, in: *COPRI Working Paper 34/2000* (Copenhagen: COPRI, 2000), http://www.ciaonet.org/wps/fem01/fem01.html (accessed on May 9th, 2005).

5   See Karsten Brüggemann, »Das Baltikum im russischen Blick: Russland und sein Anspruch auf die baltischen Staaten in der Perspektive des 19. Jahrhunderts«, in: *Nordosteuropa als Geschichtsregion,* ed. by Jörg Hackmann & Robert Schweitzer (Lübeck: Schmidt-Römhild, 2006), pp. 392–411.

6   This was reported recently by the weekly *The Baltic Times* 10 (December 8th, 2005), 486, p. 3. See also »Euroopa Liit nõuab Venemaalt piirilepingu kinnitamist«, in: *Postimees,* (December 9th, 2005). This attitude of the EU was confirmed also in a private conversation with a German diplomat (November 27th, 2005).

continue to fear that history will repeat itself. This is also exactly why any kind of German-Russian agreement at the expense of the Baltic States' interests is taken so seriously in this historically sensitive area. If Russia's stakes in the West are so high, what about the small EU and NATO partners at the Eastern coast of the Baltic Sea not having any oil or even gas?

If two years ago I argued that »thinking enlarged«[7] meant to Estonia's elite that the dominant concept of restoration in the first years of independence has given way to an »emergence of competing modes of identity politics« (Aalto),[8] then now I would like to underline that the first year of being politically part of the »West« has again brought to the agenda the need to differentiate from the East. One of the central issues in claming this difference is history. Neither Estonia, Latvia nor Lithuania became Soviet republics voluntarily. Their »escape from the East« cannot be finished without devaluating this Soviet interpretation that is prominent in Moscow to this day. History certainly did not end with EU and NATO enlargement, evidently because mentally, the Russian Federation still has not accepted that the Baltic States are no longer part of its sphere of influence.

The first two sections of this article are devoted to the ongoing process of re-regionalizing Estonian identity between »East« and »West«. The third part deals with the question of conflicting interpretations of history that not only figure prominently in Russian-Estonian relations but also divide Estonian society. Finally, some observations are made concerning the dominant mode of addressing the past in today's Estonia. Although the issue cannot be thoroughly discussed here, it is nevertheless important to stress that most Estonians claim to be victims of history, or to be more precise, victims of Soviet Communism. This self-reference is likewise crucial for an understanding of the process that I call Estonia's escape from the East.

Re-regionalizing Estonian Identity

Only a decade after having successfully restored the dominance of national Estonian narratives as a means of political legitimization for leaving the Soviet Union, different views and perspectives have emerged internally, which chal-

---

7   This term is derived from the publication *Thinking Enlarged. The Accession Countries and the Future of the European Union. A Strategy for Reform by the Villa Faber Group on the Future of the EU.* (Gütersloh: Bertelsmann, 2001), p. 1. It aims to overcome the »East-West gap in EU discourse«. See my paper »Leaving the ›Baltic‹ States and ›Welcome to Estonia‹«, op.cit.(note 1).

8   Pami Aalto, »Beyond Restoration. The Construction of Post-Soviet Geopolitics in Estonia«, in: *Cooperation and Conflict* 35 (2000), pp. 65–88, in particular p. 75.

lenge the traditional »Estonia« as a political and historical concept. First, there is an ongoing debate about economically prosperous and adapted »first« Estonia (*esimene Eesti*) and its socially and economically backward counterweight, the so-called »second« Estonia (*teine Eesti*).[9] The rather superficial unanimity of the perestroika era, which was substituted by the dominant restoration and securitizing discourses in the early years of independence, is thus lost. Although these discourses partly divided the society along ethnic lines, they were considered essential in keeping the Estonians' consensus on securing national statehood.[10] Now that external security is being secured through NATO-membership at least theoretically, it becomes clear that even during Perestroika, unanimity existed only on the anti-Moscow front. The conflict in the final years of the Estonian SSR between the centrist Popular Front, more willing to compromise with Moscow on the one hand, and the national movement of the Estonian Congress on the other hand, has left deep marks that characterize internal political divides to this day. Moreover, we still find social and political conflict sometimes overlapping with problems of ethnic integration.[11] Even if it is not the whole truth to argue that the September 2001 victory in the presidential elections by former communist and high party official, Arnold Rüütel, was a victory of *teine Eesti*, it was, nevertheless, a highly symbolic act underscoring the necessity of coming to terms with the fact that independent Estonia was not only divided on ethnic lines but even more so on social lines. All these lines of conflict are connected with the Soviet heritage, which cannot be undone simply by referring to political practices that were used in pre-war independent Estonia, as was popular in the early stages of the newly independent state in the early 1990s. This understanding may have been one of the decisive impulses for the idea to re-map »Estonia«, for in loosening the extent (and necessity) of ethnic solidarity among Estonians in an increasingly open world, it no longer corresponds to the traditional

---

9   In scholarly literature the focus has been almost entirely on foreign policy, transition successes and especially minority issues. Even in the outstanding study by Smith (2001) the »losers of transition« are barely mentioned. David J. Smith, *Estonia: Independence and European Integration* (London: Routledge, 2001); See Raivo Vetik (ed.), *Kaks Eestit. Artiklite, ettekannete ja analüüside kogmik* (Tallinn: Tallinna Pedagoogikaülikooli kirjastus, 2000), and the new publication, Tiina Raitviir & Eduard Raska (eds), *Eesti edu hind. Eesti sotsiaalne julgeolek ja rahva turvalisus* (Tallinn: Eesti Entsüklopeediakirjastus, 2005).

10   About the »politics of independence« see Smith, *Estonia*, op.cit. (note 9), pp. 65–111; Rein Ruutsoo, »Discursive Conflict and Estonian Post-Communist Nation-Building«, in: *The Challenge of the Russian Minority. Emerging Multicultural Democracy in Estonia*, ed. by Marju Lauristin & Mati Heidmets (Tartu: Tartu Ülikooli Kirjastus, 2002) pp. 31–54; Aalto, »Beyond Restoration«, op.cit. (note 8), pp. 65–72.

11   Marje Pavelson & Mai Luuk, »Non-Estonians on the Labour Market: A Change in the Economic model and Differences in Social Capital«, in: *The Challenge of the Russian Minority. Emerging Multicultural Democracy in Estonia*, ed. by Marju Lauristin & Mati Heidmets (Tartu: Tartu Ülikooli Kirjastus, 2002), pp. 89–116.

identity-shaping closed concept of *meie maa* (our country) that has belonged to Estonian ancestors for 5000 years.[12]

To find for »Estonia« a new place on their own mental map challenges this traditional view of *meie maa* that had been preserved under Soviet occupation and which eventually helped Estonians to keep their national heritage. However, it is inspired by the fact that, with the enlargement of European organizational infrastructures into the former »East«, Estonia finally »officially« became a proper and respectable member of that part of the world to which Estonians tradition-ally felt they, at least culturally, belonged. Nevertheless, integration into the »West« meant becoming its eastern frontier. It was one of the main projects of the first years of independence, nonetheless, to reassure people that the country was »Estonian« in essence and to mark an Estonian *Geschichtsraum* (historical space), that was limited to the settlement area of Estonians. However, this »return to the nation« was simultaneously accompanied by advocates of »restorationist geopol-itics«, who claimed the territories of East-Narva and Petserimaa that had been given to Estonia in the Soviet Russian-Estonian treaty of 1920 (although they are inhabited dominantly by Russians). Nevertheless, the security-first discourse that required a »purification of space« remained dominant. In fact, the second proclaimed »return«, the »return to Europe«, may have been even more decisive in abandoning this territorial claim, because a sovereign Estonia simply cannot afford to have contested borders either as part of the imagined law-and-order »West« (as opposed to the chaotic and arbitrary »East«) or as a member of the EU and NATO.[13] It was the former Estonian president, Lennart Meri (1992–2001), who took up as his main task the closing of the gap between »Estonia first« notions after fifty years of Soviet occupation and the prevalent aim of in-tegration into the »West«. If nothing else, the naming of Meri as the »European of the Year« in 1998 proves that, at least in the eyes of the »West«, he did his job quite successfully.[14]

12　Toomas Gross, »Anthropology of Collective Memory: Estonian National Awakening Revis-ited«, in: *TRAMES. Journal of the Humanities and Social Sciences* 6 (2002), pp. 342–354, in particular p. 351.

13　Aalto, »Beyond Restoration«, op.cit. (note 8), pp. 67–70, citing Mikko Lagerspetz' paper »Post-socialism as a return: Notes on a discursive strategy«, in: *Eastern European Politics and Societies* 13 (1999), No. 2, pp. 377–390. See also Mikko Lagerspetz, »The Cross of Virgin Mary's Land: A Study in the Construction of Estonia's ›Return to Europe‹«, in: *Idäntutkimus. The Finnish Review of East European Studies. Special issue: Images of the Past in Post-Socialist Politics* 6 (2001), No. 3–4, pp. 17–28. For the Estonian-Russian border issue cf. Indrek Jääts, »East of Narva and Petserimaa«, in: *Contested Territory. Border Diputes at the Edge of the Former Soviet Empire,* ed. by Tuomas Forsberg (Aldershot: Elgar, 1995), pp. 188–201; Eiki Berg & Saima Oras, »Eesti piiritlemine läbirääkimistel«, in: *Eesti tähendused, piirid ja kontekstid,* ed. by Eiki Berg (Tartu: Tartu Ülikooli Kirjastus, 2002), pp. 67–136.

14　In Meri's speeches it is possible to find elements of almost all the current possibilities to locate Estonia on the map: Estonia as part of (Middle/North) Europe or/and the Baltic area, as lo-

After internal and external independence had been secured, it now becomes possible, and increasingly necessary, to redefine »Estonia« as part of a broader regional and supranational context. Pure »Estonian« fairy tales of small nations inevitably becoming independent because of the logic of history, thus, are getting increasingly old-fashioned. Meri, nevertheless, in the preface of a book on »Estonian Identity and Independence«[15] stays in tune with the traditional national mindset in singing the old song of Estonian independence as if this had been just an implementation of historical rights. It is strange, however, that this national eschatology is attributed to a book that decidedly questions this national narrative of a historically inevitable process of Estonia becoming an independent state.[16] Moreover, this tendency to question is one of the cornerstones of the Estonian discourse on national historical legacy and identity during the last years.[17]

Thus, for instance, while taking the term »Baltic states« for granted, one can be sure that the Estonian elites do not. Their discussion on the question of being »Baltic« is part of their efforts to get rid of old mental »connections« of being part of an empire, and it represents just one aspect of the attempt to re-frame Estonian identity. A country such as Estonia, meaning a small nation that is linguistically very different from its immediate eastern and southern neighbors, tends to see itself through its own eyes. And yet, even if we have to consider a tendency of allying with the mythical »West« and escaping the »East«, especially in the first years of independence,[18] we have to remain skeptical of a historical antagonism against Russia, since Estonian history provides prominent examples

---

cated at the border of civilisation or as a bridge between the »East« and the »West«. See the analysis in Eiki Berg & Saima Oras, »Eesti mõttelise asendi kaardistamisest«, in: *Eesti tähendused, piirid ja kontekstid*, ed. by Eiki Berg (Tartu: Tartu Ülikooli Kirjastus, 2002), pp.19–65, in particular p. 56; Gert v. Pistohlkors, »Gedachte Gemeinschaften: Nationalismus und historische Erinnerung«, in: *Kollektivität und Individualität. Der Mensch im östlichen Europa*, ed. by Karsten Brüggemann, Thomas M. Bohn & Konrad Maier (Hamburg: Kovač, 2001), pp. 374–393, pp. 381–391. For Meri's speeches see Lennart Meri, *Presidendikõned* (Tartu: Ilmamaa, 1996); Lennart Meri, *Riigimured*, (Tartu: Ilmamaa, 2001).

15 Albert Bertricau (ed.), *Eesti identiteet ja iseseisvus* (Tallinn: Avita, 2001). In Russian: Albert Bertriko (ed.), *Samoopredelenie i nezavisimost' Estonii* (Tallinn: Avita, 2001). In English: Jean-Jacques Subrenat (ed.), *Estonia. Identity and Independence* (Amsterdam: Rodopi, On the Boundary of Two Worlds, 2, 2004).

16 See especially the discussions, e.g. Andrei Hvostov, Mart Laar & Harri Tiido, »Mõttevahetus«, in: *Eesti identiteet ja iseseisvus* ed. by Albert Bertricau (Tallinn: Avita, 2001), pp. 44–54.

17 See the overviews on Estonian historiography: Karsten Brüggemann, »›Wir brauchen viele Geschichten.‹ Estland und seine Geschichte auf dem Weg nach Europa?«, in: *GegenErinnerung. Geschichte als politisches Argument im Transformationsprozeß Ost-, Ostmittel- und Südosteuropas*, ed. by Helmut Altrichter (München: Oldenbourg, Schriften des Historischen Kollegs, 61, 2006), pp. 27–50.

18 Pertti Joenniemi, »The Baltic States as Deviant Cases: Small States in Search of Foreign Policy«, in: *New Actors on the International Arena. The Foreign Policies of the Baltic Countries.*

of pro-Russian thinkers. The Estonian »national awakening« during the latter part of the 19th century developed under the impact of the conflict between Russian and especially German cultural dominance; the choice was not an easy one.[19] However, although mainly fundamentally opposed to their German colonizers (and baptizers), as Lutherans, Estonians felt themselves belonging to the western European world in as much as they tended to dissociate themselves from their eastern, Slavic and orthodox neighbors.[20]

Hence, this period also witnessed the development of the Estonian *Isamaa* (Fatherland) as a region that does not know any administrative borders (C. R. Jakobson), because until 1917, the settlement area of Estonians was divided between the *Estliandskaya* and *Lifliandskaya guberniya* (provinces) of Russia. These borders were based on the historical administrative districts of the Baltic German knighthood (*Ritterschaften*). Despite this, the Estonian nation-building process imagined an Estonian *Geschichtsraum* that went far beyond these traditional borders. As early as 1870, the poet Michael Veske described it as ranging from the Lake of Peipsi to the *Läänemeri*, the »Western«, i.e. the Baltic Sea, from the Gulf of Finland to the *Munamägi*, a hill near the linguistic border between Estonians and Latvians.[21] During this »national awakening«, the notion of strong ties with Finland illustrated by the metaphor of *Soome sild* (Finish bridge) gained popularity in promoting the »own« Finno-Ugric roots of the Estonians, yet it was the Young Estonians movement that, in the years up to World War I, tried to gap the bridge between Slavic and Germanic cultures with their slogan of, »Let us be Estonians, but let us become Europeans!« However, as a small ethnos without territory, Jakob Hurt's suggestion of developing *vaimusuurus (geistige Grösse*, intellectual greatness) remained crucial for Estonians.[22]

Thus, in traditional as well as in contemporary views, there are at least two main geographical spaces in which »Estonia« finds itself conveniently mapped: »Europe« or the »West« (*Lääs*), and the »North« or the Northern countries (*Pōh-*

eds. Pertti Joenniemi & Peeter Vares (Tampere: Tampere Peace Research Institute, 1993), pp. 187–226, in particular p. 197.

19 See the discussion of the ideas of Carl Robert Jakobson, Ado Grenzstein and Johann Woldemar Jannsen in Andrei Hvostov, *Mõtteline Eesti* (Tallinn: Vagabund, 1999), pp. 293–304.

20 For more detail and various perspectives of the »national awakening,« see: Toivo U. Raun, *Estonia and the Estonians* (1991), pp. 57–80; Ea Jansen, *Vaateid eesti rahvusluse sünniaegadesse* (Tallinn: Ilmamaa, 2005); David Feest, »Die Entstehung der estnischen Nation«, in: *Estland – Partner im Ostseeraum*, ed. by Jörg Hackmann (Lübeck: Ostsee-Akademie, 1998), pp. 19–39. Toomas Karjahärm, *Ida ja Lääne vahel. Eesti-Vene suhted 1850–1917* (Tallinn: Eesti Entsüklopeediakirjastus, 1998); Gross, *Anthropology*, op.cit. (note 12).

21 Ea Jansen, »Kodu ja isamaa«, in: *Eestlane ja tema maa*, ed. by Aivar Jürgenson (Tallinn: Ajaloo institut, 2000), pp. 36–48, in particular p. 42–43.

22 Ea Jansen, »Väikerahva tugevues«, in: *Vikerkaar* (2002), No. 2/3, pp. 109–116; Toivo U. Raun, »Culture Wars in Estonia at the Beginning of the 20th Century«, in: *Acta Historica Tallinnensia* 4 (2000), pp. 49–58.

jamaad).[23] However, if integration into a Russian dominated sphere had been playing the role of an anti-German strategy prior to independence in 1918,[24] this is by no means considered an alternative today. On the contrary, it seems that integrating into the political »West« has especially underscored the necessity of differentiating itself from the »East«. In the ongoing discussion, there is, furthermore, a pragmatic understanding of being a part of *Baltimaad* in accordance with the dominant view outside of the country. However, it is now difficult to find any emphatic confession of a close connection with Latvia and Lithuania as in the days of the »Baltic way« demonstration on the 50th anniversary of the Hitler-Stalin pact in August 1989 or as in the very first years of independence.[25] EU and NATO membership did not significantly change this attitude.[26]

Estonian elites certainly are interested in leaving the old canonized borders of a limited definition of »Estonia« and aim to find new frames of identification, whether these are in historical, geographical or purely intellectual »spaces«. One of the main starting points of this endeavor of re-mapping »Estonia« is the abovementioned growing dissatisfaction with the identification of Estonia as a »Baltic« State. This stems out of the special connotations of being used, and to some extent imprinted, by the former Soviet masters, and therefore describing Estonia as ›victim of history‹.

In this context, it is important to stress that the »Baltic« States became »Baltic« only in the first half of the 20th Century.[27] As part of the *cordon sanitaire* between Germany and Soviet-Russia after World War I, Lithuania was the first

---

23   Eiki Berg, »Frontiers and Lines on Estonian Mental Maps«, in: *Cooperation, Environment, and Sustainability in Border Regions*, ed. by Paul Ganster (San Diego: San Diego State University Press, 2001), pp. 263–274; Berg & Oras, »Eesti mõttelise asendi kaardistamisest«, op.cit. (note 14), pp. 28–41.

24   Toomas Karjahärm, »Eesti rahvusluse ideed«, in: *Akadeemia* 7 (1995), pp. 2051–2077, in particular pp. 2067–2068.

25   Berg & Oras, »Eesti mõttelise asendi kaardistamisest«, op.cit. (note 14), pp. 34–37, in particular p. 61; Rein Taagepera, »The Need for Baltic Emotions«, in: *8th Baltic Conference on Intellectual Co-Operation. 15–16 June 2001, Tallinn, Estonia. Proceedings*, ed. by Mihkel Veidermaa, Galina Varlamova, & Ane Pöitel (Tallinn: Estonian Academy of Sciences, 2001), pp. 49–55.

26   Jaan Undusk, »Balti ühistunne – kas Molotovi ja Ribbentropi salaplaan?«, in: *Postimees* (December 8th, 2005).

27   For a broader discussion of the etymology of the term »Baltic« see Brüggemann, *Leaving the ›Baltic‹ States*, op.cit. (note 1), pp. 349–350; Jörg Hackmann, »Was bedeutet ›baltisch‹? Zum semantischen Wandel des Begriffs im 19. und 20. Jahrhundert. Ein Beitrag zur Erforschung von *mental maps*«, in: *Buch und Bildung im Baltikum*, ed. by Heinrich Bosse, Otto-Heinrich Elias & Robert Schweitzer (Münster: LIT, Schriften der Baltischen Historischen Kommission, 13, 2005), pp. 17–39; see also about the »Baltic« Germans: Ulrike von Hirschhausen, »Baltischer Liberalismus im frühen 20. Jahrhundert: Ein regionales Konzept zwischen Demokratie und Nationalismus«, in: *Geschichte und Gesellschaft* 29 (2003), pp. 105–137.

to be separated from its traditional Polish-Catholic context. Particularly after 1939/40, its fate was, at least *ex post,* seen as combined with its small northern neighbors. Up to 1939 however, Poland and especially Finland (as in the »Secret Protocol« of the Hitler-Stalin Pact) could also be named »Baltic«, due not only to their geographical location but also to their parallel history of formerly belonging to the Russian Empire.[28] In the Estonian geopolitical discourse of the 1920s, the traditional *Soome sild,* the »Finnish bridge,« a popular image dating back to the last quarter of the 19th century, was developed further in order to conceptualize the nation's own location on the shores of the Baltic Sea.[29] According to Marko Lehti, after declaring independence in 1918, the »Baltic Sea connection could be described quite well as an invented connection because it was in no way a return to some old connection, but [...] was of course a way of getting rid of the old Russian heritage«.[30] Edgar Kant's conception of *Baltoskandia,* which was established in the 1930s, however, envisioned a region reaching as far as the North Sea in order to construct a kind of new framework for Estonia outside of the Russian-dominated space of »Eastern Europe«. His concept was new because it aimed at an escape from the widespread Russian theory, which states that there are no geographical natural borders between the Russian mainland and the Baltic countries, and thus legitimizes Russian possession of the Baltic coast as »natural«.[31] Therefore, any kind of regionalizing of Estonia's geographical location was as much an escape from the Russian legacy in the 1920s and 1930s as it is today.

There are reasons for stating that contemporary understanding of this »Baltic« triangle can be blamed on the Soviet occupation in the middle of the 20th century. The fate of being victims of Soviet aggression welds the three countries together, not only from an outside perpective, but also from an internal point of view. In the official representation of Soviet history, the three latecomers were not allowed to play a special role as national entities. The new region of *Sovetskaia Pribaltika* was to replace the different national traditions as a newly created re-

28   Marko Lehti, »Baltoscandia as a National Construction«, in: *Relations between the Nordic Countries and the Baltic Nations in the XX Century,* ed. by Kalervo Hovi (Turku: University of Turku, 1998), pp. 22–52, in particular pp. 34–37.

29   Karsten Brüggemann, »The Eastern Sea is a Western Sea: Some Reflections on Estonia as a Baltic Sea Country«, in: *The Baltic as a Multicultural World. Sea, Region and Peoples,* ed. by Marko Lehti (Berlin: Berliner Wissenschaftsverlag, The Baltic Sea Region: Nordic Dimensions – European Perspectives, 4, 2005), pp. 59–79, in particular p. 77.

30   Marko Lehti, *A Baltic League as a Construct of the New Europe: Envisioning a Baltic Region and Small State Sovereignty in the Aftermath of the First World War* (Frankfurt am Main: Peter Lang, 1999), European University Studies Series III, History and Allied Studies, Vol. 817, p. 518.

31   Edgar Kant, *Estlands Zugehörigkeit zu Baltoskandia* (Tartu: Akadeemiline kooperatiiv, 1934), p. 32, passim; Lehti, »Baltoscandia as a National Construction«, op.cit. (note 28); about the Russian theories see Brüggemann, »Das Baltikum im russischen Blick«, op.cit. (note 5).

gional mindset. Soviet propaganda policies witnessed this trend that summarized the very distinctive histories of the three republics under topics such as »Battle for Soviet Power«, »Labor Movement« and even »Economic Geography«.[32] The aim was first of all, to form a common historical identity in accordance with Soviet eschatology among those countries having jumped later on the bandwagon, and also, to create a supranational sense of community as a kind of precondition for joining the »new community of humankind«, as Soviet civilization liked to call itself.[33] As a reaction, the republics themselves preserved in their collective pan-Baltic memory a supraregional notion of being a victim of Muscovite aggression, despite their own cultural differences. In spite of this, they did have a special status in the eyes of their Soviet compatriots: because of the higher standards of living in *Pribaltika*, the region, still foreign in Russian eyes, became known as *nash zapad* (our West).[34]

»Welcome to Estonia« – Or to Estland?

Hence, in the first years after 1991, as in other formerly Soviet dominated countries, it was the Russian/Soviet »imperial other« that was decisive in providing a negative (but productive) frame for a renewed identity.[35] Apart from focusing on antagonistic lessons of the past, it became very popular, simultaneously, to describe Estonia's role in a new Europe as heir of the Hanseatic League, as a »bridge« or as a »translator« between East and West. This »bridge« discourse, however, was never intended to be neutral, since this primarily economic way of placing Estonia on the map aimed for integration into the Western European sphere, and even gained strength when the enlargement talks with Brussels started.[36] Metaphorically speaking therefore, even the »bridge« constitutes a border in the sense of symbolizing a door that can be shut, though it does not

---

32   Cf. for example the early *Sovetskaia Pribaltika* (Leningrad: Voenizdat, 1944); *Sovetskaia Pribaltika v bratskoi semie narodov SSSR* (Riga: Zinatne,1960); *Istoriko-etnograficheskii atlas Pribaltiki*, t. 1, *Zemledelie* (Vil'nius: Mokslas, 1985); ibid. t.2, *Odezhda*, (Riga: Zinatne, 1986).

33   Cf. for example *Razvitie sovetskogo naroda – novoi istoricheskoi obshchnosti* (Moskva: Politizdat, 1980).

34   Veidemann, Rein (2001), »Eesti tee Europasse« (original written in 1998), in: Rein Veidemann, *Kusagil Euroopas*, Tallinn: Eesti Keele Sihtasutus, pp. 103–109, in particular p.106.

35   Aalto, »Beyond Restoration«, op.cit. (note 8), p. 67; Iver B. Neumann, »Russia as Central Europe's Constituting Other«, in: *East European Politic and Societies 7* (1993), pp. 349–369; Iver B. Neumann, *Russia and the Idea of Europe: A Study in Identity and International Relations* (London: Routledge, 1996); Iver B. Neumann, *Uses of the Other. The ›East‹ in European Identity Formation* (Minneapolis: University of Minneapolis Press, 1999).

36   Berg & Oras, »Eesti mõttelise asendi kaardistamisest«, op.cit. (note 14), pp. 42–47.

constitute a border in the sense of defense. As part of the securitizing discourse in Estonia, the Eastern border was partly seen, furthermore, as a border of identities. Thus it was no surprise that Samuel Huntington's »Clash of Civilizations« was gratefully taken for granted.[37] Besides being a border of identities, there is another prominent interpretation according to which Estonia will be a strategically important foothold for NATO against a virtually unpredictable Russia.[38] These identifications with the »West« being engaged in a never-ending conflict with the »East«, that partially take part on Estonian territory, are not new. Since the first centuries of baptizing these lands, the idea of a »bulwark« was topical for Baltic German interpretations of their mission in Middle-Age Livonia. In seeking for »Estonia« a new place in the space of history, this German past becomes crucial again.

Far from thinking in Huntington's dichotomies, but nevertheless engaged at least subconsciously in border-building, the literary theorist Jaan Undusk provides a new look on the *Baltikum*, i.e. the German-dominated space based on Livonia and Russia's *Ostseeprovinzen* (Baltic Provinces). In his outstanding work on Estonian and Baltic-German historiographic narratives, Undusk introduces the term *maiskondlik ajalugu*, i.e. a kind of regional history that is not based on ethnocentric principles but on something he calls a »geopolitical« or »geocultural mentality«.[39] In his opinion, the near 800 years of German, Swedish or Russian dominance and Estonian victimhood should not be a subject in Estonian historiography. In fact, he demands a history written from the standpoint of Baltic (*baltische*!) autonomy that approximately combines the settlement areas of Estonians and Latvians that were once subject to German cultural impact. He considers the continuity of the idea of regional autonomy in a specific geographic space decisive for the establishment of historical traditions. These traditions, for their part, are effective even when the »native peoples«, i.e. Estonians, Latvians and their ancestors, no longer act as bearers of this idea; in fact, these traditions must not be considered as in any way encouraging for the peoples. Undusk understands his approach as »heretical« from the perspective of ethnocentric historiography. He does not mark out a »people« or a »nation« as a constant for historical development, but rather a »geocultural mentality« which, he admits, is difficult to define.[40]

---

37   See note 3. However, it is difficult to find any mention of the notion of Estonia being located on a front and actively defending »Western« civilisation in official statements of the government. Berg & Oras, »Eesti mõttelise asendi kaardistamisest«, op.cit. (note 14), pp. 47–49, pp. 55–58.

38   Ibid., pp. 49–51.

39   Cf. Jaan Undusk, »Kuidas kirjutada Eesti ajalugu?«, in: *Vikerkkar* 8/9 (2000), pp. 188–190.

40   Jaan Undusk, »Canonical Patterns of Narrating History. In Search of a Hidden Rhetoric«, in: *Literatur und nationale Identität II. Themen des literarischen Nationalismus und der nationalen Literatur im Ostseeraum*, ed. by Yrjö Varpio & Maria Zadencka (Tampere: Tampereen

From a post-colonial perspective, the paradigms have certainly changed as compared with the 1920s. Today, no one is inclined to remove the (Baltic-) German heritage as in earlier days. On the contrary, if Estonia wants to be perceived as part of the »West« it would be counter-productive to overemphasize such a historical contrast with the Baltic Germans. German influence unquestionably brought »Europe« to Estonia in the form of Roman Law and Catholicism in the 13th century, irrespective of the methods of German baptizers in these lands. However, it has to be stressed in our case that the quite popular myth of 700 years of slavery under German rule was one of the cornerstones of Soviet propaganda in establishing a common Baltic identity. At this point, some patriotic tendencies of the 1930s melded perfectly with Soviet ideology.[41] The Soviet case, Russian imperial presence in the *Pribaltika* was to shine brightly against the background of Baltic-German subjugation. In this way, criticism of these anti-German concepts can also remove some of their own Soviet heritage. President Meri's initiative in naming the highest state decoration *Merjamaa rist* (The Cross of Virgin Mary's Land) in order to praise the impact of incorporation into the realm of Western Christianity thus becomes clear in the context of the Soviet ideology. However, this cross met with sharp protest from the media, as it was argued that it reminds Estonians of their first defeat when they lost their so-called »first independence« under the Livonian crusade. The Catholic connotation of this decoration was, to say the least, considered irritating in a Lutheran country.[42] Nevertheless, it has to be repeated that contemporary pro-German sentiments may sound strange in the traditional Estonian paradigm, which was as crucial at the beginning of the 20th century as during Perestroika and the following first years of independence.

---

yliopisto, 1999), pp. 5–13; Jaan Undusk, »Ajalootõde ja metahistoorilised žestid. Eesti ajaloo mitmest moralist«, in: *Tuna. Ajalookultuuri ajakiri* 2 (2000), pp. 114–130; Jaan Undusk, »Are we the Basques of the Baltic? The Problem of how to be represented«, in: *8th Baltic Conference on Intellectual Co-Operation. 15–16 June 2001, Tallinn, Estonia. Proceedings* ed. by Mihkel Veidermaa, Galina Varlamova & Anne Põitel (Tallinn: Estonian Academy of Sciences, 2001), pp. 121–127. The following paragraphs are based on my answer to Jaan Undusk, »Ajalootõde ja metahistoorilised žestid«, op.cit. (note 40): Karsten Brüggemann, »Rahvusliku vaenlasekuju demontaažist ehk Carl Schirren kui Eesti iseseisvuse rajaja? Märkusi Jaan Unduski ›metahistooriliste üestide‹ kohta«, in: *Tuna. Ajalookultuuri ajakiri* 3 (2002), pp. 93–99; cf. Jaan Undusk, »Eesti ajaloo kotkaperspektiivist. Minu vaidlus Brüggemanniga«, in: *Tuna. Ajalookultuuri ajakiri* 3 (2002), pp. 99–116.

41 Toivo U. Raun, »The Image of the Baltic German Elites in Twentieth-Century Estonian Historiography: The 1930s vs. the 1970s«, in: *Journal of Baltic Studies* 30 (1999), pp. 338–351, in particular p. 348; see also the paper by Jüri Kivimäe & Sirje Kivimäe, »Seven Hundred Years of Slavery‹: The Anatomy of an Historical and Political Cliché in Estonia«, paper presented at the *5th Conference of Baltic Studies in Europe* (5–7 June, University of Turku, Finland, 2003). [Manuscript sent kindly to the author by Jüri Kivimäe, Toronto.]

42 Lagerspetz, »The Cross of Virgin Mary's Land«, op.cit. (note 13).

Hence, this may simply be a consequence of changing »national others« due to two different post-colonial experiences. However, Undusk goes even further in deconstructing Estonian historical myths. In his opinion, it was not only the Estonians themselves who fought for their independence, it was a manifestation of *communis opinio* as in the classical Estonian narrative. The concept of »geocultural mentality« even allows him to see any propagandist for the German case in the *Ostseeprovinzen* as a hero of the Estonian and/or Latvian case (or as one should better call it, regional case). In Undusk's understanding thus, Baltic (*baltisch*!) regionalism, which was originally German-centered Baltic, becomes, a pillar of historical continuity far beyond the year 1939, in which the Baltic Germans followed Hitler's call *heim ins Reich* (home to the empire). In contrast to the Baltic Germans, whose »homeland« is located far away from the Baltic States, the Russians are unable to act as bearers of any Baltic autonomy because their territory borders the *Baltikum* and thus their presence is a constant menace to autonomy.[43] Nevertheless, this kind of German-Estonian *Schicksalsgemeinschaft* (common destiny) (Lennart Meri) has a common background that functions as a key factor in constructing this region from the outside. If we agree that any autonomy is framed, then it is framed by borders. Behind these borders may be an »imperial other« aiming to minimize or even destroy autonomy. This kind of »natural« antagonism between autonomy and empire is, in our case, influenced by the possibility of conflict between »Baltic autonomy« and Russia. From the perspective of the strategies of re-regionalizing »Estonia«, which is our main interest, we can conclude the following concerning Undusk. First, a core element of the region is its striving for autonomy. Second, this autonomy is clearly bordered in the East. Third, this *Balti autonoomia* historically covers Estonia and Latvia, but not Lithuania. Thus, we have an interpretation going far beyond Veske's poetic imagination of an Estonian *Geschichtsraum* in 1870 that we can call *baltisch,* and in essence corresponds to Reinhard Wittram's perspective.

Recalling the prominent Estonian sentiment at the beginning of the 20th century in which the country saw its »mission« as Russia's living wall against the German *Drang nach Osten* (push to the East) (Jaan Tõnisson),[44] or taking into account the attitude of the EU-skeptic Vello Leito, who sees a German bastion at the Narva river against the walls of Pskov as a consequence of enlargement,[45] we can imagine how heavily the waves of history can shake the position of a small state-vessel like Estonia (and that some anti-German »deep currents« remain in

---

43   Undusk, »Eesti ajaloo kotkaperspektiivist«, op.cit. (note 40), pp. 111–112.

44   Toomas Karjahärm, »Eesti rahvusluse ideed«, in: *Akadeemia* 7 (1995), pp. 2067–2068.

45   Vello Leito, *Eesti geopoliitika: Olukord, võimalused, mission* (Tallinn: Eesti Iseseisvuspartei, 1999), p. 83, as quoted in Berg & Oras, »Eesti mõttelise asendi kaardistamisest«, op.cit. (note 14), p. 46.

Estonia[46]). Nevertheless, the Estonian political elite does not suffer from a lack of imagination in searching for their own ways to move away from their big neighbors. For instance, former foreign minister Toomas Henrik Ilves, who became president in 2006, wants to get rid off Estonia's cursed »Baltic Connection« for now and forever:[47]

(M)y goal as foreign minister was to separate Estonia from being a Baltic State. I don't see any advantage in the so-called Baltic States. I don't think Estonia is a Baltic State. I think the idea of a Baltic State is a construction made up elsewhere.

Ilves had been trying to sell his country as »the only post-communist Nordic country«, because, according to him, it strictly follows the Nordic pattern in parameters such as mobile phone use, computerization, and knowledge of the English language: »it's strictly Nordic«. In Ilves' opinion, Estonia should learn from the Finnish example of re-mapping:

Finland marketed itself as a Scandinavian country: (…) My vision of Estonia is to do the same thing. (…) Why should Finland be more of a Scandinavian country than Estonia? (…) That's why I try to sell Estonia as the only Nordic, the only post-communist Nordic, country.[48]

In contrast to former restoration discourses, this vision of a new identity is not only about escaping the »East«. It is also about not wanting to be perceived as a victim of history, and may furthermore be called an escape from history. However, if Eiki Berg and Saima Oras are right in stating that in everyday politics, Estonian space is being conceptualized by its politicians depending on the context as either being a country of contact between »East« and »West« or as a country located at the eastern edge of Western security structures,[49] then Ilves' marketing strategy may be an escape to the »North« in order to leave the controversial »in-between« position behind, while still fostering a »Western« identity.

To cut off national traditions as a means of gaining a new image in foreign eyes and re-mapping the country against its historic experiences is a radical and purely intellectual strategy of the elites, which breaks all the rules. This

---

46   The Estonian historian Jüri Kivimäe, currently teaching at the University of Toronto, used the term »deep currents« (*süvahoovused*) in the context of anti-German sentiment very much present in Estonian society today. Kivimäe, »Intervjuu: Vestlus Jüri Kivimäega«, in: *Vikerkkar* 8/9 (2000), pp. 124–136, in particular p. 133.

47   The following quotations are taken from a »Marketing Estonia« forum held in Tallinn in 1998. See »Selling Estonia« (1998) http://www.balticsww.com/news/features/selling_estonia.htm (accessed on December 14 th, 2005); and Toomas Hendrik Ilves, »Põhjamaine riik ja inimene«, in: *Luup* 1 (January 19th, 2001).

48   »Selling Estonia«, (1998). Cf. the definition of Estonia's geographic location in: *EE* 11, *Eesti Entsüklopeedia*, Vol 11 (Tallinn: Eesti Entsüklopeediakirjastus, 2002), p. 8.

49   Berg & Oras, »Eesti mõttelise asendi kaardistamisest«, op.cit. (note 14), p. 54.

tendency was especially notable in the autumn of 2001, when columnist Eerik-Niiles Kross, a historian by education, tried to introduce to the public a new name for the country. In his opinion, »Estonia« sounds too much like »Latvia«, »Georgia«, »Karelia« or other parts of the former Soviet Empire. To avoid this connotation, he suggested the German *Estland* as the official name for foreign use, because the suffix »-land« would give the country a positive image thanks to its »northern« sound, as also in »Finland« or »England«.[50] Kaarel Tarand went even further in deconstructing national symbols, carrying this proposal to the extreme. Citing the example of the Olympic Games with their usage of national flags in identifying participants, he argued that it would be easy to give Estonia a positive image in the eyes of an international public by exchanging the Blue-black-white tricolor with a Scandinavian cross in the same three colors.[51] Needless to say, these somewhat naïve proposals were rejected by the Estonian public. Since changing symbols would not make Estonian society Scandinavian-like overnight, the fear of making Estonia look ridiculous in Scandinavian eyes is one of the main arguments against these ideas.[52]

However, selling a country becomes increasingly difficult if one presents one-self as only »part of« another section of the world: one needs to be something special. Eventually therefore, a state-sponsored Estonian project of developing a visual trademark for the country prior to the Eurovision Song Contest in May 2002 put an end to Kross' idea of using *Estland* in international contexts. »Welcome to Estonia. Positively transforming« was introduced as the official slogan that could be seen all over the country.[53] According to a poll, at least half of Estonia's inhabitants were satisfied with this new *bränd* for the country.[54] It also became quite popular as a motive for T-shirts even for Russian-speaking inhabitants, although it was often changed and treated with irony. In trying to explain this popularity, psychologist Voldemar Kolga sympathetically compared wearing these T-shirts with participating in a »great game« that in fact has nothing to offer for serious people.[55] Although Kolga did not explicitly mention it, wearing a T-shirt was particularly for the younger generation, and we find the accompanying advertising campaign of the logo-makers almost entirely dominated by younger people as motifs for the invitation to »positively transform« Estonia.

---

50   Eerik-Niles Kross, »Estland, Estland über alles«, in: *Eesti Päevaleht* (November 12th, 2001).
51   Kaarel Tarand, »Lippude vahetusel«, in: *Eesti Päevaleht* (December 3rd, 2001); Berg & Oras, »Eesti mõttelise asendi kaardistamisest«, op.cit. (note 14), pp. 39–40.
52   »Rahvas eelistab Estoniat ja trikoloori«, in: *Postimees* (January 21st, 2002); *cf.* Aadu Must, »Lipu, vapi ja hümni otsingust«, in: *Postimees* (December 15th, 2002).
53   For a reproduction of this logo see Brüggemann, »Leaving the ›Baltic‹ States and ›Welcome to Estonia‹«, op.cit. (note 1), p. 357.
54   See ibid., pp. 356–358, with more literature.
55   Marko Liibak, »Märk ›Welcome to Estonia‹ virgutab fantaasiat«, in: *Postimees* (September 19th, 2002); cf. »Eesti märgiga särgid ülipopid«, in: *Eesti Ekspress* (August 1st, 2002).

Hence, understanding this campaign to be part of, or at least under the impact of, the formerly dominating »return to the nation« discourse would be rather superficial. On the contrary, Aalto's suggestion concerning the decisive role of differences between divergent generations in framing Estonia's interethnic relations in order to overcome the former antagonism may be fruitful here.[56] In using the positive image of being young, the Estonian identity policy is leaving the tensions of yesterday behind and presenting a new perspective for the future. Far from being »socialist in content and national in form« Estonia thus tries to use modern marketing strategies for setting up an image of being transformed into a »normal« European country attractive for tourists and investors, not because of its past, but rather because of its future. Taking thus historical heritage and geographical location as capital for the project of »selling Estonia«, the country has the medieval hanseatic architecture of Tallinn and a long coast on the shore of the Baltic Sea to offer. However, it may be even more attractive that this country is able to create identity issues not only as an object of old men's serious patriotic discussions but also as »great games« especially for younger people.

Thus, the Estonian *political* strategy during the first years of independence of not claiming the negative role of a victim of history, but rather to present everyone the (future) success of transformation[57] has noticeably paid off, even in the internal context, which was formerly dominated by past-oriented discourses. The traditional closed concept of *meie maa,* understood as being bound to history in having been the homeland of Estonians for more than 5000 years, in its new form as »Welcome to Estonia™« now seems to be open to the challenges of globalization. However, this openness remains conditional as long as the conflict with Russia over history and identity stays alive.

The Empire Strikes Back

There are few regions left in contemporary Europe where history has the kind of influence on everyday politics that it does in Baltic-Russian relations. Russia continues to be perceived as a potential danger in its former *Sovetskaia Pribaltika.* In historical discourses today, any Estonian resistance against »Russia« or

---

56   Aalto, »Beyond Restoration«, op.cit. (note 8), p. 76.
57   See the statements of former premier Mart Laar and former foreign minister Toomas H. Ilves during the »Marketing Estonia« forum in 1998; see the quotations in Brüggemann, »Leaving the ›Baltic‹ States and ›Welcome to Estonia‹«, op.cit. (note 1), pp. 358–359, note 76; »Selling Estonia«, op.cit. (note 47).

the »East« in the past tends to be viewed in the context of the Soviet occupation in 1940. There is no doubt, however, that the Russian side does not help much in easing the situation. Thus, this legacy of the »year of horrors« 1940/41, as the first Soviet occupation is being called, affects bilateral state-relations with the Russian Federation, as well as majority-minority relations in Estonia and Latvia up to the present.[58] However, it was exactly these 12 months of uncompromising Sovietization that evoked a major change in how Estonians perceived their country's fate and looked at their eastern neighbor.[59] While the Estonian media in 1939 could not hide their relief when the Baltic Germans followed the call of Adolf Hitler *heim ins Reich* and left the country,[60] in August 1941 they greeted the invading German *Wehrmacht* units as liberators. From now on Russia served as the »main other« in securing Estonian unanimity. Therefore, fighting the Red Army on the German side in 1944 could still be perceived as a sacrifice for the fatherland, because from a common Baltic point of view, Hitler, compared to Stalin, was the lesser of two evils.[61] Although not every Estonian soldier in German uniform joined voluntarily, there were two main waves of Estonians deliberately joining the *Wehrmacht* auxiliary units and later those SS-units that were specially organized for non-Germans, after Hitler's troops had been driven back on all fronts. First, Estonians joined the German *Ostbataillone* (Eastern Battalions) in the late summer of 1941 with a very clear motivation: they wanted to take revenge on the Soviets who killed or deported their relatives, and bring back those who were sent to Siberia or forcibly mobilized into the Red Army. However, it soon became clear that the Germans looked at Estonia as a former Soviet Republic and had no intention of making it an independent state again. From late 1941 onwards up to early 1944, young Estonian men preferred to hide in the woods or to flee to Finland rather than to join the *Wehrmacht*. Furthermore, in early 1944 some 30,000 young Estonians responded to a call by the former premier, Jüri Uluots to defend Estonia's borders using German weapons. Uluots was later to become the leader of a stillborn underground government. Clearly

---

58   The minority question cannot be adequately discussed here. See for an introduction Lauristin & Heidmets, *The Challenge of the Russian Minority. Emerging Multicultural Democracy in Estonia* (Tartu: Tartu Ülikooli Kirjastus, 2005).

59   Jüri Ant, *Eesti 1939–1941: Rahvast, valtisemisest, saatusest* (Tallinn: Riiklik Eksami – ja Kvalifikatsioonikeskus, 1999); see also the forthcoming publication Enn Tarvel (ed.), *Sõja ja rahu vahel*. Vol 2, *Esimene nõukogude aasta* (Tallinn: S-Keskus, 2007).

60   Jüri Kivimäe, »Raske lahkumine. Baltisakslaste ümberasumine eestlaste rahvuslikus vaatevinklis«, in: *Looming* 9 (1989), pp. 1242–1250. Kivimäe/Kivimäe, »»Seven Hundred Years of Slavery««, op.cit. (note 41), wrote: »A member of the *Estonian Club of Nationalists* (Eesti Rahvuslaste Klubi) even corrected the old cliché and stated that it was exactly 721 years of German existence in Estonia and was joyful that their historical mission was finally over«.

61   This was once more proved during the debates about the Lihula-monument in 2005. See the contribution by David Feest in this volume.

it was the fear of a Soviet re-occupation that motivated Estonians to play the German game this time.[62]

During the summer of 2004, discussions in the Estonian media at the time of the 60th anniversary of those »defense battles« proved how contested this past continues to be for Estonians. Apart from the veterans of the battles against the Red Army, the perestroika-generation fought once again along the old front lines between nationalists and members of the Popular Front. The deep tragedy that had Estonian men at times even fighting directly against each other in the armies of the two enemies, can certainly not be denied. However, the open heroization of those Estonians, who together with Dutch, Danish and Norwegian soldiers had been trying to stop the advance of the Red Army across the Narva River near the heights of Sinimäe in North-Eastern Estonia in June 1944, and who eventually managed to defend the hill-line for two weeks, had no precedent. Not without pathos, the former right-wing premier and historian Mart Laar called Sinimäe the »Estonian Thermopyles«.[63] Indeed, this »miracle of Sinimäe«[64] forced the Soviet troops to alter their main direction of attack. Only after the Red Army broke through south of Lake Peipsi in September, were the troops at Sinimäe finally evacuated.[65] According to Laar, their heroism gave many Estonians enough time to prepare for an escape to the West. However, the political scientist and former member of the Popular Front, Rein Ruutsoo, angrily argued against this glorification of those Estonians who had been wearing German uniforms in 1944. As »shield bearers« for Hitler, they only managed to gamble away any chance of being saved by the West.[66]

From a historian's point of view, it is quite easy to agree with Ruutsoo's anger, not least because he by no means seeks to defend the following liberation of Estonia from the Nazis with the bayonets of the occupying Red Army. »Liberation«

---

62 Toomas Hiio, Meelis Maripuu, Indrek Paavle (eds.), *Estonia 1940–1945. Reports of the Estonian International Commission for the Investigation of Crimes Against Humanity* (Tallin: Inimsusevastaste Kuritegude Uurimise Eesti Sihtasutus, 2006), see also the older contributions: Seppo Myllyniemi, *Die Neuordnung der baltischen Länder 1941–1944. Zum nationalsozialistischen Inhalt der deutschen Besatzungspolitik* (Helsinki: Suomen Historiallinen Seura, Historiallisia tutkimuksia, 90, 1973); Alvin Isberg, *Zu den Bedingungen des Befreiers. Kollaboration und Freiheitsstreben in dem von Deutschland besetzten Estland 1941–1944* (Stockholm: Almqvist & Wiksell, Studia Baltica Stockholmiensia, 10, 1992); see the articles Meelis Maripuu, »Eesti juutide holocaust ja eestlased«, in: *Vikerkaar* 8/9 (2001), pp. 135–145; Argo Kuusik, »Die deutsche Vernichtungspolitik in Estland 1941–1944«, in: *Vom Hitler-Stalin-Pakt bis zu Stalins Tod*, ed. by Olaf Mertelsman (Hamburg: Bibliotheca Baltica, 2005), pp. 130–150.

63 Mart Laar, »Eesti Termopüülid Sinimäed«, in: *Eesti Ekspress* (July 29th, 2004), A24–A25; see the answer by the diplomat and historian: Margus Laidre, »Ihantala – Soome Sinimäed«, in: *Eesti Ekspress* (August 3rd, 2004), A13.

64 Villu Päärt, »Eesti leegioni võitlejad lootsid Inglismaa abile«, in: Postimees (July 27th, 2004).

65 Toomas Hiio, »Sõda Eestis 1944 a«, in: *Eesti Pevaleht* (June 26th, 2004).

66 Rein Ruutsoo, »Sõjamüütide pantvangid«, in: *Eesti Päevaleht* (August 12th, 2004).

in the Estonian context means merely another foreign occupation. Nevertheless, in contrast to his counterpart, Laar, who virtuously plays with Estonia's vulnerability in view of her unpredictable neighbor, Ruutsoo only tries to acknowledge that no matter how one names it, the end of German occupation as such was no doubt positive for Estonia. It might in fact be that, in the eyes of a Western public who is unfamiliar with Estonian history, the difference between these views on history seems rather small. The Russian Federation, however, does not accept the concept of occupation, and feels insulted (as do some parts of the Russian minority in Estonia) because Estonians do not gratefully look up to the Soviet troops as everyone else does. Was it not the Red Army that finally crushed Hitler, as the Western powers and even Germany acknowledge? How dare you, Estonians, not honor the fact that Russia again saved you? The roots of this misunderstanding are to be found, once again, in the interpretation of the events of June 1940. If Russia sees the liberation of Tallinn in 1944 as liberation of the capital of the Estonian SSR, founded in the summer of 1940 thanks to a spontaneous socialist revolution that took place simultaneously in all three Baltic States, then Estonians, along with Latvians and Lithuanians, would say that these Soviet Republics were born by the brutal force of military occupation and against the will of the people.

The St. Petersburg-based young political scientist Viacheslav Morozov recently argued that Russian-Baltic relations improved significantly after the enlargement of Western structures into the East. According to him, one of the key manifestations of the Russian crisis-ridden world-view, »the fear of isolation from Europe and doubts about Russia's belonging to the European ›civilization‹, has significantly receded«. Moreover, this has made redundant »the image of the Baltic states as an embodiment of the ›false‹, anti-Russian Europe«. Russian society, he argues, »is no longer afraid of NATO enlargement, is ready for a constructive dialogue on the issue of Russian-speakers, and is getting closer to the enlarging EU«. Thus, he concludes, »security is no longer the framework concept for Russian understanding of regional affairs«.[67] However, Morozov wrote this in the months before history again became the major object of dispute between Russia and her former colonies. Even if Morozov is right in stating that identity issues in Russia increasingly became »de-securitized« during the last years, they did not »de-historize«. The »positive« pages of Soviet history are still as important for Russian identity today as national history is in the Baltic, and, as is apparent, these identity issues are still having a distinctly negative effect on pragmatic

---

67   Viacheslav Morozov, »Russia in the Baltic Sea Region. Desecuritization or deregionalization?«, in: *Cooperation and Conflict* 39 (2004), pp. 317–331, in particular p. 330; see also Viacheslav Morozov, »The Baltic States in Russian Foreign Policy Discourse: Can Russia Become a Baltic Country«, in: *Post-Cold War Identity Politics. Northern and Baltic Experiences*, ed. by Marko Lehti & David J. Smith (London: Cass, 2003), pp. 219–252.

bilateral relations. The abovementioned border treaty quarrels do not reflect border reality, because the border regime already functions on a pragmatic basis, without a high level of contract. Essentially, this issue only mirrors the dispute over history, in which Moscow's main interest is to at least remain the historical superpower that had defeated fascism. Estonian observers, however, see as one of the intentions behind the step to reclaim the signature under the treaty, the necessity to have a foreign enemy at hand in order to address their own Russian identity crisis.[68] Finally, in the spring of 2005, the empire prepared for a final attack on the historical front at the Baltic Sea. Nothing should spoil the ceremonies of the 9th of May, and certainly not the former small Soviet Republics on the coast of the Baltic Sea.

They did spoil it, however. First, Latvia's President Vaira Vīķe-Freiberga presented her colleague Vladimir Putin on January 27th, 2005 in Kraków a sassy gift of a history book written in Russian about Latvia's history, and of course covering the years of the »Soviet occupation« in full detail.[69] Second, Freiberga's colleagues from Estonia and Lithuania, Arnold Rüütel and Valdas Adamkus, declined Putin's invitation to participate in the festivities in Moscow. Third, George W. Bush teased his comrade-in-arms in the »war against terrorism« with his startling visits to Tbilisi and Riga. It may well be that Bush's speeches irritated Putin the most.[70] In a rare moment of openness, the Russian President, who had just declared the collapse of the USSR to be the »biggest geopolitical catastrophe of the 20th century«,[71] used the opportunity to put an end to the discussion of history during a press conference on May 10th, 2005. In his answer to an Estonian journalist, who had been given the floor by chance, and who took it

---

68   Krause, »Moskvaga piirilepingute tegemine tähendab pidevat köielkõndi«, op.cit. (note 3).

69   Clearly, the Russian Foreign Ministry tried to find something wrong in this book, especially for the eyes of the West. And they found something: A sketch of the Salaspils concentration camp, drawn by a prisoner. The legend, though, repeats only the official name of the camp: *Arbeits- und Erziehungslager* (see Dajna Blejere, Ilgvars Butulis, Antonijs Zunda, & Inesis Feldmanis, *Istoriia Latvii v 20 v.* (Riga: Jumava, 2005), picture section after p. 320). The Russian Foreign ministry thus tried to exploit the fact that the Latvian president gave this book to Putin during the celebrations on the occasion of the 60th anniversary of the liberation of the Auschwitz concentration camp. See Andrei Hvostov, »Balti pelgunöör«, in: *Eesti Ekspress* (February 10th, 2005).

70   Bush »leveled his harshest criticism against Russia for acts after World War II, and seemed to lean as much toward a denunciation of postwar Soviet acts as celebratory words for the Nazi defeat. [...] Mr. Bush on Saturday seemed likely to anger the Russians even more, because he repeatedly used the word ›occupation‹ to describe the Russian acts in the Baltics - Latvia, Lithuania and Estonia – after World War II. The Russians have furiously responded that they were invited in.« Elisabeth Bumiller, »In Latvia, Bush Lectures Putin on the Joys of Democracy«, in: *New York Times* (May 8th, 2005).

71   Vladimir Putin, »Poslanie Federal'nomu Sobraniju Rossiiskoi Federacii« (April 25th, 2005) http://www.kremlin.ru/text/appears/2005/04/87049.shtml (accessed on December 14th, 2005).

upon herself to ask him why the Russian Federation does not just say »sorry for the occupation« thus signalling its readiness for a good neighborly relationship, Putin read a rather original lecture on Russian-Baltic relations. According to him, the Congress of People's Deputies of the USSR had been condemning the Hitler-Stalin Pact as far back as 1989, and as a result, he could not see any sense in repetitions – thus this should be the »end of talk«, he said. Moreover, the independence of the Baltic States in 1918, in his view, was a consequence of Germany losing the war having taken the Baltic Provinces from Russia. In 1939, these territories were finally given back to Russia by the Germans and, in 1939 (!), they »*voshli v sostav SSSR*«, i.e. entered the USSR, this obviously according to the Hitler-Stalin-pact. Thus, the Soviet Union just could not have occupied them in 1941 (!), »because they were already a part of it«. No one truly understood this curious chronology, but Putin assured people that he had had good history teachers, although he admitted that he might have had a little too much beer at university.[72] Putin's credo, however, was clear: Let's not bother each other with history. However, according to Paul Goble, former publisher of »RFE/RL Newsline« and currently a research associate at the EuroCollege of the University of Tartu in Estonia, Putin made his greatest political mistake in supposing that everyone, especially in the West, would follow exclusively the Russian interpretation of history. When Putin tried to exploit history for his own political purposes, he became a victim of history himself, according to Goble, because history has slipped out from his control.[73]

Nevertheless, the Russian media treated history almost provocatively according to the simple (Soviet) scheme that everybody who was against Stalin was (and obviously still is) on Hitler's side. Therefore, everybody who fought against the Red army in the Baltic was (and still is) a traitor. For example, Sergei Iastrzhembskii, Putin's special envoy for relations with the European Union, simply denied any occupation of the Baltic States, claiming this was merely a change of power as a consequence of bilateral treaties. He did not mention the presence of the Red army as having provided »security« for the »spontaneous revolution«.[74] At the same time, in an interview with the former Estonian president Arnold Rüütel, a journalist for the popular weekly »*Argumenty i Fakty*« asked if Mr Rüütel if he was aware of the fact that his decision not to come to Moscow »might have far reaching consequences«.[75] Unfortunately, Rüütel was not adequately prepared

72   Evgenii Rozhkov, »›Rossiia i ES dogovorilis‹. Putin: Rossiia gotova k konstruktivnoi rabote« (May 10th, 2005), http://www.vesti.ru/comments.html?sid=9&id=34919 (accessed on December 14th, 2005).

73   Paul Goble, »Putini suurim valearvestus«, in: *Eesti Päevaleht* (May 9th, 2005).

74   http://russlandonline.ru/rupol0010/morenews.php?iditem=6213 (accessed on December 21st, 2005).

75   »Prezident Estonii Arnol'd Riuitel‹. Razve my voshvaliaem nacizm? Estoncy zhdut ot russkih

to answer the journalist's demagogic questions concerning Estonia's feeling like a loser of World War II alongside Nazi-Germany, but rejoicing collectively when SS-veterans march through the streets in their old uniforms. Further, Rüütel's compassion for the fallen Red soldiers was, regrettably, not properly respected and simply taken for granted, while his argument that Estonia lost her independence thanks to the Soviet »liberation« was countered with the rhetorical question whether one could justify anything – i.e. serving with Hitler's »manslaughtering« troops – fighting for independence. Thus, Rüütel's repeated hopes of establishing good relations with Estonia's »Eastern neighbor« proved senseless, because these hopes continued to be confronted only with a rejection of dialog with Russisa, as was quite frequently expressed in the Russian media in the spring of 2005.

Simultaneously, discussions in Estonia during the campaigns for local elections in early autumn 2005 proved again the lack of unanimity even on the questions of Estonian history. Estonia also witnessed a radicalization of the discourse. This time, as the conservative historian Lauri Vahtre puts it, the debates touched on nothing less than the question of what is good and what is bad.[76] However, it was not about »good« Estonians being confronted with »bad« Russians, but about communist influence in present day Estonian society. And again, a scandal was needed to trigger this kind of discussion. This happened when the editor-in-chief of the monthly independent journal »*KesKus*« and local candidate for the right-wing populist party Res Publica, Juku-Kalle Raid, organized for a group of young people to wear red T-shirts during a football match between radio and TV-journalists at the end of September 2005. »Kommarid ahju« (commies into the oven) was the scandalous slogan printed on the front of the shirts with the names of 35 prominent leading Estonian politicians on the back, including President Rüütel and premier Andrus Ansip at the top of the list. While Ilmar Raag, head of Estonian television, prohibited Raid's idea of selling these shirts during the match, because »even as a metaphor ›Kommarid ahju‹ is a call for violence and we don't need that«, Estonian protection police, according to Raid, only said »don't worry« because »calls for social hatred« are not their business.[77] However, the public seemed more shocked when the minister of defense, Jaak Jõerüüt, used this opportunity to retire. He explained his decision in an open letter making explicit reference to the inhumanity and violence intended by the

dobrososedstva, dazhe preziraia 9 Maia i uvazhaia nacistskih prihvostnei«, in: *Argumenty i Fakty* 12 (Mai 23rd, 2005), 1273, http://www.aif.ru/online/aif/1273/12_01 (accessed on (December 14th, 2005).

76   Lauri Vahtre, »Mida siis ikkagi teha kommunistidega?«, in: *Eesti Päevaleht* (October 3rd, 2005).

77   »ETV ja raadio keelasid ›Kommarid ahju!‹ särkide müügi«, in: *Eesti Päevaleht*, (September 24th, 2005).

words *kommarid ahju*. Moreover, his employee Indrek Tarand, the director of the Estonian War Museum and a historian by education, was seen in this shirt, watching the match while sitting between former premiers Mart Laar and Juhan Parts. According to Jõerüüt, it is intolerable if the director of a NATO- and EU-state history museum supports a slogan that intends to throw the heads of state into the fire. »Then my understanding comes to an end«, he wrote, especially in view of the »dramatic historical dimension« of the wording.[78]

Jõerüüt's resignation, however, was the only serious reaction to this scandal. Not even premier Ansip, the second on the list of persons to be thrown into the fire, saw any crime in this slogan and Raid explained it to the media as being popular slang that was not intended to be understood literally. Later, literary scientist and former CP and People's Front member, Rein Veideman attacked him, claiming that party membership could not be the only criterion for the evaluation of people's morality.[79] In fact, few amongst those who commented did not take sides in the discussion. The young historian, Marek Tamm, spoke of society's schizophrenia that was crowned by the »war museum director's call for the final solution for communists in Nazi-diction«; he furthermore called Tarand's behavior »historical autism«.[80]

Vergangenheitsbewältigung (Coming to Terms with the Past) in Estonia?

One may see in these discussions two different approaches to identity debates irrespective of the particular political positions of the author. On the one hand, there are intellectuals such as Tamm or Jõerüüt who see events in Estonia from a more or less »European« point of view. On the other hand, Tamm's elaborate interpretation of missing »memory work« in order to come to terms with Estonian history evokes criticism from those who see their own »Estonian« perspective as the only possible way of orientation and who, moreover, have been constantly engaged in post-perestroika quarrels. Vahtre, for example, sees the danger of »everlasting schizophrenia« precisely in the possibility that different

---

78   »Jaak Jõerüüt põhjendab lahkumissoovi«, in: *Eesti Päevaleht*, (September 27th, 2005). See the interview with Jõerüüt in: Tiina Kaalep & Andrei Hvostov, »Ikka on lõpuks viimane tilk«, in: *Eesti Ekspress* (September 29th, 2005).

79   Kai Kalamees & Hannes Krause, »Hingevalu ajas Jõerüüdi ametit maha panama«, in: *Eesti Päevaleht* (September 27th, 2005); Juku-Kalle Raid, »Alla mõistuse!«, in: *Postimees* (September 29th, 2005); Rein Veidemann, »Häda mõistuse pärast«, in: *Postimees*, (October 3rd, 2005).

80   Marek Tamm, »Mida teha kommunistidega?«, in: *Eesti Päevaleht* (September 29th, 2005).

people in one society may simultaneously praise and condemn communism. According to him, coming to terms with one's own history only means establishing the one-and-only truth, which is by no means Tamm's intention, and indicates quite clearly the influence of the communist heritage even on the most anti-communist commentators. Thus, Vahtre's statement could be of some use in a history of Estonian historical memory as it is envisioned by Tamm, who wrote in favor of a passionate and detailed *Vergangenheitsbewältigung* such as has been practiced in Germany. Yet unlike Vahtre, Tamm is aware of what Pierre Nora has stated: while history unites, memory necessarily divides.[81] Meanwhile this has also been proven in the Estonian context in an admirable collection of live-stories written by Estonians and Russians and edited under the leadership of Rutt Hinrikus.[82]

Unfortunately, the Estonian media clearly under-represents voices like Tamm's. In fact, if one could talk of the maturity level of a society, one may argue that 15-year-old independent Estonia has reached the stage of puberty with all its plusses and minuses. The heritage of the Soviet past and the neighboring Russian Federation, which has by no means been condemning its own past, is definitely still a major burden, not only for foreign relations but also for internal political discourse. Thus, »the escape from the East« may on the one hand take a little longer, but on the other hand, it may well be that integration into NATO and the EU ends up being the catalyst to take these identity issues beyond Estonian unanimity based on anti-Communism, a unanimity which has been so essential to preserve, especially during the accession process.

Stefan Troebst recently argued that especially in the Eastern European context, the strict German model of *Vergangenheitsbewältigung* does not suit every society and that *Geschichtsvergessenheit* (oblivion of history) and *Geschichtsbesessenheit* (obsession with history) are to be perceived as different sides of the same coin.[83] In the Estonian context, however, the anti-communist consensus is secured not only by nationalists, but for the broader public thanks also to Moscow's rejection of dialog. Thus, in Troebst's scheme, the country, together with its Baltic neighbors, belongs to the first »anti-communist« category of societies that almost unanimously remembers history in the context of Soviet occupation.

81 Pierre Nora, »Nachwort«, in: *Deutsche Erinnerungsorte, Bd. III*, ed. by Etienne François & Hagen Schulze (München: Beck, 2001), pp. 681–686, in particular p. 686.

82 Rutt Hinrikus, *Eesti rahva elulood*, Pt. 1–2, *Sajandi sada elulugu kahes osas* (Tallinn: Tänapäev, 2000); Hinrikus, *Eesti rahva elulood*, Pt. 3, *Elu Eesti NSVs* (Tallinn: Tünapäev, 2003); Rutt Hinrikus [Rutt' Chinrikus] (ed.), *Rasskazhi o svoei zhizni. Zhizneopisaniia estonozemel'cev* (Tallinn: Aleksandra, 2005).

83 Stefan Troebst, *Postkommunistische Erinnerunskulturen im östlichen Europa. Bestandaufnahme, Kategorisierung, Periodisierung* (Wrocław: Wydawnictwo Uniwersytetu Wrocławskiego, Berichte des Willy Brandt Zentrums für Deutschland- und Europastudien der Universität Wrocław 7, 2005), p. 10.

As the main point of reference for a reconfirmation of being Estonian, the »good« pre-Soviet past is thus confronted with the »bad« Soviet era.[84] Although this excludes the dominant memory of the Russians living in Estonia, it nevertheless marks the country in a broader Eastern European context, while Russia belongs to category four, i.e. societies that are characterized by »consensus and general identity of ›old‹ and ›new‹ elites«.[85] However, it quite well may be that this Estonian anti-communist consensus will lose its decisive role in securing national identity. The »victim-myth«, so characteristic of Eastern European identity discourses after and even before 1989, has already been shattered in Estonia because of the de-sacrificing of the last president in the 1930s, Konstantin Päts, and because the first serious research interactions by Estonians in World War II proved the sad fact that of course, like everybody else, Estonians also committed crimes in difficult times.[86] Soon the research will also be concerned with the attitude of Estonians to their new masters after 1944 and especially after Stalin's death in 1953. Clearly, the communist past will therefore be researched with special attention given to those politicians and public figures that crossed the watershed of 1991 without scars on their reputation. Historian Indrek Jürjo, who wrote a groundbreaking study on the KGB and its contacts with Estonian émigrés as far back as 1996, is convinced that the public has the right to know, for instance, the personal history of the former president and high-ranking ex-communist, Arnold Rüütel.[87] The question as to whether or not all Estonians remained loyal to »our land« remains to be answered, and the attitude of former communists, who claim that they simply wanted to change the system from within, clearly needs closer investigation. The old lines of conflict thus will probably remain valid in the future, which may risk an even more polarized discussion when it comes to those who are now in charge of the country.

Concerning the question of re-regionalizing Estonia, as a small state, the country does not have the power to set the rules for its own image beyond its borders. Political observers already fear that other EU-countries see Estonia only as a »one-theme-country«, having its problems with Russia in mind.[88] As I have argued previously, »leaving the Baltic« remains a dream of Estonian elites because the term »Baltic States« will be even more prominent after integration into

---

84   Sigrid Rausing, *History, Memory, and Identity in Post-Soviet Estonia: The End of a Collective Farm* (Oxford: Oxford University Press, 2004), pp. 129–145.

85   Ibid. p. 12–17, quot. p. 16.

86   Brüggemann, »›Wir brauchen viele Geschichten‹«, op.cit. (note 17).

87   See the interview: Juune Holvandus, »Ajaloolane Indrek Jürjo: Valiva Mluga inimesed unustavad, et partei suunas KGB tegevust«, in: *Eesti Pevaleht* (October 22nd, 2005); Indrek Jürjo, *Pagulus ja Nõukogude Eesti: vaateid KGB, EKP ja VEKSA arhiividokumentide põhjal* (Tallinn: UMARA, 1996).

88   Hannes Krause, »Moskvaga piirilepingute tegemine tähendab pidevat köielkõndi«, in: *Eesti Päevaleht* (December 24th, 2005).

the European Union and NATO as a means of differentiating them from Russia,[89] then the same goes for the envisaged »escape from the East«. The common border inevitably binds the Baltic States together with Russia and even if these relations have been »de-securitized«, according to Morozov, different interpretations of history will continue to offer a potential discursive battlefield in the future. As long as Russia needs the Baltics to prove its own »Europeanness« for its internal and the international public (presenting itself as defending minority rights),[90] there will be no change. Thus, with Ilves' project of Estonia becoming »Scandinavian« bound to its specific historical contexts at the turn of the 20th and 21st centuries and my own proposal »Lilaest« left unnoticed (as is expected), the country will, for the moment, at least in foreign eyes, remain »Baltic«. Yet, this term has changed its meaning again after the accession process has been completed. This time, though, the change is more or less in accordance with the attitude of the people of the Baltic States, because the label »Baltic« nowadays increasingly symbolizes the easternmost countries of the »West«. From the perspective of the mid 1980s, this is clearly nothing less than a miracle.

---

89   Brüggemann, »Leaving the Baltic States«, op.cit. (note 27), pp. 359–360.

90   Morozov, »The Baltic States in Russian Foreign Policy Discourse«, op.cit. (note 67), pp. 219–252. See Iastrzhembskii's recent critique addressed to the EU: it would do nothing at all »to solve the problems facing thousands of our compatriots who have the shameful status of non-citizens«, in: *The Baltic Times* 10 (December 22nd, 2005 – January 4th, 2006), No. 488, p. 3. Nobody in Moscow these days asks if the Russian minorities actually want the Russian Federation to be their advocate for the response would be rather indifferent.

Bargaining Armenian-ness: National Politics of Identity in the Soviet Union after 1945[*]

Maike Lehmann

In 1962, Marie Kilbourne Matossian concluded her inquiry about the impact of Soviet policies in Armenia with the following consideration on Soviet Armenian identity:

> [A]n ambitious Armenian had ... to accept, at least outwardly, Communist doctrine and the Soviet system. Further, he had to acquire working knowledge of Russian language and a thorough familiarity with Soviet Russian culture. This did not necessarily mean that he had ... to deny his identity as an Armenian. But it meant that he was under the strain of resolving conflicts arising from bi-cultural affiliation. Was he satisfied with the official formula demanding a culture ›national in form, socialist in content‹?[1]

Judging from its date of publication, this quote may appear somewhat dated. But some points raised by Matossian regarding the »ambitious Armenian« are worth considering when dealing with questions about self-representation and about ways of seeing and acting in the multi-national Soviet context. This article discusses the ways in which »ambitious« Armenians – among others – voiced their concepts of being Armenian in a society in which socialism, as an idea and as state force on the one hand and national heritage on the other, played an important role. What are the ways in which Armenians interpreted »national form« and »socialist content«? And how was the thin line between the sanctioned »national form« and the officially condemned chauvinist »nationalism« defined in the process? The following discussion attempts to track down not a »real«, essentialist Armenian identity but the national politics of identity as they evolved in post-war Soviet Armenia.

Looking at the local understandings and definitions of the formula »national in form, socialist in content«, this article takes a slightly different approach than recent research on Soviet nationalities. The latter has contributed much to the

---

[*] Research for this article was generously sponsored by the DFG via the joint research project »Changing Representations of Social Order – Intercultural and Intertemporal Comparisons« at the Humboldt-University, Berlin. I would like to thank Maya Haber (London/Berkeley), Rosa Magnusdottir (Chapel Hill) and Susanne Schattenberg (Berlin) for their helpful comments on this article.

[1] Mary Kilbourne Matossian, *The Impact of Soviet Policies in Armenia* (Leiden: Brill 1962), p. 195.

understanding of the relationship between the national and the socialist for the 1920s and 1930s, modifying the view of the Soviet regime as a »breaker of people« into one of an »affirmative action empire« engaged in »nation-making«.[2] The term »making nations« seems adequate as it acknowledges the constructedness of nations.[3] While looking at the concepts of agents of the state – such as party officials or scientific researchers working on the state's behalf – this research could show how nations were »made« and what impact the central authorities had on the national republics.[4]

Due to the nature of documents at hand, however, this scholarship mainly looks at the images held by central authorities and thus, takes on a perspective »from above«. But, one might argue, even as the majority of documents are state-produced, they can still reveal concepts of Soviet national identity put forward by local agents. As the central authorities in Moscow acted according to their vision of historical development and their need for control, the nationalities in the different republics in turn not only reacted to these visions, but also made them subject to their own national interpretation. Often enough, such interpretations rested on pre-Soviet self-conceptions that did not wither away with the Tsarist Empire, forced industrialization or the Great Terror.[5] As such, nations were not only »made« from above; they were also defined by the members of the respective nationalities from below – a process that has been little researched.[6] As the space allowed for »national form« changed over time,[7] the possibilities and limits of this space were tested and challenged on the local level. Here, nationality policies of the centre turned into politics of national identity.

---

2   Terry Martin, *The Affirmative Action Empire. Nations and Nationalism in the Soviet Union, 1923–1939* (Ithaca: Cornell University Press, 2001); Ronald Suny & Martin Terry (eds.), *A State of Nations. Empire and Nation-Making in the Age of Lenin and Stalin* (New York: Oxford University Press, 2001); Paula Michaels, »Medical Propaganda and Cultural Revolution in Soviet Kazakhstan, 1928–41«, in: *Russian Review* 59 (2000), pp. 59–178; Francine Hirsch, »Toward an Empire of Nations. Border-Making and the Formation of Soviet National Identities« in: *Russian Review* 59 (2000), pp. 201–226.

3   Benedict Anderson, *Imagined Communities. Reflections of the Origins and Spread of Nationalism* (London: Verso 1991).

4   Martin, *The Affirmative Action Empire*, op. cit. (note 2); Michaels, »Medical Propaganda and Cultural Revolution«, op. cit. (note 2); Hirsch, »Toward an Empire of Nations«, op. cit. (note 2).

5   Jörg Baberowski, *Der Feind ist überall. Stalinismus im Kaukasus* (München: Deutsche Verlagsanstalt, 2003).

6   David Brandenberger, *National Bolshevism : Stalinist Mass Culture and the Formation of Modern Russian National Identity, 1931 – 1956* (Cambridge, Mass. : Harvard Univ. Press, 2002), pp. 1–3.

7   Yuri Slezkine, »The Soviet Union as a Communal apartment or how a socialist state promoted ethnic particularism«, in: Sheila Fitzpatrick (ed.) *Stalinism. New Directions*, ed. by Sheila Fitzpatrick (London and New York: Routledge, 2000), pp. 313–347.

It is these politics of national identity, this testing and challenging of the space allowed for »national form« that this article explores. While profiting from the insights into how nations were »made« from above, what follows explicitly concentrates on how »national form« and »socialist content« were interpreted at the local, national level. How did representatives of national communities define national identity and how did they try to make room for »national form«? How did this relate to Moscow's policies and which local concepts of a national identity became resonant in such definitions? In asking such questions, this inquiry draws mainly on sources that were produced in connection to the state, depicting conflicts over central policies and the reaction of the local national cadres. Therefore, a particular way of defining national identity will be at the centre of this inquiry: »bargaining« as a form of local politics of identity.

The term »bargaining« is used here as an attempt to reflect on the dynamic process of defining national identity; how it was constantly redefined and re-examined in conflicts between the visions and concepts held by the central authorities in Moscow and the national self-perceptions on the local level. It is, above all, the dynamics of bargaining that are resonant in the process, which evolved as a result of conflicts over the room to be allocated to the »national form« in the Soviet Union. The relationship between the one doing the bargaining and the one being bargained with is, moreover, a potentially uneven, and not a fixed one. Within an evolving »bargaining« process, one or the other party might gain in position to be able to convince the other of his arguments while also adjusting them to the other party's requests.

Such »bargaining« was, above all, discernable in the actions of »ambitious Armenians«: of local Party officials and members of the national intelligentsia. They not only tried to find solutions to conflicts arising over national identity in the Soviet context, but also, it was often these »ambitious« Armenians who triggered such conflicts or contributed to them when voicing their own interpretations of »national form« and »socialist content«. In the process, they did not just put forward their own views, but »bargained« over the concepts held by central authorities in Moscow in contrast with the views held by their fellow citizens. This bargaining was not just between Moscow and local elites. It also took place among the »ambitious«, who were likely to bear in mind Moscow's views, while at the same time finding it necessary to settle among each other the terms and meanings of their own interpretations of the »national« and the »socialist«.

This article inquires into such bargaining processes as they evolved in the Soviet Republic of Armenia after the Second World War. Two different conflicts serve as examples of the dynamics of the local politics of identity in bargaining by members of the Armenian political elite over the role of the »national« and the »socialist«. The first took place during the Zhdanovshchina in 1946 as a centrally incited conflict over Soviet literature was turned into a stage for the defence of Armenian historical novels and in support of members of the national intelligentsia. The second was acted out in the course of the assessment of the spontaneous commemoration of the Armenian Genocide in 1965. These two conflicts took place under quite different circumstances. But in both cases, »ambitious Armenians« bargained with the imperatives set by the socialist regime over pre-Soviet history and national memory as central reference points for Armenian self-representation.

Bargaining for National History – The Zhdanovshchina in Yerevan

On September 19th, 1946, the Armenian Secretary for Propaganda, S. T. Grigorian, addressed a meeting of Yerevan's Writers' Union, assessing the state of the republic's literature. During this speech he stated that:

– [a] considerable number of our writers display an excessive interest in the historical subject... consigning the subject of the present to oblivion. The historical subject is unquestionably not disqualified; it plays undoubtedly a positive role. However, it is impossible to establish on the historical theme the literature of a people, moving forward [to communism].[8]

These lines seem at first sight to conform to the standard Soviet rhetoric of critique and condemnation. The concession to history's »positive role«, however, appears as a slight but crucial digression from the main Soviet line. The deviation becomes apparent even more in a second remark made later on in the speech: There, Grigorian pointed out that:

– [i]t seems to me that I also express your opinion when I state, that at present among the Armenian Soviet writers we do not have anyone like Zoshchenko or Akhmatova.[9]

Those were tempting remarks, above all, as they were made in direct connection to a speech by Propaganda Secretary Zhdanov and a subsequent Central Committee (CC) decree of August 14th. Zhdanov's condemnation of the two writers Akhmatova and Zoshchenko for »aristocratic aestheticism« and »literary hooliganism« marked the beginning of a major onslaught on the Soviet intelligentsia – later to be called Zhdanovshchina – that put an end to the relative freedom

---

8   Rossiskii Gosudarstvennyi Arkhiv Sozial'no-Polititicheskoi Istorii (RGASPI), fond 17, opis 88, delo 713, l.13.
9   RGASPI fond 17, opis 88, delo 713, l. 13.

enjoyed in the arts and sciences during the Second World War. Its repressive effects were soon to be felt also by different ethnic groups, which – despite the deportations during the war of entire nationalities as enemy people – on the whole had profited from the liberalization of the war years as had the peasantry and the churches.[10]

Considering that similar decrees issued in Moscow had led to large scale arrests, imprisonment and executions in the 1930s, the way Grigorian presented the state and quality of Armenian literature in 1946 is somewhat astonishing and daring. Even if this might be a last sign of the hopes for further liberalization held by many in the months after the war, Grigorian's words point to the dynamic interpretations of a central decree on the local level. On the one hand, the CC decree does not once mention the word history. Thus, both Grigorian's criticism of the historical subject matter in Armenian literature and his immediate concession to history's positive role call for an explanation. On the other hand, Grigorian's disavowal of having sinners like Akhmatova and Zoshchenko within the Armenian community of writers contradicted Soviet practices of purging groups and individuals singled out for political persecution. So, how can we understand the apparent inconsistencies of this Armenian interpretation of Moscow's new policies? How were local perceptions accommodated with the centre's requests? What were the concessions to be made and what were the issues to be insisted upon by Grigorian as the representative of a national cadre within the Communist party?

Such questions are relevant as national history is of major importance to the formulation of Armenian identities. The stories about Armenia's greatness during medieval time played, and still play, a major role in the self-definition of Armenians. As the cultural policies during World War II encouraged the publication of novels dealing with wars against outward enemies, in Soviet Armenia a whole flood of historical novels and plays became available to the Armenian reader. Depicting the Armenians' heroic struggle throughout Armenian history, these works reaffirmed Armenian confidence, providing a sense of belonging to and pride in their nation. The popularity of books like Demirchian's novel *Vardanank,* about the Armenian struggle against Persian invaders in the fifth century, or Zorian's *Zar Pap* found expression in their omnipresence on Armenian bookshelves. Put into a broader perspective, Grigorian's remarks point to Armenian attitudes towards nationality policies and national history during a period in which the subject of history in Soviet literature had rapidly lost its legitimacy,

---

10   Ronald Suny, *The Soviet Experiment. Russia, the USSR and the Successor States* (Oxford: Oxford University Press, 1998), pp. 370, 372; Ronald Suny, *Looking toward Ararat. Armenia in Modern History* (Bloomington: Indiana University Press, 1993), p. 160.

while the publication of novels praising Armenia's long history continued to grow.

This inquiry takes the speeches by Grigorian on the matter as an example of how national identity was bargained over during the period of High Stalinism. This particular bargaining process developed in four different stages: the opening speech and the concluding remarks made by Grigorian at the meeting of Yerevan's Writers' Union on September 19th and 20th; a complaint written to Moscow by a member of the Party Control Commission; and Grigorians speech defending his position, made at the Second Armenian Writers' Conference on September 30th, 1946. Unfortunately, neither correspondence coming from Moscow, that would make the central position obvious, nor written amounts of the discussions at the Writers' Union meeting were at the author's disposal when writing this article. Nevertheless, Grigorian's speeches still echo the conflicts and discussions evolving during this particular bargaining process. In order to understand how national history could gain such significance in a conflict over »aristocratic aestheticism« and slanderous »hooliganism«, the developments set off by the CC decree and Grigorian's speech on September 19th deserves some attention.

Interpreting a Decree – Local Understandings and Patterns of the Zhdanovshchina

The CC decree of August 14th was the first public sign of a shift in Soviet cultural policies after the War. Its forerunner, Zdhanov's more elaborate speech at the Leningrad section of the Soviet Writers' Union, was not published until September 21st in *Pravda*. The decree, however, took up the central statements of Zhdanov's speech by accusing not only the Russian writers Akhmatova and Zoshchenko of »aristocratic aestheticism« and »literary hooliganism«, respectively; it also harshly criticised the two journals *Zvezda* and *Leningrad* that had published these authors' works and condemned »liberalism« towards favours based on personal relations. This criticism resulted in the expulsion of Akhmatova and Zoshchenko from the Union of Writers and the closure of the journal *Leningrad*. The appointment of the Deputy Head of the CC Propaganda Department, A.M Yegolin, as editor-in-chief of the surviving journal, *Zvezda*, is one sign of the tightening grip on the arts and, later, on the sciences.[11]

This criticism called for the re-enactment in all other local organizations and provided them with the opportunity to address local evils.[12] As had been so often the case in the pre-war years, the decree, however, left room for interpreta-

---

11   *Kultura i zhizn'*, 21. August 1946.
12   Harold Swayze, *Political Control of Literature in the USSR, 1946–1959* (Cambridge/Mass.: Harvard University Press, 1962), p. 41.

tion. A first guideline for the criticism was offered on August 23rd when *Pravda* published a summary of the Ukrainian CC Plenum. This plenum of August 15 – 17 had singled out the Ukrainian Department for Propaganda and Agitation for offering poor guidance to the Institutes of History, Language and Literature, as well as to the Union of Writers. Bourgeois-nationalist historiography, it was said, had taken root; some writers idealized the past instead of dealing with the difficult problems of the present and some works of nationalist character had been published. Conflicts about right or wrong interpretations of the party line or excuses for the wrongdoers were cut short by denying the writers the so-called »right to err«.[13]

This local interpretation of central policies was legitimized by publishing the findings of the Ukrainian CC plenum in the central organ of the Communist Party. Thus, they served as a model for the other republics. The pattern to follow was further clarified on August 24th, when another *Pravda* article identified self-criticism (*samokritika*) as the »tested armour of Bolshevism« to eradicate such evils as bourgeois-nationalistic ideology.[14] This recommendation harked back to the mechanisms developed in the 1930s, when *samokritika* became a tool to demonstrate the activity and vigilance of any Party organisation by singling out individuals and attacking them as enemies of the people.[15]

The Armenian Zhdanovshchina

As the signals had been further clarified in this way, the remarks made by Grigo-rian in his first speech at the Yerevan meeting of the Writers' Union still seem somewhat strange. Even if his criticism of history now appears to be at least in-spired by the Ukrainian example, his concessions to the »positive role« of history and his denial of the existence of an Armenian Akhmatova or Zoshchenko did not obey the established rules.

This deviation was condemned in a report on Grigorian's speeches to Mos-cow. The accusations made by Shumsharin, a member of the Party Control Commission, did not just concern the remark by the Armenian Propaganda Sec-retary regarding the non-existence of an Akhmatova or Zoshchenko in Armenia. Grigorian also failed to uncover the mistakes and flaws of Armenian writers and literary critics. The decadent, mystic and pessimistic works of the writers Emin, Kaputikian, Sarian and Demirchian were left without criticism, he wrote. Above

---

13   *Pravda*, 23.08.1946; Swayze, *Political Control of Literature in the USSR*, op. cit. (note 12), p. 41.

14   *Pravda*, 24.08.1946.

15   Lorenz Erren, »›Kritik und Selbstkritik‹ in der sowjetischen Parteiöffentlichkeit der dreißiger Jahre. Ein missverstandenes Schlagwort und seine Wirkung«, in: *Jahrbücher für Geschichte Osteuropas* 50 (2002), pp. 186–194, here 191.

all, Shumsharin made clear that Grigorian had failed to point out the »serious danger of the symptoms of bourgeois-nationalistic tendencies in Armenian literature«. This was especially problematic, since »the idealisation of the past … covers itself with the national coat – playing with the national feelings of the reader«.[16] Thus, in Shumsharin's understanding of events, Grigorian ignored the imperatives set out in Moscow and Kiev. This deviation appears to have been quite serious, as Shumsharin emphasised the power of national feelings in Armenia as highly problematic and the impact of literature in this regard. Even the Armenian Central Committee had not deemed it necessary to admonish Grigorian for his mistakes.

In his defence Grigorian sent to Moscow the Russian translations of the criticized speeches given at the Armenian Writers' meeting. They were accompanied by his somewhat weak explanation that the more explicit text of Zhdanov's speech had been received in Yerevan only a day after the writers' meeting had ended.[17] A further explanation of, or even self-criticism for, his failures are not to be found in the document. After all, the speeches seemed to follow the established pattern of Soviet speech by practicing *samokritika*, as well as praising the new Five-Year-Plan and making clear the writers' obligation to contribute to the present tasks. Further, some writers and literary works were criticized and the general fixation on the historical by Armenian writers, literary critics and the Armenian literary journals *Grakan Tert* and *Sovetakan Grakanutjun ev Arest* was judged unfavorably. Grigorian also complained about the lack of literature dealing with the Soviet present.[18]

This seemed to correspond with the guidelines set by the CC decree of August 14th and the *Pravda* summary of the Ukrainian plenum. On closer inspection, however, Grigorian appears to follow a specific rhetorical strategy, bargaining over what was imposed by Moscow with what was regarded as dear and significant in Armenia. Even as Grigorian attacked the pre-eminence of the historical subject in literature and criticised some writers – applying the important catchwords of *sovremennost'* (the contemporary) or *samokritika* – he managed not only to defend the importance of historical novels but also to shield the writers he was meant to attack. In the process, he seemed even to reintroduce some of the theories that had just been subject to harsh critique, for example the writers' »right to err«.

This becomes clear when looking at the way in which Grigorian conducted *samokritika*. When criticising the apolitical, intimate features in the works of some young Armenian writers, he refrained from naming names: »Such exam-

---

16   RGASPI fond 17, opis 88, delo 691, ll. 49–150.
17   RGASPI fond 17, opis 88, delo 713, l. 25.
18   RGASPI fond 17, opis 88, delo 713, ll. 1a-11, 17ff., 21.

ples are many in the work of our young writers, but I don't want to give examples from their work«.[19] Thus, while obeying the command to criticize, Grigorian managed to protect the young writers to some extent by refusing to identify them. A far weaker protection was given to young authors of patriotic plays, of which he mentioned only the titles.[20] These lines of Grigorian's speech seem to have been first of all a warning shot to the Armenian literary community. What had been expected of Grigorian, however, was not to only conduct a partial critique of some groups or some plays, but to undertake a thorough *samokritika* – the denunciation of individual writers. This was to become a major point of critique in Shumsharins's letter to Moscow.

The only writer Grigorian paid more attention to was the elderly poet N. Sarian, a recipient of the Stalin prize. He introduced Sarian as »our talented poet«, »known by all« for his »great dignity«, who »succeeds with great mastery to concretize in a dynamic form of poetry the very urgent problems of our days«.[21] However, as Grigorian stated, even a poet like Sarian published intimate poems about love. Thus, Grigorian had to admit »that even our progressive poets did not evade mistakes, among our writers there also are apolitical ones (*bezideinie*), committing ideological mistakes«.[22]

By criticising an individual, Grigorian fulfilled the command to show vigilance regarding the shortcomings of single writers; but only to some extent. Grigorian exposed just one single writer who should have been protected more than others by established reputation as a progressive Soviet writer.[23] Just hinting at mistakes made by »our writers« can be seen as yet another warning addressed to the literary community, though it was not a thorough *samokritika*. In addition, Grigorian made clear that »[t]he Union of our writers should *help* these writers to correct their mistakes and to understand the instruction of the Central Committee«.[24] Did Grigorian intend to reintroduce a »writer's right to err«?

While a partial critique was carried out, the solution of the problem was assigned to the Armenian community of writers and their local interpretation of *samokritika* and »help«. What this »help« implied is not entirely clear from Grigorian's speech. But what this help definitely should not be is revealed in his crucial remark: »It seems to me, that I also express your opinion when I state, that at present among the Armenian Soviet writers we do not have any like Zoshchenko and Akhmatova«.[25] Here, Grigorian presented himself not just as

---

19　RGASPI fond 17, opis 88, delo 713, l. 11.
20　RGASPI fond 17, opis 88, delo 713, l. 16.
21　RGASPI fond 17, opis 88, delo 713, l. 11.
22　RGASPI fond 17, opis 88, delo 713, l. 12.
23　RGASPI fond 17, opis 88, delo 691, l. 149.
24　RGASPI fond 17, opis 88, delo 713, l. 12, my emphasis.
25　RGASPI fond 17, opis 88, delo 713, l. 24.

Moscow's messenger, but as his audience's accomplice. This remark not only indicated that Grigorian saw no one in the Armenian community of writers who might have sinned as Akhamtova and Zoshchenko, but that, above all, their treatment was not to be repeated in Armenia – no expulsions should take place, either because of critique from within or because of unnecessary interference from outside the Armenian community. The only individual to be attacked without concession was the editor of the Armenian literary journal *Sovetakan Grakanutjun ev Arest* who had shown too much tolerance of poetry of low standards regarding language, style and content. This is, however, the only instance in which Grigorian followed the pattern established by the CC decree of August 14th without making any adjustment.[26]

Grigorian very much bargained for space regarding the definition of national merits, mistakes and their consequences under High Stalinism. While applying some elements of *samokritika*, at the same time he defused the attacks made on the literary community. But while this can be seen as a testing of the limits in regards to Moscow, the speech is both a powerful message and a concession to the other addresses of his speech. His audience was not only warned to adapt to the current central policies, but also at the same time, the Armenian writers, as powerful representatives of the Armenian elite, had to be taken into account too, if the process of bargaining over the limits and possibilities of both a national and socialist Armenian literature was to be successful.

A similarly ambivalent attitude can be detected in Grigorian's attack on the popularity of historical themes in Armenian literature. Here, Grigorian, an historian by profession, appeared to follow the Ukrainian example. However, in every comment regarding the role of history within Armenian Soviet literature Grigorian made clear the subject matter of history was not to be purged entirely from the Armenian literary landscape. Even as the »interest in the historical subject« was »excessive«, history »undoubtedly plays a positive role«, it was »not disqualified«. As the following quotes from Grigorian's speech show, all reservations voiced about historical novels were immediately followed by concessions that reintroduced the historical subject as a valuable one. Of course, the Head of the Armenian Propaganda Department made clear that the predominance of this favourite subject of Armenian writers had to come to an end, no matter ». . . how interesting the historical theme might be. . . «; especially, when bearing in mind the glaring lack of Armenian literary works on the Soviet project.[27]

This critique was much harsher than the one of intimate, aesthetic poetry made earlier; and that critique regarding the »majority of our able literary critics

---

26   RGASPI fond 17, opis 88, delo 713, ll. 18ff. At the time of writing, it could not be clarified, whether the editor suffered from the same fate as the editor of the journal *Leningrad*. However, he might have been the possible scapegoat needed.

27   RGASPI fond 17, opis 88, delo 713, l. 16.

[who] deal with old literature«, who left the questions of the Soviet literature to »accidental people«.[28] Apparently, the more competent people refrained from dealing with the Soviet present.

Weighing the strong insistence on the need for Soviet literature against the concessions made, an adjusted hierarchy of values becomes apparent. Of course, the »Soviet« had to take pre-eminence over every other subject such as national history. Though demoted and downgraded, history remained part of the permissible topics within this hierarchy.[29]

This downgrading was obviously subject to much discussion at this writers« meeting. From Grigorian's concluding remarks a day later it seems like some »well-known writers tried to cover the insufficiencies and mistakes«. Criticising them, Grigorian declared that »here the question is not about giving up the historical subject, but about observing a sense of proportion«[30] – a proportion, which in the Armenian community of writers, apparently would have been defined in different terms. Such local politics of identity seem to have been taken into account again by Grigorian, together with the limits set by Moscow's policies. When »warning« his audience again, he made clear at the same time that history did not have to be given up:

Don't forget that [in the work of] some writers the idealization of the past develops into national conceit, which prepares a favourable field for manifestations of bourgeois-nationalistic sentiments. Our writers once and for all should know that, while not giving up the historical subject, the central and fundamental theme of a writer's work should be the present Soviet life.[31]

The warning shot of the evil slogan »bourgeois-nationalist« seemed to be addressed primarily to the Armenian community of writers, reminding them of the possible repercussions if they tested Moscow's limits too much.

This message was expressed in an even harsher way on September 30th, when Grigorian addressed the Second Soviet Armenian Writers' Conference. After Shumsharin's criticism, Grigorian consequently announced the necessity of a »vigilant and critical approach to … literature and its cleansing (*ochistka*) of all rubbish.« Then he declared that »with the decision of the Central Committee a new era begins, for Soviet literature as well as for Armenian Soviet literature«.[32] Was the time of historical novels and the protection of the national

---

28   RGASPI fond 17, opis 88, delo 713, l. 21.
29   This demotion of history appears much less harsh than the centrally conducted degradation of aesthetic values. See Swayze, *Political Control of Literature in the USSR*, op. cit. (note 12), p. 38.
30   RGASPI fond 17, opis 88, delo 713, l. 46.
31   RGASPI fond 17, opis 88, delo 713, ll. 46f.
32   RGASPI fond 17, opis 88, delo 713, l. ll. 26–27.

cadre of Armenian writers over? Since Gigrorian then singled out the young poet Sil'va Kaputikian for writing intimate poems and advising her compatriots not to forget the Armenian language,[33] this speech is likely to have been influenced by Shumsharin's negative report to Moscow. Thus, Grigorian's remarks in this speech would attest to Moscow that he was putting definite limits to Armenian national self-assertion.

But as the slogans of *ochistka* and »bourgeois-nationalistic« tendencies were further emphasised in the course of Grigorian's speech, here again are signs of bargaining for this national self-assertion:

You all very well remember that the Communist Party of Armenia did a lot of work cleansing the Armenian Soviet literature from bourgeois-nationalistic elements. Our party succeeded in the years 1937–1938 to destroy the bourgeois-nationalistic elements.[34]

This remark appears to be, first of all, a strong threat to the Armenian writers. However, the actual presence of bourgeois-nationalistic elements is ascribed to the past.

And while Grigorian threatened possible wrongdoers among the Armenian writers, he again defended the historical subject matter. When referring to comrades who had criticised the one-sidedness (*odnostoronnost'*) of the subject, he stated that they

– ran to extremes when proposing the absolute renouncement of the historical subject. This is not right; the historical subject persists, as it is indispensable in order to throw light upon … the historical past of our people. But the task lies in not losing the feeling for measure and in understanding that the fundamental and principal should be the Soviet subject.[35]

From this insistence on the »indispensability« of the historical subject it becomes clear that Grigorian turned against interpretations of Moscow's new policies that would bar any further treatment of this reference point for national identity. Whether this might be because of more definite orders from above or eager criticisers from within Armenian lines.[36] Again, space for national history was bargained for by emphasising the imperative of the Soviet subject, while defending history's place as a possible if not preferable topic.

33 RGASPI fond 17, opis 88, delo 713, ll. 33–34.
34 RGASPI fond 17, opis 88, delo 713, l. 31–32.
35 RGASPI fond 17, opis 88, delo 713, l. 36.
36 RGASPI fond 17, opis 88, delo 713, l. 40

Bargaining for National Identity under High Stalinism

The »national« and history as such were never attacked by Moscow, not even under the Zhdanovshchina. However, if in the formula »national in form, socialist in content« the »national« never lost its validity, the pre-eminence of the »socialist« was not to be questioned. In the bargaining process examined above it becomes clear how even a representative of the Stalinist ruling elite interpreted, tested and bargained over this relationship between the »national« and the »socialist«. Being a conflict over high politics, Grigorian's speeches attest both to the significance that national history had in the Armenian community and to the community's concerns for the preservation of its own views on national history. This was not necessarily a questioning of the validity of socialist values from the Armenian side. But this conflict over local views on national identity indicates the crucial role of conflicting interpretations of the formula »national in form, socialist in content«.

How ambivalent and conflicting such interpretations continued to be becomes apparent in subsequent developments in this bargaining process over national literature and identity. For example, shortly after being criticised, the poet Sil'va Kaputikian was chosen to travel to Moscow for the First All-Union Young Writers' Conference and received the Stalin prize in 1952.[37] Of course, not all Armenian writers and academicians escaped accusations for nationalistic-bourgeois writings. In November 1948, the Congress of the Armenian Communist Party launched another attack against writers and historians who allegedly ignored the class struggle in Armenia's history and idealized the past.[38] In 1952, the historians Nersisian and Parsamian were accused of nationalistic interpretations of 19th century Armenian history.[39]

But history seems to have remained »indispensable«; the publication of historical novels and positive references to the Armenian past did not cease. In fact, the ongoing interplay between Armenian publishers and writers on the one hand and the central Party institutions in Moscow on the other attests to a continued negotiation for an Armenian view of Armenian history and literature. The reverence for historical literature became obvious as pre-Soviet Armenian classics that had been purged from the Soviet canon were published once again. In 1947, the Armenian authorities permitted the publication of the 19th century writer Raffi – condemned in the 1930s as nationalistic – only to be criticized for this in 1951.[40] Armenian publishers also continued throughout these post-war years to bring out new publications on Armenia's historical past, some of them to be

37   Kaputikian, Sil'va, *Stichotvorenie* (Moskva: Gosizdat 1959), pp. 13–14.
38   Matossian, *The Impact of Soviet Policies*, op. cit. (note 1), pp. 167f.
39   Suny, *Looking toward Ararat*, op. cit. (note 11), p. 160.
40   Suny, *Looking toward Ararat*, op. cit. (note 11), pp. 154, 160.

later interpreted as nationalistic. This was also the case for books by »ambitious« higher ranking Armenian Party members. A book entitled »Soviet Armenia« written by the Head of the Armenian Council of Ministers received disapproving reviews entitled »Against the remnants of bourgeois nationalism«.[41] The author had failed by declaring the medieval Armenian King Tigran II to be »one of the greatest, most progressive Armenian kings«.[42]

A book called »Journey through Soviet Armenia« by Marietta Shaginian[43] set off a huge controversy, which the editor of the Moscow publishing house *Molodaja gvardija* tried to settle the issue by writing to Stalin in 1950 after two years of discussion.[44] According to his evaluation of Shaginian's book, her description of Armenia was dominated by monasteries and old Armenian princes, ghosts and heroes, which by far outnumbered the Soviet Armenian *kolkhozy* – which were allegedly mentioned only twice in the whole book.[45] Other reviewers held, however, nothing against such a depiction of the Soviet Republic of Armenia.[46]

Bargaining National Memory – The 50th Anniversary of the Armenian Genocide

Bargaining not only took place in conflicts over centrally formulated policies. The »national« also had to be bargained over within the Armenian community, especially, if it was concerning national history and national memory. In the following section, another example of bargaining is examined during a time when the more liberal period of the »Thaw« was drawing to an end and the Soviet regime had acquired some experience in the forceful suppression of national and social uprisings after the death of Stalin.[47]

Within this environment, the 50th anniversary of the Armenian Genocide in 1965 gave rise to public demands for the acknowledgement of national memory and national rights, both previously subject to political repression. The mas-

---

41   *Literaturnaja gazeta*, 31.07.1948.
42   RGASPI fond 17, opis 88, delo 908, pp. 160–162.
43   As a member of Moscow's literary elite, Marietta Shaginian took part in Gorky's publication on the Belomorcanal. She became famous for anti-American novels writing under the pseudonym Jim Dollar.
44   RGASPI fond 17, opis 132, delo 398, ll. 53–54.
45   RGASPI fond 17, opis 132, delo 398, ll. 80–137.
46   RGASPI fond 17, opis 132, delo 398, ll. 50–60, 62.
47   Jeno Györkei & Miklos Horvath (eds.), *Soviet Military Intervention in Hungary 1956* (Budapest: Central European University Press, 1999); Samuel Baron, *Bloody Saturday in the Soviet Union, Novocherkassk 1962* (Stanford: Stanford University Press, 2001).

sacres of 1915, which had begun on April 24th with the arrest of Armenian intellectuals by the ruling Young Turks, had been a forbidden topic under Stalin; many families refrained from passing on the memory of the Genocide to their children. Yet, many members of the Armenian elite had experienced the Genocide themselves or were descendents of refugees. This was also the case for the First Secretary of the Armenian Communist Party at that time, Ja. N. Sarobian, and the previously mentioned poet Sil'va Kaputikian. As a so-called repatriation campaign started in the late 1940s – to be continued throughout the Soviet era[48] – more and more information and materials on the massacres were brought to Soviet Armenia and found keen readers especially among Armenian students and the intelligentsia. Independent of the Komsomol, youth groups started to form, printing leaflets and starting heated discussions about setting aside April 24th as a national day of mourning.[49] As the 50th anniversary approached, there was allegedly the saying that »[w]ho does not go out to Lenin Square on April 24th is no Armenian!«[50]

As the comment of a Member of the Armenian Central Committee on April 29th, 1965, shows, the duty to observe this anniversary not only applied to the national, but also to the political community:

> Comrades! I argue against the remarks regarding whether we should have or should not have marked the tragedy of the Armenians … If we had not observed the 50th anniversary of the slaughters, we would have been very bad communists.[51]

Not just Armenians, also Communists should mark such an anniversary. The justificatory tone of this last comment, however, indicates that the open expression of national memory still needed some defence. The comment about the »remarks« made concerning the commemoration of the anniversary refers to a conflict over national memory, identity and their implications. If such remarks were made, then how was Armenian national memory and identity voiced at the time? Sources that could inform us about the concepts held by a wider range of Armenians are hard to access, although the officially unapproved demonstration which took place on April 24th, 1965 is part of many of today's oral narratives. Therefore, the conflicts within the Armenian Central Committee – a whole assembly of »ambitious« Armenians – over how to assess the demonstration may serve as another example of bargaining national identity in a Soviet republic.

---

48   This »repatriation«-campaign invited Diaspora Armenians form all over the world to settle in their »homeland« of Soviet Armenia from 1946 onwards.

49   Gosudarstvennyi Arkhiv Rossisskoi Federazii (GARF) fond 8131, delo 36s, opis 5728; Omari Chechoian, »Revoljuzija v Umach«, in: *Aniv*, No,1 (2005), pp. 6–9.

50   Emanuil Dolbakian, »Eto Bylo Sorok Let Nasad«, in: *Aniv*, No.1 (2005), pp. 2–5, here p. 2.

51   Nazional'nyi Arkhiv Armenii (NAA) fond 1, opis 45, delo 2, l. 39.

April 24th, 1965

In order to understand the conflict that took shape among the members of the Armenian Central Committee after April 24th, one should take a closer look at the events leading up to the discussion.

On the initiative of members of the Armenian Academy of Science and high Party officials,[52] the Armenian Communist Party decided in accordance with the Central Committee in Moscow to end the silence about the Armenian Genocide of 1915. A closed commemorative ceremony at Yerevan's Opera house, the erection of an obelisk symbolizing the rebirth of the Armenian people under Soviet rule, a scientific conference at the Academy of Sciences and at the University and the publication of articles about the anniversary were approved by the centre. All of these measures are quite astonishing within the Soviet context. Whether these concessions originated in the transition of power from Churshchev to Breshnev or as a result of a cautious approach to national sentiments after the experiences of Hungary would be mere speculation at this point.

These measures, however, did not meet their ends. As the obelisk was not erected and the articles published in the press did not directly refer to the anniversary of Armenian Genocide,[53] the commemoration excluded the majority of the Armenian population. In the course of the anniversary day, an unofficial demonstration took place on Lenin Square, at the heart of the Armenian capital. Several thousands Armenians came together to observe publicly their day of grieving, and to voice their demands for Armenian lands by chanting and holding posters. Another group assembled north of the Opera House at the statue of the Armenian composer Komitas – a symbol of the sufferings as he had gone insane during the Armenian Genocide and died thirty years later in a Parisian asylum. According to the reminiscences of one of the organizers of the demonstrations »[a]lmost 20.000 people went out onto the street, demanding the return of the historical Armenian lands«.[54]

Although some Party members and representatives of the Armenian intelligentsia like Sil'va Kaputikian talked to the crowd and pleaded for peacefulness and orderliness, the people only partly dispersed. A fraction of the demonstration which started at Lenin's square paraded through the city, attracting more people. In the evening, the crowd arrived at the square in front of the Opera house, where the official commemoration ceremony had just ended. Several windows were smashed and some demonstrators managed to enter the theatre. It was only when the demonstration became disorderly that the militia intervened and attempted to disperse the crowd with water cannons.

---

52 NAA fond 1, opis 46, delo 54, ll. 66–73, 75ff.
53 *Pravda*: 24.04.1965; GARF fond 8131, opis 36s, delo 5728.
54 Chechoian, »Revoljuzija v Umach«, op. cit. (note 49), p. 7.

Bargaining Meaning – »Nationalism«, »Nationalistic Elements« and
»Hooligans«

The demonstration and its claims for national memory and homeland as well as
its escalation at the Opera house were likely to become interpreted as »chauvinist
nationalism«; a label that despite the officially sanctioned »national form« had led
not just to critique and condemnation but to harsh repression and persecution
in the Soviet Union. Thus, the events of April 24th called for an appropriate
condemnation and satisfactory assessment that would at least satisfy Moscow.
Accordingly, a plenary session of the Armenian Central Committee was con-
vened to decide on what should be the consequences of the disorder. But even if
the decree (*postanovlenie*) to be decided upon was to be also a message to Moscow
and had, therefore, to comply with certain views and policies, the discussion in
the Armenian CC plenum had primarily a local character. Here, the definition
of the national was bargained over by Armenian party officials who tried to make
sense of the events of April 24th.

The speakers at these plenary sessions on April 29th and 30th 1965 were
primarily concerned with justifying the anniversary and with differentiating between »nationalism« and »nationalistic elements«. Most felt compelled to defend
the fact that the anniversary had been observed and that it had been no mistake
to do so.

As First Secretary Sarobian opened the session, he declared that the decision
to commemorate the anniversary had been made taking into account all possible
problems.

> It was impossible not to think about [the fact] that in 1915 as a result of genocidal
> politics ... more than 1.5 million Armenians died, e.g. half of the population. ... With
> the 50th anniversary of the slaughters (*resni*) approaching, the national feelings, above
> all among parts of the intelligentsia and students, manifested themselves stronger and
> stronger. [Therefore,] ... the Armenian Central Committee decided to commemorate
> this date, in order to give these feelings and attitudes the right direction.[55]

Sarobian already offered two justifications for commemorating the Genocide,
which would later be used by many of his comrades. First, that »the question of
the slaughter of the Armenians had been for a long time on the mind of all«.[56]
And secondly, that the national feelings among important groups of the population had to be guided into a proper direction by an official commemoration.
To the question whether the anniversary of this »tragedy without precedent in
the history of humankind«[57] should have been commemorated, »there can be

55   NAA fond 1, opis 45, delo 2, l. 32.
56   NAA fond 1, opis 45, delo 2, l. 38.
57   NAA fond 1, opis 45, delo 2, l. 48.

only one answer:« One would have been a bad communist, if one had suggested ignoring the anniversary. And, above all, »[i]f we had not observed it, the people would not have understood us«.[58]

Since none of the speakers suggested that the anniversary should not have been commemorated, this repeated justification can be interpreted as the conviction of being in the right in having paid due respect to the Armenian victims. This conviction, it seems, had to be defended against any possible doubt or attack, whether from Moscow or, potentially, from within the Armenian national cadre. Several speakers pointed out that there had been no previous experiences, since this had been the first time the Armenian Genocide was officially commemorated.[59] The disregard for the Genocide prior to 1965 was criticised not merely as a non-communist practice, but in fact as a result of the cult of personality.[60] Thus, April 24th as a national day of mourning was defended passionately by all speakers. Two speakers even suggested that it would have been appropriate to observe the anniversary in the Caucasus or even the Soviet Union as a whole.[61] But while there was a common agreement that the official commemoration of the Genocide was justified and that even an annual commemoration would be necessary, understanding of the phenomena observed on April 24th of that year varied.

A heated discussion took place about two formulations of a draft of the *postanovlenie*, where »some nationalistic elements« were said to be responsible for the events and the »struggle against some manifestations of nationalism« was declared.[62]

Accordingly, the First Secretary Sarobjan stated »some nationalistic and malevolent elements« organized this demonstration, which had been turned into disorder by »disgraceful hooliganism«, by »drug-addicts, drunkards and criminals«.[63] Some speakers seemed to support this position by calling for the punishment of all those who supported or participated in the disorder.[64] Only a few of them, however, declared the disorder to be explicitly nationalistic.[65] The general tendency of these remarks was to assign the responsibility to »elements«, to individuals who could not however be identified.[66] This line of reasoning tried to establish the view that it was not the measures taken but an unidenti-

---

58   NAA fond 1, opis 45, delo 2, l. 53.
59   NAA fond 1, opis 45, delo 2, ll. 34, 45, 53.
60   NAA fond 1, opis 45, delo 2, l. 50.
61   NAA fond 1, opis 45, delo 2, l. 44.
62   NAA fond 1, opis 45, delo 2, l. 58.
63   NAA fond 1, opis 45, delo 2, ll. 32ff.
64   NAA fond 1, opis 45, delo 2, ll. 38, 40.
65   NAA fond 1, opis 45, delo 2, l. 60.
66   NAA fond 1, opis 45, delo 2, l. 36.

fiable group of »nationalistic elements« and »hooligans« which were to be held responsible for the escalation.

The proposed criminal persecution of either hooligans or participants of the demonstration and the formulations presented in the decree draft, however, were not supported by the majority of the CC plenum. And many speakers turned primarily against the formulations of »manifestations of nationalism«. A member of the Plenum, identifying himself as a representative of a rural district, argued that »one should not look for nationalism where there is none«.[67] Another CC member from the city of Leninakan advised against a careless treatment of the term nationalism. Referring to Lenin, he warned against incautious treatment of national feelings. »[If we] ... call it nationalism when they smashed windows and talk about the [Armenian] lands, then we go quite far«.[68] Apparently, this speaker could not see anything negative in the claims to the Armenian lands in Turkey. A similar view is discernable in the comments of the following speaker, who declared:

Don't write in the decision, that the disorders [were] the result of the deeds of nation-alistic elements. It is more the result of the organisational short-comings. I think that the majority of this crowd ... [were] devoted people and did not have any nationalistic inclination.

Therefore, the term nationalism, he said, should be deleted from the decree.[69] This proposal was supported by many other speakers.[70] One member of the Plenum raged:

[o]ne should not call nationalist or nationalism the sincere indignation and anger that is directed against the Turkish oppressors. ... [It is not possible that] anti-social deeds of hooligans are classified as nationalistic instead of hooliganistic. ... To search for something like nationalistic tendencies and tie them to our intelligenzija – this is political slander.[71]

As many thousands Armenians had participated in the demonstration, among them also high Party officials, this differentiation between hooligans and hon-ourable representatives of the Armenian nation appears to have been the main

---

67 NAA fond 1, opis 45, delo 2, l. 48. How much this national anniversary did in fact stir up national feelings is shown by the number of illegally dispersed leaflets dealing with the Armenian Genocide. According to a KGB report, the following tendencies were to be observed around the anniversary: While in 1963 only six leaflets were picked up, in 1964 this number increased to 577, in 1965 to 2038 and in 1966 to 10902. See RGANI Fond 5, opis 58, delo 3, l. 4.
68 NAA fond 1, opis 45, delo 2, ll. 38ff.
69 NAA fond 1, opis 45, delo 2, l. 39.
70 NAA fond 1, opis 45, delo 2, l. 40.
71 NAA fond 1, opis 45, delo 2, l. 49.

concern. This does not mean that the plenum was not outraged over the disorder at the Opera house: »Is there one sincere person to be found, a sincere Soviet citizen and, above all, sincere Armenian, who would not be filled with indignation because of the disorder?«[72] However, it was the disorder that was seen as outrageous, not the illegal demonstration of thousands of Armenians who had carried on without major interference on the part of the authorities.

The national-turned-nationalist was by no means understood to contradict socialist values. On the contrary, commemorating a national anniversary of oppression was consistent with being a good communist. National feelings were legitimate and declaring national feelings to be nationalistic was seen to be a misinterpretation as the remarks of two speakers show. They equated the incorrect interpretation of the demonstration as nationalistic and anti-Soviet with »misunderstandings« about Armenian General Andranik.[73] The latter had been declared to be a member of the Armenian nationalistic party *dashnaktsutiun* by the Party paper *Kommunist*. Andranik, however, according to his defenders »was the sworn enemy of the Turkish oppressors… Throughout his life he sympathized with Soviet Armenia«.[74] Here, the bargaining over the assessment of the national anniversary on April 24th was even broadened into a discussion about national heroes and national memory in general, ascribing to them an inherent socialist quality. On top of that, to be anti-Turkish was equated with being pro-socialist. This can be seen as formulating Soviet identity in a quite nationalist way. Above all, this bargaining for national memory reveals the problematic relationship between the positive formula about »national form« and the officially condemned nationalism in the Soviet Union.

When the draft was brought to a vote, several members of the plenum raised the question of whether »nationalism« would be erased from the decree. In the heated exchange that followed the Armenian Central Committee seemed to split into two. One faction around Sarobian and the chairman of the meeting, both members of the CC Presidium, wanted to cut short any discussion about formulations. They offered to edit the decree after the plenum's vote. The other faction of the CC Plenum, however, denied the vote since »[i]f I vote, I must know, for what I vote.« Another member of the plenum stated that »such an important document, like the decree on the disorder on April 24th« could

---

72   NAA fond 1, opis 45, delo 2, l. 40.

73   General Andranik was an active member of the Armenian Liberation movement in the Ottoman Empire and was widely acclaimed among Armenians for defending Eastern Armenia against the Turks in 1918. His reputation in the Soviet Union, however, was an embattled one. See for example Zatur P. Agaian, *Andranik i ego epocha* (Moscow: Meshdunarodnyi gumanitarnyi fond armenovedenija im. Z.A.Agaiana, 1997), introduction.

74   NAA fond 1, opis 45, delo 2, ll. 46, 49.

not be just edited by the Presidium. »Every member should know for what he votes.«[75]

As the attempts to secure the Presidium's prerogative were questioned, the following dispute evolved:

Sarobian: Comrades, ... now two-three comrades [are] against the word ›nationalistic elements‹... No member of the CC Presidium is interested in not being objective; to the contrary, we criticize everyone, who wants to see nationalism everywhere. But were the organizers of these disorders in your opinion internationalist?
From the auditory: Those were hooligans.
Sarobian: No, the hooligans joined them. Those were the nationalistic elements. This is about *some* people. Taking into account your remarks, the CC Presidium will edit [the decree] anew. If there are no objections, we approve this decision that has been read. Who is in favour of approving this decision?[76]

Although Sarobian agreed that the term nationalism or nationalistic elements did not apply to all participants of the demonstration, he was not successful in inducing the plenum to vote. The discussion about the formulations carried on, until another session was scheduled for the next day. By then, the plenum demanded that the decree be corrected.

In this bargaining over »nationalism« and »nationalistic elements«, the local seems to have played a major role. As far as the speakers could be identified in terms of their position and local background, it seems that the strong defence of nationalism came from CC members who were either in the lower ranks of the Party hierarchy or not from Yerevan. They declared – contrary to Moscow's policies – the popular wrath against the Turkish perpetrators to be legitimate. One speaker even attacked the Soviet Ministry of Foreign Affairs for »fearing Turkey very much«.[77] From the same group came the warning against playing with the national feelings of the Armenian people as well as the strong defence of the national hero Andranik. These CC members argued as one that the word »nationalism« was not at all applicable to the individuals responsible for the disorder. Apparently, hooliganism could not be seen an expression of nationalism.

The arguments against these views held by some members of the CC Presidium like Sarobian, who were higher up in the hierarchy and most likely to be held responsible for the disorder, proved to be unsuccessful. The rejection of their original formulation of the decree by the lower rank and local representatives of the CC Plenum proved to be a strong factor in the bargaining process and made the significance of the »local« evident. The decree was re-edited, the formulation »some nationalistic elements« was replaced by the »some individu-

---

75   NAA fond 1, opis 45, delo 2, l. 55.
76   NAA fond 1, opis 45, delo 2, l. 56, my emphasis.
77   NAA fond 1, opis 45, delo 2, l. 45.

als« and the »struggle against certain manifestations of nationalism« was turned into one against »nationalistic attitudes«.[78]

These adjustments are presented to the CC Plenum on the following day, however it did not end the discussion. One member of the plenum even proposed erasing from the decree the announced criminal proceedings against all participants of the demonstration. In his view, they should not even apply to the persons that had been arrested for hooliganism, because hooliganism »should not be treated as a criminal offence«.[79] On the question of the chairman as to whether there would be any objections to the removal of this part of the decree, the plenum's reaction was – »No«.[80] Consequently, criminal prosecution was removed from the decree.

Yet another speaker from the Plenum proposed the erasure of any hint of nationalism from the whole decree »since this would leave a black stain on the Armenian Party organisation«.[81] To this the Armenian First Secretary Sarobian reacted almost sarcastically: »Sure (*Jasno*). Comrade Ter-Grigorian proposes to erase that paragraph that we reedited on the order of the plenum«. In reply he got a »Right! (*Pravil'no!*)« from the audience.

How far this bargaining process went is explicit also in the last desperate exclamation of Sarobian, trying to prevent the erasure of all central points from the decree: »Comrades, for two days we have been discussing this, because the plenum should have been state its attitude on this important issue. We should not insist on the measures, but show our attitude!«[82] After all, the decree had to satisfy the central authorities in Moscow.

All negative consequences tied to hooliganism or nationalism, were successfully deleted from the decree, and the national memory and national pride was saved from being put on trial. But even after this considerable adjustment of the decree to the local demands, the vote of this – Soviet – political organ was still marked by one abstention.

Bargaining National Identity in Soviet Times

This bargaining process over the national memory turned the logics of Soviet hierarchy and prerogative upside down. The daring discussion in the Armenian Central Committee, however, was followed not by repressions from Moscow, but by further concessions to Armenian interpretations of »national form«. Of the responsible politicians, only the First Secretary Sarobian had to abandon

---

78   NAA fond 1, opis 45, delo 2, l. 59.
79   NAA fond 1, opis 45, delo 2, l. 61.
80   NAA fond 1, opis 45, delo 2, l. 61.
81   NAA fond 1, opis 45, delo 2, l. 61.
82   NAA fond 1, opis 45, delo 2, l. 61.

his position. Some participants in the demonstrations were expelled from the Komsomol.[83] The initially approved obelisk was turned into a whole memorial complex on a hill above Yerevan's city centre. This memorial was opened in 1967 and became the national sanctuary, visited every year since then by a huge crowd. These pilgrimages were observed with caution but were accepted. And as many of the »ambitious« high party officials were the first each year to lay wreaths at the memorial even in Soviet times, this march acquired a semi-official character.

These two cases of bargaining, the Armenian Zhdanovshchina and the debate over the response to the demonstration for observance of the anniversary of the Armenian Genocide, might appear quite different in terms of time, setting and style. This second case of bargaining shows first of all how confident »ambitious Armenians« bargained for their own interpretation of »national in form, socialist in content« in a post-Stalinist setting. These ways of seeing and acting, the confidence, the relatively minor repercussions following the events and the liberal attitude towards national memory are quite astonishing within the Soviet context. Apparently, the local bargaining over the meaning and interpretation of the national memory was successful. But in Grigorian's speeches also, held under High Stalinism in a more cautious manner than the later discussion of 1965, there are many indicators of an obstinate, self-confident defence of the national, equal to the historical reference points of Armenian identity and the placement of writers as the guardians and perpetuators of the glorious past.

Both examples exemplify the possible ways used by members of the national elite in Soviet Armenia to bargain for space for the national. They show the insistence on pre-Soviet references for Armenian identities, which for most of »ambitious Armenians« did not contradict the socialist. After all, they mapped their interpretations of the national and the socialist in the Bolshevik idiom. This is not an argument in favour of an essentialist inquiry about either clever tactics or true beliefs. Rather, what is of interest are rather the ways in which the national and the socialist became reinterpreted by »ambitious Armenians« in a dynamic bargaining process. Here, the official formula, centrally initiated conflicts or political imperatives, were not only shaped from above, but were redefined and acted out on the local level. It is local bargaining process that calls for further investigation. To amplify the insights gained from the perspective »from above« in an affirmative action empire by putting more emphasis on the processes in which this affirmative action became defined and acted out provides an insight into the dynamics and the development of the Soviet system. To analyse the ways of seeing and acting according to particular self-representations

---

83   GARF fond 8131, opis 36s, delo 5728; Chechoian, »Revoljuzija v Umach«, op. cit. (note 49), p. 9.

put forward by local agents might contribute much to the understanding of the terms and logics of a multi-national Soviet society.

Armenian Statehood and the Problems of European Integration as Reflected in School Education

Artur Mkrtychian

The Return of Ethnicity

The concept of »globalization« has an increasingly sustained impact on the debate in the social sciences, and social scientists find themselves continually confronted with the new world order – and not only because the international economic competition has intensified with globalization, forcing a serious reduction in government expenditures for social causes. Globalization also brings a corresponding generalization of foreignness, since everyone is integrated into the various social systems only as the possessor of a certain function. Personal identity is no longer bound within the territorial borders of nations, and political actions no longer have exclusive territorial limits; rather, they can also make themselves felt trans-territorially.

In the age of globalization, everyone can communicate directly with everyone else without taking spatial distance into account. Yet, the global society which can be characterized as the guiding idea and the macro-organization of the modern processes of communication[1] is still hardly acknowledged by the greater part of the population, since »the picture of the global society that its members have is marked to a high degree of being structureless. Being structureless implies unpredictability and in the extreme case, chaos«.[2] An increasing disintegration of societal orientation processes can be identified, in the course of which many of the received notions of state and political order and the patterns of value and interpretation bound to them lose their binding force.

Within the global society, the indices of an increasingly heterogeneous and diverse formation of social self-perception are multiplying – a self-perception in which ethnic, cultural and religious demarcations continue to play an essential role as arguments in struggles over political power and distribution. Social conflicts in the global society play themselves out more and more in ethno-religious form, since people's self-identifications seek to anchor themselves by

---

1 See Rudolf Stichweh, »Zur Theorie der Weltgesellschaft«, in: *Soziale Systeme. Zeitschrift für soziologische Theorie* 1 (1995), pp. 29–45, in particular p. 43.
2 Peter Heintz, *Die Weltgesellschaft im Spiegel von Ereignissen* (Diessenhofen: Rüegger, 1982).

ethnic and confessional affiliation. National identity gets equated with ethnic identity which also finds linguistic expression.[3] Starting with various distinguishing features, certain processes of exclusion and inclusion are set in motion, directed both outwardly and inwardly, and new trans-territorial ethno-national groups are formed along with an ensuing new global ethno-nationality.[4] This results in the formation of ethnic diaspora communities and a heightened potential for conflict that manifests itself in various forms (up to bomb attacks). The latest events in France demonstrate the relevance of ethnic forms of self-organization, especially when, due to globalization processes, the nation-state, as a centrally-guided organization, is »weakened in its ability to exhaust tax resources, stimulate growth and thus secure the essential foundation of its legitimacy«[5].

The basis for the long persistence of ethnicity is its role as a point of reference for collective identity. It is precisely because of the ethnic group's particular ability to fulfill the needs for belonging, recognition, and self-esteem that ethnic solidarity offers itself as a point of reference for the »core identity«. Global ethno-religious identities come into being as a consequence of modern de-spatializing processes within the global society. Global networks and communication in fact allow the construction of ethnically based post-national and supra-national spaces where these groups can pursue their own political interests. The distinction between »us« and »them« (or »not-us«, »other«) thus traces a new line of demarcation, such that foreignness is close by and the manifold ethno-cultural differences can seem to become even more sharply palpable (often as problems resulting from hypertrophic state apparatuses whose crises can not least of all be traced back to the neglect of socio-economic problems).

Earlier, the general and reciprocal foreignness that goes along with the functional differentiation of global society was made invisible by the self-descriptions of modern states as nations with general national interests determined by territory.[6] But the loosening of the previously solid bonds between national-territorial states transforms the basis of cultural identity and exerts a radical influence on the identity politics of European states. The structural change in statehood, such as is occurring with the process of European integration, makes a new point of

---

3   Some semantic traditions distinguish between ethnicity and nationality. In the USA one can be American and at the same time still be Italian- or African-American. However, many other languages do not allow for the possibility of such distinctions.

4   See Artur Mkrtichyan, »Ethnonationalität und ethnokulturelle Konflikte bei der Bildung von Diasporagemeinden«, in: *Berliner Blätter: Ethnographische und ethnologische Beiträge* 33 (2004), pp. 69–85, in particular p. 70.

5   Jürgen Habermas, »Die postnationale Konstellation und die Zukunft der Demokratie«, in: *Blätter für deutsche und internationale Politik* 7 (1998), pp. 804–817, in particular p. 811.

6   See Alois Hahn, »›Partizipative‹ Identitäten – Ausgrenzung aus systemtheoretischer Sicht«, in: *Wiederkehr des »Volksgeistes«?: Ethnizität, Konflikt und politische Bewältigung*, ed. by Roland Eckert (Opladen: Leske+Budrich, 1998), pp. 143–181, in particular p. 178.

reference necessary, since the concepts shaped by the nation-state no longer have any symbolic binding force. Now it is the global society rather than the nation-states that serves as the primary point of reference for the development of Europe as a »space of communication« spanning across nations, and the national systems are increasingly reliant on the coordinating function of the European system of negotiation. Within the European Union the centralizing of organizational competences aims at the political and legal homogenization of large spaces. This corresponds to a policy of expanding Europe. In order to compensate for functional differences and remedy contentious divergences of interest, the European Union tries to come to terms with foreignness in Europe by establishing general rules in a broad cultural-political space that includes all of Europe (eastern expansion) as well as outer-European states (»new neighbors«). In offering those states willing to join the concrete prospect of accession, the European Union acknowledges its political responsibility in Europe on the one hand while on the other hand pursuing tangible economic interests, not only in its core region but also in terms of its eastward enlargement and its »new neighbors«.[7]

The European integration is also directed towards not just changing the procedures of political coordination and legislative practices, but also forming a common European political culture. The European Union is thus conceived as the creative director whose promulgated cultural concepts and paradigms are made available alongside offers of a material nature. But since culture is essentially bound up with a common language, the idea of a European culture seems hardly capable of being realized. In order to develop at least common language-games spanning the differentiated national linguistic forms, the possibility of a common civic culture has to be formulated in terms of a culture of institutions. Only by continuing to develop and propagate the common culture of institutions can the modern European states function as a point of reference for social integration as they previously did. But the institutional cultures are bound to certain levels of representation and are only accessible to those groups that already operate within certain relevant structures. The broad mass of the European population would thus remain excluded from participation in a common political culture. Yet the problem can be solved with the aid of schooling; since every culture is essentially the result of the transmission from one generation to the next of knowledge, values and other factors relevant to conduct by means of teaching and education. The unification of an originally quite socially and culturally diverse entity might then be the indirect but very much intended

---

7   On March 12th, 2003 the European Commission declared the beginning of a new politics of close cooperation between the EU and its »new neighbors« (Russia, Ukraine, Moldavia, the south Mediterranean countries). On September 25th, 2003 the European Parliament recommended the accession of three southern Caucasian countries (Armenia, Azerbaijan, Georgia) in the course of this politics.

result of the homogenizing effect of a standardized school system with a corresponding logic of identity formation. Using the example of Armenia, one could illustrate which problems need to be dealt with in forming identity in Europe through schooling in order to avoid a »return of the ethnic«[8] concomitant with the enlargement of the EU.

Dimensions of Statehood

Following the breakdown of the Soviet system, the Republic of Armenia is today an independent state with a democratic constitution. On January 25th, 2001 the Republic of Armenia was adopted into the Council of Europe and recognized as a European country[9] after a decade of fundamental change. Since then, the transformation of Armenian society can be called Armenia's Europeanization. Yet the problems of this transformation are by no means solved.

The process of Europeanization presupposes that European norms are in fact adopted, first in legislation and secondly in the attitude of the people and, thirdly, that this results in their expression in public (as well as in private) forms of life. The content of these norms is given in the Charter of Fundamental Rights of the European Union (December 2000). In light of the Armenian constitutional referendum (November 27th, 2005) it can be demonstrated that the Armenian legislative system has been »Europeanized«. Yet this does not imply a corresponding »Europeanization« of the attitudes of the people and above all of the Armenian elite. The »indigenized« Soviet legacy has not yet been overcome in the consciousness of the people. Whereas Western Europeans emphasize above all the positive freedom of individuals (participation in political processes), the

---

8   See Anton Pelinka, »Die Wiederkehr des Ethnischen«, in: *Ästhetik und Kommunikation* 80/81 (1993), pp. 166–171.

9   Geographically Armenia lies in the Orient: the Republic of Armenia is located in Transcaucasia and borders on the Republic of Azerbaijan in the East, on the Republic of Georgia in the West, on Turkey and the Nakhichevan Autonomous Republic in the West and Southwest, and on Iran in the South. Armenia and its inhabitants were first mentioned in the Hittite cuneiform texts from 1388 to 1347 BCE. The Armenians trace their ancestry directly from the Indo-Germanic tribe of the Hayasa (ca. 2000 BCE) and call themselves »Hay« and their country »Hayastan«. The cultural identity of the Armenians relates first and foremost to their language, Armenian (an independent Indo-Germanic language), their alphabet (with 39 letters) developed in the year 405 by Mesrop Mashtots, and to the oldest Christian national church in the world, the Armenian Apostolic Church. Around 3 million Armenians live in the Republic of Armenia.

population of the former Soviet republics sees democracy primarily as the people's freedom from state »incursions«[10].

The quintessential points for the desired political and economic transformation of post-Soviet societies are the introduction of Western political institutions, privatization of the economy including property, the most comprehensive investments possible from the highly developed industrial countries in the form of capital and sophisticated technology, and the fastest possible opening of economies towards the global market. And although almost all of those in authority were and are in agreement about the goal of the transformation, the »transition to democracy and market economy«, and were only able to establish the formal elements of a democracy in the country through a comprehensive privatization of property and the means of production as well as the very rapid construction of a pluralistic political system (1990) and the enactment of a democratic presidential constitution (1995), yet, as Bischof notes, Armenia received no significant economic aid from the West that could further expedite the transformation process.[11] And it is not only economic and financial problems, but also political and cultural problems as well, that require corresponding solutions.

Due to a lack of complementarity between the new democratic institutional framework and old notions among the population, democracy is often understood as »organized irresponsibility« in the name of the people. Thus, the democratic forms of social activity operate highly selectively and in dependence on the interests of those in power. This is not only the result of economic and communicative intertwinement, but also the indirect, yet very much intended, result of the extension of the administrative apparatuses of state power – the enormous magnification of their formal possibilities of control through administration, the media, police, and the military. Democratic reforms are greatly impeded by the lack of »feedback«, which also has to do with the legacy of the Soviet system of command. This includes the repercussions of an authoritarian school system, which contributes significantly to preserving old attitudes by means of images and political stereotypes from the Soviet era. Either the networks based on traditional values continue to be used in place of the official institutions, or the democratic institutions introduced get »indigenized« in the form of personages playing a greater role in Armenian elections than their political platforms, personal associations having more weight than the institutions structured according to democratic criteria, and the access to the state apparatus becoming a question of survival.

Hence various factors hindering Armenia's Europeanization have to be ac-

---

10   See Gevorg Poghossian, *The Armenian Society in Transformation* (Yerevan: Lusabaz, 2003), pp. 354–355 [in Russian].

11   Henrik Bischof, *Der Karabach-Konflikt: Moskaus Hand in Transkaukasien* (Bonn: Friedrich-Ebert-Stiftung, Abt. Außenpolitikforschung, 1995), p. 10.

counted for. Armenia is characterized by a chaotic transformation, as the various components of the functional sub-systems in Armenian society are directed »outwards« and are not at all synchronized with each other as regards their degree of development. The economy is dependent on »input from without« and, as a result, the greater part of industrial capacity lie fallow. Privatization seems to be incapable of creating a domestic labor market, and the wage and salary levels are too low to stimulate work activity. Many companies can only subsist because the taxes due are not always paid. Thus, part of economic activity takes the form of an the underground economy. Advanced science, previously oriented toward the Soviet Union's global level of communication, has now ended up without support. The legal system »copies« Western legal norms without harmoniously tying these into Armenian legal reality. External conditions also have a negative impact: the Karabakh conflict and the continual traffic blockade by Azerbaijan and Turkey.

One can thus group the problems of Europeanization into social-economic, institutional, and identity problems. The latter type of problem is frequently »neglected« and is hardly the subject of any research in Armenia, even though it is accepted that the establishment of a market economy and a regime of democratic governance presuppose the formation of a democratic identity among Armenian citizens.

To come to terms with this problem, it is necessary to shape schooling in Armenia in a way that enables the realization of a new politics of identity.

Armenia's officially adopted course of Europeanization can only succeed if the country proves to be a unified political entity structured according to the European model. This requires, above all, that a European culture of institutions an of educated citizens be established within Armenian society. Because the socialization processes in schooling contribute so decisively to the formation of a national identity, and because the state schools have shown themselves everywhere to be the most important institution in terms of creating identity, school education should be a crucial tool for the formation of a future Armenian society, in order to anchor the elements of a civic consciousness of statehood in the structure of schoolchildren's national identity. This relates to the phenomenon of imprinting.[12] The basis of this phenomenon, which has been investigated by many psychologists, lies in the fact that there are particular emotional stages of life when what is seen and learned can no longer be forgotten. The age group of 9 to 13 presents the most important emotional stage for children's primary political socialization. The acquisition of fundamental political values and knowledge occurs at this age and these values can only be altered later on with great difficulty. In various life crises, an adult will with great probability fall back on these

---

12   See Albert Naltschadzyan, *Ethnic Pedagogy* (Yerevan: »Zangak-97«, 2002) [in Armenian].

values and knowledge. The question is how the work of education is organized in Armenian schools and which strategy for the formation of the schoolchildren's identity is pursued.

On the other hand, identity politics in Armenia's transformational society are reflected in the practices of schooling and upbringing, and by examining these practices we can attain a systematic overview of the processes by which identity is being formed in Armenian society. School education is exposed to various influences from politics, the economy, the media, etc. and reflects them. It in turn influences social life. When we take these mutual influences into account, we can recognize the problems associated with forming schoolchildren's national identity as well as modern Armenian statehood.

The Republic of Armenia proclaimed its independence following a plebiscite on September 21st, 1991 and subsequently has found itself confronted with the necessity of building a new state identity. Armenia's very young statehood gives a new dimension to the problem of national identity. Although Armenia lacks a long history of modern statehood, there are at the moment two Armenian states (the Republic of Armenia and the Republic of Nagorny Karabakh). It is important to present both states adequately in school education and to thereby foster the students' self-identification with the nation-state. The traditional ethno-cultural identity is to be supplemented by a national identity adequate to the conditions and circumstances of Armenia in its present process of Europeanization. Armenian statehood should no longer (and can no longer) be neglected in implementing educational policy, since Armenian identity cannot develop further without this. It is a very important component of national identity, since the ongoing worldwide processes of globalization threaten the existence of »weak« and unstable states in which state identity and the political self-sufficiency of the society are not to be taken for granted and the educational strategies only result in a »nationalizing« of traditions. Yet only modern states can also profit from the ineluctable processes of institutional »de-state-ification«.

The current Europeanization of Armenia presupposes above all the formation of a modern state. As defined by Habermas, »the modern state arose as an administrative and tax state and a territorial state endowed with sovereignty that could develop into a democratic state of law and welfare within the context of the nation-state«.[13] Thus, it follows from this definition that the modern state emerges first as a functional administrative and tax state, secondly as a sovereign territorial state, thirdly as a legitimate nation-state with a corresponding collective identity and fourthly as a welfare state founded on a legal basis. The extent

---

13   Habermas, »Die postnationale Konstellation«, op. cit. (note 5), p. 807.

to which the current Armenian state is a modern state in this sense can be seen from an analysis of the practices of identity politics in Armenian schools.[14]

Problems of the Legal and Welfare State

Following the Habermasian logic of the development of the state, our analysis begins with the reflection of this last stage of development in school education. Here we are dealing with the problematic of human rights. In order to instruct children in »civic feelings« and ultimately in the »awareness of legal solidarity«, the significance of such values as social solidarity, a democratic disposition, the exercise of civic activities etc. should be particularly emphasized in the educational practices of identity politics. This presupposes the introduction of new subjects in Armenian schools. According to the »state program for educational development (2001–2005)«, subjects such as »human rights«, »civil education«, and »the foundations of law and of the state« should be introduced as of the 8th grade with the goal of teaching an active civic and universal disposition. But given the lack of an adequately developed methodological basis and qualified instructors, this has all taken a back seat in schooling. It is to be noted that the subject of human rights and obligations, despite its current relevance, occupied only a very small space in children's schoolwork (essays, drawings, etc.). In the Soviet Union, children's scouting organizations were used to convey Soviet patriotism. These scouting organizations no longer exist. In some schools, new organizations for students (above all »student republics«) now operate. These »student republics« could ingrain the new civic culture in the Armenian school, since with the activities of these organizations (elections, discussions of statues, educational measures, etc.) the children begin to seriously take note of the problems that arise in civic life and the importance of the civil solution of problems; but only very few schools have such organizations.

---

14   The question is how national and state identity is anchored in Armenian schools and which strategy is pursued to shape the identity of the youth. In order to answer this question, in 2006 I conducted thirty guided interviews with school teachers and principals in five different schools in Yerevan and the city of Abovjan (6 interviews each) and two focused interviews with groups of schoolchildren and analyzed the relevant publications about school education and official documents (»The Law of RA of Education«, »The exemplary statutes of the state establishment for general education of the RA«, »The state program of educational development, 2001–2005«), lesson plans from the state middle-school for 2004–2005, and schoolbooks, essays, drawings, and craftwork of students. The practices of identity politics were also visible in school names, exhibits, wall newspapers, etc.

Civic identity[15] cannot be formed by a special school subject but rather through all educational means in the course of all educational activities in close connection with the curriculum material. The analysis of this material and of the schoolwork reveals that the pre-state ethno-cultural presuppositions of national unity are much better and more frequently elucidated than the mechanisms of social solidarity.

Armenia's transformation has taken on a chaotic form. The basis is still missing for the necessary changes in the institutional conditions of the state, and nowadays Armenian society finds itself in a transformation that is marked by the lack of a systematic approach. This produces the non-synchronicity and the deviations in the degree of development of the various sub-systems. The system of values and legal norms is also affected by this lack of system, and Armenian citizens often find themselves confronted with a chronic anomie.[16] But »the status of citizen must have a utility value and be payable in the currency of social, ecological, and cultural rights«[17]. Yet Armenia today has become a society of great tensions and grave social imbalances. The access to material and immaterial goods in Armenia is somewhat contradictory, depending on one's status. Based on their prestige, people have a claim to certain goods (income, education, etc.) but cannot make good on this claim.[18] New societal goals are adopted along with the market economy (for the individual the concern is above all with financial success), but no adequate means for reaching these goals have been presented either in a *de facto* or legally institutionalized *de jure* manner.[19] These tensions neutralize themselves due to the »formless« rules that the Armenians have developed over centuries for dealing with foreign rule. Traditional, culturally established mechanisms of familiar affiliation and friendly loyalty are observed instead of the official game rules.

This is reflected in schooling, where the formation of the »pre-state« perceptions reinforcing the ethno-cultural and historical peculiarities of Armenians in the identity of schoolchildren continues to play the most important role, as in the continuance of traditional education policy; even though specialists recognize the necessity of a civil education and thus assign Armenian schools a decisive role in the dissemination of civic culture. Yet it appears that the current Armenian school system has not yet been able to cope with the problems associated with teaching a consciousness of legal and social justice. The fact that the cur-

---

15 Civic identity is here understood as the representation of the discursive processes of the society.
16 Armenia is rich in laws but poor in their application.
17 Habermas, »Die postnationale Konstellation«, op. cit. (note 5), p. 809.
18 There is a lack of strong institutions, e.g. independent courts.
19 In the face of the lack of these means, the comprehensive privatization of industry, agriculture, and housing has displayed a low level of efficiency.

rent Armenian state, in terms of its Europeanization, is neither a legal state nor a welfare state is reflected in school education.

The Efficaciousness of the Nation-State

The problem of constructing a legal and welfare state is bound up with the problem of the democratic legitimacy of the nation-state. The young Armenian state is the guarantor of national existence and as such should provide a basis for the legitimacy of national identity. Yet as our analysis of Armenian schooling shows, the current state has yet to find an adequate place in the practices of identity politics in Armenian schools, and is therefore limited in its efficaciousness in forming identity. In the schools examined it, became clear that not very much space is devoted to the topic of current national statehood in decorating classrooms with pictures and visual aids. Armenian history and cultural accomplishments are frequently depicted, but the symbolism of the nation-state has taken a secondary role.

The great value placed on the use of national and political state symbols for educational goals in the USA is praised by Armenian schoolteachers.[20] Yet only a few of the schools examined displayed the national symbols of the flag, the national crest, and the text of the hymns, or celebrated the Day of Independence. In most, there are no special events commemorating the state's independence. The day of the Armenian Republic's constitution is not celebrated at all. In their essays the children do not write at all about the dangers facing our current statehood (the indifference of citizens about their rights and obligations or the lack of trust in state institutions and especially in political elections) even though these topics are very current. Only seldomly does one see the national flag in the elementary schoolchildren's drawings (primarily on the peak of Ararat) and generally the symbols of modern Armenian statehood play no noticeable role in children's schoolwork. The knowledge that students in the last grade of school have about the Republic of Armenia's political system and about their civic rights and obligations is obviously insufficient. All this points to the fact that the students do not identify with the state and are not yet self-aware regarding the question of being the constituents of the young Armenian state.

In the course of the centuries, the ethno-cultural Armenian identity was

---

20   A specialist said the following about the American school system: »In classrooms in the USA there are many large and small national flags and texts of the pledge of allegiance to the American flag, pictures of American presidents with information on their accomplishments for the benefit of the USA, and figures of donkeys and elephants.«

formed under the conditions of statelessness, and the fourteen years of state independence are of course not a sufficient period of time to form an adequate new consciousness of the nation-state. For this reason the following components above all become clear in the structure of schoolchildren's national identity: they are members of a people dispersed throughout the whole world, which »lost« a large part of its territory as a result of genocide. They represent the legacy of a great 1700-year-old Christian culture and a pagan culture almost twice as old, embracing very valuable national and universally human cultural goods, especially since the invention of the Armenian alphabet by Mesrop Mashtots. It is these notions that are formed and anchored in the schoolchildren's national identity by the identity politics in Armenian schools.

Thus in contrast to many West European states, the Republic of Armenia is founded on an ethno-cultural basis. But Armenia faces very dangerous geopolitical and civilizational challenges and the formation of a modern national-political self-awareness is an important condition for the Europeanization of Armenian society. Otherwise, the official course of Armenia's Europeanization will take on the non-official form of a migratory movement in the direction of Europe, and emigration as the traditional strategy for dealing with problems during social crises is becoming a significant feature of Armenian transformation.[21] The analysis of schoolbooks and children's schoolwork reveals that Armenians see themselves as a world nation, which brings additional difficulties for their self-identification as a territorially demarcated nation-state. And because the Armenians are in fact a diaspora and have networks based on traditional values at their disposal, they frequently seek to secure their subsistence outside of the borders of Armenia. When the official politics of identity fails, the problem of social integration is solved at the community level. The national consciousness thus hardly gets »modernized« and comes to be marked by a confrontation between old stereotypes and new innovative ideas. This sort of consciousness is very unstable, contradictory, and exposed to both mass-euphoria and general pessimism. Despite the rapid enactment of laws that were to have enabled the establishment of a nation-state, the people primarily rely on traditional norms, since the application of these laws has proven to have no »universality«. Therefore we also still do not have an effective nation-state.

It was above all the ethno-cultural components of collective identity rather

---

21   The reasons for the current emigration of Armenians are to be found in the social situation of the Armenian population as well as in Armenian history and the traditional cultural mechanisms for coping with problems and crises. The strong familiar relations and the aid coming in from the worldwide Armenian diaspora play a large role in the transformation of Armenia. The family and not the state is seen as the institution that offers protection. The strong flow of emigrants in the last years is primarily to be explained as a lack of apprehension of the strategic advantages of the national unification within the state.

than national ones that took on the primary functions of protection and unification in securing Armenias' national existence. Thus, in school what children learn to see as the important components of national identity are their common ancestry (the legend of Haik, the patriarch), the homeland as the historical and cultural space of their existence, the Armenian language as the precondition of Armenian cultural identity, the old Christian faith and the protective role of the Armenian Apostolic Church in the course of their history, the heroic stories of the great forefathers, and the tragic era of genocide. These historical and cultural components are very important and have to be preserved; but Armenian history itself has led to the independent statehood of today. It is not viable to persistently ignore the state independence of the Republic of Armenia that has been won and to continue to identify only with the tragic history and the ethno-cultural accomplishments of the Armenian people. Only a people with an identity based on the symbolism of statehood can live up to the requirements and challenges of Europeanization.

Thus in this respect, educational policy has to be fundamentally rejuvenated. In concrete terms this involves teaching the sort of content (such as the significance of statehood and of the nation-state and of respect for the presidents of the Republic and other state institutions and for civic activity and loyalty) that would contribute to the students' education in civic characteristics and »constitutional patriotism«. This reformation should not be limited to the higher school grades, as appears to be the case today, since the particularities of children's socialization mentioned above (the significance of the age group of 9 to 13) require that students receive the relevant knowledge in middle school. The whole work of education in Armenian schools has to be led towards the formation of structures of civic identity as early as elementary school and for this an appropriate methodology has to be used. In this way, the feeling of ethnic belonging should be complemented and thereby reinforced by the feeling of state affiliation.

In fact, nothing of this sort occurs in Armenian schools. Instead the schools reinforce the cult of the fallen heroes and statesmen of earlier eras and of recent history.[22] In many schools there is a special gallery room named for historical national heroes. For example in the city of Abovjan school number 11 has the Njdeh Gallery of National Education, in which children learn ethno-national songs and listen to lessons on patriotic subjects surrounded by ethnographic finds, old weapons, pictures of the freedom fighters, and the books of the military commander and philosopher Garegin Njdeh.

Yet the present and the future have been pushed into the background of

---

22   Thus instead of the slogan »unite with the army« one sees the call to »honor those fallen in war« on the walls of school-buildings. The students are thus called on to identify primarily with spiritual commemoration and not with a state structure (the army).

school practices and are hardly given any space either in schoolbooks or in wall decorations or in outside events. And since national identity is to be conceived as a process, a true national self-identification can only occur if the present national activities and visions of the future are accounted for alongside past history. The Armenian school system above all should contribute to this, since national identity is formed in school-age children primarily through the processes of socialization.

Our Land

In early phases of socialization, national symbols, legends, sagas, and myths play a large role in the formation and preservation of national identity. In the A-B-C book schoolchildren already find a reference to important components of national identity, the ethnonym »Hay« (Armenien), under the letter »H«. The self-given name of »Hay« reflects the course of the formation of the original ethnic group. Elementary schoolchildren learn from the ancestral legend of the patriarch Haik that they are all his descendents. This legend is, so to speak, the founding charter of the Armenian people and possesses a great capacity to form identity and is, thus, very often used by teachers for the purposes of education. In the subsequent school years, ancestral conceptions are anchored more deeply in the schoolchildren's identity in literature and history classes. The students identify psychologically with the person of Haik, his tribe, and his heroic deeds and glorify him and thereby their own nation and themselves. A significant function of the legend of Haik is his creation as the paramount ethno-national symbol of the Armenian people. At first Haik the patriarch, his deeds, and his descendents are symbolized – pictorial symbols of Haik are already to be found in the A-B-C book. The first symbols are then carried over to the ethnic territory. Schoolbooks – the literature book for the fourth grade, the history book for the fifth grade – show that many Armenian settlements and locations were given names by the first descendents of Haik: »our country was named *Hayq* after Haik«. Then the other territories settled by Armenians »were named after Haik's sons (and grandsons): *Aragaz* – after Haik's son Aramanjak, *Armavir* – after his grandson Aramais, *Schirak* – after Schara, *Eras'ch* – after Erast, *Masis* – after Amasia, *Sjunik* – after Sisak, etc.«[23] In this way, the whole territory of the Armenian highlands are ethnicized and perceived as a fatherland. This conception of territorial commonality is a very important basis of national identity.

---

23   *Schoolbook for Armenian history* (5th grade) (Yerevan: Lujs, 2000), p. 32 [in Armenian].

The spiritual-psychic character of Armenians emerged in the Armenian highlands and is still borne today in memories of the »home cradle«. Historical spaces of settlements in the Armenian highlands become a homeland through the symbols of ethno-national culture. During the Soviet Union the schoolbooks depicted the »unified« greater Soviet homeland above all. They were supposed to generate loyalty among schoolchildren to the »guiding force« of this homeland, the communist party. Now the schoolbooks convey the following picture: historical, architectonic, and ethnographic monuments shape the cultural landscape of the fatherland, which was made holy by the blood spilled in battles with enemies and the graves of the legendary ancestors and is preserved in the national-cultural memory in the form of folk-legends, epic narratives (e.g. the epic »David of Sasun«), and folklore songs and fairy tales. The Armenian ethno-national traditions, customs, linguistic particularities, specific national character traits, and national self-awareness have formed on this holy territory in the course of four-thousand years. In this context the images of the »lost homeland« of the Armenian people were also visualized and appear as effective means of ethno-national socialization. The colorful pictures of the historical homeland in the schoolbooks present themselves as holy land, as the land of the Armenian kings and great poets, and thus as »our land«.

The reconstruction and reconfiguration of the »lost homeland« by means of artistic and literary school exercises occupies a large space in the practices of school education. The depictions and glorification of the holy mountain *Masis* (Ararat) in particular appear very frequently in schoolbooks. The concern is clearly to overcome the humiliation and great defeat suffered due to the genocide through the exalting praise and continual preservation in spiritual and cultural activity of the »ethno-national symbol taken into captivity«.[24] Thus the will to survive is particularly emphasized in narrating the history of the genocide as the Armenian people's entitlement to historical existence. With such historical narratives, the schoolteachers want to educate the schoolchildren in the feeling of loyalty to the homeland and prepare them for the further struggle for the »lost homeland«. Yet, as a result of these identity politics we now see a clear contradiction in the national consciousness between the notions of nation-state and of national territory, between state and fatherland. Strictly speaking, Armenia is not perceived as a territorial state.[25] Rather the perception is much more of

---

24   It is no coincidence that those works of Armenian authors have found a place in current schoolbooks who praise the holy mountain of Ararat, Mother Araks (the river on the Turkish border), the heroic region of Sasun, the Akdamar island in Lake Van (both in Turkey today) etc.

25   The Armenians' very high degree of readiness to emigrate is also to be explained by the ambiguity in the national self-identification with the current territorial borders. Most Armenian diaspora hold the Armenian highlands »Erkir« (land) to be their homeland.

a state that could not attain to its complete territorial sovereignty due to the genocide. The genocide of 1915 is thus a national tragedy not only due to the murder of around 1.5 million Armenians in Turkey[26] but also because of the loss of the largest part of the historical territory of the fatherland. National security is put into question by this loss, and the Turks made the primary enemy.[27] And because the Armenian people has diverged from the »true path« of national development due to their enemies, in school education the roots of the current problems are very often sought in the tragic history of the Armenian people. For centuries the Armenians had no state sovereignty and thus could not develop an adequate civic identity and an institutional culture.

Thus it can be said in summary that the Republic of Armenia, as reflected in state school education, is neither a legal, welfare, national, nor territorial state in the usual sense. The current Armenian state is only a taxation state and has formed itself out of the Soviet system of command. »This system gave absolute priority to the administrative levers above the economic and political ones...«[28] Whereas horizontal cooperation and the interconnectedness of state and societal actors developed in the EU states, a strict vertical, hierarchic relationship between state and society is characteristic of the Republic of Armenia. Whether such a taxation state« founded primarily on administrative practices can exercise administrative functions effectively is questionable.

Translated by Karsten Schoellner

---

26 See for example Johannes Lepsius, *Der Todesgang des armenischen Volkes. Bericht über das Schicksal des armenischen Volkes in der Türkei während des Weltkrieges* (Potsdam: Missionarshandlung und Verlag, 1930).

27 The historical antagonism between Armenians and Turks or Aseri-Turks emerged with the »ethnic cleansings« of the traditional space of the Armenian people carried out over the last several centuries and the resistance of the Armenians to this politics. The memory of the history of Turkish violence towards Armenians, of the greatest tragic event in Armenian history, the genocide of 1.5 million Armenians in Turkey, and the expulsion of the Armenian population from a large part of their traditional homeland have very strongly marked the Armenian consciousness of national history with an enmity for Turkey, which finds expression also in history schoolbooks. Armenians see themselves as victims of a terrible crime and demand »historical justice«, which relates not just to Turkey but to Azerbaijan as well (the massacre in 1988 of Armenians in Sumgait also remains unforgotten).

28 S. Korolev, »Das administrative Kommando-System: die Genesis und die Evolution«, in: *Quintessenz: der philosophische Almanach*, ed. by Mudragej & Usanov (Moskow, 1990), pp. 106–132, here p. 122 [in Russian].

Soviet Armenian Identity and Cultural Representation

Hrach Bayadyan

This article attempts to observe the issue of Armenian identity in the Soviet Union in general terms; more precisely, to give answers to the following questions: How can Soviet Armenian identity and its different dimensions be characterized? What factors, forces and circumstances have affected the shaping of Soviet Armenian identity? We believe that Soviet nationalities policy and the ways of maintaining its rule over Soviet nations and the formation of the united Soviet people had peculiarities which could be characterized as Russian-Soviet Orientalism. The main thesis this article will advance concerns the pressure that was exercised over national identity through restraining cultural representation in the Soviet Union(SU). First of all, this relates to the sphere of visual representation – cinema. To this end I will focus on the 1960s. Those were the years we consider as turning point in terms of the changes that the Soviet nationalities policy and the perception of the national identity underwent. The main arguments pertaining to this issue are derived from the novel »Hangover« written by the Soviet Armenian Hrant Matevosyan.

I would like to start with two quotations. Manuel Castells, the author of the three-volume work »Information Age: Economy, Society and Culture«, depicts the post-Soviet situation in the following way:

When the obvious enemy (Soviet Communism) disintegrated [...] [it turned out that] the ex-Soviet people didn't have any collective project, beyond the fact of being ›ex‹.

Then he goes on:

The most enduring legacy of Soviet statism will be the destruction of civil society after decades of systematic negation of its existence. Reduced to networks of primarily identity and individual survival, Russian people, and the people of the ex-Soviet societies, will have to muddle through the reconstruction of their collective identity, in the midst of a world where the flows of power and money are trying to render piecemeal the emerging economic and social institutions before they come into being, in order to swallow (in) their global networks. Nowhere is the ongoing struggle between global economic flows

Figure 5.1: The monument to »Mother Armenia« that replaced the monument to Stalin in 1962. Yerevan, 2005. Photo: H. Bayadyan.

and cultural identity more important than in the wasteland created by the collapse of the Soviet statism of the historical edge of the information society.[1]

The philosopher Boris Groys thinks that:

[...] the contemporary Western cultural market, as well as cultural studies, require the Russians, Ukrainians, etc., to rediscover, to redefine, and to manifest their alleged cultural identity. To demonstrate, for example, their specific Russianness or Ukrainness, which as I have tried to show, these postcommunist subjects do not have, because even if such cultural identities ever really existed, were already completely erased by the universally Soviet social experiment.[2]

He defines the communist project as the ultimate denial of the history is past

1   Manuel Castells, *The Information Age: Economy, Society, and Culture, vol. 3: End of Millennium* (Oxford: Blackwell Publishing, 1998), p. 68.

2   Boris Groys, »Beyond Diversity: Cultural Studies and Its Postcommunist Other«, in: *Democracy Unrealized: Documenta11 Plattform*, ed. by Okwui Enwezor (Ostfildern-Ruit: Hatje Cantz, 2002), pp. 303–19, in particular p. 304.

history, as a fundamental and absolute split from any kind of distinct cultural identity and diversity.

The considerations of different scholars such as Castells and Groys partly confirm and partly complement each other. To sum up briefly, it can be concluded that the absence or the crisis of post-Soviet national cultural identities is a consequence of the Soviet modernization project. Even if we assume that there had been some national identities before the establishment of Soviet Power, according to the authors referred to, they have disappeared. On the other hand, the elimination of national identities has not been replaced by the shaping of a new Soviet identity. Addressing the failure of the Soviet attempt to shape a new individual (*sovetskii chelovek*) and a new community (*sovetskii narod*), Castells writes: »Communities may be imagined but not necessarily believed«.[3]

Furthermore, a closer look is useful to complement and to a certain extent, balance the afore-mentioned views. Ugo Vlaisavljevic, a Balkan researcher, notes that the discourse on Yugoslavian communism refers to the ethnic tradition of making sense of reality. What was happening was a fusion of two discourses and dictionaries, when, for example, »communist revolution« coincides with the »national liberation war«. He then goes on:

A hypothesis might be advanced that in all Eastern Europe, the adoption of communism after the Second World War bore a strong ethnic mark. The majority of people warmly welcomed the idea of revolution, at least in the beginning, not only because of the strong ideological pressure of the lure of industrialization and electrification, but also because of the collective »ethnic experience« of the replacement of cultural paradigms through war. These two revolutions – industrial and cultural – ensured the exterior of the »social-proletarian« revolution. [...] Long time communism successfully protected from big effects of modernization – individualization, disenchantment and the power of instrumental thinking. To that extent, at least in this part of the world, communism can be described as a modern strategy against modernization; a strategy in the foundation of which »*ethnic resistance*« can be detected.[4]

Perhaps the ethnic dimension of Soviet republics and their opportunities for »ethnic resistance« were not as significant as those in Eastern European countries. However, Soviet Armenia was basically perceived as a restored Armenian state (after a long break) by the Armenians. It is true that Soviet Armenia was not a national state in the strict sense, though it allowed the shaping of some of the attributes of a modern nation (establishment of some state institutions, de-

---

3 Manuel Castells, *The Information Age: Economy, Society, and Culture, vol. 2: The Power of Identity* (Oxford: Blackwell Publishing, 1997), p. 39.
4 Ugo Vlaisavljevic, »The South Slav Identity and the Ultimate War-Reality«, in: *Balkan as Metaphor: Between Globalization and Fragmentation*, ed. by Dusan I. Bjelic & Obrad Savic (Cambridge, MA: The MIT Press, 2002), pp. 191–207, in particular p. 203.

velopment of the literary Eastern Armenian language, dissemination of literacy – all characterized by unavoidable ambiguities intrinsic to the Soviet reality).

Therefore, thinking over the »Soviet Armenian identity« we should account for the years of Soviet power and Soviet order as an historical era and way of rapid modernization for Eastern Armenians. This means in particular, the adoption of modern ideas of development and progress; self-definition through renarration of one's own history; foreseeing the future and self-reflection, as well as shaping some notions of culture, nation and national identity. Thus, the »Soviet Armenian« – the bearer of the modernized Armenian identity, is a hybrid construction, where »the Soviet« and »the Armenian« seem to be inseparable from each other. In this sense it is impossible to imagine any »pure Armenianness« free from Soviet mixtures, the same way as it is difficult to imagine a Soviet nation or Soviet community free from ethnic/national attributes.

At this point, before moving on to the consideration of national identity, it would be relevant to refer to the correlated issues of modernity and nation. With respect to Russia and later the USSR, researchers often speak of imperfect or incomplete modernization. It is clear that if we define modernity »as the emergence of nation-states, the establishment of parliamentary democracy, and the spread of industrial capitalism in Western Europe«, we will then have to ascertain that »Clearly none of these aspects of modern political and economic systems pertained in the Imperial Russian and Soviet cases«[5]. On the other hand, if we are guided by such definitions which ear-mark a number of characteristic aspects of transformation, namely industrialization, urbanization, secularization, universal literacy, etc. we will see that many aspects of modernization were fully incorporated into the objectives of the Soviet power. In the meantime Soviet society was characterized by aspects of the Enlightenment such as the belief in progress, faith in reason and science. The Soviet universalism project is comparable to »a mode of historical consciousness, a manner of situating oneself in time. Modernity, in this sense, manifests itself as an awareness of the disjuncture between present and past and the impermanence of present-day reality as history moves along a clearly discernible path of development«.[6] Eventually, the idea of socialism was the product of Western modernity.

Thus, if we elaborate on the concept of modernity we can speak of the Soviet modernization or the Soviet version of modernization. However, the issue of modernization of Soviet nations is more complicated and ambiguous. On the

---

5   David Lloyd Hoffmann, »European Modernity and Soviet Socialism«, in: *Russian Modernity: Politics, Knowledge, Practice*, ed. by David L. Hoffmann & Ianni Kotsonis (Houndmills: Macmillan Press, 2000), pp. 245–260, in particular p. 246.

6   Nathaniel Knight, »Ethnicity, Nationality and the Masses: *Narodnost'* and Modernity in Imperial Russia«, in: *Russian Modernity: Politics, Knowledge, Practice*, ed. by David L. Hoffmann & Ianni Kotsonis (Houndmills: Macmillan Press, 2000), pp. 42–64, in particular pp. 41–42.

one hand it would not be correct to insist that the paths of modernization were closed for the Soviet national republics, but at the same time it was clear that the newly built society was a socialist one; that the modern identity was reserved for the newly shaped Soviet society or the people rather than individual nations. In order to perceive the Soviet model of the settlement of the relationship of national and all-union socialist identities within the Soviet program of modernization as well as the means of its implementation it is necessary to at least to some degree revert to the Soviet nationalities policy.

According to researchers, two opposite trends were paradoxically combined in the Soviet nationalities policy. On the one hand there was attention given to Soviet nations and support for the development of national identities and cultures, on the other hand there was the process of the merging of Soviet nations and shaping of the Soviet people.

Some researchers believe that this ambiguous policy was one of the reasons why the Soviet Union collapsed. One can find different interpretations concerning the Soviet nationalities policy. Let us refer to two of them, which complement each other.

The first explanation is based on the »depoliticization« and overcoming of the Soviet national identities, and the idea of the formation of a united Soviet people – the bearer of a common Soviet high culture which implied the guidance of the Soviet power.[7] The second interpretation is based on the logic of the Soviet geopolitical strategy for disseminating communism throughout the world.[8] In conformity with the first interpretation embodying Stalin's principle »national in form, socialist in content«:

Soviet policy sought to decouple high culture and national identity. [...] Socialism would provide the basis for a new Soviet high culture; a statewide cultural idiom inculcated through a universal, standardized, and yet multilingual, system of education and propaganda. Socialism, not nationalism, would be the state's unifying principle. National identity was accepted, and indeed propagated, by the Soviet state in order to avoid the emergence of a defensive nationalism. National identity was systematically promoted at the sub-state level in the form of national republics, with their own national elites, languages and cultures. Of course, these national cultures had to accommodate the new Soviet high culture, but not a common national identity. According to Gellner's theory, in modern world, such an outcome was impossible.[9]

Irrespective of the extent to which this goal was feasible even if it was viewed

---

7   Terrry Martin, »Modernization or Neotraditionalism? Ascribed Nationality and Soviet Primordialism«, in: *Russian Modernity: Politics, Knowledge, Practice*, ed. by David L. Hoffmann & Ianni Kotsonis (Houndmills: Macmillan Press, 2000), pp. 161–82.

8   A. M. Salmin, *SNG: Sostoyanie I perspektivy razvitiya* (Moscow: Gorbachev Fund, 1992).

9   Martin, »Modernization or Neotraditionalism?«, op.cit. (note 7), p. 167.

as a long-term prospect, it seems that this explanation completely ignores the external vector of the Soviet nationalities policy that makes up the core of the second approach.

The second explanation is guided by the Soviet logic of on-going enlargement to reach the ultimate goal – world communism. With the aim of bringing new nations into the communist camp it was necessary to pursue a proper nationalities policy, to have respect for and pay proper attention to national identity in a world in which nationalism was such a decisive factor and which was impossible not to take into account. Based on this model proposed by Salmin, Castells arrives at the following conclusion: »This constant tension between the a-historical, class-based universalism of communist utopia and the geopolitical interest of supporting ethnic/national identities as potential territorial allies determined the schizophrenia of Soviet policy toward the national question«.[10]

The arguments and observations in Terry Martin's article are interesting from the angle of the main thesis of this article. However, it is not possible to agree with the requirement to separate high culture and national identity from each other, even if it was one of the basic targets of the nationalities policy of the Soviet Power. Did this mean that literature, which deserved to be called »high culture«, was being created solely in Russian or were there no national high cultures, which were produced in national languages. Hrant Matevosyan's work written in the last period of Soviet Power is a good example. It is true that some of his works were first published in Russian translation in Moscow, and only after that they were published in Armenian in Yerevan. Another truth is that Matevosyan's books printed in Russian were read throughout the entire Soviet Union. He was awarded the State Prize – the highest Soviet literary prize. However, Matevosyan's works first of all constitute part of Soviet Armenian high culture.

Generally speaking, the idea of separating the form and the content from each other is not convincing either. It is difficult to imagine how it is feasible to allow »purely national forms« and demand »purely socialist contents«. This was truly an unsolvable task. During Soviet nation-building socialist nations came forth: Soviet modernization was sovietization of nations. And with the failure of the merging of nations project, national units came forth which were, perhaps similar to each other, but also different and the difference was not only in the form.

It seems as if it would be more correct to seek the forms binding, restricting, and in the future »transcending« or marginalizing the national features in other places, including the modes by which, according to Benedict Anderson,

10   Castells, *The Information Age: End of Millennium*, op.cit. (note 1), p. 42.

the communities are imagined: »Communities are to be distinguished, not by their falsity/genuineness, but by the style in which they are imagined«.[11]

The article aims to show that in the SU the availability of some means of cultural representation, which made the modern forms or »styles« of imagination possible, were restricted for national cultural production.

Russian-Soviet Orientalism?

Needless to say, by pushing the Anderson criterion of nation-ness and nation-alism as »cultural artifacts of a particular kind« and by attaching importance to the means and forms of representation, »the place of ethnicity in the national imaginary«[12] should not be neglected. In the final analysis, researchers explaining the consequences of the Soviet nationalities policy as well as of the Soviet modernization project basically do not differentiate between the various Soviet nations being guided by the principle »the Russians and the other nations« thus, this could be called a Russian-centric approach, which, in its turn, seems to be a consequence of Eurocentrism. This is the reason why the explanation often remains abstract and general, and the nations are perceived as a single mass: both, those having an ancient history, and those which acquired a name and history only during the Soviet years.

Referring to the 1960s, let us recall that those were the years of Khrushchev reforms: »A new outward-oriented and competitive nationalism, forward- rather than backward-looking, replaced the blinkered chauvinism of Stalin's last days«.[13] The expression of global competitive ambitions was combined with the new wave of industrialization of national republics, in particular Armenia. Perhaps this was a response to the Western initiative for Third World's development, which started after World War II. This was also a period of shifting attention towards national cultures and supporting their development, and the emergence of nationalistic moods: »Apart from human rights generally, intellectuals in republican capitals (particularly in the Caucasus, the Ukraine, and the Baltic States)

11 Benedict Anderson, *Imagined Communities: Reflections on the Origin and Spread of Nationalism* (London: Verso, 1991), p. 6.

12 Seteney Shami, »Circassian Encounters: The Self as Other and the Production of the Home-land in the North Caucasus«, in: *Globalization and Identity: Dialectics of Flow and Closure*, ed. by Birgit Meyer & Peter Geschiere (Oxford: Blackwell Publishing, 2003), pp 17–46, in particular p. 19.

13 Catriona Kelly, »The Retreat from Dogmatism: Populism under Khrushchev and Brezhnev«, in: *Russian Cultural Studies: an Introduction*, ed. by Catriona Kelly & Shepherd David (Oxford: Oxford University Press, 1998), pp. 249–73, in particular p. 256.

were active from the 1960s onwards in the cause of national liberation from central control«.[14]

However, on the other hand it was also an era of consolidation of the Soviet people and extending the shaping of Soviet identity. The declared competition with the West was also an appeal to and an incentive for the Soviet people. Some of Khrushchev's initiatives such as the space race and the virgin-land campaign had the same ideological significance – the consolidation of the Soviet people around unprecedented and ambitious projects and self-identification with those »great achievements«. The Great Patriotic War became the central symbol of the identity of the Soviet people, in which the messianic role and mission of the SU was once again revealed. The Victory Day, The Tomb of the Unknown Soldier, the Eternal Fire, etc. were among the mythologized attributes and rituals of the war.[15]

Those were the years of undisguised efforts of Russification, even if we admit that before this the Soviet authorities were consciously avoiding such a policy. Yet, it was implemented in various forms: by restricting use of national languages in favor of Russian and by transforming the Russian language into the second native language, which was easy to do since the system of education and the media were under strict control, by promoting the growth of the role of Soviet realities in education and culture, by increasing the proportions of the native elite co-opted into the ruling Party, etc.[16]

Following all these issues it is appropriate to ask the question: How can the status of a former colony of the Russian Empire, later a Soviet republic, Soviet Armenia and its relationship with the Centre be characterized? Obviously there was something of colonialism which can be qualified without reservation by the word Orientalism,[17] Russian or Soviet Orientalism – for the time being without attempting to go into the details.

However, it is worth referring to some of the characterizations and observations by researchers clarifying a number of characteristic features and aspects of

---

14   Kelly, »Retreat from Dogmatism«, op.cit. (note 13), p. 252.

15   Kelly, »Retreat from Dogmatism«, op.cit. (note 13), p. 262.

16   John L. H. Keep, *Last of the Empires: A History of the Soviet Union 1945–1991* (Oxford: Oxford University Press, 1995).

17   Edward Said argues that »Orientalism can be discussed and analyzed as the corporate institution for dealing with the Orient – dealing with it by making statements about it, authorizing views of it, describing it, by teaching it, settling it, ruling over it: in short, Orientalism as a Western style for dominating, restructuring, and having authority over the Orient. [...] My contention is that without examining Orientalism as a discourse one cannot possibly understand the enormously systematic discipline by which European culture was able to manage – and even produce – the Orient politically, sociologically, militarily, ideologically, scientifically, and imaginatively during the post-Enlightenment period.« Edward Said, *Orientalism* (Harmondsworth: Penguin, 1978), p. 3.

the Russian Empire and colonialism providing room for thought regarding Russian and Soviet Orientalism. Discussing the theoretical and practical issues of literary and cultural translation in 19th century imperial Russia, Andrew Whachtel underlines that unlike »the elites of other imperializing nations, whose explicit or implicit assumptions of cultural superiority caused them to view their own values as universal and as something to be imposed on others, members of the Russian cultural elite proposed a model that emphasized their nation's sponge like ability to absorb the best that other people had to offer as the basis for a universal, inclusive national culture«.[18] Such an approach »while compensating for the perceived cultural inferiority vis-à-vis West European powers, also propagated an image of Russia as a mediating civilization between East and West and of Moscow as ›the third Rome‹, the fabled instance of a culture of translation«.[19]

In her work, dedicated to the relationship between Russian literature and colonialism, Ewa Thompson critiqued the West-East bipolar model, from which the Russian Empire actually is left out. She writes:

The world has never been divided into two neat compartments, West and non-West. The bilateral vision disregards the fact that Russia engaged in a massive effort to manufacture a history, one that stands in partial opposition to the history created by the West on the one hand, and on the other to the history sustained by the efforts of those whom Russia had colonized. In doing so, Russia has successfully superimposed portions of its own narrative on the Western one, either blending the two or including its own voice as a kind of universally acknowledged commentary or footnote. Entering Western discourse through a side door, as it were, reinforced Russia's invisibility as a third voice.[20]

The »translation« mission of introducing Western modernity into the East was actually one of the aspects of Russian modernity allowing the Russian Empire to shape and export to colonized nations the Russian modern world picture and to establish its cultural hegemony over them. Elements of Orientalism are evident in this attitude of the empire towards the colonies, and later towards the Soviet nations, in its ways of dominating over them and maintaining power. The entirety of these elements can tentatively be called »translated« or »second hand« or simply Russian-Soviet Orientalism.

If we recall that in the first half of the 19th century most people linked the only possibility of the liberation of Eastern Armenians from Persian rule and

---

18   Andrew Whachtel, »Translation, Imperialism, and National Self-Definition in Russia«, in: *Alternative Modernities*, ed. by Dilip Parameshwar Gaonkar (Durham: Duke University Press, 2001), pp. 45–67, in particular p. 52.

19   Dilip Parameshwar Gaonkar, »On Alternative Modernities«, in: *Alternative Modernities*, ed. by Dilip Parameshwar Gaonkar (Durham: Duke University Press, 2001), pp. 1–23, in particular p. 20.

20   Ewa M. Thompson, *Imperial Knowledge: Russian Literature and Colonialism* (Westport, Conn.: Greenwood Press, 2000), p. 23.

coming into contact with the Western modernization process to Russia, one can come to the conclusion that the idea of modernization of Eastern Armenia was at the outset born and embodied within the framework provided by the Russian mediatory mission, first as a Russian Armenian, later as a Soviet Armenian, project.[21]

In this respect, for post-Soviet researchers, a research project focussing on the Balkan region taking an approach incorporating colonial discourse and post-colonial cultural studies could be very helpful.[22] Here the relationship between the West and the East of Europe by analogy with Orientalism is called Balkanism, consistently revealing the existing similarities and important differences between Orientalism and Balkanism. Thus the comparison between Orientalism and Balkanism could be beneficial in the discussion of Russian-Soviet Orientalism.

The Issue of National Identity in »Hangover«

Hrant Matevosyan was certainly linked to the Soviet literary orientation called »village prose« which appeared in the 1960s. The works of Russian writers such as Valentin Rasputin, Vasily Belov and Victor Astafiev, addressing traditional natural and human values, were anti-modern in orientation:

During the 1960s and 1970s, the nostalgic portrait of the Russian village on the brink of extinction in Siberia or in the Russian North was received as progressive, sometimes even as dissident, relative to the official Soviet cultural ›monolith‹.[23]

However, though admitting the similarities between Matevosyan and Russian rural writers one cannot identify him with this movement. He was a national writer, to be more correct, a Soviet Armenian writer. Avoiding the label »dissident« in his case, it would be correct to speak about a cultural resistance against the Soviet imperial ideology. Matevosyan was not a party member: publishing his first writings required some effort as they often underwent censorship. Besides we can find resistance not only in the writer's behavior but also in his

---

21   It is suffice it to recall the novel »Wound of Armenia« by Khachatur Abovyan, the first work of modern Eastern Armenian literature.

22   Dusan I. Bjelic & Obrad Savic (eds.), *Balkan as Metaphor: Between Globalization and Fragmentation* (Cambrigde, MA: The MIT Press, 2002).

23   Thomas Lahusen, »The Ethnicization of Nations: Russia, the Soviet Union, and the People«, in: *Nations, Identities, Cultures*, ed. by V.Y. Mudimbe (Durham: Duke University Press, 1997), pp. 121–42, in particular p. 123.

writings, not only in the fact of bringing »undesirable« topics into literature, but also in the writer's discourse strategies.

A summary of Hrant Matevosyan's novel is as follows: People from all national republics, basically writers, were to take the two-year Advanced Course for Scriptwriters organized at the Moscow Cinema House. The novel describes one day in the life of the attendees at the course; the conversations of the narrator, Armenian writer Mnatsakanyan, with different people; reminiscences of rural life, etc. Each and every participant in these courses was to write a scenario giving the basis upon which a film could be shot. Mnatsakanyan writes a scenario highlighting the problems of an Armenian village: industrialization, modernization, a devastated rural community, etc. The head of the course, Vaksberg, suggests introducing changes into the scenario – a long conversation, in the end almost an argument – but Mnatsakanyan refuses to do so. Most probably he could be kicked out of the course. The events of the novel take place in 1965. This is an autobiographical novel based on the personal experience of the author.

Many Russian and Soviet writers have traveled to Armenia, and there are many texts on Armenia written by Russian and Soviet writers. Andrei Belyi, Osip Mandelshtam, Vasilii Grossman and Andrei Bitov are among the most famous authors writing on Armenia. We could start the enumeration by Aleksandr Pushkin's work, »Journey to Arzrum«. Ewa Thompson examines the colonialist and orientalist aspects of this text. I do not know of similar readings of texts by Soviet authors, and in Armenia the writings of the afore-mentioned authors on Armenia as a rule are perceived in the context of the »centuries-old friendship between the Russian and Armenian peoples«. Here, I do not intend to discuss this issue, but it is at least appropriate to quote a few lines from the article of a Soviet critic of O. Mandelshtam's writing, »Journey to Armenia«. The work was first published in 1933, in the magazine »Zvezda«. »Mandelshtam's images smell old, rotten ... great-power chauvinist who, paying compliments to Armenia, praises its exoticism, its slavish past, since Mandelshtam has not written anything on its present«.[24] If we leave aside the accusations in Mandelshtam's address about »not understanding what proletarian literature is«, not seeing »Armenia that is blossoming and building socialism with rejoicing« then »great-power chauvinism« and »exoticism« do not seem to be unsubstantiated characteristics, even if this vocabulary was part of the arsenal of the Soviet criticism in the first half of 1930s.

In this regard it would be particularly interesting to read Bitov's book »The Lessons of Armenia«, especially for the reason that Bitov like Mandelshtam was

---

24   Pavel Nerler »Notes«, in: *Works. Volume 2*, Mandelstam, Osip (Moscow. Khudozhestvennaya literatura, 1990), pp. 378–461, in particular p. 421.

not at all a champion of Soviet ideology and did not belong to the mainstream of Soviet literature.[25]

It's true that Matevosyan's novel differs from Bitovs book and those of the afore-mentioned authors. It differs also from the texts of Western authors (Gide, Benjamin, Steinbeck) written as a result of their trips to Russia. The text stands on its own in that it is written from the perspective of a person from the province about the empire at the centre.

I shall present in brief the aspects of national situations reflected in the novel, which allow it not only to describe a crisis of identity but also to address the issues. First, in the course of Soviet modernization as a result of industrialization the rural community is destroyed, including the forms of pre-modern social organization, which, according to Matevosyan, had been part and parcel of the Armenian national existence for millennia.

Secondly, Armenian culture is marginalized and national cultural heritage is featured by the tourist industry. Armenian history and culture are identified with tradition and the museum.[26] Hence, there are different national cultures, but there is one modern Soviet civilization. The national tradition is exotic, and Soviet tradition is the norm. Modernization thus comes to, mean sovietization. Hence, it is understandable why modernization is perceived as violence, as the forceful elimination of the pre-modern.

Thirdly, again in a very brief and simplified way, pressure on national intellectuals to become part of the Soviet intellectual elite was quite obvious. The novel shows very well the process of building of the Soviet intellectual's identity through the establishment of an intellectual elite from the various nations, and the representation of the Soviet people as an imagined community: »They are my friends – in their presence for me a warm climate of safety is being knitted: it is pleasant to feel their existence from Yerevan to Moldavia, Tbilisi, Leningrad«.[27]

The following observation of Frederic Jameson, American philosopher and cultural critic, is applicable, without reservations, to »Hangover«:

All third-world texts are necessarily, I want to argue, allegorical, and in a very specific way: they are to be read as what I will call *national allegories*, even when, or perhaps I should say, particularly when their forms develop out of predominantly western machineries of representation, such as the novel. [...] The story of the private individual destiny

---

25　　I wish to stress that Bitov and Matevosyan not only knew each other but also were good friends, Bitov has written some essays about Matevosyan.

26　　In the essay »Metsamor«, Matevosyan recalls the well-known expression: »The foreigners call our country a museum under the sky.« In so doing, he emphasizes that it is outsiders who see his country in this way.

27　　Hrant Matevosyan, *Tsarere* (Yerevan: Sovetakan Grogh, 1978), p. 128.

is always an allegory of the embattled situation of the public third-world culture and society.[28]

These are genuine rites of passages, a transition from the »national« to the »Soviet« through building the Soviet identity of the subject. If he/she wishes to do so it will involve the setting aside of »anachronistic« and »out of date« national issues and engaging in common human and global issues so as to have a real career, success, wealth and fame. Meanwhile, according to Jamesone's statements, this transformation of national intellectuals into Soviet ones symbolizes an implied national perspective.

Identity and Visual Representation

Ever since the first years of the Soviet power the famous statement of Party leader V. I. Lenin has been well-known: »Of all the arts for us the most important is cinema«. Here is the People's Commissioner for Enlightenment Lunacharsky's comment: »the main task of cinema in both its scientific and feature divisions is that of propaganda«. Subsequently, Stalin also argued: »Cinema is the most important means of mass agitation. Our task is to take it into our hands«.

Generally speaking, as Walter Benjamin observed in his Moscow diary, the more popular the culture is, the stricter the Communist Party control is. Till the last years of the Soviet empire the cinema was an all-union enterprise, which was actually the monopoly of the centre. This included education and personnel fraising, the infrastructure and technologies of film production, the norms and standards and censorship.

In this respect, the Russian philosopher Mikhail Ryklin's comment on Soviet culture of the Stalin era is interesting, a comment that we can take also as a description of dominate regimes of visual representation. Given that the Russian cultural tradition was oriented toward the word and was non-visual by its nature, Russian philosophers characterized the cultural process during Stalin era as a total verbalization of culture, as elimination of visual aspects of human experience and replacing them with so called »speech vision of collective bodies«. The influence of this tendency on Soviet cinema was devastating. Thus, it is not surprising that critic Mikhail Yampolsky describes Soviet cinema as »cinema without cinema«.[29] In terms of regimes of representation this striving for total

---

28   Fredric Jameson, »Third-World Literature in the Era of Multinational Capitalism«, in: *Social Text* 15 (1986), pp. 65–88, in particular p. 69.
29   Mikhail Ryklin, *Terrorologiques* (Eidos, 1992), p. 19.

verbalization can be understood as censorship of visual expression. So, within the dominating regimes of visual representation not only was cultural expression subject to distortion, but also visual expression was essentially restricted.

Within this context, one can feel the refreshing spirit of the 1960s and the comparatively free situation in the novel. Matevosyan's work became possible only in this period. However, the limits of the freedom allowed were also clear: the attendees of the course could watch Antonioni and Bergman freely discussing films, but while writing their own scripts they encountered tough restrictions.

Let me sum up the long Vaksberg-Mnatsakanyan argument over the question of »what requirements should the Soviet (national) film meet?« Narrow national topics: the problems of an Armenian village, the national-liberation movement, the Armenian genocide, cannot become a basis for a good film, since they cannot interest the Soviet and, moreover the foreign, audience. They lack general-human interest, they do not relate to urgent modern issues, in the contemporary world, in particular they do not play the required role in the fight to the death between the SU and the capitalist world: the cinema should serve this struggle both in the commercial and in the ideological sense. And furthermore if one wishes to shoot a film about shepherds, a young girl or a love story, etc. should be added so that the film »is saved from boredom«, i.e. the national element is either fully withdrawn from the cinema or is orientalized.

Hence, there is no way to be both national and modern at the same time. It is impossible to enter modern times without being Soviet. The Soviet is in the real world, thus it is modern and actual, and the national is »outside the world«. It is in the traditions and museums, and is condemned to oblivion. In order to be modern, to master the cultural capacities of new technologies, to work and to create, the national intellectual was obliged to separate himself/herself from the »national« and to move on to the »Soviet« and become »Soviet«.

Here is a remark by Stuart Hall on the Caribbean »black movie« from his article »Cultural Identity and Diaspora« written in the early 1990s – a remark that is instructive in emphasizing the crucial role of representation and the means of representation in constituting new identities:

We have been trying to theorize identity as constituted, not outside but within representation; and hence of cinema, not as a second-order mirror held up to reflect what already exists, but as the form of representation which is able to constitute us as new kinds of subjects, and thereby enable us to discover places from which to speak. Communities, Benedict Anderson argues in ›Imagined Communities‹, are to be distinguished, not by their falsity/genuineness, but by the style in which they are imagined. This is the vocation of modern black cinemas: by allowing us to see and recognize the different parts and histories of ourselves, to construct those points of identification, those positionalities we call in retrospect our ›cultural identities‹. [30]

As I have tried to demonstrate the new and the most powerful cultural means were made to serve Soviet ideology and its »universalist project«: the building of the Soviet individual and the identity of the Soviet people. Thus, the dominant regimes of visual representation within Soviet culture served to the highest degree of the implementation of cultural power and functioned as a means of normalizing and homogenizing cultural expression operating against the so-called Soviet nationalities cultures.

Consequently, the contemporary means of representation, i.e. cinema, later also the TV, were by and large inaccessible for national cultures. If we agree with Hall's statement that identities are not only inherited but also constructed and that they are constructed in and through representation, then we can conclude that in the Soviet Empire through cultural representation strict restrictions and limitations were established on national cultures. These limitations marginalized national cultures and cultural identities.

---

30 Stuart Hall, »Cultural Identity and Diaspora« in: *Identity: Community, Culture, Difference*, ed. by Jonathan Rutherford (London: Lawrence & Wishart, 1990), pp. 222–37, in particular p. 235.

Yet Another Europe? Constructing and Representing Identities in Lithuania Two Years after EU Accession

Asta Vonderau

Definition Ceremonies

As Susan Parman notes, the disciplinary community treats some Western European fields of ethnological and anthropological research simply as an »excuse for a holiday«,[1] because they are supposed to be not »different« enough. In contrast to that, anthropological studies dealing with postsocialist contexts and being conducted in Eastern European societies never experience any lack of legitimacy. Far from it, these studies are regarded as challenging tasks. Sponsors of scientific projects generally expect them to be highly politically and socially rewarding. The Eastern sites of ethnological and anthropological fieldworks are imagined as being full of social problems and tensions. These tensions are assumed to emerge not as the result of single social developments but rather as deriving from the collapse of entire social and political systems, being the result of complex social crises and all-embracing societal transition. Such an understanding of postsocialism indeed seems to make it the only possible interpretative framework for the study of Eastern European societies. It is not my intention to question the legitimacy of research done from this perspective. However, I find it necessary to point to some assumptions which often have been taken for granted in this context and are still very dominant within postsocialism studies. I take this general discussion as a starting point for the analysis of Lithuanian collective identities because it is directly linked to the topic of my essay.

As this dominant research paradigm would have it, postsocialism stands for a social and cultural existence which is only defined by the fact of »being *post* (that is, coming *after*)«.[2] Consequently, the so-called socialist heritage appears to be a phenomenon so complex and indefinable that it exceeds the capacities of normal research. Even well known scholars acknowledge that after a decade of researching and writing »no clear direction for post socialism and the study of

---

1   Susan Parman, »Introduction: Europe in the Anthropologic Imagination«, in: *Europe in the Anthropological Imagination*, ed. by Susan Parman (Upper Saddle River, New Jersey: Prentice Hall, 1998), pp. 1–16, in particular p.1.

2   Zygmunt Bauman, *Moderne und Ambivalenz. Das Ende der Eindeutigkeit* (Frankfurt/Main: Fischer Verlag, 1996), p. 333.

›transition‹ has emerged«[3]. Again, this fact gives reason to ask if postsocialism can be regarded as a self-evident category and as a useful framework for analysis. It is quite understandable that researchers of postsocialism tend to defend the legitimacy of this category and the perspectives it opens up. As Christopher Hann notes in the German foreword of his standard volume *Postsozialismus*, even if the category »postsocialist« increasingly adopts a kind of mystical meaning, it will stay relevant as long as socialist ideas, ideologies, and practices constitute a point of reference for many people's understanding of their present situation.[4] I would like to stress that postsocialism as an analytic frame works out only if it is regarded and used as one category amongst others, a point of reference comparable to europeanization, globalization, or nationalization – terms which refer to and mutually depend on each other. As Caroline Humphrey argues, »it makes sense, at least for a time being, to keep a category ›postsocialism‹ in order to maintain the broadest field of comparison«.[5] Leaving aside the question as to how many people in Eastern Europe still regard socialism as a point of reference, I rather would like to draw the attention to the stereotyped thinking guiding so often comparative studies in one or the other direction. These binary ways of thinking tend to lock up socialism and / or postsocialism within the »ghetto« of Eastern Europe.[6] This kind of research is based on the idea of Eastern Europe as the »utter other«[7] or the »internal other«[8], ideas ingrained in European modernity which are solely based on a perceived difference to Western Europe. During the time of the Cold War, such one-sided images made Eastern European societies appear to be identical with the socialist political system, as Peter Niedermüller argues.[9] Scientific research on these societies generated the obligatory comparative studies of socialism and capitalism. Correspondingly, after the

---

3   Katherine Verdery, »Whither Postsocialism?«, in: *Postsocialism. Ideas, Ideologies and Practices in Eurasia*, ed. by Christopher Hann (London: Routledge, 2002), pp.15–21, in particular p. 15.

4   Christopher Hann (Ed.), *Postsozialismus. Transformationsprozesse in Europa und Asien aus ethnologischer Perspektive* (Frankfurt/Main: Campus, 2002), p. 7–11, in particular p. 7.

5   Caroline Humphrey, »Does the Category ›Postsocialist‹ Still Make Sense?«, in: *Postsocialism. Ideas, Ideologies and Practices in Eurasia*, ed. by Christopher Hann (London: Routledge, 2002), pp. 12–21, in particular p. 12.

6   Verdery, »Whither Postsocialism?«, op.cit. (note 3), p. 20.

7   A. David Kideckel, »Utter Otherness: Western Anthropology and East European Political Economy«, in: *Europe in the Anthropological Imagination*, ed. by Susan Parman (Upper Saddle River, New Jersey: Prentice Hall, 1998), pp. 134–147.

8   Trenholme Junghans, »Marketing Selves. Constructing Civil Society and Selfhood in Postsocialist Hungary«, in: *Critique of Anthropology* 21/4 (2001), pp. 383–400.

9   Peter Niedermüller, »Ethnographie Osteuropas. Wissen, Repräsentation, Imagination. Thesen und Überlegungen«, in: *Ethnographisches Wissen. Zu einer Kulturtechnik der Moderne*, ed. by Köstlin & Nikitsch (Wien: Selbstverlag des Instituts für Volkskunde, 1999), pp. 42–67, in particular p. 51.

breakdown of socialism, political, social, and cultural developments were first and foremost seen as a post-existence. According to this perspective, Eastern European societies are imagined to undergo a constant change which aims at smoothing out political, economic, and cultural deficits and to catch up with the West. In this perspective, it seems consistent to compare postsocialism with socialism and to set them against each other. Comparing East European post-socialism to West European capitalism in order to measure the backwardness of the first one against the progress of the latter is another seemingly self-evident strategy. The Eastern European countries therefore always remain sites of difference, associated with problems still to be solved. As Sabine Hess notes, many surveys undertaken by social scientists use culturalistic arguments to explain the transformation processes in Eastern Europe. These arguments are based on a traditionally oversimplified understanding of culture as a set of static, unchangeable ways of behavior. Accordingly, the reasons for social and economic problems in these societies are seen as being caused by the cultural incompetence or passive mentality of the Eastern Europeans.[10]

A comparative perspective is certainly not unproductive in general, yet a more nuanced ethnological approach would have to recognize the fact that experiences with postsocialism and the effects of the Cold War left their marks on societies in Western as well as in Eastern Europe.[11] Political, economic, and social changes taking place in postsocialist societies cross geographic borders and are part and parcel of European processes as well as global ones. Complex processes of change are multidirectional and therefore not easy to compare. We also have to bear in mind that continuities make up the flipside of discontinuities and that differences do not necessarily indicate social and cultural superiority or inferiority.

These and other problems inherent in researching postsocialism could lead us to accept Europe and europeanization as alternative frameworks for analysis. However, stereotypes and mental images of self and other as well as dualist arguing function well within this framework, too. Comparisons of East and West, old and new are easily to be found in scientific, political, and media discourses on europeanization. Changes in Eastern European societies become a long and never ending way »back to Europe«, while those societies regularly are described as children »needing tutelage in the ways of civil society, yet having a potential that needs only to be cultivated«.[12] My critique, then, is to be understood rather as a plea for a more sensitive and self-reflexive ethnological approach than as an attempt to replace one concept with another. From my point of view, the

---

10   Sabine Hess, *Globalisierte Hausarbeit. Au-pair als Migrationsstrategie von Frauen aus Osteuropa* (Wiesbaden: Verlag für Sozialwissenschaften, 2005), p. 56.

11   Verdery, »Whither Postsocialism?«, op.cit. (note 3), p. 20.

12   Junghans, »Marketing Selves«, op.cit. (note 8), p. 397.

main challenge for such an approach lies in the fact that the postsocialist societies themselves seem to be overwhelmed by the idea of their post-existence.
»With the breakdown of the socialist model of modernization, the iconography
of a ›modern‹ West and a ›backward‹ East became crucial for the positioning of
›self‹ and ›other‹ within East-West relations«[13]. The same images and perspectives, which dominate scientific research dealing with postsocialist societies, are
adopted in Lithuanian public discourse. Here, I am referring in particular to
the images mentioned above such as the vision of a backward Eastern Europe
standing in opposition to the modern West which is deterministic and leads to
the specific perspective on the postsocialist countries as being fundamentally different from the western societies. Or rather the idea of a socialist society being
identical with the socialist political system which can be instrumentalized for
denying the socialist past and negating the legitimacy of socialist experience.

In the following, I will describe the current social situation in Lithuania as
it is reflected in local public discourses. What images of self and other exist in
today's Lithuania? Are there any attempts to define a collective »we«-feeling in
this particular societal situation? I will also show how certain social actors, in
particular the Lithuanian economic elites, position themselves within this social
context, and investigate which identification strategies and »modes of subject
making«[14] are being adopted by these social actors in order to obtain and to
maintain their social elite status.

Without being able to provide definite solutions to the methodical problems discussed above, I will restrict myself here to describe actual social tensions
which accompany the identification processes, without defining clear-cut models of identity. I will refer to public as well as scientific discourses in Lithuania
and especially to texts published in German and English which explicitly formulate Lithuanian self-images and address readers outside the country with their
analysis of the political, social, and cultural situation.[15] Observations from my
fieldwork in Lithuania and statements from interviews conducted there are to
be included as well.[16] Even if my empirical examples refer to single social actors

---

13 Hess, *Globalisierte Hausarbeit*, op.cit. (note 10), p. 60.

14 Aihwa Ong, *Flexible Citizenship. The Cultural Logics of Transnationality* (Durham & London:
    Duke University Press, 1999), p. 19.

15 I refer mainly to the following anthologies: Paulius Subačius (Ed.), *Fortsetzung folgt. Essays über
    Litauen und Europa* (Frankfurt /Main: Inter Nos, 2002), published in German on the occasion
    of the Frankfurt book fair; and Almantas Salamavičius (Ed.), *Forms of Freedom. Lithuanian
    Culture and Europe after 1990* (Vilnius: Knygiai, 2005), a »collection of essays written by
    Lithuania's leading cultural and art critics« in an »attempt to communicate to the readers the
    ideas of Lithuanian culture in a new, European, and the global context« (Salamavičius, book
    cover).

16 I refer to my fieldwork conducted in the Lithuanian capital Vilnius in 2005. This fieldwork is
    part of my PhD project on consumption and career strategies of economic elites in Lithuania.

only, they nevertheless give insights into the interplay between political ideologies, public images, and personal life and career strategies.

Social Moods

More than ten years ago, most Lithuanians were dreaming about a ›return‹ to Europe. However, they soon realized that the average Lithuanian citizen had not much in common with the Europe they were dreaming about. As a result, they voluntarily switched on to ›Russkoje Radio‹, ›Svoboda‹, as well the Russian-dubbed ›Animal Planet‹ and other western TV channels.[17]

Society Images

If one tries to visualize how society is imagined as a geographic and symbolic space in Lithuanian public debate, the one-way street seems to be the most appropriate image. The front page of the weekly magazine *Veidas*[18], issued on the occasion of the first anniversary of Lithuanian membership in the EU, may serve here as an example. »The Long Way to Europe« (caption) is divided into three periods, each of them being represented by a stereotype, i.e. »*Homo Sovieticus*«, »*Homo Lituanus*«, and »*Homo Europaeus*«. The way to Europe is understood here as evolutionary, leading to civilization and progress. As it can be seen from this example, political and ideological borders of this imagined social space are clearly defined and social developments are pointing in only one direction, that is, the West. Or rather vice versa, »not to join the post-Soviet Unions in the East«[19] makes up the strategic goal the country is committed to according to its constitution. NATO and EU membership are understood as further steps towards the realization of this goal.

As Katherine Verdery notes, »›democracy‹, ›civil society‹, ›markets‹, and other features of post socialist politics are partly a symbol [...]. One of its functions has been to generate external and internal support by signifying the end of socialism.«[20] Similarly, Europe and Europeanization seem to function partly as a

---

17   Algimantas Prazauskas, »Globalizacijos išbandymai mūsų dar laukia«, in: *http://www.delfi.lt /archive/index.php ?id=6445315* (2005) (accessed on December 21st, 2005).

18   *Veidas* is a weekly magazine dealing with social, political, and economic issues.

19   Evaldas Nekrašas, »Litauen: Auf der Suche nach einer regionalen Identität«, in: *Fortsetzung folgt. Essays über Litauen und Europa,* ed. by Paulius Subačius (Frankfurt/Main: Inter Nos, 2002), pp. 196–216, in particular p. 201.

20   Katherine Verdery, *What Was Socialism and What Comes After?* (Princeton, New Jersey: Princeton University Press, 1996), p. 210.

Figure 6.1: The long way to Europe. A title page of Veidas magazine, Lithuania 2005. Photo: Natalija Chiterer

symbol in Lithuanian politics today. Europe stands for the end of the transition period and a country's new beginning, a country that »finally has arrived in Europe«. This symbol has both legitimacy and acceptance within the society: »Europe« is an important political keyword, Lithuanian economy is oriented towards the European market, and the majority of the population feels positive about it, as recent polling shows.

However, the one-way character of social space does not permit easy orientation since alternative directions are missing in the general picture. Local analysts claim that the political left vanished; both rightist and leftist parties follow a pro-capitalist and liberal agenda dominated by topics like, for example, the free market economy, EU and NATO, independently of which parties have a ruling majority in the country. Outside party politics, a leftist intellectual tradition is missing as well. Since Marxist thinking is usually associated with the Soviet regime, outing yourself as a leftist is »such an incomprehensible action, that it necessarily leads to speculations about your activities as an agent«[21]. The duality of East and West dominates the public discourse: Everything that is identified as wrong or immoral can in turn be explained as resulting from affinities for the socialist past or even the present political system of Russia. While some commentators see these views as being instrumentalized in order to discriminate against people who think differently,[22] others question whether it makes any sense at all to speak about leftist or rightist traditions in the Lithuanian context. As Tomas Daugirdas notices, many Lithuanian intellectuals understand Marxism as the rightist ideology against which they were fighting during the »singing revolution«[23]. The well-known Lithuanian translator and essayist Laimantas Jonušys describes this understanding as follows: »When I see those Austrians protesting against Jörg Haider, crowding town squares with red flags, this is just as hideous to me as Haider is to the Austrians.«[24]

It is not only the significance of left or right, but also the idea of social order that remains unclear in the public discourse. According to media reports, the

---

21   Gintaras Beresnevičius, »Linkes Vakuum in einem postkommunistischen Staat«, in: *Fortsetzung folgt. Essays über Litauen und Europa,* ed. by Paulius Subačius (Frankfurt/Main: Inter Nos, 2002), pp. 176–188, in particular p. 185.

22   See for example Beresnevičius, »Linkes Vakuum«, op.cit. (note 21).

23   Tomas Daugirdas, »Warum haben die Linken Sokrates umgebracht?«, in: *Fortsetzung folgt. Essays über Litauen und Europa,* ed. by Paulius Subačius (Frankfurt/Main: Inter Nos, 2002), pp. 189–195, in particular pp. 189 ff.; *singing revolution* is a term used to describe the Lithuanian independence movement of the 1990's and the political change following it. The term emphasizes the peaceful character of the movement, during which traditional patriotic songs were extremely popular and functioned as means of demonstrating the political will.

24   Laimantas Jonušys, »Von Osten her gesehen sieht einiges anders aus«, in: *Fortsetzung folgt. Essays über Litauen und Europa,* ed. by Paulius Subačius (Frankfurt/Main: Inter Nos, 2002), pp. 140–147, in particular p. 140.

only social group, which can be identified precisely, are the political and economic elites. Making up about five to ten percent of the population, these are the winners of the transformation, overexposed in all the media, earning several times above the average salary. In contrast, all other social groups seem to merge into a rather undefined crowd. Experts disagree on the question whether there is a middle class in Lithuania and how big this group could be. A local representative of an international agency for social research told me that definitions of social class, which developed with regard to the European population, are problematic in the Lithuanian context. Definitions based on criteria like education and income, for example, can not be applied in the case of teachers who, according to their education, should be found at the top of the social hierarchy but stand quite at the bottom according to their income. Analysts agree, that the majority of the population does not belong to a middle class but has to cope with severe material shortage and restricted possibilities for social mobility. Despite these uncertainties, diverse polls and statistics help to classify people and to create new types of subjects which in turn are presented every day in the media and constitute a popular and powerful means to justify different ideologies and argumentations: »Statistics play a key role in creating new classifications of people [...] and new types of subjectivities [...] not just by creating administrative rulings but by determining classifications within which people must think of themselves and the actions that are open to them.«[25] Attempts to impose prefabricated socio-demographic categories on people cause uncertainty and social tension. They create feelings of immeasurable social differences, whereas ways to overcome these differences remain completely unclear. These tensions are present not only in public debates and official ideologies but in individual life strategies as well. In order to clarify one's position in society one might for instance ask if it is really worth striving for a university education when a degree only guarantees a minimal income? Would it not be more reasonable to save time and immediately start working on a construction site in Ireland or the UK, sending money home regularly? Contradictions like these make it quite clear that concepts developed with regard to Western Europe cannot automatically be used for the analysis of postsocialist contexts, be it in a public or scientific discourse.[26]

The European dimension of Lithuanian society is not only defined ideo-

---

25 Cris Shore, »Forging a European Nation State? The European Union and the Question of Culture«, in: *Building Europe: the Cultural Politics of European Integration*, ed. by Cris Shore (London: Routledge, 2000), p. 30.

26 Ingrida Gečienė, »Democracy and the Middle Class: Western Theoretical Models in a Post-Communist Context«, in: *After Communism. Critical Perspectives on Society and Sociology*, ed. by Harrington, Salem & Zurabishvili (Oxford, u.a.: Peter Lang, 2004), pp. 235–255, in particular p. 244.

logically but takes a geographical and physical shape as well, first of all due
to the streams of immigrants to the West. It has been estimated that about
300.000 qualified and unqualified workers emigrated from Lithuania in recent
years. Whole small towns and villages suffering under poverty and unemployment left the country and the lack of a work force as well as the brain drain will
surely have consequences for the future. In the meantime, almost everyone has
friends or family members working and living in Great Britain, Ireland, Spain,
Portugal, or Scandinavia. These »activists of mobility« and »balance contraban-
dists«, as Karl Schlögel calls them, »have a hybrid identity. They are ›multilingual‹ in several ways, knowing well how to make advantage of difference for their
everyday needs.«[27] By sharing experiences and income, emigrants make Europe
tangible for those social groups which do not have the same opportunities as the
political and economic elites. Migration thus becomes a means of compensation for inequality in society. Transnational strategies for life planning, however,
cause new social problems, for instance for emigrants' children abandoned in
Lithuania and lacking legal status. Migration creates new social spaces within
which new meanings and new concepts of distance and proximity, of self and
other emerge and new strategies of constructing Lithuanian identity develop. In
this respect, it is worth mentioning that the collective identities of emigrants are
not only based on national affiliation, but on shared experiences of socialism,
postsocialism and of transnational life as well.[28] In contrast to former émigrés
who are supposed to have left the country during the First or Second World
War (out of necessity), emigrants today seem to turn their back on Lithuania
voluntarily. Therefore, the current emigration bears an implicit criticism of, or
protest against, the Lithuanian state which appears to be unable to provide its
population with opportunities for a good life in their own country. The official
position towards emigration has not always been clarified, especially since the
formerly illegal status of Lithuanians abroad only recently has been legalized by
Western European countries. The passivity of the state was criticized by some
as a conscious political attempt to sort out unwanted citizens: »The ability to
change belongs to the younger generation which hasn't been fed [the] falsehood
and aggression of the communist surroundings but who are now immigrating
to foreign countries because they are unwanted in their native land. This emigration is part of a consciously but ›imperceptibly formed‹ policy«.[29] When

---

27   Karl Schlögel, »›Europas Comeback‹. Marijampolė oder die stille Verfertigung eines Konti-
     nents«, in: *http://www.lettre.de/archiv/64_Schloegel.html* (2005) (accessed on December 21st,
     2005), here p. 2.

28   Vytis Čiubrinskas, »Transnational Identity and Heritage: Lithuania Imagined, Constructed
     and Contested«, in: *Communicating Cultures,* ed. by Ulrich Kockel & Mairead Nic Craith
     (Münster, u.a.: Lit.Verl., 2000), pp. 42–66, in particular p. 58.

29   Daiva Tamošaitytė, »The Price of Boredom«, in: *Forms of Freedom. Lithuanian Culture and*

Lithuania joined the EU, local politicians finally recognized the political and social importance of emigration. The issue is handled in a traditional manner, however, by mostly ignoring the transnational lifestyles of emigrants, instead maintaining contact with them in terms of national affiliation. Programs have been developed which aim to bring the so-called Lithuanian intellect back home to the country, and Lithuanian schools as well as communities abroad get regular support. Focusing on cultural and national bonds, in fact, seems to be the only consequence since public opinion agrees on that the failure of the state's social promises was and is one major reason for emigration.

While Europe seems gradually to come closer, there is uncertainty about Lithuania being a genuine part of it. If one follows public debates more closely, trying to reveal how social moods are expressed, it soon becomes clear that two years after Lithuania joined the European Union there is a strong feeling in Lithuanian society that the state and other influential groups regard EU membership as mere formality. This common feeling provokes speculation about the absence of »real« Europeanness in Lithuania. For some, this uncertainty stems from the distrust of Lithuanian EU politics. There is a gap perceived to exist between a formalized EU membership, the activities of state institutions, and informal relations that seem to become influential under the surface. In public discussions these processes, assumed to take place under the surface, are mystified or at least characterized negatively as socialist heritage, mafia-related, or due to Russian influence. In any case, such processes arouse suspicion as deviating from legal and formal structures and patterns of behavior. Public uneasiness about activities under the surface can be interpreted in terms of a »transformation of social visibility«, as Katherine Verdery calls it. While the socialist state created the illusion of submitting everything to social control, the change to a free market economy was perceived by many as replacing »the visible hand of the socialist state by the invisible hand of the market«. This perception suggested »there is still a hand, but it has disappeared into the shadows«.[30] But the wide-spread hope that EU membership would set an end to those dubious manipulations under the surface, clarifying social structures again, obviously will not come true. It is precisely because of these unfulfilled expectations of social visibility that power relations and social structures seem to remain opaque, incomprehensible, and therefore immutable for many members of Lithuanian society.

The economic elites differ from this social context by virtue of their demonstrated self-assurance, inner balance, and contentedness. According to a survey by the Lithuanian sociologist Irmina Matonytė, more than 90 percent of the

---

Europe after 1990, ed. by Almantas Salamvičius (Vilnius: Kultūros barai, 2005), pp. 35–48, in particular p. 40.

30   Verdery, What Was Socialism, op.cit. (note 20), here p. 181.

local elites are satisfied with their social and economic situation as well as their personal and professional life. They neither feel overworked nor lonely and they probably constitute the only social group in Lithuania which does not consider emigration as a possible future perspective.[31] Members of the elites feel at home both within official institutional and unofficial, national and transnational power structures and networks. Many of these people were active in the soviet shadow economy or were founders of the first legal private companies in Lithuania. In addition to their private business activities, many of them hold high positions within state-owned companies and were also active in the communist party or related organizations. In other words, members of the Lithuanian elites always used to maneuver between legality and illegality, formality and informality. For these people, the transformation from socialism to capitalism has not necessarily meant a change of property forms (from state to private), but rather a change in the organization of their social relations and the necessity to adopt this relationship with the new social and political system. When I asked representatives of the economic elites whether they did not find it difficult to establish a legal and functioning business within continuously changing social structures, their answer usually was negative. As the second wealthiest man in Lithuania told me: »Any change is painful if you are not able to reorientate. I would not call such changes a crisis for the whole society. For me every change is good, it has a big exploding energy and opens many possibilities. I am extremely happy that we live in a dynamic time and it makes me feel like a fish in the water«.[32] While many social actors feel confused about the changes, which appear to come down to them from the state, the EU, or simply those holding power, members of the elites on the contrary claim that they themselves created or at least implemented these changes by their own will and energy. As the president of an agricultural corporation replied to me: »It was not like awakening one morning in a totally new world. We were ourselves initiating and enforcing the change: we brought western pesticides, fertilizers, and medicines to Lithuania, we saw how they became a norm, how they were consumed, what people's opinion was about them«.[33]

---

31   Irmina Matonytė, *Posovietinio elito labirintai [Labyrinths of the Postsoviet Elite]* (Vilnius: Kny-giai, 2001), here p. 207.
32   Please see the note 16.
33   See the note 16.

Social Memory

In socialist modernity, a »new historical community« was propagated in the sense of a »›super-modern‹ type of society more advanced than any nation state«.[34] This, consequently, led to the idea that »the national question« had been left behind.[35] With the refoundation of the nation state during the first years of postsocialism, the national question came up again. When Lithuania joined the EU, this historical event again reorganized the collective imagination concerning the national question. Today, commemorative ceremonies such as national holidays and the cultivation of ethnographic traditions, which both had been extremely popular at the beginning of the nineties, clearly have lost their symbolic value. Folklore festivals now are a major tourist attraction, while the new pagan movement is regarded as only one of many existing subcultures.[36] According to opinion polls, the popularity of politicians who once were celebrated as heroes of the singing revolution has sharply decreased. The romantic image of the Lithuanian farmer as the archaic and authentic personification of Lithuanian national culture has been replaced by the image of the so-called *sugar beet*: an apolitical, passive and uneducated »*Homo Sovieticus*« voting in favor of populist« parties and indulging in nostalgia for the soviet past. This labeling functions as a means of discriminating against the political and social position of provincials as illegitimate and primitive.[37]

Commemorating the national suffering of a Lithuania on its way »back to Europe« is less present in public discourse as well. New public events such as the celebration of Lithuanian's admission to the European Union join the official calendar of national festivities, therefore placing it in the European context. The official strategies of commemoration try to escape the former popular self-victimization and to find a more self-confident and future-oriented interpretation of historical hardship. National historical events are reinterpreted as Lithuania's contribution to European civilization. For instance, as the known Lithuanian historian Alfredas Bumblauskas claims, Lithuania has already since the middle ages been one of the most tolerant states and one of the most seden-

34   Vytis Čiubrinskas, »Identity and the Revival of Tradition in Lithuania: an Insider's View«, in: *Folk. Journal of the Danish Ethnographic Society*, 42 (2000), Special Issue: *Anthropology and the Revival of Tradition: Between Cultural Continuity and Invention*, ed. by Otto & Pedersen, pp. 19–40, in particular p. 23.

35   Čiubrinskas, »Identity and the Revival of Tradition«, op.cit. (note 32).

36   Egidija Ramanauskaitė, *Subkultūra. Fenomenas ir modernumas* (Kaunas: Vytauto Didžiojo Universitetas, 2004).

37   The term *sugar beat* emerged and became popular in the years 2003–2004 during the election campaign and later impeachment process of the former Lithuanian president Rolandas Paksas. Paksas was especially supported by the provincial population which was accused by his opponents of being uneducated and primitive and therefore believing his populist promises.

tary (genuine European) nations in Europe. In his opinion, the Lithuanian resistance against Soviet occupation after the second World War made an essential
contribution to the European civilization of the 20th century, and by regaining
its independence as the first of all the Soviet republics, the country played a key
role in the europeanization of the whole former Soviet Union.[38]

The Lithuanian position within the EU is subject to intensive negotiation.
Political developments of recent years are seen as being historically determining
for Europe's future. Lithuania is imagined not simply as enjoying EU membership but rather as fulfilling the function of teaching other European states –
especially Western ones – a lesson. »For about 200 years we've been ›taught‹ that
we can't rule our nation state, that we are losers. Well, we have to learn now that
we are able to do so, and even more, that it was wrong to believe the contrary.
This is a lesson the West is learning very unwillingly.«[39]

In political terms, Lithuania is seen as a stubborn and non-conformist country. It wants to push through its own projects acting like a thorn in the flesh of
the powerful states. Lithuania's support for the war in Iraq was interpreted as
such an independent decision made in opposition to the supposed Western European anti-Americanism: »We are participating in a war in Iraq. It is a sign that
we don't want to be on the side of the defeated any more.«[40] With regard to economics, Lithuania is seen in the role of an economic tiger[41] due to its having the
highest economic growth rates Europe-wide.[42] And also culturally, the country
is supposed to become a special spiritual site in Europe. Very different characteristics, regarded as being national virtues, such as religiosity, strong bonds with
nature, industriousness, strong family ties, or warmth of human relations are
being related to this rather nebulous notion of spirituality in different contexts.
»Everything that is preserved in the collective memory of this region can be instructive to Western civilization on the condition of course, that we agree that
history has meaning and is able to teach something to somebody«.[43] According
to this kind of argument even the very feeling of Europeanness appears to be of
a special depth in Lithuania. Its spiritual quality emerges out of the sufferings

---

38 Alfredas Bumblauskas, »Litauische Gegenwartsgeschichte: Litauen als Zentrum Europas«, in:
    Fortsetzung folgt. Essays über Litauen und Europa, ed. by Paulius Subačius (Frankfurt/Main:
    Inter Nos, 2002), pp. 27–43, in particular pp. 28ff.
39 Tamošaitytė, »Price of Boredom«, op.cit. (note 29), p. 42.
40 Tamošaitytė, »Price of Boredom«, op.cit. (note 29), p. 41.
41 *Economic tiger* is a very popular characterization of the Lithuanian success, being used by
    politicians and the media in a variety of contexts.
42 It is worth pointing out the problematic nature of such argumentations which more or less
    ignore the fact that Lithuania is still one of the poorest countries in the EU.
43 Almantas Salamavičius, »Europe's East as Spiritual Space«, in: *Forms of Freedom. Lithuanian
    Culture and Europe after 1990*, ed. by Almantas Salamvičius (Vilnius: Kultūros barai, 2005),
    pp. 49–60, in particular p. 59.

which Lithuanians went through while maintaining European identity under Soviet suppression. In contrast, countries which »for centuries had no necessity to insist on their [...] belonging to Europe«[44] seem to have a rather superficial feeling of being European.

All these political, economic, and cultural views of Lithuania, which form part of public discourses, then quite obviously address the West teaching it »lessons« about Lithuania's possible prospects in the European Union: this country will bring economic growth, political opposition, and a new spirituality to Europe which currently is undergoing some economic and cultural crises. As has been noted by the Lithuanian philosopher Nerija Putinaitė, Europe and Lithuania are not equated in these visions as the problems of the EU are not understood to be Lithuanian ones.[45]

Despite the current attempts to reorganize social memory, one aspect of the country's self-image remains unchallenged: the socialist past, that is, the one-sided image of evil socialism dominating public discourse and the official version of history (although not necessarily of collective memory). This image of the past is perceived as authentic by members of the younger generation who did not experience socialism, while the rest of the society had to sort out socialist reminiscences already a long time ago. The gap in history resulting from such attempts to bring the past under control can be seen as one reason for political passivity in the population. Since historical references are missing, social relations cannot be explained out of past experiences and therefore seem unchangeable. Social actors act and communicate within the collective »mental spaces« of their respective social groups and their memories not only shape social space but are mirrored in mental and material milieus as well.[46] It is, however, not easy to relate for example the memories of the fifty to sixty year old Lithuanians to such a collective mental map. The memories of many people today are underrepresented in the society because most of them »do not belong to ruling elites or experience the history of their own lives primarily in the context of the life of such elites«.[47]

Since the socialist past is not accepted as a legitimate point of reference for the present, the economic elites develop strategies of symbolic representations of their social status conforming to this dominant ideology. Officially the social function of these social actors is formalized under the notion of the economic elite of a EU member state. They are recognized in the public as the »winners of

44   Salamavičius, »Europe's East as Spiritual Space«, op.cit. (note 41), p. 59.
45   Nerija Putinaitė, *Šiaures Atėnų tremtiniai Lietuviškos tapatybės paieškos ir Europos vizijos XX a.* (Vilnius: Aidai, 2004), p. 199.
46   Paul Connerton, *How Societies Remember* (Cambridge, New York: Cambridge University Press, 1992), p. 37.
47   Connerton, *Societies,* op.cit. (note 44), p.18.

transformation«, important people for the further advancement of the country, who are able »to teach lessons« not just within the country but also in a European context. But on the other side, their activities are just as often suspected to be opaque and based on the old socialist informal networks. Consequently, while creating their public elite image, the economic elites cannot rely on their past socialist experiences or their current eastward directed activities. On the contrary, these kind of experiences and activities are kept socially invisible within their lives and career paths. Instead, west-oriented lifestyles and images are publicly presented.

As Elisabeth Dunn explains, due to the negation of the socialist past the »outer signals«, symbolizing a western orientation, become especially important: »[...] job histories and track records were of little value because of their ties to the socialist past. Instead, they had to rely on the idea that the outer self signals changes in the inner self. They used changes in dress, personal professions, and personal space to display their supposed transformation from a socialist being to a capitalist being.«[48] Similarly, many of the Lithuanian businessmen are incorporating the idea of their transformation to the European elites by imitating the imagined habitus of European or Western entrepreneurs instead of relying on their long term experience or knowledge.

Self-inventions

Just when Central Europeans are being told that what was once dissimulation – deceptive and manipulative self- invention – is now legitimate self-actualisation, a new group of Others is being defined according to a ›civilisationally‹ determined inability to self-invent, legitimately or otherwise.[49]

The connection between the project of social order and the project of personal life can be regarded as an integral part of modernity, as Zygmunt Baumann argued.[50] Socialist, postsocialist and European modernity involve their own variation of this connection by propagating respective images of a new human being. If in socialist society the new human being was a representative of the working class serving the collective, the postsocialist reorganization changed this image into the image of the Lithuanian farmer serving the nation by preserving national culture.[51] In today's Lithuania, the new human being is seen as a westwards oriented, young, and dynamic individual, a »*Homo Europaeus*« who is self-

48   Elizabeth C. Dunn, *Privatizing Poland. Baby Food, Big Business, and the Remaking of Labor* (Ithaca and London: Cornell University Press, 2004), p. 81.

49   Junghans, »Marketing Selves«, op.cit. (note 8), p. 397.

50   Zygmunt Bauman, *Unbehagen in der Postmoderne* (Hamburg: Hamburger Edition, 1999), p. 40.

51   Čiubrinskas, »Identity and the Revival of Tradition in Lithuania«, op.cit. (note 32), p. 23 ff.

responsible for his or her route of personal success through society. Images and identity patterns of this new social role model are promoted in Lithuanian public discourses. Lifestyle magazines again and again tell the story about people who use these west-oriented identity patterns for a successful and happy life, not reflecting upon the fact that they are actually impossible to implement in the given social milieu in which the majority of Lithuanians are living. As Tatiana Zhurzhenko stresses, those patterns are not seen as the result of social change and democratization but are imagined as pre-existing these processes. As for example, »The image of successful women entrepreneurs promulgated by the mass media fulfils the function of legitimating a new market order, much like the image of the happy female Soviet worker in communist propaganda was used in the past for the legitimation of the communist regime«.[52] Since identities are imagined to exist independently from social circumstances, one can use them as a recipe for personal luck, making success dependent on personal will and industriousness only. »This is precisely the universalizing assumption which underpins the view of democracy as offering ›freedom‹ for the expression of pre-existing political identities [...] which, is argued, communism has simply ›suppressed‹«.[53] According to the logics of such assumptions, the responsibility for social success or failure can then be delegated to the individual alone, and what formerly might have been blamed on the state now solely lies on the individual's shoulders. People successfully using these identity patterns are recognized as the winners of transformation, while »a person unable to conform to this orientation cannot expect honor in today's society«.[54] In this way the losers are being sorted out, people are left alone with their social failures without being aware about the power mechanisms crossing their personal lives.

The economic elites are perceived in public as an incorporation of the new human being and *Homo Europaeus*, and depicted in the media as an example for other social actors of a successful transformation and orientation.

During my research, I observed that the economic elites are working hard to adopt their official social role. They try to live up to this role both professionally and personally, by way of lifestyle and personality. This includes acting dynamically and west-oriented, demonstrating that your business is successful and transparent. In the professional context, activities such as participating in beneficial events, paying employees for training or coaching, and holding mem-

---

52   Tatiana Zhurzhenko, »Free Market Ideology and New Woman's Identities in Postsocialist Ukraine«, in: *The European Journal of Woman's Studies* 8/1 (2001), pp. 29–49, in particular p. 42.

53   Peggy Watson, »(Anti)Feminism after Communism«, in: *Who's Afraid of Feminism?*, ed. by Ann Oakley (New York: The New Press, 1997), pp.144–161, in particular p. 145.

54   Mindaugas Degutis, »Social Structure and Social Changes«, in: *http://www.tspmi.vu.lt/files /leidpubl/str081.pdf* (2001) (accessed on December 21st, 2005), p. 3.

bership in clubs and public organizations are all still relatively new in the Lithuanian context and regarded as a part of the elite role. Privately (as well) many of
these people are trying to live up to the idealized images of successful persons,
as portrayed in lifestyle magazines. Leisure time and sports activities, beauty
procedures and cultural events are regarded as necessary for family life or rather,
for the reputation of a successful European businessman. Many of the persons
I spoke to admitted to suffering as a consequence of the popular imagination
which makes criminals of businessman. Accordingly, decisions in everyday live
are often made with the intention to distance one-self from the so-called »bandits«. Of course, there exist generational and other differences and not all elite
members conform to the image of the successful person which dominates the
Lithuanian media and public space. However, stressing their west-orientation
seems to be still important for these businessmen because, as one of them puts
it: »It would be self- destruction to be east-oriented, at least regarding your image. You would be rejected by colleagues.«[55]

As Elisabeth Dunn explains, the neoliberal vision of an autonomous, active,
self-responsible and flexible person was introduced in postsocialist societies already in the beginning of the nineties. It seems, that the Lithuanian EU access
has put this imagined person into a new frame of action. According to the expec-
tation of my informants, their special abilities of an »enterprising self«[56] would
guarantee their social elite status not only within the national but also within the
international context and even enable them to achieve a special position among
the European elites. The ability to adapt to new situations, the absence of rigid
attitudes, the capability to deal with chaos are indeed core skills identified by
members of the Lithuanian economic elite as for people in their position. It
is worth stressing here that a readiness to switch between western and eastern
economic cultures and the ability to mediate between them has also been highly
valued in this context. A certain feature which my interviewees called »hunger«
has also been seen as important. »Hunger« stands for the will to follow personal,
material aims as a guarantee not only of personal success in Lithuania but in the
European Union as well. »The new generation of managers and businessmen
have some positive aggressiveness. They are hungry in a positive way. They are
clever and well educated, they want to come and conquer and win. They want
to earn money and this motivates them, while in Western Europe they are all
relaxed, inert, and lazy. I think that Eastern Europeans will very fast take high
positions in the EU. It will be like a positive injection for ›Old Europe‹.«[57]

In fact, in the case of elites, the »enterprising self« can be regarded as a strat-

---

55   See the note 16.
56   Dunn, *Privatizing Poland*, op.cit. (note 46), p. 22.
57   See the note 16.

egy of self-making which is exploited in order to achieve and to maintain social elite status. Although the dominant social and political orientation toward Europe and the West excludes other possibilities for orientation and denies their legitimacy and social visibility, the possibility and capability to develop activities in both directions (West and East) seems to be necessary in order to ensure the achievements of the economic elites within Lithuania and Europe. Consequently, at least two codes for the »enterprising self«, the organizing of personal life and career models seem to be important for this particular social group. One has to be aware of these codes and be able to identify situations in which they are used in order to make both a successful business career and to be publicly perceived as a member of the European elite.

Lack of Culture

In spite of all efforts to demarcate social space and to bring past and present under control, cultural homogeneity in society, which is supposed to be necessary, is felt to have been lost and to be impossible to re-establish.[58] Anomie as in the »rejection of cultural goals« is spreading in Lithuanian society, as experts claim.[59] Different social groups accuse each other as well as the Lithuanian state of lacking culture. This lack of culture seems to represent a collective feeling encompassing diverse meanings of culture, which are held by different social groups or actors in different situations.

Thus, due to Lithuania's seemingly superficial EU politics and in the face of the ongoing struggle for money from EU structural funds, the politicians and state bureaucrats are seen to lack political culture. Darius Kuolys for instance, the director of the Civil Society Institute in Lithuania recently claimed that Lithuanian politicians had ratified the EU constitution without even having understood what it is actually about and why most of the EU states instead

---

58 Peter Niedermüller describes the special character of Eastern European constructions of collective identity in the following way: »It is a view which transforms *the* culture into *my* culture which can exclusively (and is willing to) understand the cultural phenomena in the frame of their own cultural terminology. Homogeneity – an image of cultural consistency – constitutes a substantial characteristic of this view of life, culture, and society.«(Peter Niedermüller, »Politischer Wandel und Neonationalismus in Osteuropa«, in: *Kulturen – Identitäten – Diskurse. Perspektiven Europäischer Ethnologie*, ed. by Wolfgang Kaschuba (Berlin: Akademie Verlag, 1995), pp. 135–151, here p. 143).

59 Degutis, »Social Structure«, op.cit. (note 52), p. 1.

had decided to organize a referendum before approving it.[60] In his view, public discussions concerning current political issues are missing while state institutions are self-contained »black boxes« from which no information is passed on to the population. Those critized meet his kind of critique with evidence of economic growth and, in turn, tend to explain social problems as the inevitable consequence of progress. As already mentioned, the economic elites – which embody collective visions of success – actually have a Janus-faced reputation as well. While on the one hand they are accepted and celebrated as »the winners« of the transformation process, they are on the other hand often accused of being criminal, materialistic, selfish, in short: personifications of »money without culture«,[61] that is people giving up cultural and spiritual interests in favor of the comforts of material life. Whenever possible, the reasons for this lack of culture are seen in the socialist past which is brought into the present by former Soviet bureaucrats or others who are suspected of maintaining strong bonds with the Soviet regime in one or an other way: »These cynical chameleons, some cold-blooded, some hot-headed, are now trying to rewrite history, to be at the head of all possible movements, and in addition to gather all regalia, awards, bonuses, and medals which are being handed out according to one's devotion to the present state of Lithuania.«[62] The biggest lack of culture, nevertheless, is attached to the provincial population mentioned before as »sugar beets«. They are seen to be uneducated, conservative, easy to manipulate in their political as well as moral attitudes, retreating from social life rather than contributing to it in productive ways. In this context, the Lithuanian philosopher Leonidas Donskis used the term »culture of poverty« to designate social groups accepting the role of innocent victims in society. »Consciousness of victimhood is motivated by the belief of malevolent and sinister forces manifesting themselves through secret and elusive human agencies (...). The principle of evil is permanently ascribed to the powerful majority, while the principle of good is reserved exclusively for the powerless minority. It follows that I can not err because I happen to belong to a small vulnerable and fragile group or vice versa.«[63]

The new migrants are also under attack, mostly by other generations of migrants who accuse them of lacking culture in terms of inherent and genuine

60   Darius Kuolys, »Valdžios atotrūkis nuo visuomenės – kaip 1940–aisiais«, in: *http://www.delfi.lt /archive/ article.php?id=7524329* (2005) (accessed on December 21st, 2005).

61   Steven L. Sampson, »Money without Culture, Culture Without Money: Eastern Europe's Nouveaux Riches«, in: *Anthropological Journal on European Cultures. World View, Political Behaviour and Economy in the Post-Communist Transition* 3/1 (1994), pp. 7–30, in particular p. 7.

62   Tamošaitytė, »Price of Boredom«, op.cit. (note 29), p. 39.

63   Leonidas Donskis, »The Unbearable Lightness of Change«, in: *Forms of Freedom. Lithuanian Culture and Europe after 1990*, ed. by Almantas Salamvičius (Vilnius: Kultūros barai, 2005), pp. 11–34, in particular p.14.

Lithuanian culture patterns. Furthermore, it is assumed that they have lost certain qualities and even have become »contaminated« by being exposed to the Communist culture.[64]

Finally, even intellectuals are seen to lack culture, to be passive and conformist in their analysis of dominant ideologies, unable to adapt to the current cultural and social context. »The professors, many of them old communists, are praising the free market economy while the students constitute one of the most passive social groups in the country. Their ideal is to find a well-paid job as quickly as possible or to emigrate as soon as they have got their diploma.«[65] The social role of intellectuals actually seems to be eroding. While some of them were occupied with creating the official culture of Soviet Lithuania and the others maintained and (re-)invented national culture during the Soviet occupation and later, their former roles have become superfluous in the face of ready-made patterns of cultural identity which obviously do not need to be legitimized further. For politicians oriented towards the market economy, intellectual statements are unimportant since statistics of economic growth are regarded as telling all. Even if material poverty is recognized to be a problem for intellectuals, it is not so much seen as a social problem but rather as resulting from their inability to leave behind their accustomed role in the Soviet times when they were supported by the state. Lack of culture then stands for a collective feeling relevant to all social groups in their respective situations.

If we understand culture to be the main symbolic system by which collective cultural identities are construed,[66] the strong feeling of lack of culture documented in Lithuanian public discourses could be interpreted as expressing a fragmentation of collective identity or at least as a disagreement on the question what collective identity is all about. Social moods indicate that there is not one single collective identity but rather a variety of black box-identities having little connection to each other. Their only common ground is the very feeling of lacking culture. Most of those participating in public debates regard this fragmented identity as a problem (if not a tragedy), first of all because it makes Lithuania's place in Europe look like one of uncertainty and discontinuity – one which is not in accordance to the envisioned role the country should take. Consequently, the Lithuanian participation in EU institutions is being compared with an empty ritual, »sitting in the meetings which is an aim in itself«,[67] just as the observed passive behavior of major parts of the population becoming »an end in itself, it leads to no other goal and thus in fact is a ritual«.[68] This situation is understood

---

64   Čiubrinskas, »Transnational Identity and Heritage«, op. cit. (note 28), p. 61.
65   Beresnevičius, »Linkes Vakuum«, op.cit. (note 21), p. 186.
66   Peter Niedermüller,»Politischer Wandel«, op.cit. (note 54), here p. 143.
67   Kuolys, »Valdžios atotrūkis nuo visuomenės«, op.cit. (note 56).
68   Degutis, »Social Structure«, op.cit. (note 52), p. 6.

to be a local problem by which an essential difference between East and West becomes apparent: »What in Western Europe was one of the greatest civilization shaping movements in centuries, in Central and Eastern Europe took the form of the mandatory economic and political programs to be implemented by the successor states of the Soviet Union.«[69]

Conclusions

In this paper, I have described social tensions and uncertainties which accompany processes of identity construction and representation in today's Lithuania. In doing so, I have analyzed the interplay between political ideologies and collective as well as individual images of a successful European life and the European person. I have also shown how some stereotyped images of self and other, East and West, which can be found in an anthropological research on postsocialist societies, are being internalized in Lithuanian society and integrated on different levels as part of these complex identification processes. The social uncertainties described here are often discussed within the Lithuanian public discourses and understood to be specific Lithuanian problems. By trying to lock all these uncertainties and discontinuities of a modern globalized state into its own national »ghetto«, consequently bringing past und present under control, Lithuanian society is making strenuous efforts towards being »really European«.

The economic elites are seen as representing the »*Homo Europaeus*« or the »real Europeans«. On the one hand, due to their publicly recognized image and privileged social position, these social actors feel free from collective uncertainties. The seemingly missing collective identity, which is regarded as problematic for many social actors, does not deter their efforts in constructing elite identities according to the neoliberal idea of a self-responsible and independent person. On the other hand, the elite status of these persons is tightly linked with and dependent on the political and social contexts within which they are active. So they realize the necessity of reorganizing their professional activities and networks and private life models and adepting them to the new political, social, and economic situation of Lithuania as an EU member state.

The lack of material resources and social competences, which makes it impossible to live up to the western oriented European identity models, can be seen as one reason why Europe still seems to be a place far away for many other Lithuanians. More important to me, however, is the basic dualism underlying

---

69   Donskis, »Lightness of Change«, op.cit. (note 59), p. 25.

the construction of Lithuanian self-images. The internalized stereotyped images of backward East, different from the West, which I described above in the context of research on postsocialist transformation, are dominating the Lithuanian public debate in which collective visions of present, past, and future are negotiated. Problematic issues are seen only as a result of the socialist past, differences between East and West are exaggerated and the continuities between past and present are ignored and only specific ways of being European are regarded as legitimate. As a consequence of this dualism, the »socialist heritage« turns out to be still deeply rooted within the society, provoking the common feeling of living in »yet another Europe«.[70]

It therefore seems reasonable to work towards achieving a more sensitive and differentiated analytical approach to these self-images both within the particular local Lithuanian public discourse as well as within the more general scientific discourse on postsocialism.

In the case of Lithuania, this approach would give a possibility to distance oneself from dominant westwards oriented ideologies to cross the symbolic borders and to imagine Lithuanian society as a social space where different streams of people, commodities, and money cross the territory. In addition to those emigrants heading westwards, one would discover other entities and even immigrants crossing the borders to the East, highlighting economic relations, cultural influences (mostly on the level of popular culture), and migrant workers from the GUS as well as other countries. One could therefore claim that in fact there is not one single social space but rather a multiple one having visible as well as invisible sides, both equally real and important for social life, but not equally represented in public discourse and political ideology. Even if the eastern side of this space is almost invisible, the western part of it cannot be regarded as being the natural or the only one. If this particular differentiated approach were to be pursued, it probably would become easier to feel free from the so called »socialist heritage«, different visions of history and future would be accepted as valid, and other forms of constructing and representing identities would gain legitimacy and social visibility.

---

70   Donskis, »Lightness of Change«, op.cit. (note 59), p. 25.

Histories of Violence: National Identity and Public Memory of Occupation and Terror in Estonia

David Feest

The twentieth century has been a violent century for Estonia. But not all violence is remembered alike. The punitive expeditions after the upheaval of 1905 at most occupy a small corner in collective memory. Even World War I and the struggle for independence after the withdrawal of the German troops play only an indirect part in the public consciousness. Apart from being beyond the scope of the life-time experience of most contemporaries, these images have been overshadowed by the experience of mass terror during the first Soviet occupation and the memories of World War II, as well as of the hardships of the postwar years that proved to be everything but a time of peaceful reconstruction.

The remaking of Estonia is still connected to the commemoration of painful parts of history, yet, as the late Maurice Halbwachs has pointed out, memory is not a depository or storage. It is reconstructed within the changing social frameworks of present life, and only those facts that have a place in them are remembered.[1] This paper deals with collective memory, that is, the construction of memory by groups.

Of course, just as identities are manifold, there is no single way of commemorating in a society. In Estonia, those who remember the events of the 1940s generally have a different approach to that of the post-1991 generation, and former dissidents have a different relationship to Estonian history as compared with former members of the Communist Party. Therefore, I will first try to point out which historical discussions have special significance for the forming of national identity and who is leading them in public. Then I will move on to one of the most controversial topics in recent times in coming to terms with World War II outside the academic world: the erection and eventual removing of a statue commemorating Estonian soldiers in German SS-units. I will try to show how different memory cultures partly overlap, while they are incompatible in other respects. This is an article about the public discourse of memory that operates in

---

1 M. Halbwachs, *Das Gedächtnis und seine sozialen Bedingungen* [Memory and its Social Conditions] (Berlin: Luchterhand, 1966), p. 390.

conflicting modes of remembering the past and the diverse strategies of making sense of historical experiences.[2]

Institutions of Commemoration and Their Functions

Memory serves functions in a society that, while not determining wholly what is remembered, yet do influence which aspects are stressed and which ones are neglected or omitted. The most explicit expressions of such functional aims can be found in the programmatic statements of the organizations that are directly in charge of coping with the past. This is especially true for the institutions researching the crimes committed against the Estonian people.

In the narrowest sense of the word, their function is to offer (and demand) that acknowledgment be given to the victims by showing the historical scale of terror as well as by drawing legal conclusions.[3] Since in Estonia there has been no truth commission as in South Africa, some organizations are trying to satisfy this need on their own. Apart from non-governmental victims organizations, most of which since 1989 are organized under the umbrella of the »Estonian Association of the Illegally Repressed Memento«, a »State Commission for the Examination of the Politics of Repression during the Occupations« was founded in 1992 to evaluate the damages committed under the Soviet and German occupations. Meticulously adding up the results of repression in a long row of single research projects, the commission has mainly been engaged in basic quantitative research.[4] The interpretation of the facts, however, had been fixed beforehand

2   Since my paper deals with the Estonian identity, the point of view of the Russian minority will not be dealt with here. I acknowledge, however, that for an adequate overall picture of history culture in Estonia this would be a welcome addition.

3   E. Sarv, »Õiguse vastu ei saa ükski: Eesti taotlused ja rahvusvaheline õigus« [No one can Challenge the Law. Estonian Claims and the International Law], in: *Okupatsioonide Repressiivpoliitika Uurimise Riiklik Komisjon* 11 (Tartu, 1997).

4   H. Lindmäe, »Suvesõda Viljandimaal 1941« [The Summer War in Viljandi County, 1941], in: *Okupatsioonide Repressiivpoliitika Uurimise Riiklik Komisjon* 21 (Tartu, 2004); I. Paavle, »Saksa okupatsioon 1941–1944: hukatud ja vangistuses hukkunud« [The German Occupation 1941-1944], in: *Okupatsioonide Repressiivpoliitika Uurimise Riiklik Komisjon* 17 (Tartu, 2002); V. Salo, »Population losses 1940–1941: citizens of Jewish nationality«, in: *Okupatsioonide Repressiivpoliitika Uurimise Riiklik Komisjon* 18 (Tartu, 2002); A. Kurgvel & H. Lindmäe, »Pro Patria. Auraamat teises maailmasõjas langenud Eesti vabadusvõitlejaile« [Pro Patria. Book of Honours for the Estonian Freedom Fighters who died in World War II], in: *Okupatsioonide Repressiivpoliitika Uurimise Riiklik Komisjon* 12 (Tartu, 1998); E. Sarv, »Õiguse vastu ei saa ükski«, op.cit. (note 3); P. Varju, »Eesti rahva inimohvrid nõukogude ja saksa okupatsioonide ajal 1940–1953« [Human Victims amongst the Estonian People during the Soviet and German Occupation, 1940–1953], in: *Okupatsioonide Repressiivpoliitika*

in the program of the »State Commission«, when the exploration of the »genocidal crimes« committed by the Soviet occupational force was set as the aim of research.[5] In doing so, the »State Commission« is dedicated to a clear-cut dualism between the Soviet occupational force set to destroy the Estonian people and the victims of these efforts throughout the Soviet years. It is not surprising that under these premises there is hardly an area of life that cannot be described as having been damaged by Soviet force, be it in education, the economy, ecology, culture, public health, or mental health.[6] Also, this perspective implies strong assumptions about Estonian identity, mainly that Estonian lifestyle and culture is seen as a clear antipode to Soviet lifestyle. Thus, the »State Commission« also implicitly provides an ideal image of an untainted Estonian identity beyond Soviet corruption.

Other organizations have been more explicit regarding the *identity-building* function of their work. The Kistler-Ritso Estonian Foundation was founded by Olga Kistler-Ritso in Washington State in 1998 to »help to determine an identity, to define and consolidate a national consciousness« and to »teach the importance of statehood to a young nation«.[7] In the Estonian section of its

Uurimise Riiklik Komisjon 10 (Tartu 1997); U. Tõnnus, »›Soomepoiste‹ langenud« [The Perished »Finnish Boys«], in: *Okupatsioonide Repressiivpoliitika Uurimise Riiklik Komisjon* (Tartu, 1996); P. Lotman & A. Lõhmus, »4000 Eesti raamatute hävitamine nõukogude võimu poolt« [The Destruction of 4000 Books through the Soviet Power], in: *Okupatsioonide Repressiivpoliitika Uurimise Riiklik Komisjon* (Tartu, 1995); J. Vessik & P. Varju, »Saaremaa inimkaotused esimese nõukogude okupatsiooni tagajärjel« [The Loss of People on Saaremaa as Result of the First Soviet Occupation], in: *Okupatsioonide Repressiivpoliitika Uurimise Riiklik Komisjon* 6 (Tartu, 1995); Salo, »E. V. kaadriohvitseride saatus: 1938–1944« [The Fate of The Officers of the Estonian Republic: 1938–1944], in: *Okupatsioonide Repressiivpoliitika Uurimise Riiklik Komisjon* 7 (Tartu, 1994); J. Kangilaski & E. Lamp, »Eesti kunstielu ja okupatsioonide repressiivpoliitika« [Estonian Art Life and the Politics of Repression during the Occupations] in: *Okupatsioonide Repressiivpoliitika Uurimise Riiklik Komisjon* 3 (Tartu, 1994); Varju, »Eesti laste küüditamine 14. juunil 1941 kui genotsiidikuritegu« [The Deportation of Children on July 14th, 1941 as Genocidal Crime], in: *Okupatsioonide Repressiivpoliitika Uurimise Riiklik Komisjon* 2 (Tartu, 1994); Varju, »Eesti poliitilise eliidi saatusest« [On the Fate of Estonias Political Elite], in: *Okupatsioonide Repressiivpoliitika Uurimise Riiklik Komisjon* 1 (Tartu. 1994); A. Oll, *Nõukogude kaug-põhja vangilaagrid ja eesti poliitvangid kolõmal* [Soviet Prison Camps in the High North and Estonian Political Prisoners in Kolyma], in: *Okupatsioonide Repressiivpoliitika Uurimise Riiklik Komisjon* 14 (Tallinn, 1999).

5   »Okupatsioonide Repressiivpoliitika Uurimise Riiklik Komisjon« [State Commission for the Research of the Politics of Repression during the Occupations], http://www.okupatsioon.ee /koostoo/orurk.html (accessed on December 12, 2005).

6   The research of the State Commission was summarized recently in Ülo Ennuste et al. (Eds), *Valge Raamat. Eesti Rahva kaotustest okupasioonide läbi. 1940–1991* [The White Book. The Losses of the Estonian Nation throughout the Occupations. 1940–1991] (Tallinn: Eesti Entsüklpeediakirjastus, 2005).

7   Põhisuunad, »Teadustegevuse põhisuunad ja prioriteedid« [The main Directions and Priorities of Research], http://www.okupatsioon.ee/sihtasutusest=koikfreimid.html (accessed on December 12, 2005).

web page (and only there) the foundation makes very straightforward remarks regarding how to achieve this: »The main aim of the scholarly work is to seek and find answers to the central questions of Estonian contemporary history: Who are our heroes? Who are our friends? Who are our enemies?«[8] In spite of such somewhat sappy slogans the foundation has been quite differentiated in its actual work. Research and conferences granted by the Kistler-Ritso Foundation included basic research as well as methodological discussions.[9] Furthermore, the main project of the foundation, the »Museum of the Occupation and Fight for Freedom« in Tallinn opened in July 2003, is surprising in its focus on everyday life in Soviet Estonia.[10]

The so called »president's commission« (actually the »Estonian International Commission for the Investigation of Crimes against Humanity«), founded in October 1998 under the auspices of the late former president Lennart Meri,[11] has put an even more differentiated approach on its agenda. According to its description of itself, the commission is not only committed to researching crimes against humanity in Estonia, but also »to overcoming the stereotypes about groups« that were the basis of many of these crimes«.[12]

The differences between these organizations are not as large as they may seem. Their personnel overlaps a great deal, cooperation has been fruitful, and coordination has been provided by the S-Center (*S-Keskus*) that was formerly called the »Research Center for the Soviet Times«, but which broadened its view

---

8 Ibid.

9 For instance: Otsinguil, *Ajaloolise tõe otsinguil* [Searching for Historical Truth], Volume I–III, (Tallinn: Umara, 1999–2000); E. Tarvel, *Kõrgemad võimu vahendajad ENSV-s. Eestimaa Kommunistliku Partei Keskkomitee sekretärid 1940–1990* [The Higher Intermediaries of Power in the ESSR. The Secretaries of the Central Committee of the Communist Party of Estonia 1940–1990] (Tallinn: Kistler-Ritso Eesti sihtasutus, 2000); Tarvel, *Eestimaa Kommunistliku Partei Keskkomitee organisatsiooniline struktuur 1940–1991* [The Organizational Structure of the Central Committee of the Communist Party of Estonia 1940–1991] (Tallinn: Kistler-Ritso Eesti sihtasutus, 2002).

10 The historical work is being coordinated by the renowned historian Enn Tarvel. About the museum see: H. Ahonen & E. Tarvel, *Asjad ja esemed: Eesti Okupatsioonide Muuseum. Items and objects: Museum of the Occupation of Estonia. Die Dinge und die Gegenstände: Das Estnische Okkupationsmuseum* (Tallinn: Lähimineviku Okupatsioonide Muuseum, 2002); there is also a short movie on the founding of the museum: *Okupatsiooni ja Vabatusvõitluse muuseumi rajamine* [On the Construction of the Museum of Occupation and Fight for Freedom], DVD 2003.

11 The board includes such diverse international celebrities as the former Danish foreign minister Uffe Ellemann-Jensen, the chairman of the International Relations Commission of the American Jewish Committee Nicholas Lane, the journalist Paul Goble and the chairman of the Russian »Memorial« Arseny Roginsky.

12 *Eestimaa Kommunistliku Partei Keskkomitee organisatsiooniline struktuur 1940–1991* [The Organizational Structure of the Central Comittee of the Communist Party of Estonia 1940–1991] (Tallinn: Kistler-Ritso Eesti sihtasutus, 2005).

to cover the German occupation as well.[13]   None of these organizations has provided radically new interpretations of the past, but they all had their part in picking up existing ones, collecting memories and interpreting them in a broader context so as to help make sense out of them and result in their wider acceptance.

Topics and Modes of Memory

Estonian historical memory draws directly from the lively experience of the 1940s, beginning with the pact between Hitler and Stalin and the invasion of the Soviet army, and covering war and mass terror. These events are still sensitive points in the collective memory.

The shock of being deprived of independent statehood in 1940 without a single shot being fired can hardly be overestimated. The Republic, whose self-esteem so dominantly relied on the memories of the Independence War, was given away without calling its veterans to arms or giving the younger generation a chance to live up to the heroic images with which they had been raised. To make matters worse, the sovietization of the country was soon accompanied by terror that drew increasingly wider circles. While the initial elimination of the old elites could still be perceived as clear-cut violence against individuals, the deportation of almost 11,000 people in June 1941 made such an interpretation virtually impossible.[14] The terror seemed arbitrary, directed against the Estonian nation as such and made practically everyone a potential victim. By this point, individual suffering was merged into a collective fate. When the German troops crossed the border of the country in the summer of 1941, they were greeted as liberators by a majority of the population. However, independence was not restored and the terror continued, although on a smaller scale for the Estonians. The re-occupation by the Red Army in 1944 was followed by attempts to crush resistance and to get on with introducing Soviet structures in the country. Secret police and army units alike practiced excessive force. The post-war terror culminated in the deportation of some 20,000 people to Siberia in March 1949, the majority of whom were women and children. Again, it was difficult to foresee who would be hit and who would be spared.[15]   People, even party secretaries,

---

13   S-Keskus, »S-Keskus. Lähiajaloo uurimiskeskus« [S-Center. Research Center for Contemporary History] (2005), http://www.s-keskus.arhiiv.ee (accessed on January 19, 2006).

14   A. Rahi-Tamm, »Inimkaotused« [Loss of People], in: *Valge Raamat. Eesti Rahva kaotustest okupasioonide läbi, 1940-1991* [The Losses of the Estonian Nation throughout the Occupations. 1940-1991]/Okupatsioonide repressiivpoliitika uurimise riiklik komisjon, 2004, ed. by Ennuste et al. (Tallinn: Eesti Entsüklpeediakirjastus, 2005), pp. 23-42, in particular p. 25.

15   Officially, many were family members of the already arrested, meaning that even in Soviet

expected further deportations of a much greater number or even the deportation of all Estonians.[16]

It is hardly astonishing that the mass deportations of 1941 and 1949 were central issues when memories of repression could openly be discussed during the late 1980s. The public debate focused on the aims and character of mass terror, as well as on the number of victims.[17] Thorough research followed soon after. Publications of the most important documents were edited and lists of victims compiled.[18]

However, in order to make sense of experiences of violence, people tend to refer to bigger frames of explanation. In the Estonian case, different dominant interpretations have given the devastating experiences meaning in a broader context, or provided an expansion of the basic types of memories. On the most general level, two major modes of memory can be distinguished that appear as two sides of one coin. The first is the understanding of Estonia as a victim nation; the second is the self-image as a rebellious people. Both are supported by connections to historically remote events.

The first mode can itself be cut down into different types. In the most general form the victim image appears as an understanding of the Estonians as being, and always having been, victims of foreign forces. The fact that since the time of the »national awakening« in the nineteenth century Estonian history has all along been perceived as a history of oppression made the Soviet Terror fall in place with the long history of domination by foreign powers: by the Knights of the Cross, by the Baltic Germans, by the Russian Empire, by the German Army in World War I, and by the Soviet Union and Nazi Germany. (For some, the European Union seems to be taking over this function). Less generally, the victim image is often narrowed down to being the victim of Russian aggression. The enduring threat from the East is confirmed historically by the invasion of the Swedish provinces by Ivan the Terrible in the course of which the city of Tartu/Dorpat was completely destroyed, by the brutal conquering of the same

---

terms, they carried no individual guilt. Others were the so called »kulaks«, farmers who were accused of having exploited their fellow men – a more than problematic point in a country that had undergone one of the most radical agrarian reforms of Europe in the mid-twenties. The actual aim seems to have been to force the farmers to join the kolkhozes, but probably also to cut off the anti-Soviet guerilla forces from their food supplies.

16   M. Arold (ed.), *Märtsivapustused* [The Successions of March](Tartu: Tungal, 1995), pp. 34-38.

17   For a concise summary of the discussion see: A. Rahi, *1949. aasta märtsiküüditamine Tartu linnas ja maakonnas* [The Deportations of March 1948 in the and County of Tartu] (Tartu: Kleio, 1998); A. Rahi, »Massirepressioonide uurimine ja Balti koostöö« [Research on Mass Repression and Baltic Cooperation], in: *Ajalooline Ajakiri* 1 (1999), 104, pp. 87–92.

18   Rahi, *1949*, op.cit. (note 17); Rahi, »Massirepressioonide uurimine ja Balti koostöö«, op.cit. (note 17); »Dokumente, 1949. aasta märtsiküüditamisest« [Documents on the March-Deportations of 1949], in: *Akadeemia* 1-10 : 11 (1999), pp. 620–630; 821–831; 1051–1068; 1283–1291; 1510–1517; 1736–1743; 1993–2016; 2176–2181; 2648–2655.

provinces by Peter the Great during the Great Nordic War, by the politics of Russification in the late nineteenth century, by the Bolshevik attempts to form a Soviet state in Estonia after 1917, and by the war of independence against Soviet Russia up to the occupation of 1940. These events are all taken as instances of the general rule concerning Russia's eternal thrust westward.[19] Even in 2003, an expert on the armed resistance described the historical dimension of Bolshevik terror in Estonia as going back to Ivan the Terrible.[20]

Now and again, the aim behind this historical thrust westward has been seen in a century-old attempt to annihilate the Estonian troublemakers once and for all. »The Soviet Union«, Enn Sarv of the ›State Commission‹ wrote, »obviously aimed at uniting the Baltic region with Russia for all time and cleansing it of the peoples there that had already caused the Great Russian imperialism trouble for some centuries«.[21] As a former deportee, Sarv is perhaps the most consistent exponent of the genocide thesis, which is basically shared by the »State Commission«.[22] For Sarv, Russification was the ultimate goal behind all other plans. He interprets industrialization as merely a pretext for Russian immigration by explaining that the bombing of Tallinn was an instrument used to make room for larger buildings. These in turn were intended for Russian immigrants, whose privileges Sarv sees as part of a strategy to make life too uncomfortable for Estonians to keep up with reproduction.[23]

Convincing arguments have been put forth against the genocide thesis, stressing the clear correlation between industrialization and immigration, as well as the important role that nationality continued to play in Soviet times.[24] Neverthe-

---

19   In the nineteenth century, the nationalist movement was still undecided about the image of Russia and a pro-Russian wing existed that sought Russian aid in opposing the Baltic Germans. Consequently, in Soviet times, attempts were made to establish a counter-myth that figured the Russians as allies of the Estonian people in their fight against the German oppressors.

20   T. Noormets (ed.), *Metsavennad Suvesõjas 1941: Eesti relvastatud vastupanuliikumine Omakaitse dokumentides* [The Forest Brethren in the Summer War 1941: The Estonian Armed Resistance Movement in Documents of the Self-Defense] (Tallinn: Riigarhiiv, 2003), in: *Ad fontes* 13, p. 23.

21   Sarv, *Õiguse vastu ei saa ükski*, op.cit. (note 3), p. 65.

22   See for instance: Varju, *Eesti laste küüditamine 14. juunil 1941 kui genotsiidikuritegu*, op.cit. (note 4); Vessik & Varju, *Saaremaa inimkaotused esimese nõukogude okupatsiooni tagajärjel*, op.cit. (note 4); and the above remarks on the aims of the Commission).

23   Sarv, *Õiguse vastu ei saa ükski*, op.cit. (note 3).

24   The ideology of industrialisation is stressed in: Parming 1980. It seems more plausible that the terror was not directed against the Estonian nation as such, but aimed at remolding it into the kind of nation that would fit into the Soviet framework. In the same vein the politician and publicist Jaak Allik sees the terror mainly as an instrument of power and states: »In the Estonian SSR the Estonian statehood was not prohibited as such, but only a statehood, that separated itself from the USSR.« J. Allik, »Jäi kestma Kalevite kange rahvas ...« [The Strong People of the Kalev's Lasted ...], in: *Eesti identiteet ja iseseisvus* [Estonian Identity and Independence], ed. by A. Bertricau (Tallinn: Avita, 2001), pp. 167-175, in particular p. 169.

less, the Genocide Thesis has to be taken seriously as a method by which many Estonians cope with their history and specifically the mass terror of the Forties. And after all, there have been deportations of whole nations under Stalin. And horrid facts such as the high number of deported children, many of whom died on the trip to Siberia, are hard to make sense of outside such grand designs.[25] The feeling of being endangered as a nation is very real for many Estonians.

The positive counterpart to the victim image is that of the freedom fighter. Especially the so-called »forest brethren«, who fought the occupation from the dense woods, have become legendary symbols of the Estonian urge for freedom. Being criminalized as »bandits« by official Soviet historiography, the anti-Soviet partisans lived on in oral tradition as well as in the surveys of the Western exile; facts and legends thus became intertwined. In the last decade, much work has been done to base accounts on reliable sources.[26] Nevertheless, the »war in the woods« has remained a highly symbolic topic and serves all of the aforementioned functions. Most notably, it has been used to substantiate the claim to independence as future Prime Minister Mart Laar put it in an early book: »a nation that does not fight for its independence does not deserve it«.[27] Also, the freedom fighters serve as a role model for patriotic behavior and self-sacrifice. By showing that despite the painful »silent submission« of 1939[28] the Estonian nation was not ready to give itself up, the resistance is an important reference point for contemporary Estonian identity.

Research has shown that the resistance in the woods was many-sided. Shortly before the German army invaded, partisan groups had already begun attacking Soviet positions and participated in driving the Soviet troops and the newly founded »destruction battalions« out of the country. Analogous to the Finnish winter war – and to distinguish their own war actions from the German aims

25 Varju, *Eesti laste küüditamine 14. juunil 1941 kui genotsiidikuritegu,* op.cit. (note 4).

26 E. Laasi, ed., *Vastupanuliikumine Eestis 1944–1949: dokumentide kogu.* (Tallinn: Näomm, 1992); M. Laar, *Metsavennad* [Forest Brethren] (1993); compare the later account: Laar, »The Armed Resistance Movement in Estonia from 1944 to 1956«, in: *The Anti-Soviet Resistance in the Baltic States,* ed. by A. Anušauskas (Vilnius: Du Ka, 1999); Noormets, *Metsavennad Suvesõjas 1941,* op.cit. (note 20); T. Tannberg, »Relvastatud vastupanuliikumine Eestis aastatel 1944–1953« [The Armed Resistance Movement in Estonia, 1944–1953], in: *Tuna* 1; comparative overview in the Baltic States: Anušauskas, op.cit., pp. 24–30.

27 M. Laar, *Eesti 1944. Tundmatu autori silme läbi* [Estonia 1944. Through the Eyes of an Unknown Author]. (Olion: Tallinn, 1993). [First published in: *Vaba Eesti* (Toronto), vol. 69-91, September 20th, to 1983 December 6th, 1983] Later he took a less moralistic point of view by stating: »A country that does not fight for its freedom will loose it«, M. Laar, »The Armed Resistance Movement in Estonia from 1944 to 1956«, op.cit. (note 26), p. 209.

28 This is the title of a book about the entanglement of the political elite in the events of 1939, that recently stirred up some emotion. See: M. Ilmjärv, »Silent Submission: Formation of Foreign Policy of Estonia, Latvia and Lithuania: Period from mid-1920s to Annexation in 1940«, in: *Studia Baltica Stockholmiensia* 24 (Stockholm, 2004).

– these activities have later been termed the »summer war.«[29] While resistance against the German occupation force remained scarce and was hardly ever militant, after the war, many of the former soldiers continued fighting as partisans in the woods; joined by a very mixed crowd of mainly young men, who tried to evade Soviet conscription. Others who joined hoped that the allied forces would soon set an end to the Soviet occupation. Thus, by far not all »forest brethren« were taking part in fighting; sometimes even whole families took to the woods along with their farm animals, continuing to farm on small plots between the trees.[30] The most active resistance took place in 1945, and after the mass terror in 1949 resistance revived again briefly. It is estimated that about 30.000 people hid in the woods.[31]

In order to fulfill the identity-building function, memories of the resistance have to be selective. It is striking how the armed resistance has been in the center of attention, being most apt to demonstrate an heroic, unconditional will and national strength. »The Estonian forest brethren knew how to fight and knew how to die.«[32] Also, the resistance against the Soviet occupation remains dominant, while the fewer instances of anti-German resistance, let alone the Communist one, are hardly ever mentioned. While the quantitative relations can partly explain this phenomenon, it also echoes the functions that memories fulfill today. It is the material and mental heritage of the long lasting Soviet occupation that is troubling the people now, not the short lived German occupation more than 65 years ago. This also accounts for the fact that the term »collaboration« is strictly reserved for members of the Communist Party and hardly ever applies to cooperation with the Nazi forces. While collaborating with the »lesser evil« in order to prevent worse can be a patriotic act, siding with the »greater evil« is seen as collaboration in the negative sense of the word.

Concerning Estonia's relations with Western Europe, however, the cooperation with Nazi Germany is one of the most controversial issues. While the harm that was done to the small state and its people during Soviet times is increasingly acknowledged in the West, the participation in German army units remains a bone of contention; the question has also remained unsettled within Estonia. As I will try to show in the following paragraphs, attempts to adapt to the Western European understanding without giving up essential elements of a uniting identity have only begun.

---

29 Noormets (ed.), *Metsavennad Suvesõjas 1941*, op.cit. (note 20), p. 69.

30 Laar, »The Armed Resistance Movement in Estonia from 1944 to 1956«, op.cit. (note 26), p. 218.

31 Tannberg, »Relvastatud vastupanuliikumine Eestis aastatel 1944–1953«, op.cit. (note 26), pp. 26, 29; Laar, »The Armed Resistance Movement in Estonia from 1944 to 1956«, op.cit. (note 26), p. 217.

32 Ibid. p. 228.

Ambiguous Allies: Estonians in World War II and the »Localized Interpretation«

Estonians were not the natural allies of the Germans. The Estonian image of Germans was shaped through the Baltic German minority that had been the dominant group up until World War I. Many Estonians perceived them as a threat even during the years of independence from 1918 to 1940 and in particular until their resettlement in 1939. Furthermore, Germany and Russia were both seen as potential dangers in foreign policy.[33] It was one year of Soviet terror that altered the situation and led to Estonians greeting the German troops as liberators. Although hopes of a restoration of Estonian independence under German occupation proved futile, active resistance was scarce. There were three reasons for this. First, Estonians were not among the main victims of Nazi ideology and the Jewish minority was relatively small. Before the war, 4.500 Jews lived in Estonia; 1.000 remained in the country when the Nazi troops invaded. They were all killed.[34] Secondly, plans for settling Germans in the Baltic as part of the *Generalplan Ost* (General Eastern Plan) were postponed due to the war effort.[35] The third factor was the common enemy. The closer the Soviet Army moved to the Estonian border, the more Estonians took on the belief that it was best to fight the war on the German side in order to prevent a recurrence of 1941. While conscription numbers had been modest in 1943, indicating a minor interest in assisting the Germans in their war efforts, the numbers changed as the Red Army advanced towards the Estonian Border.[36] Some 50,000 men were mobilized to fight at the front in the 20th *Waffen-Grenadier-Division SS* (1st Estonian, Estonian SS-Division).[37]

Recently, a collection of memories has been published by the »Estonian Club of Fighters in the East-Battalions« (*Eesti Idapataljonide Võitlejate Klubi*) that very

---

33   J. Kivimäe, »›Aus der Heimat ins Vaterland.‹ Die Umsiedlung der Deutschbalten aus dem Blickwinkel estnischer nationaler Gruppierungen« [»From the Home Country to the Fatherland« The Resettlement of the Baltic Germans seen from the Point of View of Estonian national Groups], in: *Nordost-Archiv* 5 (1995), pp. 453–478.

34   A. Kuusik, »Die deutsche Vernichtungspolitik in Estland 1941–1944« [The German Policy of Destruction in Estonia, 1941–1944], in: *Vom Hitler-Stalin-Pakt bis zu Stalins Tod. Estland 1939–1953*, ed. by O. Mertelsmann (StateHamburg: Bibliotheca Baltica, 2005), pp. 130–150, in particular p. 139. See also: E. Gurin-Loov, *Eesti juutide katastroof 1941* [The Catastrophe of the Estonian Jews, 1941] (Tallinn: Eesti Juudi Kogukond, 1994).

35   S. Myllyniemi, *Die Neuordnung der baltischen Länder 1941–1944. Zum nationalsozialistischen Inhalt der deutschen Besatzungspolitik* [The Reconstruction of the Baltic Countries, 1941–1944. On the Content of the National Socialist Occupation Policy] (Helsinki: Vammalan Kirjapaino Oy, 1973), Dissertationes Historicae II, Historiallisia Tutkimuksia, 90, pp. 206 ff.

36   Ibid. p. 229.

37   Ibid. p. 276.

well echoes the way the war experiences are remembered by the veterans.[38] First of all, these memories are individual accounts of people who experienced the Soviet occupation and terror as young men. They joined the army voluntarily or by indirect force, lived through battles and saw fellow men die. They were sent to Germany for schooling, were wounded or taken as prisoners of war. Most tried to reach their home villages or they hid in the forests after their units disintegrated. Many were eventually arrested by the Soviet authorities and deported to Siberia. It is not as much a book about the big story as one about many little stories that add up to a general impression. The memories cover many aspects of everyday life at the front and only a few bear a heroic undertone.

Nonetheless, there are some general notions that go beyond the personal experience. First, due to the public controversies of the last years, most veterans today feel the need to justify themselves for having joined the German side. The decision is explained mostly by their direct experience of violence. The motivation of the young men was often to seek revenge for having personally or through their families suffered under the Communist terror.[39] »Let's go to Russia and bring home the deported and arrested« was a popular slogan among Estonians at the time of their conscription.[40]

In a somewhat larger frame of interpretation, the men often viewed the service in direct continuity to the service in the army of the Estonian Republic. »Most of us had not served in the Estonian army,« one man explains his decision, »and now a good possibility emerged [...].«[41] The soldiers interpreted their army service in a specifically Estonian tradition as the »Freedom War« of 1918–1920, that in many ways formed the founding myth of the first Estonian Republic. »What happened in 1944 on Estonian soil [!] was actually our Second Freedom War«, one veteran explained.[42] Some called the service in the German army the »follow-up war to the Estonian Freedom War«.[43] In the same vein, many soldiers thought of the action as a way to make good what the Estonian Army had failed to do in 1940.[44] That way, many veterans today are convinced of having fought their own war within their own tradition, which was clearly distinct from the German war aims: »We did not join the German army but the Estonian army. Through the creation of these units it was possible to get

---

38   A. Adamson (ed.), *Eesti idapataljonid idarindel 1941–1944/Eesti Idapataljonide Võitlejate Klubi* [Estonian East-Battalions on the Eastern Front, 1941–1944] (Tallinn: Argo, 2004).

39   Ibid. pp. 155, 158.

40   Ibid. p. 116, see also p. 200.

41   Ibid. p. 65, see also pp. 60, 213.

42   Ibid. p. 269.

43   Ibid. p. 90.

44   Ibid. p. 91.

equipment and arms from the German state. We didn't fight *with* the Germans but *against* communism.«[45]

I would like to call this interpretation a localized understanding of the war action Estonians took part in. However, the character of the Estonian military duty within the German army was in fact far more ambiguous. While the rising demand of soldiers made the German forces more ready to include Estonian units, it was not always granted that they would fight in Estonia. Respective promises were already broken in the case of the early recruited East-battalions that assisted in the blockade of Leningrad, while auxiliary police units (*Schutzmannschaften*) fought partisans in Belarus. The Estonian SS-Division, that was eventually to incorporate most of the Estonian men under arms, ended up serving in Czechoslovakia, and the »Narva« battalion fought in the Ukraine as part of the SS-Tank-Division »Viking« before being integrated into the Estonian SS-Division. The fact that in many cases the fighting action did not take place in Estonia, or even near the Estonian border, presents a strong challenge to the »localized« interpretation. In the case of the Leningrad blockade, the geographical connection was still a given. It is telling, however, that in the accounts of 2005, not a single veteran bothered to spare a thought for the question as to what was going on behind the ring of the blockade. This would not have fitted into the picture, because the enemy in the veterans' memories is Communist aggression, and not civilians enduring an ordeal beyond imagination. The actions in the Ukraine, Belarus or in Czechoslovakia are even harder to integrate into the localized picture because they were remote from Estonia, and in many cases directed against partisans fighting an occupation force – just as some of the Estonian soldiers had been or were thought to be doing after the war. Finally, the image of the soldiers as »Estonian freedom fighters« is impossible to maintain for the Estonian soldiers that retreated with the German army after Estonia had fallen to the Soviet Union. The participants felt this painfully. According to the memory of a veteran, »the mood was bad because the fatherland was lost and there was no sense in fighting anymore. But there was no other possibility either.«[46] Estonian soldiers had ultimately become part of the bigger picture and had to suffer it to the end. The horrific last days of the Estonian SS-Division has a firm place in the memories of the participants and are termed the »Czech hell«. After having been engaged in anti-partisan activities in Czechoslovakia, most members of the division were taken prisoners during the days of the »Prague upheaval«, when popular wrath was unloaded most of all against captured SS-men. In most cases, attempts by Estonians to explain the differences between German SS-units and

---

45 Ibid. p. 201, emphasis added.
46 A. Kartau. »Sõjalõpupäevad võõrsil« [The Last Days of the War in a Foreign Country], in: *Postimees* (May 8th, 1995).

foreign units of the Waffen-SS to their enraged attackers proved futile, and many soldiers were shot on the spot.

These explanation problems remain to this day. The fact that Estonians did not usually fight in regular units but were subordinated to the SS has resulted in severe justification problems in the international arena. Historically, it was connected to the rising dominance of the SS in the last years of the war. When Hitler ended recruitment through the *Wehrmacht* in February 1942 and more so when in February 1943 an Estonian SS-Legion was founded (that was later to become the Estonian SS-Division), these units became virtually the only possibility for Estonians to be armed against the approaching Red Army. However, there were many different ways of entering the *Waffen-SS*. Some units, such as the East-Battalions of the *Wehrmacht*, were *nolens-volens* integrated into the SS in August 1943 while others, such as the Security Groups (*Sicherungsgruppen*) of the *Wehrmacht* were disbanded and their members transferred.[47] Furthermore, service was not always voluntary as many men had to choose between working duties in the military industry, auxiliary duties in the *Wehrmacht*, or the Legion, where the latter was strongly propagated.[48]

The situation was different with the *Self-Defense* (*omakaitse*) that was modeled after the »Defense League« (*kaitseliit*) of the inter-war years and consisted of former anti-Soviet partisans. It was subordinated to the SS.[49] Contrary to the Estonian SS-Division *Self-Defense* can be unconditionally called a voluntary organization. As the *Self-Defense* fulfilled police tasks under the control of the occupation force, they were also in charge of persecuting Communists, »antisocials« and Jews. Although their contribution in the murdering of Jews was only indirect, since the responsibility lay with the *Einsatzkommando 1a*, the activities of the Self-Defense nevertheless seriously taints their aura as freedom fighters. It has been pointed out that racist thinking, although not dominant among them, maintained a necessary connection between Communism and Judaism.[50] In

---

47   The status of the border defence regiments remained ambivalent by being transformed into an Estonian SS-border security regiment while keeping the uniforms and ranks of the Wehrmacht (T. Hiio, A. Niglas & P. Kaasik, »Eesti üksused Saksa relvajõududes Teise maailmasõja ajal« [Estonian units in the German Armed Forces during World War II], http://www.-okupatsioon.ee/1940/koikfreimid.html, (accessed on May 1, 2006).

48   Myllyniemi, *Die Neuordnung der baltischen Länder 1941–1944*, op.cit. (note 35), p. 230.

49   The same goes for diverse auxiliary police units that were later integrated into the Estonian SS-division.

50   R. B. Birn, »Collaboration with Nazi Germany in Esastern Europe: the Case of Estonian Security Police«, in: *Contemporary European History* 10 (2001), 2, pp. 181–198, p. 108. Birn shows this with the example of a Jewish woman in Haapsalu whom the Estonian security forces actually tried to save from persecution by proving her innocent of communism. Needless to say, it is an argument that the SS leadership did not follow.

their eyes the persecution of the Jews was part of the anti-Communist struggle, and understood as an act of revenge for the Communist terror of 1940.

Apart from the fact that this interpretation hardly seems convincing, taking into consideration that the small Jewish Community in Estonia proportionally suffered worse than the Estonians during the Soviet deportations of 1940,[51] it is another example of a »localized« interpretation, by being completely insensitive to the larger context of the Holocaust. Among the veterans, there is a general feeling that foreigners with no predisposition towards understanding the local reading of the events have no right to stick their noses into exclusively Estonian affairs. Nazi-hunter Efraim Zurov's tour of Estonia fueled this notion of exclusiveness when he sought information on the alleged war criminal Harry Mannil and made some very general statements about Estonians‹ involvement in the Holocaust. Insisting on having fought their own private war against Bolshevism, the foreword of the recent collection of memories stubbornly states, »the Estonian freedom fighters were not connected to the Jewish problem. They neither owe the Jews a single cent, nor do they want anything from them.«[52] The President's Commission tried to find a compromise by condemning *all* kinds of generalizations. Just as the membership in the *Self-Defense* is no proof of criminal action, it stated, real criminals should not be allowed »to shelter behind a cloak of victim-hood.«[53]

This approach seems valid not only for the Estonians on the German side. Just as the Nazi occupation force recruited soldiers into their ranks, so too did the Soviet forces. Beside the mainly voluntary formation of so called »destruction battalions«, young men were also recruited into the existing 22nd Territorial Corps. Those who were not trusted to be reliable were forced into so-called »work-« or »construction colonies« and »construction battalions«, which were generally called »work battalions.«[54] They were subordinated to the *NKVD* (People's Commisariat for Internal Affairs) and run like prison camps.[55] The 22nd Territorial Corps was disbanded in the autumn of 1941, as it turned out

---

51   Kuusik, »Die deutsche Vernichtungspolitik in Estland 1941–1944«, in: *Vom Hitler-Stalin-Pakt bis zu Stalins Tod. Estland 1939–1953*, op.cit. (note 34); Salo, *Population losses 1940-1941*, op.cit. (note 4). The latter is a publication by the »State Commission«.

52   Adamson, *Eesti idapataljonid idarindel 1941–1944/Eesti Idapataljonide Võitlejate Klubi*, op.cit. (note 38), p. 14.

53   »Conclusions of the Estonian International Commission for the Investigation of Crimes Against Humanity«, http://www.historycommission.ee/temp/conclusions_frame.htm (accessed on January 1st, 2006).

54   U. Usai, »Sissejuhatus«, Introduction in *Eestlased tööpataljonides 1941–1942. Mälestusi ja dokumente* [Estonians in Working-Battalions 1941–1942. Memories and Documents], Vol. @ 1 (Tallinn: Olion, 1993), pp. 5–18, in particular p. 5.

55   The number of deaths due to hunger, disease and executions have been estimated at 10–12,000. (»Population Losses«, in: *World War II and Soviet Occupation in Estonia: A Damages Report*, ed. by J. Kahk (Tallinn: Periodika Publishers, 1991), pp. 33–41, in particular p. 36).

to have a high rate of defection and the soldiers were sent to the work battalions. However, in December 1941, two Estonian rifle divisions were founded, which from September 1942 on formed the 8th Estonian Rifle Corps.[56] The Corps gave some inmates of the work batallions the chance to become soldiers again, where they fought side by side with Russians or Russian-born Estonians. That way, the prospects of the members of the corps were manifold. To be sure, there may have been those who were dedicated fighters for the cause of Communism. But others had been mobilized by force, survived the work battalions and saw the Rifle Corps »as the only possibility to escape the death camp«.[57] Furthermore, many soldiers simply wanted to get home as fast as possible.

In contemporary Estonia, the forced recruits of the Red Army are remembered as victims and perpetrators alike. On the one hand, in general statistics the illegal character of the recruitment is stressed, and the soldiers appear as victims of communism. On the other hand, their direct, and propagandistically intended, involvement in the conquering of Tallinn in September 1944 made them symbols of collaboration with the Soviets. Having been on the winning side for some five decades, the men of the Estonian Corps had trouble finding their place in the master narrative of the re-established Republic. World War II was a »brothers‹ war« in Estonia, in some cases even in the literal sense.

Ultimately, a common ground between the Estonian soldiers on the German and on the Soviet side was an illusion they shared. One veteran of an East-Bataillon admits that his aims of normalizing life in his home country and restoring independence were shared by the Estonians fighting in the Red Army. He soberly concludes, »but we both did not reach our aims.«[58] A collection reflecting the experiences and expectations of the Corps‹ men going beyond the Soviet propaganda would be a worthwhile project.

Memory and Public Space: The Lihula Memorial

But the veterans feel misunderstood in their home country as well. Their experiences are neither shared by the following generation that grew up in Soviet Estonia, nor by the current younger generation adapting to the western Euro-

56   *Ülevaade Eestimaa Kommunistliku Partei ajaloost* [Overview over the History of the Communist Party of Estonia], Vol. 3 (Tallinn: Eesti Riiklik Kirjatus, 1972), p. 479.

57   V. Selge, »Eesti Korpus II Maailmasõjas« [The Estonian Corps in World War II], in: *Eesti riik ja rahvas teises maailmasõjas*, ed. by A. Purre, Vol. 7 (Stockholm: Spanga, 1959), pp. 157–164.

58   Adamson, *Eesti idapataljonid idarindel 1941–1944/Eesti Idapataljonide Võitlejate Klubi*, op.cit. (note 38), p. 201.

pean discourse. The collection of memories contains more than one bitter sentence about the lack of recognition and gratitude, and about the misinformation dissemisated by the press and historians, who are not interested in their story.[59] A recurring topic in the memories is also the young generation of today, which is taking freedom and independence for granted and avoids military service by all means.[60] The current government as well as the parliament ranks among the most unpopular of institutions. According to the one veteran, it should be »chased down the stairs of Dome Hill [the location of the parliament building] with a club.«[61] The background to the latter comment is the controversy surrounding that classic place of memory, which is the monument in Lihula County.

In December 2003, the founder of the Estonian Legion Museum, Leo Tammiksaar, and other Estonian World War II veterans erected a monument in the seaside town Pärnu. It bore a bas-relief depicting an armed soldier in an Estonian Legion army coat and a caption that read: »To all Estonian soldiers who died in World War II for their home country and for a free Europe, 1940–1945«. The local authorities removed it after only nine days, accusing the organizers of playing down the Nazi occupation and war aims. Seeking a compromise Pärnu's mayor Väino Hallikmäe offered his assistance in building a new monument that would not »directly refer to the SS-Legion, but would be dedicated to everybody, who fought for the freedom of Estonia in World War II«.[62]

But the veterans wanted the old monument. In 2004, they found an ally in the somewhat notorious former dissident and political prisoner, Tiit Madisson, who agreed to put up the monument in Lihula where he served as county elder. To emphasize the patriotic motives of the Estonian men, the caption was changed to the localized version: »To the Estonian men that in 1940–1945 fought Bolshevism in the name of reestablishing Estonian independence«. In spite of this change, its erection was prohibited once again. The opening ceremony on August 20th, 2004, which was attended by some one thousand people, became the starting point of a power struggle not only between the veterans and a young political elite, but also between the local and the central authorities. Madisson had hired private security personnel to maintain order while the state police forces left their positions a safe distance away only to escort a Russian television crew past the security men who had initially denied them access to the site. Less than two weeks later, on November 2nd, the situation escalated to

---

59 Ibid. pp. 17, 70.
60 Ibid. p. 60.
61 Ibid. pp. 44, 60.
62 Tigasson, »Pärnusse rajatakse sõjameeste mälestusmärk« [In Pärnu a Monument for the Soldiers is Being Erected], http://www.vabaeuroopa.org/Article.aspx?ID=4080425B-B1A5-432D-8445-83283CD1ED60&m=7&y=2003 2003 (accessed on December 8th, 2005).

Figure 7.1: Lihula Monument in Tallinn

the point where the government in Tallinn took action and had the monument removed despite violent protest of the bystanders, who threw stones and were pushed back with the help of rubber clubs, dogs and tear gas.[63]

The young Prime Minister, Juhan Parts, justified the action by demanding that the soldiers should be remembered by »honoring their actual aims and motives and not a uniform that has been forced onto them.«[64] Just as important, however, was the impression that the government feared the monument would make on the international community. The statements suggest that the problem was not in the first place a lack of understanding for the way the veterans wanted to remember the war, but rather the fear that this could not be communicated to foreign countries, especially to Western Europe. »In the world the Lihula monument is not understood«, the press department of the ministry for foreign affairs quoted Minister Kristiina Ojuland, and stated the concern that the democratic world would equate the German uniform with Nazism.[65] Many newspaper commentators shared this position of being worried about instantly ruining Estonia's international reputation that had taken so long to build up.[66]

This argument was received very badly by proponents of the monument. Giving in to foreign interests fits well into the general historical picture of oppression by alien forces. Madisson, who is also known to adhere to theories of freemasonry and to deny the Holocaust, reacted by writing a book that depicts Estonia as being enslaved by a »spiritual occupation«, as still being run by Communists, and as a victim of international conspiracy and false friends in the West. The book sold out in no time.[67]

However, the uneasiness over the monument was by no means provoked only by strategic concerns about the reaction of the western countries. For many, the issue was not so much what the rest of Europe would think about it, but rather, regarding how European Estonia is. After all, the concept of belonging to Europe was already dominant during the national awakening in the nineteenth century, and remains one of the uncontested elements of Estonian national conscience. While people like Madisson criticized the influence of Western political correctness, in the overall discussion, Europe still worked as an argument. »In Europe

---

63 Rahvas, »Rahvas loopis Lihula mälestussamba mahavõitjad kividega« [The People threw Stones at Those Who Removed the Memorial], in: *Postimees* (February 9th, 2004).

64 Ibid.

65 Ojuland, »Ojuland: maailmas ei mõistetud Lihula monumenti (Välisministeeriumi pressitalitus)« [Ojuland: in the world the Lihula monument is not understood (press department of the ministry for foreign affairs)] (2003), www.vm.ee/ee/est/kat_42/aken_prindi/4790.html (accessed on December 5th, 2005).

66 See for instance: »Inimesed, tulge mõistusele!« [People, be Reasonable!], in: *Valgamaalane*. (December 5th, 2005).

67 T. Madisson, *Lihula õppetund* [The Lesson of Lihula] (Tallinn: Rahva Raamat, 2005).

it is simply not the custom to fight over the dead and over memorials.« One commentator tried to call on Estonians to behave »in a more civilized way.«[68]

Ironically, the Estonian soldiers thought they were fighting for the maintenance of a European ideal in their country in World War II. Why do the veterans, one might ask, so stubbornly hold on to a monument whose aesthetic qualities have been doubted even by some of its proponents and which would stand like a wall between Europe and Estonia? The answer is that they want to be remembered as members of Estonian army units. In a letter to the president, they demanded, among other things, to be acknowledged in the line of the freedom fighters of the first Estonian Army.[69] Therefore, the Nazi character of the uniform was downright denied. It was argued that the uniform had neither a swastika nor SS-runes applied to it, but on the contrary displayed an Estonian crest and a freedom cross, both Estonian symbols that the legion was allowed to carry.[70] In order to check the validity of these arguments, the police even engaged Peeter Torop, the director of the renowned Department of Semiotics at the University of Tartu, to prepare an expert analysis. The professor could only confirm that all Nazi-symbols had been thoroughly eliminated on the figure. Still, he remarked on the similarity of the monument to wartime mobilization posters, and eventually qualified it as »rude or ambiguous« in the present day context.[71] Yet for the veterans, it was neither one nor the other. After being denied a place in public memory for so long, while the Red Army soldiers were hailed with monuments and parades for allegedly liberating the country, the men of the SS-Division now claim the same honors for themselves. This is why they do not want new symbols that are more adequate for the present, but on the contrary, wish to have their well-earned share of established and traditional forms of commemoration. Maybe not so paradoxically, the Estonian veterans want to be remembered in the same way their enemies were: with a classical heroic war monument, counterweighing those Red Army monuments that have not been removed in Estonia so as not to strain the relationship with the Russian-speaking minority any further. The so-called Bronze Soldier in Tallinn has often entered discussions as a prominent example. It is a bulky figure in Red Army uniform, built in 1947 and, originally, bending his head in memory of the Soviet soldiers that fell while conquering Tallinn in 1944. After 1991 its place remained on

68 »Inimesed, tulge mõistusele!« in: *Valgamaalane*, op.cit. (note 66).

69 Pöördumine, »Eesti vabadusvõitlejate pöördumine Riigikogu poole« [Appeal of the Estonian Freedom Fighters to the Parliament], http://kultuur.elu.ee/ke477_vabadusvoitlejad.htm (accessed on December 12th, 2005).

70 V. Kallas, »Võõra vormi kandmine ei ole häbiasi« [Wearing an Alien Uniform is no Disgrace] (2004), www.hot.ee/relvaleht/eestlased.htm (accessed December 5th, 2005).

71 »Semiootik Torop: Lihula mälestussammas pole natslik« [Semiotic Torop: The Lihula Memorial is not Nazistic], in: *Eesti Päevaleht* (September 14th, 2004), http://www.epl.ee/_artikkel-274069.html (accessed on December 5th, 2005).

Figure 7.2: The Bronze Soldier in Tallinn, Source: Erik Raiküla, *Tallin* (Tallin: Kirjastus-Eesti Raamat, 1975), p. 107.

Tõnismägi, opposite the national library, but the caption changed, dedicating the monument now to all the victims of the war. Despite this change, it is still perceived as a Red Army monument. Consequently, after the removal of the Lihula monument, the Fatherland-party, »Isamaa,« called for the removal of the Bronze Soldier as well. Others took to direct action by vandalizing former Soviet statues all over the country.[72] Discussions about the »Bronze Soldier« have not been resolved to this day.

Integrating Memory?

As of now, no common understanding has been reached about how to commemorate the different histories of violence. A plurality of memories exists in Estonia, and while institutions like the »State Commission«, the »President's commission« or the Kistler-Risto Foundation have contributed greatly to research on the topic, the Lihula incident shows that they are far from succeeding in creating an integrated collective memory – a master narrative that everyone can relate to. The hope of the historian Tiit Noormets that there could at least be a clear lesson in the suffering, that it educated the Estonians »to be a united, fighting people that never yields to exploitation, violence and pressure, irrespective from which direction or with which crooked slogans they come« sounds more normative than descriptive.[73] As many of the veterans disappointedly note in their memories, the young generation is not primarily interested in the Estonian self-identification that the veterans have to offer.

In fact, most young people today would probably agree with the historian and journalist Andrei Hvostov, who called the veterans' attitude »Soviet style under opposite signs«. Without condemning the veterans' claims as a whole, he interprets the wish for an unambiguous culture of commemoration as a typical heritage of the totalitarian Soviet state, where people were raised to think, »when the memory isn't total, it doesn't exist at all«.[74] Today, however, there is no authoritarian state to implement such a memory and a variety of different notions do exist.

»Can we cope with our history?« the writer and essayist Jaan Kaplinski asked in a recent article. For him, the pseudo-history of the Soviet time is often being replaced by a counter-version that, albeit an understandable reaction, is just as

---

72   »Inimesed, tulge mõistusele!« op.cit. (note 66).
73   Noormets, *Metsavennad Suvesõjas 1941*, op.cit. (note 20), p. 256.
74   A. Hvostov, »Vastasmärgiline sovetlus« [Soviet Style under Opposite Signs], in: *Eesti Ekspress*, (September 1st, 2005).

one-sided. Kaplinksi sees a possible remedy only in facing the »painful spots« of the Estonian past more honestly, and not leaving them to Finnish or German historians or even to the »likes of Tiit Madisson«. Otherwise, the memories would remain in opposition: »Some are bringing flowers to the place of the Lihula statue, the others to the bronze soldier«.[75] Maybe as Eva-Clarita Onken has remarked concerning Latvia, it will have to live with a plurality of histories for some time to come, is also true for Estonia.[76]

---

75 J. Kaplinski, »Meie vältimatud vastasseisud« [Our inevitable oppositions], in: *Eesti Päevaleht* (October 4th, 2005).

76 E.-C. Onken, *Demokratisierung der Geschichte in Lettland. Staatsbürgerliches Bewusstsein und Geschichtspolitik im ersten Jahrzehnt der Unabhängigkeit* [Democratization of History in Latvia. Civic Consciousness and History Policy in the First Decade of Independence] (Hamburg, 2003).

Rites

Troubles and Hopes – Armenian Family, Home and Nation

Levon Abrahamian

The political enlargement of Europe has naturally raised many questions about the cultural remaking of national identities on the margins of the New Europe. In these remote regions of the New Europe one can find a vast number of governmental and non-governmental organizations, wide-scale and narrow-focused local projects which try to demonstrate how ready these regions are for the implementation of European standards, or at least how eager they are to become a true Europe – however vague this image might be in the minds of such Europe-oriented persons and organizations. Sometimes the »European standards« are used to achieve openly non-European goals, as it was the case, for example, in Armenia during the referendum on constitutional changes on November 27th, 2005: authorities used all the power of the state machine (including methods which hardly could be classified as European) to demonstrate to Europe that the constituency said »yes« to the constitutional changes approved by the European experts, while the majority of the constituency simply boycotted the referendum[1] using quite another rhetoric, which was opposed to the local authorities and not to European political values.

This is to show that the terms »European«, »Western«, »democratic« are often used on the margins of New Europe in quite different contexts than in Old Europe. Or, to say figuratively, in Armenia, underneath the *evroremont*[2], one can see a less visible »Asian« mode of life and values. It was also said after the referendum that Europe actually was not interested in thorough democratic repairs in Armenia, but preferred just a cosmetic repair. This repair symbolism is not just a metaphor: we will see later that home is one of the main symbols of Armenian identity. In this article, I will try to show, in a sense, what is not European on the margins of New Europe, namely in Armenia. This does not mean, of course, that Armenia is not integrating into the new European realities or that is indif-

---

1   However, this boycott was simply neglected, the estimated 350,000 participants of the referendum (the opposition's version) being declared as nearly 1,5 million (the official version).

2   The Russian word *evroremont* meaning »Euro-repairs« is used in Armenia for prestigious repair using modern European building materials, technology and design. A completely »Euro-repaired« apartment has very little (if any) resemblance to a traditional Armenian home interior.

ferent to the changing boundaries, both geographical and cultural.[3] (Although the state of European-oriented processes in Armenia is often exaggerated, if not just declared.) One has to know the local specificities to understand the challenges of new ideas and trends. Here I will try to show from the anthropological perspective, how the notions of family and home shape the Armenian nation, especially during critical periods in the history of this society.

Nation-state or Family-state?

Armenians have a long tradition of translating foreign words, sometimes even untranslatable ones, into their own language, or creating new »telling« words. However, this was not the case with the word *nation*. When the modern concepts of nation and nationalism emerged in the European discourse in the 19th century, Armenians gave preference to the Armenian word *azg*, since, like the original Latin *natio*, it embraces such meanings as »tribe«, »clan«, »people«, »order«, »class«. However, by acquiring this new meaning,[4] the Armenian *azg*, in contrast to the foreign word *nation*, nevertheless did not lose its traditional »tribal« and »family« meaning.[5] Let us recall the commonly used word *azganum* meaning »family name«, literally »name of the *azg*«, or *azgakan* meaning »relative«, which are both devoid of the nuances of the new abstract meaning and, on the contrary, seem to pull the concept of *azg*-nation back to tribal realities. This »tribal« worldview is not a result of the magnetic force of the word *azg*, it still seems to have strong roots in the Armenian mentality – confirming the neo-pagan trends in the »tribal religion« *Tseghakron*.[6]

Recently, Armen Petrosyan made an interesting comparison between the Ar-

---

3   On the democratic (rather pseudo-democratic) trends during the mass national rallies of the late 1980s see Levon Abrahamian, »Civil Society Born in the Square: The Karabagh Movement in Perspective«, in: *The Making of Nagorno-Karabagh: From Secession to Republic,* ed. by Levon Chorbajian (Basingstoke, U.K.: Palgrave, 2001), pp. 116–134.

4   In an Armenian explanatory dictionary of the mid-1940s (St. Malkhasiants', *Armenian Explanatory Dictionary.* Vol. 1 (Yerevan: HSSR pet. hrat, 1944), p. 8) this new meaning is listed under point 3.

5   In this sense Armenians fit Anthony Smith's description of the non-Western model of nation as a fictive »super-family« (see Anthony D. Smith, *National Identity* (Reno, Las Vegas & London: University of Nevada Press), p. 12). On *azg* as the traditional kindred group among the Armenians, see E. T. Karapetian, *Armenian Family Community* (Yerevan: Izd. AN Arm. SSR, 1958); E. T. Karapetian, *The Kindred Group »Azg« among the Armenians (the second half of the 19th – beginning of the 20th centuries)* (Yerevan: Izd. AN Arm. SSR, 1966).

6   On Tseghakron see Mushegh Lalayan, *Tseghakron and the Taronakan Movements and the Public Work of Garegin Nzhdeh* (Yerevan: Azgaynakan Akumb, 2001).

menian traditional extended family, which proved to represent one of the most archaic Indo-European kin groups, and the Armenian *azg*-nation. Following E. Karapetian's[7] definition of *azg* as a familial-kin group – which includes families of several generations, usually six to seven, rarely eight – deriving from an ancestor-founder, whose name becomes the generic term, Petrosyan concludes that the Armenian progenitor Hayk's large family (with seven descendants) could present the mythological prototype, the most archaic version of the Armenian patriarchal family. This consideration shows that »the ethnonym *Hay* and the dialectal *hay* »husband, head of family« are affined with the name of the patriarch Hayk (*Hay-ik*). The name of Hayk would have become the generic name of Hayk's *azg*-family and *azg*-nation. ... The historical Armenian *azg*, i.e., the nation of Hayk, would have been regarded as the current state of Hayk's initial (divine) family«.[8]

Although the word *azg* does not have the literal meaning of »family«, which, in the meaning of »extended family« is occupied by the word *gerdastan*, it nevertheless is close to the same semantic field. It is not a mere chance that in the streets of present-day Yerevan a young man will address an unfamiliar man or woman of his age as *aper* (colloquial from *ełbayr* »brother«) or *k'uyrik* (diminutive from *k'uyr* »sister«) respectively, while unfamiliar representatives of his parent's generation would be addressed usually as *hopar* and *mork'ur* (colloquial from *horeghbayr* »father's brother« and *morak'uyr* »mother's sister«, respectively); elderly women are addressed as *mayrik* (diminutive from *mayr* »mother«). The *hayrik* (diminutive from *hayr* »father«) address is used relatively less frequently, at least among those who use the *aper* and *hopar* forms.[9] Younger persons address those much older than themselves as *tati*/*papi* (»grandma«/»grandpa«). That is, the Armenian society – *azg*-nation as a whole – is modeled as a family: children, father and mother and their brothers and sisters. In this system of address, one will rarely meet a *hork'ur* (»father's sister«) and *k'er'i* (»mother's brother«) – the Armenian terms of kinship include this gender specification for parents' relatives. But this does not mean that the modern mode of address reflects some ancient family forms among Armenians, as those supporting Henry Lewis Morgan's views might think. It simply shows that the nation is modeled in the classic family form: father, mother and children, the *hopar* »father's brother«

---

7   Karapetian, *The Kindred Group »Azg« among the Armenians*, op.cit. (note 5), p. 25.

8   Armen Petrosyan, »The Indo-European and Ancient Near Eastern Sources of the Armenian Epics«, in: *The Journal of Indo-European Studies Monograph* 42 (Washington: Institute for the Study of Man, 2002), p. 161.

9   And, on the contrary, those who use the *hayrik* form of address (mainly the elite), as a rule, don't use the *hopar* one. The prevalence of the *mayrik* form of address as compared with *hayrik* could be correlated with the »victory« of *tikin* (the Armenian equivalent of *Madame*) over *paron* (»Sir«), even under the conditions of the post-Soviet rehabilitation of the *paron* form of address.

and *mork'ur* »mother's sister« presenting, respectively, an »extended« father and an »extended« mother.[10] If we also add here the *axpar* »brother« used in Armenia to basically denote the Armenian diaspora, we will have the entire Armenian nation. This »extended family« context of the *azg*, which is absent in the word *natio* and its derivatives, would inevitably introduce some family nuances into the *azg*-nation and related Armenian concepts. In particular, it may explain the paradoxical trend of the Armenian nation-state toward a kind of a »family-state«. Thus, the clan system in Armenia, which has often been brought up in the scientific literature[11] actually embraces all institutions from families themselves, to NGOs[12] and the few working collectives of the period of economic decline[13] to the supreme power (e.g., the former president Ter-Petrossian and his brothers[14]). Even the terrorist group that attacked the Armenian parliament on October 27, 1999, had a pronounced family/clan nature. It is characteristic that the position of the assassinated Prime Minister Vazgen Sarkissian thereafter was shortly occupied by his brother, and the son of the Speaker, Karen Demirchian, soon became the leader of the party, which had been headed by his murdered father.

Let us note that the individualism of the Armenians, this often-stated traditional endo-stereotype,[15] also involves the family: an Armenian individual always implicitly represents the family, so that the Armenian word for »indi-

---

10   The absence of similar specification of parents' sisters and brothers in Russian (*tiotia* and *diadia* – equivalents of the English *uncle* and *aunt*), do not allow for similar speculations about Russian society, which could be classified as otherwise close to the described Armenian situation, according to some informal »family-oriented« forms of address, although the possible avoidance of the Soviet general address *tovarishch* »comrade« without gender specification by the late Soviet times had brought the Russians to a strange »biological« society – judging from the widely used forms of address *muzhchina* and *zhenshchina* meaning, respectively, »man« and »woman«.

11   See, e.g. Nora Dudwick, »Political Transformations in Post-communist Armenia: Images and Realities«, in: *Conflict, Cleavage and Change in Central Asia and the Caucasus*, ed. by Karen Dawisha & Bruce Parrott (Cambridge: Cambridge University Press, 1997), pp. 69–109, in particular pp. 89–91.

12   Lusine Kharatyan & Gayane Shagoyan, »»Family« in the Context of Contemporary Non-Governmental Organizations«, in: *Problems of the Study of Family. Materials of the Republican Conference in Memory of Emma Karapetian* (Yerevan: Akunk', 2001), pp. 49–54.

13   The traditional family/clan orientation in rural Armenia today hinders some commune-oriented international aid projects (see Vahe Sahakyan, *Manifestations and Trends of Communes and Communalism in Armenia (A Sociological Analysis)*, Ph.D. thesis (Yerevan: State University, 2002)). One may compare this with the opposite situation concerning Stolypin reforms in pre-revolution Russia, which were directed, to the contrary, against traditional communal peasant structures.

14   Two brothers of the President were controlling, respectively, the privatization of former-Soviet industry, international economic relations and new construction activity.

15   This stereotype is reflected in many anecdotes, jokes and sayings and usually criticizes Armenians' incapacity to form a solidary group (»we can't even form an ordinary queue«) in contrast to the alleged solidarity of other nations (e.g. Georgians or Jews).

vidualism« – *anhatapaštut'yun*, meaning literally »worship of an individual«, is in fact a specific kind of »family-worship«.

The word for »family« in Armenian is *əntanik'*, which is nominative plural of *əntani* »relative« or rather »the one of the home,« if we follow the Armenian word literally, which has *tun* »home« in its structure.[16] Hence, the meaning of the Armenian »family« is »everybody at home«. On the other hand, *tun* not only means »house« as a construction, but also its dwellers, clans of the discussed *azg* type, tribe and nation.[17] Thus, the Armenian word for »family« shows the importance of home for the Armenian identity, the *azg*-family is perceived as collected within the home. So, this well-known fact of the crucial role of family and home for Armenians, which is supported by ample ethnographic and socio-logical evidence, is also etymologically supported.[18] *Tun* also means »country«, »world« in a broader sense of the word, which has, according to anthropological evidence, in addition to geographical meaning, also a cosmological meaning.[19] That is, the Armenian nation-state seems to be not only a »family-state«, but also a »home-state«.

Home

While the home of an Englishman is said to be his castle, the home of an Armenian seems to be his universe, where he plays the role of the Creator. In the traditional »head-house«, he »creates stars« on the »dome of the sky« during some principal festivals – by putting flour spots on the ceiling,[20] and when sett-

---

16 Hr. Acharian, *Etymological Dictionary of the Armenian Language*. Vol. II (Yerevan: Yer. hamals. hrat, 1973), p. 132.

17 After E. Benveniste's (see Émile Benveniste, *Le vocabulaire des institutions indo-européennes. 1. Économie, parenté, société* (Paris: Minuit, 1970), chap. I.3.2.) analysis of the Indo-European *domos* / *domus* (the Armenian *tun* derives from this form), its social aspect, like the one present in the Armenian word *tun*, has been regarded as the original and most principal one (see O. N. Trubachev, *Etymological Dictionary of the Slavonic Languages. Proto-Slavonic Lexical Fund*. Vol. 5 (Moscow: Nauka, 1978), p. 73).

18 Hr. Acharian, *Etymological Dictionary of the Armenian Language*. Vol. IV (Yerevan: Yer. hamals. hrat, 1979), pp. 427–428.

19 Cf. H. Marutyan, »Home As the World«, in: *Armenian Folk Arts, Culture, and Identity*, ed. by Levon Abrahamian & Nancy Sweezy (Bloomington & Indianapolis: Indiana University Press, 2001), pp. 73–97.

20 H. Marutyan, »Home As the World«, op.cit. (note 19), p. 86. The »head-house« with corresponding inhabitants, both real and mythological, could be correlated with the tripartite structure of the Cosmos: hearth or *t'onir* corresponding to the lower world, the *yerdik* smoke-hole – to the higher world, and the home space proper – to the middle world, the terrestrial

ling into a modern new apartment, he often completely changes the plan of the apartment in order to create his own universe.[21]

According to Gellner[22], the modern nation is supposed to have enough mobility to ensure its homogeneity within the boundaries of nation-state. In the United States this principle is well realized at the level of both family and home. This is reflected, for instance, in the mode of building contemporary, usually family-oriented houses: at speedy rates, like stage properties, made for seven to eight years of inhabitance. In Armenia, on the contrary, the building of a house follows quite different models: a house is to be built solidly to face eternity.[23] This does not seem strange, if we recall the cosmic aspect of the Armenian home. During Soviet times, the rule of obligatory registration fastened the house to the ground even more strongly, giving it an additional »eternal« value. Every Soviet citizen had to be linked with some dwelling place, and should have an address which was fixed in his/her passport. In this sense, the words of a popular Soviet-time song »My address is neither a house, nor a street, my address is the Soviet Union« being an ideological metaphor, were actually nonsense within the totalitarian Soviet state. This linking of any man/woman with a house/place continues in post-Soviet period. In Moscow (later elsewhere in Russia), it took the form of the obligatory registration of everybody who entered the capital, a kind of anti-hospitality law introduced by the Moscow mayor Yu. Luzhkov. In Armenia, this registered link with the place of living is said to be used by the authorities for falsifying elections results, since many *émigrés* from Armenia do not rush to »register out« officially – this hope for returning home making them a kind of »ghost elector«.[24]

The door, being an important part of the home,[25] its safeguard and presently its calling card, often represents the home as a whole, especially under the condi-

---

space being represented by people (the family) and animals, traditionally kept under the same roof in old times.

21   This is the source of a Soviet-era joke which said that Armenians were never allowed to stay more than three days in the huge hotel »Rossiia« in the center of Moscow – in order not to give them enough time to cover the hotel's open balconies with glass frames, which is a usual minor »act of creation« in any of Yerevan's many apartment buildings. (Stephanie Platz, »The Shape of National Time: Daily Life, History and Identity during Armenia's Transition to Independence, 1991–1994«, in: *Altering States: Ethnographies of Transition in Eastern Europe and the Former Soviet Union,* ed. by Daphne Berdahl, Matti Bunzl & Martha Lampland (Ann Arbor: University of Michigan Press, 2000), pp. 114–139, in particular p. 120 uses this joke in the context of analysis of living space in Soviet Armenia.)

22   Ernest Gellner, *Nations and Nationalism* (Oxford: Basil Blackwell, 1983), p 73.

23   The destructive earthquake of 1988 cast doubt on this ideal perception.

24   A joke on another type of »ghost elector« relates that a person was offended by his passed away father who came to vote but did not visit his son's home.

25   See H. Marutyan, »Home As the World«, op.cit. (note 19), pp. 87–89 for an ethnography and mythology of the door in the traditional Armenian worldview.

tions of modern house planning on a mass scale. In present-day Armenia, many people install expensive and beautiful entrance doors even in large multi-unit buildings, a rather strange luxury in contrast with the usual gloomy interior of the stairways and entrances. The following characteristic story illustrates the Armenian attitude toward the door-and-house. In 1945, during the first days following the end of World War II, the Soviet army headquarters tried to prevent marauding on the occupied territory of Germany by creating special commands and commissions. A former head of one such commission, Grigor Arzumanian, who later became a prominent statesman in Soviet Armenia, told how he released a soldier, an Armenian by nationality, who was charged with an extraordinary act of looting. While other marauders had robbed different types of valuable things, this soldier carried a heavy, beautifully designed door on his back. He said that he removed the door from an abandoned house and wanted to take it back with him to his native village somewhere in the Lake Sevan basin to build a new house for his family.[26]

The collapse of the Soviet regime brought about a social and economic crisis in almost all the former Soviet republics. However, Armenia suffered even more as a result of the destructive earthquake in 1988 and the blockade by Azerbaijan, which was a response to the national-liberation movement in Nagorno-Karabagh (an autonomous district with a majority Armenian population in former Azerbaijan SSR), which developed into ethnic conflict and war. No wonder that this post-Soviet crisis struck most painfully at the level of the family and home – the principal paradigms of Armenian identity. Thus, taking into account that for an Armenian the house is the Universe, one can say (following modern cosmological theories stating that there is no other reality outside the borders of our Universe) that any change in the attitude toward the home could be an evidence of serious changes in the psychology of the Armenian people. If judging only from the well-known formulas of the home ideology – *Tund šen mna* »Let your house be prosperous«[27] and *Tund k'andvi* »Let your house be ruined« – one may think that the documented cases of Armenians pulling down their houses in order to sell the components as building materials[28] should be a signal of the collapse of the Armenian »Cosmos«. True, such destruction of one's own

---

26   I am grateful to Gagik Arzumanian, the son of Grigor Arzumanian, for this story.

27   *Tund šen mna* could be etymologically interpreted as »Let your house stay standing« – *šen* is of the same root as *šinel* »to make«, also in the sense of building, constructing. Cf. *Tund šinvi* »Let your house be built« as a euphemistic substitution for *Tund k'andvi* »Let your house be ruined«.

28   H. Marutyan, »Have Armenians Changed? (Anthropological Notes)«, in: *Stories on Poverty*, ed. by Hranush Kharatyan (Yerevan: Lusakn, 2001), pp. 392–406, in particular p. 400. In many villages the building materials are more expensive than an already built house. (On the other hand, this also shows that these materials are needed for building new houses – evidently for the new rich of Armenia.)

house mainly refers to the Armenian refugees from Azerbaijan, who are going to eventually leave Armenia – they have already lost their former homes-»Cosmos«, while their new homes in Armenia did not have enough time to achieve »cosmic« features. The local Armenians leaving Armenia, whose number alarmingly continues to increase, as yet seem to preserve their houses, leaving them to a relative – as a precondition of their future return. This refers more to the emigrants from rural regions who mainly leave for Russia to join the »internal diaspora«, as it was called in Soviet times.[29] As for those who plan to join the »external diaspora«, the situation is different – even if we judge only from the advertisements looking for people who would like to sell their real estate, which appeared in the late 1990s in the neighborhood of the American consulate in Yerevan, the place where the long line of waiting people illustrates the problem of emigration.

There are also cases where a local resident of a village has sold only a part of his/her house as »building materials«.[30] These cases, however, can be compared with the widely practiced cases in Yerevan, where people sell their houses (larger apartments) to buy a more modest and/or less prestigiously located dwelling in order to use the rest of the money for survival. In principle, this process could proceed in several steps – up to losing the last dwelling to become homeless, *bomzh*[31] (I know of at least one such dramatic case). If we take into account that the houses are not just »ruined« (directly and metaphorically) and lost, but merely change their owners, one can say that we are dealing with transformations in the social structure expressed in the »language of homes«. The process of this new social restructuring is more visible in the cities, in the first instance in Yerevan introducing new »editions« in its still »draft text«.[32] That is, judging from the home paradigm, we may conclude that although the Armenian »Cosmos« has not yet collapsed, it is nevertheless in serious danger.

---

29 The Russians define the similar but opposite situation of Russians living in the former Soviet Republics as »near abroad«.

30 See material tellingly entitled after her informant's words »I ruined my house to pay my debts«. Gayane Shagoyan, »Aid: Voluntarily or Under Constraint?«, in: *Stories on Poverty*, ed. by Hranush Kharatyan (Yerevan: Lusakn, 2001), pp. 350–369.

31 *Bomzh* is the abbreviation of the Russian *bez opredelennogo mesta zhitel'stva* »without definite place of residence«, which, unfortunately, became a common word in the modern Armenian vocabulary.

32 On the ethnosociological and urban processes in pre-crisis Yerevan see Yu.V. Arutiunian & E.T. Karapetian (eds), *The Population of Yerevan. An Ethno-sociological Study* (Yerevan: Izd. AN Arm. SSR, 1986).

Family

One may also see some alarming signs in the other home-bond paradigm, the family. We cannot go into the details here, since this problem requires a large-scale and long-term sociological analysis.[33] Especially, as the inertia of the traditional family may for a while resist changes in the family structure. For example, one case study by H. Kharatyan on poverty in present-day Armenia[34] shows that the head of the family or, in Armenian terms, »the man of the home« is commonly out of his work and cannot help his family to survive. Now this function is passed on to his daughter. However, he still holds his role as head person, decision-maker and master of the home.[35] In other similar cases I observed a more rapid change in the family hierarchy: the possibility of earning some money by baby-sitting immediately gave a young woman some privileges, including upgrading relations with her mother-in-law – the most rigid sphere in the traditional Armenian family. Changes in the principal structural oppositions within society, like man – woman, elderly – young, rich – poor, are very important for sociological evaluations and forecasting, since these are the most sensitive elements that may signal fundamental changes in a society. Some of these oppositions or even all of them can change dramatically during festivals and festival-like political mass rallies and also during crises. Such transformations in the social structure are usually not too long lasting, and the society, as a system of stable structural oppositions, tends to return to the original state, as happens after carnivals. That is the reason why after revolutions, only by force is it possible to fix the inverted oppositions. As for a crisis, the transformed oppositions could return to their initial position, if the crisis does not last too long. For example, during the first phase of Gorbachev's economic chaos, women's activity in trade became accentuated, which was a kind of gender revolution in this traditionally male sphere. The so-called shuttle-traders were mainly women, which, as a matter of fact, should not surprise us, since crises often resurrect archaic modes of production. And the shuttle-trade could be compared with gathering, the most archaic women's »economy«: the shuttle-traders »wander« through the »market-lands« picking up any saleable goods. However, the mo-

---

33 Cf. notes by an American anthropologist on the changes in personal and group identities during the first years of post-Soviet Armenia (Stephanie Platz, »The Shape of National Time«, op.cit (note 21), p. 127 ff.).

34 The study of poverty in Armenia was carried out in 1994 -2000 by a group of social anthropologists in the frames of different projects sponsored by the World Bank. The results of the research (case studies, interviews, analytic articles, comments, etc.) were collected in a book – see Hranush Kharatyan (ed.), *Stories on Poverty* (Yerevan: Lusakn, 2001).

35 Levon Abrahamian, » ...Indeed, Poverty Is the Origin of All Misfortunes«, in: *Stories on Poverty*, ed. by Hranush Kharatyan (Yerevan: Lusakn, 2001), pp. 406–419, in particular p. 414.

ment the phase of considerably large-scale commodity turnover began, women gradually surrendered their place in trade to men, the women's »gathering« being replaced by men's »hunting«. Only the homeless *bomzh* made gathering their constant mode of life.[36] It is characteristic that during the initial days of crisis after the 1988 earthquake, women in Leninakan again immediately »regained gathering« by looking for food in the ruined city for the surviving members of their families. Examples of such crisis returns to archaic modes of production or crisis transformations of certain economies are well known in the history of humankind. Thus, the impoverished nomads are forced to lead a settled life by engaging in primitive agriculture, until they find an opportunity to return to nomadic cattle breeding. In turn-of the century-Armenia, on the contrary, some impoverished peasants are now forced to leave traditional agriculture.[37] So that the long-lasting crisis may deprive the present-day Armenian villager and Armenian culture, in general, of their centuries-old agricultural way of life and characteristics.

It has to be said, however, that despite the already mentioned uncertainties and other real problems that threaten the modern Armenian family, it is often considered endangered and even already dead in the imagination of the observers. To illustrate here is one example of a situation in which I was just a passive observer. An informant residing in Yerevan told a foreign journalist that family ties had become very loose in Armenia as a result of the crisis and supported this statement with the fact that her mother's sister could not come from a distant village recently to be present at an important family event. The foreign interviewer later concluded that the present-day crisis resulted in considerable destruction of the family among Armenians, without specifying what his informant understood by the term »family«. In reality, the informant's words referred to other transformations of the traditional Armenian family. The crisis has actually favored the development of the small family, typical of the city – by cutting ties within the traditional extended family, which was formerly conjoined with the village.[38] In the given example one can say that the crisis has accelerated urban processes in Yerevan.[39] While paradoxically, in other cases, the same crisis may produce a quite opposite result. Thus, to resist the recent energy crisis, many small families were forced to swell into a large artificial family – including parents who had lived separately or more distant relatives and friends. Because such types of families did not fit American standards, they were usually overlooked by American aid projects, which were aimed to help Armenia during the

---

36 Shagoyan, »Aid: Voluntarily or Under Constraint?«, op.cit. (note 30), pp. 364–365.
37 Kharatyan (ed.), *Stories on Poverty*, op.cit (note 34), p. 339.
38 Stephanie Platz, »The Shape of National Time«, op.cit (note 21), pp. 122, 134.
39 For the characteristics of urban families in Yerevan, both small and extended, in Soviet times, see Arutiunian & Karapetian (eds), *The Population of Yerevan*, op.cit. (note 32), pp. 114–153.

fuel and energy crisis in the early 1990s.[40] The aid itself, as the sad stories collected in the volume on poverty in Armenia show,[41] could in turn transform the family – by artificially breaking down the family into units that correspond to the aid-providers' requirements. Let us note that the latter phenomenon – the unintended role of aid projects in the transformation of the family – can be seen beyond Armenia. For example, the US welfare programs favored the unintended artificial transformation of poor, small Afro-American families into large ones of matriarchal nature, since only families without able-bodied men could benefit from these programs.

In some cases, an informant's evaluation of the collapse of kinship ties may confuse an observer who may not have enough ethnographic background regarding the situation described. A telling example is one given by G. Shagoyan[42] about a »good« sister, who helped the informant in a critical situation, although traditionally, as a member of another family after marriage, she was not obliged to do so, and a »bad« brother, who actually helped her to survive in accordance with his family obligations, but was not able to provide additional aid, thus deserving the label »bad«. In another example, an informant blamed the crisis for her and her children's distancing from relatives of the same generation (respectively, third and fourth, counting from a common ancestor) after the death of her parents (representing the second generation), only because this natural process coincided with the difficult 1990s.

However, let us keep in mind that under the difficult conditions of the crisis, when the state was unable to effectively realize life-sustaining programs for its citizens, many people nevertheless survived thanks to their kindred ties, especially thanks to the aid coming from their relatives who had left the country. This is a kind of permanent feeding capillary from the new and as yet not so well established segment of the Armenian diaspora, in contrast to the impressive donations of the old diaspora like the St. Grigor the Illuminator Cathedral in Yerevan. In any case, the network of the family, this paradigm of the Armenian identity, seems to be at the core of the riddle of Armenians' survival during the most difficult years. One may say that the Armenian »*azg*-family« helps the Armenian »*azg*-nation« to survive and keeps its »home-Cosmos« still standing.

---

40   The energy crisis was caused by the specificities of the post-Soviet crisis in Armenia mentioned earlier in this article. The nuclear heating plant was brought to a stop after the earthquake, and the Georgian–Abkhazian conflict halted the railroad communication with Russia, deepening the fuel crisis caused by the Azerbaijani blockade.

41   See Kharatyan (ed.), *Stories on Poverty*, op.cit (note 34).

42   Shagoyan, »Aid: Voluntarily or Under Constraint?«, op.cit. (note 30), p. 368.

Always Between East and West

The post-Soviet crisis favoured emigration from Armenia.[43] This was not the first time that Armenians had left their homeland. The history of the Armenian Diaspora contains many pages of similar and much more dramatic situations.[44] However, in this forced or voluntary (many times seemingly voluntary) dispersion one can see a strange coincidence: Armenians always seem to appear on the borderlines between East and West. This coincidence is such a constant in the course of history that one is even tempted to call it »the fate of the Armenians«.

Presently this phenomenon is mainly expressed in the Europe/Asia controversy when identifying the Republic of Armenia and the Armenians. Since there is no distinct natural borderline between Europe and Asia,[45] it is drawn differently. Mainly this borderline varies in the area between the Caspian and the Black Sea. Usually it is drawn along the Central Caucasian mountain ridge or a little to the north of it, across the Kumo-Manych valley, leaving Armenia, together with Transcaucasus, in Asia.[46] But sometimes Transcaucasus is included in Europe,[47] so that Armenia finds herself in Europe. However, according to other divisions, Armenia finds herself in Europe with greater permanence. For example, the Armenian soccer team is a member of the European Soccer League or Armenia is admitted to the Council of Europe,[48] from where it is threatened with expulsion if it will not behave like a European, that is a civilized country. Such »European encouragement« from the outside is met with a counter-reaction from the inside: Armenians usually consider themselves Europeans anyway. However, this seems to be a civilizational self-appraisal of many, maybe even all, peoples living near a geographical borderline. Thus, Turkey has been seeking to enter the European Union, while Georgians, after the recent find of the most ancient scull of European appearance, often treated by Georgians as an

---

43   For an anthropological analysis of the emigration processes in Armenia see Hranush Kharatyan (ed.), *Emigration from Armenia* (Yerevan: Hazarashen, 2003).

44   On the specificities of the Armenian diaspora see Levon Abrahamian, »Armenia and Armenian Diaspora: Parting and Meeting Again«, in: *21st Century. Journal of »Noravank« Foundation* No. 2 (2005), pp. 137–155 and Levon Abrahamian, *Armenian Identity in a Changing World* (Costa Mesa & CA: Mazda Press, 2006), ch. 15.

45   See E.G. Rabinovich, »Europa propria?«, in: *Inner Structure, Semantic Aura, Context. Summaries of the scientific conference. Part I* (Moscow: Inst. of Slavic Studies RAS, 2001), pp.59–61 for the original scope of the Europe mentioned in a Homer hymn.

46   Cf. *Encyclopedia Britannica*, any edition, article »Europe« (section »Geography and Statistics«).

47   See, e.g. *Bol'shaia Sovetskaia entsiklopediia* (Moscow: Glavnoe nauchnoe izdatel'stvo Bol'shaia Sovetskaia entsiklopediia, 1952), pp. 383–384, article »Europe« (sections »General Data« and »Physical-Geographical Essay«).

48   Cf. A.V. Kukhianidze, »A Caucasocentric Concept of Democracy«, in: *Nauchnaia mysl' Kavkaza* 4 (1995), pp. 66–72, in particular p. 68 for a similar situation in the case of Georgia.

»ancestor of the Europeans«, begin also to consider themselves Europeans in a paleoanthropological sense.

At the same time, present-day Armenia semiotically manifests its closeness to Asia. For example, the first »Western free market« in Yerevan (represented on the level of small vendors) was introduced through a typical Asian bazaar structure, or Western consumer goods were introduced in their Eastern disguise.[49] The same situation is evident in the sphere of music: the part of the Armenian populace oriented toward European music co-exists with a greater part of the populace oriented toward *r'abiz* music, which itself is a synthesis of Oriental and Western musical styles.[50] And all the *r'abiz*, jazz or flamenco type phenomena indicate that we are dealing with a borderline situation, an intermediary space between at least two cultures. In the case of Armenia, in addition to the mentioned geographical intermediary position, many signs also indicate her being (or imagining herself) in a borderline intermediary position between Asia and Europe. A good illustration of the Armenians« »fixed idea« of their intermediary position could be the results of one brainstorming session and sociological investigation carried out in Yerevan in the autumn of 1990. This investigation was aimed at locating the future Europolis, a city that was planned to be built after the earthquake of 1988 but never was. The majority of the respondents wanted this illusive city with its telling name to be built near the village of Yeraskhavan in the Ararat valley, a site that is simultaneously the closest to Turkey, Iran and Azerbaijan.

The present Asia/Europe controversy presupposes, and was preceded by, a more general East/West controversy. Unlike the borderline between Asia and Europe, which may shift a little in the minds of geographers, policy makers and borderline territory dwellers, the border between East and West is much more flexible and mobile. Thus, this border shifted toward the West as a result of the Seljuk expansions. And suddenly an Armenian kingdom of Cilicia appeared just on this border in the 12th–14th centuries, away from the ethnic territory of the Armenians.

For relations between Russia and Oriental countries, the East/West direction corresponded to the South/North direction, in cases when the road to the East passed via the Caucasus. And it is just in this borderland that we find the

---

49 L. Abrahamian, A. Gulyan, H. Marutyan, G. Shagoyan, H. Petrosyan, »Ethnography of the Armenian Market: Towards a Statement of the Problem«, in: *Modern Ethnocultural Processes in Armenia. 1.* Abstracts of the Republican Scientific Conference (Yerevan: HH GAA hnagit. ev azg. institut, 1997), pp. 5–6.

50 On the *r'abiz* phenomenon see L. Abrahamian & Hr. Pikichain, »Observations on the Ethnography of a Modern. The Example of Yerevan. I. The *Rabiz* and the Variability of the Urban Social Hierarchy«, in: *Soviet Anthropology & Archeology* 29 (1990), 2, pp. 34–44. Abrahamian, *Armenian Identity in a Changing World*, op.cit. (note 44), ch. 5.

Cherkezogai (Circassian-Armenians),[51] who played the role of an important intermediary link between South (East) and North (West).

Another example is the dramatic end of Jugha, a city in Armenia, which was a flourishing trade center in the 16th century. When the Persian king Shah Abbas decided to move the borderline between East and West toward his country, he accomplished this by destroying Jugha, the former intermediary point between East and West, and by moving its population to Persia in the beginning of the 17th century to found New Jugha. Soon it became a new intermediary point between East and West. Nearly two centuries later, when this borderline moved further to the East, to India, this time as a result of the activities of the Dutch and later British East India Company, the British found Armenians, who had already created a trade network there, at just this borderline. The Armenians, who were tradesmen from New Jugha, helped the Company in its initial stages to penetrate into the Indian market and played the role of a buffer between Western and Eastern merchants.[52]

There are many more such examples and each example has, of course, a different and specific history ranging from deportations to adventurous trade expeditions, which are hard to fit into a common model. But, however different the reasons for these moves were, the result was the same: wherever the flexible borderline between East and West shifts, Armenia and/or the Armenians are in some mysterious way right there, as if waiting to become intermediates between the newly distributed East and West. Usually this happens against their will. It is as if Armenians are doomed to become intermediates. But sometimes it becomes part of a political strategy, as it is, for instance, in the case of present-day Armenia's ambiguous intermediate position between Iran (South [East]) and Russia (North [West]), which takes aback and annoys the West, especially the United States.

The many minor cases, in which Armenians play the role of intermediates

---

51   The name *Cherkezogai* was composed from the Russian *Cherkes* »Circassian« and Armenian *Hay* »Armenian« – with the russified initial »g«. This was a small group in the Northwest Caucasus, which was formed, according to one probable opinion, in medieval times by a group of Armenian warriors who married Circassian women. On the Cherkesogai group see Arakelian 1984. Cf. V.P. Grigorian, *History of the Armenian Colonies of the Ukraine and Poland (Armenians in Podolia)* (Yerevan: Izd. AN Arm. SSR, 1980), pp. 49, 61 on a similar intermediary role of the Armenians of the Ukraine and Poland.

52   Armenians were even granted the privileges of the British in India in 1688 due to this important intermediary role, but were deprived of them when they supported the rebel Bengal nawab Mir Kasim (Kasim Ali-khan) in the early 1760s (R. Abramian, *Eighteenth Century Armenian Sources on India*. (Yerevan: Acad. Sci. Arm. SSR Press, 1968), p. 70). On this anti-British rebellion and Gergin-khan, the legendary Armenian commander-in-chief of the Bengal army, see Mesrovb Jacob Seth, *Armenians in India* (New Delhi, Bombay & Calcutta: Oxford & IBH Publishing Co., 1983), pp. 383–418; Abramian, *Eighteenth Century Armenian Sources on India*, op.cit. (note 51), pp. 50–71.

in local East/West divisions, for example, between the British and the Turks in Cyprus, show that we are dealing with a universal model of an Armenian way of life. The last example also illustrates that this model is not always a successful model of survival. In Cyprus, the Armenians that fled Turkey during the Genocide first settled in the part of the island inhabited by local Turks (that is why they played the role of intermediates between the British and the Turks), but after the Greek/Turkish conflict they had to move to the Greek part of the island.[53] There are two sides of the coin and this is a cost to »being in between«: this fate of being in between has brought many misfortunes to Armenia and the Armenians, since the West and the East not only cooperate, but also go to war, and those in between become the immediate victims of such wars.

This »trend« of always being between East and West also refers to the diaspora-forming processes in one way or another. Both sides of the coin contribute to these processes. Let us recall if nothing else the division of Armenia between Persia and Byzantium in 387. Nowadays, when caravans do not cross Armenia any more, Armenians look towards new models that fit the old intermediary model to survive in the modern world of airplanes flying over the former busy crossroads of East and West – especially as the East/West borderline seems to be preparing for a new shift. This mystical logic gives us a clue, a litmus test for prognosticating the location of the new borderline between East and West: one just has to look for large accumulations of Armenians on the world map. Presently, such a place is California. The increasing numbers of Asian people living there gives a visible »confirmation« of such a possible future shift. The trend by the US since the 1980s to realize trade communications via the Pacific instead of the Atlantic Ocean[54] also points in this direction.[55] So, perhaps, it will be the Armenian diaspora with its internal structure of successive intermediary components (including the new immigrants from post-Soviet Armenia and all other different old and new diaspora groups with their many levels of social and professional standings) that might play an important role in establishing a new model of homeland-diaspora relations and thus enter a new and hopefully more prospective stage for the Armenian family, home and nation.

53　Susan Paul Pattie, *Faith in History. Armenians Rebuilding Community* (Washington & London: Smithsonian Institution Press, 1997), pp. 50–51, 108, 119–122.

54　Rod Hague, Martin Harrop & Shaun Breslin, *Comparative Government and Politics. An Introduction* (London: Macmillan, 1992), p. 116.

55　A.V. Kukhianidze, »A Caucasocentric Concept of Democracy«, in: *Nauchnaia mysl' Kavkaza* 4 (1995), pp. 66–72, in particular pp. 67–68, uses this possible Pacific orientation of the future world center to prognosticate a new East/West division of the world, but sees the Caucasus as the possible intermediate point between a future Eurocentre and the Pacific centre.

Celebrating Identities in Post-Soviet Georgia[1]

Florian Mühlfried

Introduction

[Presenter] Davit Gamqrelidze [leader of the New Right] has given Interior Minister Irakli Okruashvili and Tbilisi Mayor Zurab Chiaberashvili two weeks to replace English writing on police cars with Georgian, otherwise he will lodge a complaint with the Constitutional Court and call for their impeachment. Gamqrelidze made this statement a short time ago at a parliamentary session. He also attacked the director of the National Library for criticizing the Georgian *supra* [traditional banquet] and other traditions.

[Gamqrelidze] This is very troubling. It is just like communist times when the Bolsheviks tried to promulgate the idea that Russian was top and that the Georgian mother-tongue was second-rate. I will give Batoni Irakli Okruashvili, the interior minister and Batoni Chiaberashvili, who seems not only to hate Kartlis Deda but everything Georgian, two weeks to rectify the problem. If not, I will go to the Constitutional Court and I am sure that this violation of the constitution will be grounds for their impeachment.

Similarly, I want to raise an issue which is currently worrying the public. Batoni Emzar Jgerenaia apparently described the Georgian *supra* and other traditions as homosexual acts. It is disturbing when the director, or acting director, of the National Library, comes up with such ideas. I ask Nino Burjanadze, as speaker of parliament, to look into this and take the appropriate decision. [2]

Why should a speaker of parliament deal with attitudes concerning tradition and homosexuality? Why is the Georgian banquet a matter to be discussed among high-ranking politicians?

The above quotation from Georgian TV channel »Imedi TV« broadcast in December 2004 raises questions about Georgian tradition, culture, politics, and the politicization of culture. In his speech, the leader of an opposition party refers to the Georgian language and the Georgian banquet (*supra*) as key elements of national identity. By criticizing the official usage of the English lan-

---

1   Some parts of this article have been published previously in Florian Mühlfried, »Banquets, Grant-Eaters and the Red Intelligentsia in Post-Soviet Georgia«, in: *Central Eurasian Studies Review* 4/1 (2005), pp. 16–19; and Florian Mühlfried, *Postsowjetische Feiern – Das Georgische Bankett im Wandel* (Stuttgart: Ibidem, 2006).
2   Imedi TV, Tbilisi, Georgia, 9 December 2004, 10.00 o'clock GMT, in Georgian; translated by the author; I would like to thank Adam Jasinski for letting me know about this news.

guage on police cars and Jgerenaia's association of the *supra* with gay culture,[3] Gamqrelidze discredits central figures of the post-Rose Revolutionary political and intellectual elites as anti-national. Just as in the Russian and Soviet times, Gamqrelidze argues, the Georgian elites are sacrificing their national identity, preferring English (formerly Russian) to Georgian and water (formerly vodka) to wine. Following this argument, the West is Georgia's new Russia, and the task of a truly patriotic opposition is to prevent the loss of self-esteem and to protect language and tradition.

Although no action came of the English inscription on the police cars, the *supra* and its proper perception remained an extensively and controversially debated topic in the months following Gamqrelidze's speech. The heyday of the controversy stirred by Gamqrelidze was marked by a TV discussion between him and his opponent Jgerenaia in March 2004. In a tense atmosphere, Gamqrelidze accused Jgerenaia of insulting »holy« Georgian traditions, whereas Jgerenaia questioned his opponent's personal integrity and intellectual ability.

A few weeks later, a new director of the national library had to be appointed by the parliament.[4] With his long experience as acting director, Jgerenaia would have been a reasonable candidate. Instead, though, the parliament elected Zaza Abashidze, a modest intellectual and professor of history from a well-known family, and whose father was a famous toastmaster.[5]

Among other factors, Jgerenaia's reading of the Georgian banquet as a culturally accepted institution for expressing homosexual feelings cost him promotion. It must be stressed, however, that it was not Jgerenaia who started or maintained the public debate. It was a leader of an opposition party who used the debate to discredit Jgerenaia as anti-national.[6] Thus, discourse on the *supra* (as with the Georgian Orthodox church) is a tool for silencing dissident thinkers in Saakashvili's Georgia – the same people who were among the forerunners of the Rose Revolution.

When Jgerenaia first published his provocative article on the *supra* in 2000,

---

3   In his paper from 2000, Jgerenaia described the Georgian banquet as a »geipi« – a blend of the words »keipi« (party) and »gay« – while pointing to the sentimental and often exaggeratedly demonstrative male bonding that can occur at the banquet table, especially after a certain quantity of alcohol has been ingested; Emzar Jgerenaia, »kartuli supris sociopilosopia da zogierti sxva ram« [The social philosophy of the Georgian »supra« and some other things], in: *kartuli supra da samokalako sazogadeoba [The Georgian »supra« and civil society]*, ed. by Gia Nodia (Tbilisi: Caucasian Institute for Peace, Democracy, and Development, 2000), pp. 31–42.

4   Following the example of the US Library of Congress, the Georgian National Library is a state institution. Thus, its leader has to be elected and appointed by the parliament.

5   A toastmaster is the ceremonial leader of the traditional Georgian banquet. There will be much more about this in the next section.

6   Other strategies for discrediting public figures are labeling them as homosexuals or Armenians.

his words did not resonate as they would four years later. The article was part of a booklet on the *supra*, summing up the results of an NGO-sponsored conference called »The Georgian Feast (*supra*) and Civic Society«.[7] Jgerenaia's work is included with four other articles, one dealing with Georgian toasts written by German socio-linguist Helga Kotthoff, and the others authored by Georgian intellectuals. Two of the Georgian authors (Bregadze and Nizharadze) state that despite the popular perception of the *supra* as being an »eternal tradition« existing since times immemorial, it actually originated as late as the 19th century.

As a response to this publication a couple of anthropologists and historians from official academic institutions dismissed the Georgian authors as incompetent amateurs.[8] Until 2004 the dispute concerning the *supra* was limited to the intellectual scene and communicated in academic journals (e.g. *Lit'erat'uruli Sakartvelo* [Literary Georgia]). During this period, the protagonists in the dispute could be divided into two groups: the first is the authors of the booklet and their associates – mostly young, well-educated people who work for NGOs instead of taking badly paid academic positions. As most of these people are dependent on money from Western institutions, they are sometimes referred to as »grant-eaters«. The second group is their opponents – mostly older representatives of the established academic system (e.g. the Georgian Academy of Science). These people are commonly referred to as »red intelligentsia« by the »grant-eaters« in order to stress their ties to the Soviet past.[9]

Thus, in the late years of the Shevardnadze regime, the discourse on the *supra* helped to differentiate a new intellectual elite. Most of the members of the new elite were somehow connected to the oppositional movement, and some of them were among the most influential brainstormers. It comes as no surprise that after the Rose Revolution some former »grant-eaters« assumed high-ranking positions in the state university, administration, and even in politics.

As the case of Jgerenaia illustrates, however, the »anti-traditionalists« have not won the battle. Saakashvili's strong nationalist rhetoric led to a second wave of political patriotism, unmatched since the times of Gamsakhurdia.[10] The critical, »unorthodox« voices within the former Georgian opposition become significantly weaker.[11] As a discursive marker, the *supra* has been experiencing a revival

7   Gia Nodia (ed.), *Kartuli Supra Da Samokalako Sazogadoba [The Georgian »supra« and civil society]* (Tbilisi: Caucasian Institute for Peace, Democracy, and Development, 2000).

8   See for example Giorgi Gociridze, »Vin Ebrdzvis Kartul Supras?« [Who is fighting the Georgian »supra«?], in: *lit'erat'uruli sakartvelo [Literary Georgia]*, Vol. 23–29 (2001), p. 7.

9   See on the same topic: Zaza Shatirishvili, »'Old' Intelligentsia and 'New' Intellectuals: The Georgian Experience«, in: *NZ/Eurozine* (2003) (http://www.eurozine.com/articles/2003–06–26–shatirishvili-en.html (accessed November 15, 2005).

10 Zviad Gamsakhurdia (1939–1993) was the first president of independent post-Soviet Georgia.

11 Ironically, the perception of Saakashvili in Western countries is as equally biased as the perception of his predecessor, Shevardnadze. Shevardnadze was primarily seen as a clever, pragmatic

these days. Formerly an antipode of the new intellectuals, it is now identified with national identity and pride. Thus, the »*supra*-turn« in recent Georgian politics marks a shift in the practice of discourse: from liberal thought after the Rose Revolution to a new patriotism – though more or less virtual in nature.

In the following pages, I intend to investigate further the reasons for and consequences of the »*supra*-turn« in Georgian culture and politics. Accordingly, some contextual knowledge must be elaborated. I will start by defining the *supra* and explaining its role in the maintenance of Georgian national identity over the past hundred years.

Structure and Past of the *Supra*

The *supra* is a highly formalized banquet, structured by toasts and ruled by a toastmaster (*tamada*). The toasts follow a generally uniform, yet not entirely fixed, structure. Certain topics are obligatory, such as toasts to the family and the deceased, and a certain pattern is prescribed, such as following a toast to the deceased by proposing a toast to life, often presented as a toast to children. In addition to this, toasts to attributed identity (e.g., family, gender) are most commonly proposed before toasts to acquired identity (e.g., profession, hobbies).[12]

Some toasts reinforce national values (especially the toast to the motherland, but also more subtly expressed in toasts to culture, song, and history), gender identity (particularly the obligatory toast to women), family values, and peer group identity. Generally the toasts should express honor to the addressee or the topic in hand and should not contain any colloquial expressions, let alone swearwords, gossip or criticism. The language used is itself characterized by the use of certain formulas (e.g., *gaumarjos* [»May victory be with you!«] at the end of each toast) and a high, grammatically complex, level of speaking.[13]

A good toastmaster is generally defined as a person with an extensive knowledge of history, poems, songs and traditions. He (or, in very rare cases, she) should not merely repeat formulas – that would be considered a bad perfor-

---

foreign affairs politician. Saakashvili is famous for his democratic, pro-Western orientation. In both cases, their domestic policy is widely ignored: the full range of the corrupt system Shevardnadze established in Georgia was only fully realized in the West after the heavy street protests in 2003 which led to the Rose Revolution. Now Saakashvili's autocratic governance and nationalist ideology are barely touched upon by Western media or policy analysts.

12   Mary Ellen Chatwin, *Foodways and Sociocultural Transformation in the Republic of Georgia, 1989–1994* (Tbilisi: Metsniereba Press, 1997).

13   Note especially the frequent use of a grammatical form almost exclusively reserved for toasting (the third subjunctive).

mance. It is very important that the toastmaster is able to improvise and propose toasts in an original, personalized way. Thus, the topics of the main toasts and the general structure are given, but the transmitted factors, or »tradition«, have to be acquired and integrated into personal, intentional behavior to complete the performance and make it successful. Consequently, a »correct« performance of the *supra* is not based on a faithful reproduction of an »authentic« or »true« procedure, but on the willingness and ability of the performers to integrate the formulas into their personal habitus.

At a Georgian banquet it is impossible to drink alcohol without relating it to a toast. Sipping wine is a deadly sin. The ritual consumption of wine and its connection to food bears obvious parallels in the Christian Holy Communion. But wine in the context of the Georgian banquet is not exclusively attributed to the blood of Christ. As many Georgians believe Georgia to be the birthplace of wine, and as there are many traces in Georgian culture that indicate the prior importance of wine for Georgian identity, wine becomes a metaphor for Georgian blood, and those who share wine at a *supra* become virtual kinsmen.

The rules of etiquette at the *supra* are very strict and function as a formalized system for distributing honor. Everybody should be included in this process of distribution, but a certain hierarchy based on social structure is reinforced. Who is addressed by the *tamada*, when and how, who speaks after whom and for how long, who drinks when and how much – all these factors can be considered to be part of a performance of status. Boys show that they have become men when they stand up during a toast to women or the deceased, while women and children remain seated. Men who have stopped actively participating in the process of drinking and toasting are most likely no longer considered the head of their family.[14] Generally, toasting encompasses both competition and solidarity.

Both in Georgian scholarly and popular discourse, the *supra* is considered to be an essential part of the Georgian tradition, too old to be dated accurately. Historical sources would suggest, however, that the *supra* in its current form is a product of the late 18th/early 19th centuries, and closely related to the rise of bourgeois and aristocratic culture in Tbilisi as well as the formation of a national movement. Western travelogues from the 15th-18th century[15] indicate

---

14 In some cases I could relate the refusal to drink wine at a *supra* by men in their 50s to the loss of a prestigious job after Georgia acquired independence. These men were deeply depressed about their current situation and unwilling to »try again«.

15 Such as Ambrosio Contarini, »The Travels of the Magnificent M. Ambrosio Contarini«, in: *Travels to Tana and Persia by Josafa Barbaro and Ambrosio Contarini*, ed. by Lord Stanley of Alderley (New York: Franklin, 1873), pp. 108–173; Ogier Ghiselin von Busbeck, *Vier Briefe aus der Türkei von Ogier Ghiselin von Busbeck*, ed. by Wolfram von den Steinen (Erlangen: Philosophische Akademie, 1926 [1589]); Jean Chardin, *Journal du Voyage du Chevalier Chardin en Perse & aux Indes Orientales, par La Mer Noire & par La Colchide – Première Partie* (London: Pitt, 1686); Archangelo Lamberti, *Relatione della Colchida, poggi della Mengrelia*

the long and vivid history of ritualized drinking, but the Georgian words for toastmaster and toast cannot be found in these sources, nor can the description of cultural practices comparable to these concepts.[16] Additionally, according to the travelogues, wine was frequently drunk without any ritual framing.

These observations are backed by Georgian literature and historiography. Since the »Golden Age« in the 11th-13th century the description of feasts has been a common topic in Georgian sources, but no hint of explicit toasting or toastmastership can be found. Even in the 19th century the poet Ak'ak'i C'ereteli noticed in his writings that »the ancestors« did not propose toasts at a table and would be ashamed if they witnessed the present-day phenomenon.[17] In the famous and extensive dictionary from the early 18th century by Sulxan Saba Orbeliani,[18] the words for toastmaster and toast are absent, an omission that would be difficult to explain if the Georgian banquet at that time were structurally the same as today's. Consequently, the Georgian banquet is an example of an »invented tradition«[19] and fulfills the function of creating and reinforcing national identity.

In written form, the Georgian word for toast first appears in a cycle of poems by the Georgian aristocrat Grigol Orbeliani (1800–1883),[20] often considered to

---

nella quale si trate dell'origine, costumi e così naturali di quei paesi (Naples: [no publisher], 1654).

16   In his portrayal of a 17th century wedding banquet at the court of king Vakhtang V. in Tbilisi, Chardin describes something he calls »drinking for [somebody's] health« (»boire la santé«): A group of eight men sitting close to the king is served with equally large drinking vessels filled with wine. The men get up and drink the wine to the end – in pairs of four. After they sit down again, the neighboring eight people get served wine in the same vessels and drink precisely in the same way. This drinking game continues all night with ever-larger drinking vessels and »santés« to more and more prominent people – up to the king.
      When it comes to the word, drinking to somebody's long life (»santé«) could be called »sadghegrzelo« in Georgian, which is derived from the roots »long« and »day« and effectively translates as »a toast.« On the other hand, Chardin does not mention that the »santés« are verbally formulated, repeated or elaborated – a crucial function of toasts at the *supra*. Whereas in the *supra* of recent years a »sadghegrzelo« is foremost a mode of speaking, it is not this particular genre that Chardin is writing about here. Furthermore, there is no trace of a *tamada* in Chardin's description (unless we assume that the king implicitly assumed this function); Chardin, *Journal du voyage*, op.cit. (note 15), p. 239.

17   Ak'ak'i C'ereteli, »Tornik'e Eristavi [tornike eristavi]«, in: *rcheuli nac'armoebebi xutt'omad, t'omi 2: p'oemebi, dramat'uli nac'erebi leksad [Selected Works in Ten Volumes, Volume 2: Poems, Dramatic Writings in Verses]* (Tbilisi: Nakaduli, 1989 [1884]), pp. 24–82, in particular p. 25.

18   Sulxan-Saba Orbeliani, *Kartuli Leksik'oni [Georgian dictionary] I-II*, ed. by Ilia Abuladze (Tbilisi: Merani, 1991 [1716]).

19   Eric Hobsbawm & Terence Ranger (Eds.), *The Invention of Tradition* (Cambridge: Cambridge University Press, 1983).

20   Grigol Orbeliani, »Sadghegrdzelo Anu Omis Shemdgom Ghame Lxini, Erevnis Siaxloves« [Feast in the night after the war in the vicinity of Yerevan], in: *txzulebata sruli k'rebuli [Complete collection of writings]*, (Tbilisi: sabchota sakartvelo [Soviet Georgia], 1959), pp. 89–106.

be one of the »fathers« of the national movement.[21] The poems are written in the form of toasts and remember national heroes, and their deeds.[22] This genre quickly became popular at banquets. Remembering the past as a toast became a form of national education after the Russian annexation of Georgia in 1801 and the consequent suppression of national sovereignty. In this context, the verbal evocation of the past becomes a patriotic mission at the table.

As a dramatization of the national narrative, the *supra* distinguished Georgian from Russian culture. This may be the reason why the culture of the *supra* spread so quickly all over Georgia in the 19th century. Unlike former occupiers of Georgia, the Russians shared the same religion as Georgians. Consequently, religion could no longer be a distinguishing factor between »us« and »them«. Despite its aristocratic (and possibly bourgeois[23]) origin, the *supra*, as a distinct way of feasting and as a manifestation of »Georgian« hospitality, became synonymous with »folk culture« and a symbol of cultural otherness.

In Soviet times the *supra* continued to be a sign of national identity and aroused suspicion from the authorities. In a law adopted in 1975 in Soviet Georgia, large banquets associated with crucial events like births, marriages, or deaths, were dismissed as a public display of a traditional attitude opposed to the ideal of the *homo sovieticus*. The *supra* became a »harmful custom«[24]. As religious activities were banned, ceremonial *supra*s also worked as a compensation for church rituals. Additionally, for ethnic Georgians *supra*s were a privileged place for creating networks, reinforcing alliances and trading information – important factors for coping with Soviet life.

---

21   See for example Ronald Grigor Suny, *The Making of the Georgian Nation* (Bloomington: Indiana University Press, 1994 [1988]), p. 125.

22   The Georgian literature journalist Levan Bregadze argues that Orbeliani copied the style of the Russian author Zhukovskii in his poem. This would present the possibility that the Georgians adopted the art of toasting from Russian aristocratic circles.

23   Possibly in the late 18th or early 19th century a particular bourgeois culture developed in Tbilisi. The culture was based on a trans-guild social club of craftsmen. A member of this organization was called »qarachogheli«, had to follow a certain dress code (black wool coat called a »chokha«, a belt, and fur hat or cap) and a codified set of honors. Qarachogheli men were famous for the poetic verses they recited with a raised bowl of wine in hand – definitely a form of toasting. In lower social strata, their culture was reflected and ironized by the k'int'os – street vendors and merchants famous for their stories, jokes, and songs. Unfortunately, there are no primary sources on qarachogheli- or k'int'o-culture. The most profound and popular source is Grishashvili's book on Old Tblilisi: Iosif Grishashvili, *Dzveli T'pilisis Lit'erat'uruli Bohema [Old Tbilisi's Literary Bohemia]* (Tbilisi: Sakhelbami, 1928). Though detailed and well informed, the information provided cannot be verified or properly dated. Thus, the influence of bourgeois and working class culture on the origin of the *supra* remains speculation.

24   Compare the decision of the Central Committee of the KPG from November 15, 1975 on »Measures to increase the fight against harmful traditions and customs«; in: Jürgen Gerber, *Georgien: Nationale Opposition und kommunistische Herrschaft seit 1956*, (Baden-Baden: Nomos, 1997), in particular p. 261 [in German].

Those Georgian intellectuals who considered defending Georgian culture to be their main task, but were well established in the Soviet academic or administrative systems, saw the *supra* as an important means of education. Historians like Shota Meskhia presented a completely different version of Georgian history at a *supra* than the one he taught at the university. For »orthodox nationalism« the *supra* was a »true academy«, as a popular saying from this time states. The representatives of »unorthodox nationalism« used the socially acceptable form of the *supra* to disguise their meetings.[25]

The Taste of Independent Georgia

For a compact and vivid description of *supra* culture in Georgia, I will differentiate the spheres of the national and the transnational. I will address the national mainly in reference to bourgeois and low-class social circles, and the transnational in reference to the Georgian diaspora.

In Georgia, drinking alcohol is a key element of national identity. This causes some difficulties for those Georgians who are Muslim by faith, e.g. in the Western-Georgian republic of Ajara, which borders Turkey. According to recent observations in Ajara by Pelkmans, refusing to drink alcohol at a *supra* or to serve alcohol to guests could be treated as a breach of »Georgian« hospitality. Thus, most Muslim Georgians in official positions who cannot avoid attending meetings and receiving guests act according to Georgian codes in public and observe Muslim codes at home. As one of Pelkmans' Muslim informants states in reference to his Christian neighbors: »People would think badly of you if you said that alcohol was prohibited in your house. It would be the same as saying that you are not Georgian«.[26]

Without a doubt, the *supra* remains a major way of performing the nation. As such, it is a powerful tool for inclusion and exclusion. This is not restricted

---

25 The concept of »orthodox« and »unorthodox« nationalism was used and popularized by Suny in his monograph, *The Making of the Georgian Nation* (Suny, *Georgian Nation*, op.cit. (note 21), here p. 307).

26 Mathijs Pelkmans, *Uncertain Divides – Religion, Ethnicity, and Politics in the Georgian Borderland* (PhD dissertation, University of Amsterdam, 2003), p. 72. – This double strategy challenges the popular self-perception of Georgian national identity as being based on religious and ethnic tolerance. One of the strongest national narratives has it that Georgia is characterized by its centuries-long tradition of peaceful cohabitation of different ethnic and religious groups. A popular example is that the Jews have never been persecuted in Georgia, and a popular image for the religious tolerance of the Georgians is the intimate neighborhood of churches, a synagogue and a mosque in the old district of Tbilisi.

to national identity: who is included in the *supra* – and how – makes a significant difference for setting the socio-cultural boundaries of the given group. Every *supra* states, reinforces and symbolizes the organizing principles of one social network or overlapping networks. These principles are commonly based on neighborhood, kinship, friendship, gender, age, region, interest and/or professional collaboration.

Inclusion also means incorporating foreigners in the community. In the process of turning the foreigner into a guest, he or she is implicitly informed about acceptable and unacceptable ways of comportment. Thus, the *supra* includes and excludes not only people, but also modes of behavior.

Apart from networking (including the exchange of sensitive information and confidential knowledge), reinforcing social boundaries, including and excluding modes of behavior or being, and revitalizing social hierarchies, the *supra* is most of all about making sense – something sought-after in times of drastic change characterized by a high level of social and cultural uncertainties. Males over 40 have lost significantly in social status and prestige since the Rose Revolution – and some have lost their jobs, too. The *supra* allows them to remember a past which was theirs, to bridge a gap in time, and to link the past to the present. In the *supra* ritual, the toast-givers blend their voices with those of their imagined ancestors. By integrating formalized modes in personal habitus and genetic heritage in individualized speech acts, the performer not only compensates for what is lacking in his life, but also actively creates sense, meaning and consistency.

With the real emotional involvement of the performers, the *supra* works as psychotherapy. For Vitebsky, the ability to envision the future from the past and thus make sense of the present is a prerequisite for a satisfied and successful life.[27] From his point of view, many inhabitants of Siberia still suffer from traumatic experiences stemming from the Soviet times, unable to reconcile their past with their present and thereby heal their wounds.[28] In Georgia, the traumatic experience of losing a safe and stable basis of life is at least partly processed during a *supra*.[29]

When it comes to the younger generations, the situation is far more complex indeed. Many young people (especially from urban contexts) overtly dislike and discredit the Georgian *supra*. Their reasons are based on changing gender roles,

---

27   Pierre Vitebsky, »Withdrawing from the Land: Social and Spiritual Crisis in the Indigenous Russian Arctic«, in: *Postsocialism – Ideals, Ideology and Practices in Eurasia,* ed. by Christopher Hann (London, New York: Routledge, 2002), pp. 180–195.

28   As true as this may be, it should not be forgotten that, according to Adorno, »Wrong life cannot be lived rightly.« (Theodor W. Adorno, *Minima Moralia – Reflections from Damaged Life* (London: NLB, 1974 [1951]), p. 39).

29   This partly explains why some elderly male Georgians will not stop drinking or participating at *supra*s despite serious warnings from their doctors.

an attributed backwardness of customs like the *supra* in the face of pro-Western orientation, and a differing understanding of authenticity. With the latter I refer to a commonplace criticism from young Georgians who state that friends turn into strangers during the *supra*, acting in a fundamentally different and disconcerting way. Thus, for some young Georgians the *supra*'s function has changed from a vehicle of hospitality to one of alienation.

On the other hand, most urban youths in Georgia do not simply ignore the rules of the *supra*. During an informal gathering called a *keipi*[30], members of a peer group take liberties with toasting and the institute of a toastmaster. Despite the informal atmosphere in such situations, gender distinctions are strictly observed. Men and women hardly ever engage in common *supras*, as in most cases only the young men are active speakers. On their own, however, young women in bars sometimes engage in toasting as well, albeit in a more or less informal or jocular manner. Here the rules of the *supra* work as an affirmation of peer group identity.

But there is more to it: For young men, the successful performance of »toast-mastership« (*tamadoba*) earns them status as honorable men. Within this context, the *supra* takes over the function of a school: the school of the table. Young men challenge each other during the process of toasting. Sometimes open dismissal is expressed of someone who does not manage to speak intoxicatingly, failing to entertain his friends or display charisma. In the school of the table ability to enforce is crucial. Apart from personal traits, this ability is based on mastership of public speaking, and this mastership is in turn a prerequisite for successful conflict management. As Koehler states, even for settling conflicts on the streets of Tbilisi the tongue is more important than the knife.[31] Sometimes the form of the *supra* is applied directly to conflict resolution. This is primarily due to the *supra*'s implicit demand for consensus: participating in a *supra* forces the participants to find solidarity openly with common principles of belonging and justice. In rare cases, I have even seen participants who were directly involved in confrontation arrange a *supra* in order to settle the conflict.[32]

If in Georgia the performance of the *supra* evokes the nation in quotidian and festive life, this is all the more true in diasporical contexts in which tangible reference to the »motherland« becomes a scarce resource. The role of the *supra* in

---

30   This word stems from Arabic and originally means, »to be in a good mood«. Variants of the words also exist in Russian and German. The Russian word »kajf« is a slang word for »being high« or for the colloquial »phat«; the related German verb »kiffen« means to smoke marijuana.

31   Jan Koehler, *Die Zeit der Jungs – Zur Organisation von Gewalt und der Austragung von Konflikten in Georgien* (Münster: LIT, 2000), p. 63.

32   Florian Mühlfried, »Sharing the Same Blood – Culture and Cuisine in the Republic of Georgia«, in: *Anthropology of Food* (forthcoming 2006).

the diaspora is twofold: On the one hand, socializing with fellow Georgians more often than not takes place at a table. Georgian dishes and the »Georgian way of drinking« evoke a feeling of home in this context. It is observable, however, that the rules of the *supra* are not strictly applied. Here, sipping wine is not a deadly sin, and some of the people gathered take pleasure in having escaped the rigidity of the *supra* in Georgia. Consequently, it is possible to toast and to remember, to evoke and to dream of home – but it is not obligatory. The *supra* becomes an option, and the procedure becomes more virtual.

On the other hand, the rules of the *supra* often serve as a way of explaining Georgian culture to non-Georgians – both as a distinct cultural practice and as a manifestation of »Caucasian« or »Georgian« hospitality. Georgian »national character« is often phrased in the form of a popular narrative on the origin of the Georgians. According to this story, the Georgians arrived late when God was distributing the land among the peoples of the world, and they were late because they had been feasting. When God told the Georgians that all the land had already been distributed, the Georgians apologized and said that they had stayed so long at the feast because they had been drinking in His honor. God was so touched by this statement that he gave the Georgians the land he had reserved for himself. Thus, according to the story, the Georgians came to live on God's land. This narrative inscribes feasting and toasting as core elements of Georgian culture and the Georgian nation as God's chosen.

In the sphere of the transnational, actions and artifacts sometimes change their meaning, becoming designators of the nation from outside. As an example, I would like to explain how a particular sauce called *tqemali* (popularly served at banquets) becomes the »third blood« of the Georgians and a culinary marker of national belonging.[33]

The sauce is made from wild plum (*prunus cerasifera*) grown almost exclusively in Georgia and Eastern Turkey. In Georgia, the fruit is a major ingredient in national cuisine. The sauce is made with various spices and greens such as coriander, some garlic and sometimes lemon juice. Its preparation varies from household to household, allowing for variation according to individual taste. Additionally, the transmission of individual modes of preparation manifests family wisdom and encodes family identity.

The popularity of *tqemali* in Georgia is comparable to that of ketchup in the USA. In some circles of the Georgian diaspora, the question of its acquisition becomes a question of the availability of national resources. Consequently, the availability or production of *tqemali* is vividly discussed in a German Internet forum on Georgia: what matters most are the »connections to home« in order to

---

33   The sauce is popular among Armenians with roots in Tbilisi as well.

secure »supplies«.[34] *Tqemali* is also known in Hungary because »wherever there are Georgians, there will be *tqemali*, too«.[35] It tastes »like mom's«,[36] is consumed like »manna and ambrosia« and is the »third blood of every Georgian«.[37] This is why *tqemali* sauce is a popular gift for Georgians living abroad.[38] According to a popular saying, wine is the second blood of the Georgians. The strict rules of alcohol consumption exemplify the sacredness of metaphorical kinship. *Tqemali* in turn becomes closer the farther the distance is from home. Both wine and *tqemali* epitomize Georgian national identity – wine as a way of world making, and *tqemali* as a product and producer of home in the diaspora.

Patriotic Discourse and Culturalization of Politics

In order to predict the future development of Georgian society and its approach to the *supra*, it will be helpful to reexamine the recent *supra* controversy and the revival of Georgian patriotism.

In the first months following the Rose Revolution, Georgian society was in a state of limbo. Former values and practices were questioned and new social concepts had not yet been stated explicitly. It was during this time that the *supra* seemed to be the »other« *supra* of a society catapulted into a new era. I will quote from an email that I received in January 2005 from a British colleague working in Georgia: »I just thought I'd write to say hello from Georgia. I've been here a couple of weeks now and I've had to work very hard. I thought the whole point of being in Georgia was to drink and eat, but it seems these post-revolutionary government officials do neither. No *supra*s for me – in fact, they might even be illegal now.«

This somehow impressionistic and non-representative statement illustrates a new spirit that seemed to have dominated the public sector in Georgia: no more wasting of time at endless banquets, and hard work instead. In former times, *supra*s were an important and integral part of networking, negotiating

---

34   See http://www.georgienseite.de/magazin/forum.php. The first contribution is from March 15, the last one from March 18, 2002. All contributions are saved in the archive of the forum. The following translations are mine.

35   Quotation from a contribution from »Anna«; March 16, 2002, 02:37.

36   Quotation from a contribution from »Dato«, March 15, 2002, 14:50.

37   The last two quotations are from a contribution from »Kavabata« from March 15, 2002, 13:00.

38   When traveling from Georgia to Germany, my Georgian acquaintances frequently asked me to take *tqemali*, »Svanetian salt« and/or homemade schnapps (*ch'ach'a*) for their friends or relatives living in Germany.

and business-making, spreading the smell of corruption and nepotism. The new officials seemed eager to get rid of this culture.

Those highlighting the ideology and practice of the *supra* were easily identifiable as belonging to the old generation. In the intellectual and academic sphere, they were the members of the »red intelligentsia«. In the realm of politics, they were associated with the corrupt machinations of the Shevardnadze apparatus.

Among other groups, the opposition against the old regime united NGO bureaucrats, unruly intellectual thinkers, and those who saw themselves as true patriots, striving for a better future for their country. President Saakashvili, as the »winner« of the peaceful revolution and strongest politician in the country, uses democratic pro-Western discourse in his foreign policy and a national, sometimes nationalistic discourse when he addresses his fellow citizens and politicians.

As Saakashvili was elected president in January 2004 with more than 96% of votes cast, and as the parliament is extensively dominated by allied parties, opposition to the new government is rather weak. Although the main internal problems of the country are social in nature (unemployment, high rate of poverty, significant price inflation, etc.), the opposition is engaged in a nationalist, sometimes ultra-orthodox discourse, blaming the current regime for neglecting Georgian values or interests and selling the country to Westerners.

Thus, the domestic debate is about who the real patriots are. To win this battle, Saakashvili and his fellows started an enthusiastic campaign, widely visible in the capital city of Tbilisi. The main elements of the campaign are posters, flags, architecture and monuments.

Apart from the central square of Tbilisi (called Freedom Square) and in front of the city hall, a huge poster states, »The patriots are coming«[39]. The poster shows young people dressed in orange and blue, waving the new Georgian flag, which is five red crosses on a white background. This flag was a symbol of the National Movement and replaced the old flag used under Gamsakhurdia and Shevardnadze. The latter flag stemmed from the time of the independent socialist Georgian government, which ruled Georgia from 1918 until it was abolished by the Red Army in 1921. The new flag was originally used in the Middle Ages, designating Christian Georgia.

On almost every prominent building at every location in Tbilisi, the national flag with its Christian symbolism waves, spreading the flair of pride and power. In many cases the Georgian flag is next to the European flag, perfectly manifesting the Georgian double strategy: outwardly European, inwardly patriotic. Although far from becoming a member of the European Union, Tbilisi has more European flags than almost any city in Europe.

---

39   The »patriots« is a youth movement strongly supported by the government and comparable to the Russian »Nashi« promoted by Russian President Vladimir Putin.

Figure 8.1: Tearing down the Soviet symbol called »Andropov's Ears« in Tbilissi, 2005. Photo: F. Mühlfried.

But the campaign is not limited to posters or flags. Entire squares, monuments and buildings are being demolished and rebuilt, inscribing the new spirit into architecture. The central plaza for Soviet parades known as Republic Square (which has supposedly been renamed Revolution Square) has been freed of Soviet architecture. For the last couple of decades, the place had been dominated by enormous concrete arches, which were dubbed »Andropov's Ears« by the Tbilisians because the arches were constructed during Andropov's reign and represented the almighty presence of the KGB (»ears«) for some locals. Although undoubtedly ugly, the arches represented a significant chapter of the country's past, and their demolition is a symbolic rejection of Soviet heritage.

Republic Square has yet another victim: The monument to King David The Builder has been relocated to the outskirts of Tbilisi. In the game of demolition, relocation and construction, a gigantic monument to be built at Freedom Square has recently been worrying intellectuals. In the middle of the square, surrounded by traffic, dominating the view of the city's old town, a 33-meter-high pillar is to be erected with a statue of St. George slaying the dragon at the top. The mayor of Tbilisi made the decision to build the monument without any public selection process. During the celebration for the second anniversary of the Rose Revolution in November 2005, Saakashvili and the presidents of Ukraine, Romania, and Estonia ceremonially laid the monument's foundation. The statue itself is a gift from Moscow-based Georgian sculptor Zurab Tsereteli, a much-beloved artist of the former Soviet authorities.

The aforementioned plans, strategies and activities have been challenged. Some artists and intellectuals dismiss the architectural practice as megalomaniac, nationalist and reactionary, some opposition politicians call it a loss of identity and a waste of money, and the Orthodox Church argues that saints like St. George may not be depicted three-dimensionally. The events as such clearly indicate, however, that the public sphere and the realm of culture have been politicized and that the field of politics itself has been culturalized by the recent political elite. The dominant discourse is built around nationalized values and expressed in words and objects. When talking about the *supra* it is impossible to avoid this discursive context.

External Actors

Grant Donors and NGOs

After the Rose Revolution, Georgian political, social and cultural matters were frequently discussed at international conferences on developments in post-Soviet space. For certain reasons, the influence of Western players was either downplayed or simply ignored in most cases. Recent political events were commonly presented as a self-made internal affair, with no significant contribution from the outside.

This is all the more surprising, as activities like those of George Soros and his Open Society Institute (OSI) in Georgia are well documented on various websites and controversially debated within the country. For example, the OSI supported a trip for the Georgian opposition student association *k'mara* (»enough«) to Serbia, where they were trained in effective oppositional organization and civil disobedience techniques by their counterparts at Otpor, a national student organization that played a significant role in the overthrow of Serbian President Slobodan Milosevic. After the successful change of power in Georgia, Soros contributed to the salary of the Georgian president and some of his most influential ministers. Apart from Soros, US institutions like the World Movement for Democracy (headquartered at the National Endowment for Democracy) and military experts for peaceful revolutions like Robert Helvey are active throughout the post-Soviet sphere.

Currently, former NGO representatives are well represented in the Georgian government and parliament. The minister of education, for example, is the former head of the Open Society Georgia Foundation (OSGF), and the minister of defense was a prominent figure in an NGO called the Liberty Institute, which received funding from USAID and OSGF. The recent strategy of OSGF (as stated in autumn 2005[40]) is directly oriented towards influencing state policy. The aims mentioned in reference to the slogan, »dialogue with the government« include attempts to influence the legislative and executive powers in the fields of the economy, education and the military, health, media, and minority rights. On another plane, the OSGF has taken a strong interest in grassroots movements. Here the aim is to create or strengthen a civil society based on liberal values. Localized strategies supporting »civic action« have concrete results in shaping the notion and practice of citizenship.

Consequently, the activities of NGOs like OSI affect both politics and socio-cultural life. As a side effect, a middle class consisting of people paid by NGOs has emerged, legitimized by values primarily defined by Western donors.[41] To neglect this input on local and national levels indicates a failure to understand the current shaping of the Georgian nation. Additionally, it includes the danger of misinterpreting dominant discourses and cultural practices.

The above mentioned indicates that the very term NGO (Non-Governmental Organization) has become obsolete in Georgia recently: Institutions like OSGF or the Liberty Institute are so closely intertwined with the government that they can hardly be separated. The consequences are: loss of legitimate status as independent voices, a change in the discourse praxis, and a silencing of fundamental critique. The most powerful and influential NGOs are less interested in challenging the system and provoking the political elite. Changes are still encouraged, but within the framework of values set and propelled by the Rose Revolution.

The influence of NGOs is not limited to the sphere of politics. In the course of recent reforms in higher education, the academic sphere has become more and more dependent on financial and personal support from NGOs. In the times of Shevardnadze the academic field was an intellectual antipode to the field of NGOs, but now it is evaluated according to criteria more often than not developed by NGOs. Thus, the discursive practice of academicians and intellectuals is contextualized in the normative framing of NGO policy.

This shift in the framing of discourses is reflected in the controversy over the

---

40   Open Society Georgia Foundation, *Quarterly Newsletter* 3/4 (2005).
41   I would like to thank Lasha Bakradze, who shared this observation with me.

supra. Jgerenaia first presented his thoughts on the *supra* in 2000 at a conference organized by a Georgian NGO called the Caucasian Institute for Peace, Democracy and Development. At this particular time, critical discourse on Georgian identity, values and traditions functioned to help overcome the old mentality. After the old regime was by de-facto overcome, this discourse lost its function. Rethinking Georgian identity and culture has been postponed.

Tourism

Culture and discourse are not shaped exclusively by political interactions, but by face-to-face interactions as well. Tourism is one kind of face-to-face interaction, implying contact with inner and outer perspectives. Most foreigners visiting Georgia immediately notice the great importance of the *supra* for socio-cultural life. Some of them perceive the impossibility of escaping hospitality in the form of everlasting banquets as a plague.[42] Others praise the Georgian spirit and something they interpret as cultural authenticity. As an example, here is a toast made by a woman from the US:

I would like to speak about Georgia, because I've noticed as I've grown older in my own country I've seen a lot of fakeness. There are lots of fake smiles, lots of fake food [laughter], lots of fake ... clothes, people are just ... plastic. And I came to Georgia, and the food wasn't fake, the music wasn't fake, and the people weren't fake, and I felt this real quality of life that I think I've been missing. And I was very relieved to find it here. And I don't want to go home, but I know I've things to do there. And I know I'll be back. [applause]

In contrast to her own culture, this woman attributes authenticity to Georgian food, music, and people, and thus to culture and society. This understanding is sharply contrasted by the statements of most of my young informants. One well-educated women in her early thirties said:

I have problems understanding people whom I know really well ... and suddenly [these people] behave completely differently [at a *supra*]. And then this kind of behavior becomes so normal, it's a kind of blurring of borders.

And further:

The borders between the real me and this imagined me which I want to play become so blurred that you don't know who you are. And the people with whom you interact are also kind of lost.

---

42   For example, German writer Clemens Eich, who complains that everywhere he goes to, a *tamada* is already waiting and the table is already set; Clemens Eich, *Aufzeichnungen aus Georgien* (Frankfurt am Main: Fischer, 1999), p. 38ff..

The distinction between »real me« and »imagined me« parallels the dichotomy of »authentic« and »fake«. Thus, for the young Georgian the performance of the *supra* is fake, whereas for the young American it is a harmonic blend of »true« feelings and culture. Consequently, the statement of the woman from the US cited above provides a positive feedback to the *supra* system, and tourists' expectations of authentic experiences in Georgian culture keep Georgians »playing the game«. This act of playing, in turn, is dismissed by some Georgians. Once again, the attitude towards the *supra* differentiates inward from outward perception, and belonging from rejection. But here it is the other way around: not belonging creates the desire for inclusion and the notion of authenticity, whereas belonging means rejection and dismissal of the rules of the game.

Conclusion

»Celebrating Identities«, the title of this paper, refers both to the practice of banqueting and to recent emergences of new socio-cultural identities in the republic of Georgia. Within a set of pre-coded actions (including speech-acts), the performance of the *supra* formulates and celebrates the social identities of the attendees, who are also the performers. Discourse on the *supra* plays a role in the self-ascription and attribution of identities, particularly in intellectual elitist circles. If new emerging social identities and dominant discourses are sanctioned by state policy, they are immediately manifested in architecture (including monuments). Here – as always – the spheres of the political and social are inseparable, and culture is the playground for both.

The method applied in this article could be called »parallel close reading«, as I have tried to »read« cultural (focus: the *supra*) and social elements (focus: elites) at the same time. The disadvantage of my approach is that it is highly dependent on time. Future developments in Georgian society, culture and politics may fundamentally alter the image. Recapitulating my observations and conclusions, however, I will now try to outline some possible directions for socio-political developments in Georgia.

The autocratic tendencies in the governance of the new political leadership, its patriotic rhetoric and urbanistic practice are not unquestioned in Georgian society. Three fields can be distinguished which may provide the grounds for new social movements and the formation of new intellectual elites:

The protest against the erection of the St. George monument in front of the city hall mainly focuses on the nationalist, anti-modernist and megalomaniac symbolism of the post-revolutionary government. The recent fore thinkers of the movement (namely, artist Mamuka Japaridze and historian Lasha Bakradze) are neither directly involved in politics nor in the activities of NGOs. Here, the future of the country is debated in aesthetic terms, but reflecting the development of Georgian society in general.

Apart from a recently-established movement called »Anti-Soros«, which mainly consists of ultra-orthodox-nationalists and followers of Georgia's deposed president Zviad Gamsakhurdia, a younger and not necessarily nationalist generation, most of them students, has been questioning the actions of NGOs. Given the loss of legitimate status of NGOs as independent voices, criticizing them may paradoxically support the formation and consolidation of a civil society based on the values of freedom, political independence, and cultural autonomy. This might lead to an anti-globalization movement that is not steeped in subconscious wishes or conscious attempts to restore a glorious past.

The same applies to a third possible tendency, which remains the least developed: replacing culturalist with social discourse. Instead of debating the outcomes of symbolic politics, issues like class, wealth, employment, solidarity etc. would be at stake here. As in most other post-socialist societies, social discourse is highly discredited as a follow-up to Bolshevik ideology. The growing reception of Western anti-globalization discourses in academic circles is likely to have an impact, however.

Discourses, like currencies, have their trade-cycles. The discourse on the *supra* has reached its peak and is on the decline. It played its role in the shaping of a post-post-Soviet mentality, but lost its functionality once the old dogmas were abandoned. However, as a cultural practice designating uniqueness and identity, the *supra* will remain important – especially in the circles of diaspora, and in an increasingly virtualized form.

Barth, »Yeraz«, and Post-Soviet Azerbaijan: Inventing a New Sub-Ethnic Identity

Bahodir Sidikov

As a result of The European Neighbourhood Policy, relations between the EU and Azerbaijan have improved.[1] This South Caucasian country would even geographically come closer to Europe if Turkey became a member of the EU. The concepts of the »West«, such as modernization and democracy, are now in Azerbaijan associated not only with the United States and Western Europe but also with Turkey. Turkey as a member of the Euro-Atlantic community has played, and still plays, a vital role in keeping Azerbaijan on the path of transition towards democracy and market development.[2] Therefore, it would be interesting to discuss in the following paper[3] specific *challenges* to collective identity in post-Soviet Azerbaijan, a Muslim country with a pronounced secular orientation, that is now »on the outskirts« of the enlarged EU.

Demise of the Soviet Union: New Boundaries, New Identities

The disintegration of the USSR has resulted not only in the formation of new political borders but also in the strengthening of sub-ethnic boundaries within the so-called titular ethnic groups (*titul'naia natsiia*) in the Caucasus. In Soviet times, belonging to a certain sub-ethnic group was of secondary and even tertiary importance and was manifested largely by means of minor cultural differences in private life.

---

1 http://europa.eu.int/comm/external_relations/azerbaidjan/intro/index.htm.

2 About the role of the »West« in Azerbaijan see Arif Yunusov, »Azerbaijani Security Problems and Policies«, in: *The South Caucasus: a Challenge for the EU*, ed. by Dov Lynch (Paris: Institute for Security Studies, 2003), pp. 143–157.

3 This article is based on the author's field work in Azerbaijan in 2004 within the framework of the research project *Accounting for State-Building, Stability and Conflict: The Institutional Framework of Caucasian and Central Asian Transitional Societies* at the Institute of East-European Studies, Free University, Berlin. It also uses some data from Bahodir Sidikov, »New or Traditional? ›Clans‹, Regional Groupings, and State in Post-Soviet Azerbaijan«, in: *Berliner Osteuropa Info* 21 (2004), pp. 68–74.

After 1992, sub-ethnic identity, due to the new socio-economic environment, again began to surface and revealed itself not only in private life but was also used by the elites of the new independent states in the Caucasus as an important mechanism for political mobilization as well as for building informal networks for resource distributions in the economy. This was possible only as it became advantageous to create a network of clientele designed as a »we-group«[4] when competing over the newly accessible resources. Before, in Soviet days, the economy and politics were spheres in which sub-ethnicity did not play any significant role.

Despite obvious identity shifts and changes among the people of the Caucasus in the post-Soviet period, most of those researchers who studied this region either simply »overlooked« the process of sub-ethnicity strengthening or, having noticed it, distorted its essence almost beyond recognition.[5] Strategic groups[6] that misused sub-ethnic identity for the purpose of political mobilization were labeled as »clans«. If one takes a careful and unbiased look at the names of »clans« in the Caucasus, one may find that these are self-ascriptions and/or nicknames (ascriptions by others) of sub-ethnic communities within corresponding ethnic groups.

In other words, the entire post-Soviet literature on the »rebirth« of »clans« and »clannishness« in this region is nothing but distorted evidence. In fact, along with the process of consolidation of Caucasian ethnic groups, also an ongoing process of internal differentiation or, more precisely, disintegration can be observed. It was this process of disintegration that enabled the central authorities of the former Soviet Republics in the Caucasus to create client networks by employing sub-ethnic identity strategically.

This may appear to be contradictory. However, the contradiction is resolved if one agrees with the two following points. Firstly, the processes of consolida-

---

4   Georg Elwert, »Switching of We-group Identities: the Alevis as Case Among Many Others«, in: *Syncretistic Religious Communities in the Near East*, ed. by Krisztina Kehl-Bodrogi & Barbara Kellner-Heinkele & Anke Otter-Beaujean (Leiden: Brill, 1997), pp. 65 – 85, in particular p. 66.

5   See for details Bahodir Sidikov, »Novoe ili traditsionnoe?   Regional'nye gruppirovki v postsovetskom Azerbaidzhane«, in: *Vestnik Evrazii* 2 (2004), pp.151–169; see also Sidikov, »New or Traditional?«, op. cit. (note 3).

6   A strategic group comprises individuals united by a shared interest in retaining or expanding their opportunities to capture resources. Resources shall be understood not only as material benefits but also as power, prestige, knowledge, or religious ends. Shared interest leads to strategic actions, that is, it enables the implementation of a long-term »program« for maintaining or enhancing opportunities to capture resources. See Hans-Dieter Evers & Tilman Schiel, *Strategische Gruppen: vergleichende Studien zu Staat, Bürokratie und Klassenbildung in der dritten Welt* (Berlin: Reimer, 1988), in particular p.10. In the context in question the term »strategic group« refers to an informal group acting as part of a strategy to capture and exploit resources.

tion and disintegration of an ethnic group occur virtually simultaneously and it is only a question of which of the two processes dominates in a given historical period and what it is leading to. Secondly, forces behind the processes of consolidation and disintegration of ethnic groups in the Caucasus are qualitatively different. This alone is a good enough reason to see no contradiction in the fact that the said processes occur simultaneously. Whereas the process of consolidating ethnic groups into nations within the newly formed nation-states in the Caucasus is primarily encouraged by political and cultural elites through predominantly ideological measures and cultural policies (»imagined communities« and »invention of tradition« policy), new socio-economic realities, resource distributions in particular, have an effect in a completely opposite direction as actively facilitating the process of disintegration of ethnic groups. However, one should not completely forget about the engagement of elites in this process. In some instances, being removed from the distribution of the »public pie«, a part of the political elite took intensive measures to strengthen and secure the results of ethnic disintegration in order to create for themselves a large basis of support from below – which is primarily from members of a corresponding sub-ethnic group.

A Methodological Problem

The processes of ethnic group consolidation in the Caucasus have been covered widely by scientific research. So far, however, no attention has been paid to the disintegration of the said ethnic groups. Therefore, in this article, I will pay special attention to the picture of how the state authorities and a certain part of the Azerbaijani cultural elite were making targeted efforts between 1992 and 2002 to »invent« and impose a specific sub-ethnic identity on a group of Azerbaijanis originating from Armenia.

I am compelled to disregard the question of how successful these efforts have been for the answer would require extensive sociological surveys among the representatives of the group in question. Sociological surveys are associated with major difficulties not only due to the current political situation in Azerbaijan but also regarding the methodology to determine whether people belong to a group that has not yet come into existence.

The identity of Azerbaijanis, like of any other ethnic group, is multi-layered and situational. Furthermore, »mixed« marriages between Azerbaijanis from Azerbaijan and those from Armenia represent specific challenges to a researcher trying to define their identity. The children of these »mixed« marriages have also been subjected to the imposition of a distinct sub-ethnic identity by the authorities and cultural elites of this country.

Some Remarks on Terminology

But first of all some brief remarks should be made on the sense in which I will use the terms »ethnic group« and »sub-ethnic group«. Barth considers ethnic groups to be a form of social interaction and not culture-bearing units. According to Barth, »... ethnic groups are categories of ascription and identification by the actors themselves, and thus have the characteristic of organizing interaction between people«.[7]

Barth believes, meanwhile, that the self-identification by group members is a decisive criterion for identifying an ethnic group. On top of that, the self-identification is in complex interaction with the identification from the outside (ascription by others). Hence, an ethnic group is stable only if its self-identification is reflected in its being identified as such a group from the outside. Self-identification (some Russian authors use the term »ethnic self-consciousness«) and identification from the outside are reflected in the self-referential term and nickname respectively.[8]

What has been said about ethnic groups could, with certain reservations, be applied to sub-ethnic groups too, namely, that it is possible to identify a sub-ethnic group on the basis of self-referential terms and descriptions from the outside while the nickname may or may not match the self-reference term. In all other situations, a researcher is on precarious ground because, as Barth stated, there is »... no simple one-to-one relationship between ethnic units and cultural similarities and differences.« There are no »objective« features that could help to differentiate between ethnic groups. We may take into consideration only »those, which the actors themselves regard significant.« Barth refers to them as »diacritical features«, that are features that are unsubstantial and incidental, emphasizing that choosing any of them as a symbol of group identity is absolutely arbitrary and unpredictable for we cannot predict »... which features will be emphasized and made organizationally relevant by the actors«.[9]

---

7 Frederik Barth, »Introduction«, in: *Ethnic Groups and Boundaries: The Social Organization of Culture Difference*, ed. by Frederik Barth (Boston: Little Brown & Company, 1969), pp. 9–38, in particular p. 10.

8 Georg Elwert, *Ethnizität und Nationalimus: Über die Bildung von Wir-Gruppen* (Berlin: Das Arabische Buch, 1989), in particular p. 23.

9 Barth, »Introduction«, opt. cit. (note 7), p. 14.

This point is of special significance for my analysis. Addressing activities of state authorities and elites in Azerbaijan that »invent« and »create« a new sub-ethnic identity as well as impose it on Azerbaijani re-settlers and refugees from Armenia in Azerbaijan, I will focus specifically on these »diacritical« features and their inclusion into the collective memory of that particular community.

Azerbaijanis: Three Levels of Identity

When addressing processes in the sphere of ethnicity in post-Soviet Azerbaijan, it is necessary to make the following distinction. The term »Azerbaijanis« (*Azär-baycanlılar*)[10] has a dual meaning. In the first instance it denotes a »titular« ethnic group, in another – a supra-ethnic group (the community of all residents of the country regardless of their ethnic origin).

The Russian anthropologist Bruk remarked in discussions on sub-ethnic groups that all peoples evolved during a lengthy period from numerous elements, often ethnically heterogeneous, and it is not surprising that selected portions of those peoples that have not reached a high degree of consolidation have special self-reference terms (self-ascriptions).[11] This certainly applies to Azerbaijanis as well, among which, based on self-reference terms, researchers identify the following sub-ethnic groups (in alphabetical order): Bakiners, Borchaliners, Ganjiners, Karabakhers, Nakhichevaners, Shekiners, and others.[12] After 1992, the so-called »Western Azerbaijanis« (Azerbaijanis originally from Armenia) have been distinguished. This group will be discussed later in this article.

In addition to the above mentioned sub-ethnic groups there are representatives of some non-Turkic, by now assimilated people who are living side-by-side with Azerbaijanis as, for example, Lezgins, Kurds, Talyshs, Tats. A noteworthy peculiarity is that, despite the complete assimilation of language and culture as well as a change in self-ascription, these non-Turkic elements within Azerbaijani sub-ethnic groups usually remember their origin. More precisely, the

---

10 Note on the transliteration: Azerbaijan ə in the Latin script, reintroduced in December 1991, is rendered as ›ä‹ and ğ as ›gh‹.

11 Sergei Bruk, »Vse gorazdo slozhnee«, in: *Rasy i narody* 18 (1988), pp. 36–41, in particular p. 37.

12 Arif Abbasov, *Azerbaidzhantsy: istoriko-etnograficheskii ocherk* (Baku: Elm, 1998); Aliaga Mamedov, »Vliianie regionalizma na politicheskuiu zhizn' trebuet nauchnogo izucheniia«, in: *Ekho* 86 (2002), p. 8.; Rasim Musabeyow, »Die politischen Parteien und die Elite in Aserbaidschan«, in: *Diaspora, Öl und Rosen. Zur innenpolitischen Entwicklung in Armenien, Aserbaidschan und Georgien*, ed. by Heinrich-Böll-Stiftung (Berlin: Heinrich-Böll-Stiftung, 2004), pp. 205–215.

origin is remembered depending on changes in the political environment. A well-known parallel is the memory of origin of the Chechen *taips*: depending on ethnic elements a certain *taip* is traced back to, a *taip* can be regarded as either »pure«/aboriginal or »non-pure«/alien. In this regard there has been a lot of speculation concerning the origins of the particular *taips*, to which the late Chechen President Jokhar Dudaev belonged.[13]

I shall not go deeper into contemplating the factors that contributed to the preservation of sub-ethnic boundaries among the people of Azerbaijan. But I will mention that the presence of different »ethno-genetic« components (I am using the term from the article by Bruk) among the people of Azerbaijan as well as the existence on Turkic khanates on the territory of contemporary Azerbaijan and Armenia prior to the Russian conquest have resulted in the fact that the Azerbaijanis now consist of the above mentioned sub-ethnic communities that differ from one another in terms of dialect[14], in one instance even in language, in the peculiarities of lifestyle and culture, and partly in their anthropological type. The analyst Vagif Guseĭnov noted that in this respect Azerbaijan is somewhat similar to neighboring Georgia. It has the same intricate interweavement of two mutually excluding dispositions – nationalism and ineradicable regionalism [sub-ethnicity – B. S.]. To flesh it out, Guseĭnov cites the words of Aslan Abashidze, the former leader of the Autonomous Republic of Ajaria in Georgia: »No matter how hard you try to create new administrative divisions, the ancient names of Kakhetia, Migrelia, Guria, Ajaria live on in the nation's historical memory«[15].

In connection with this, I would like to make one comment with regard to the historical prerequisites for the emergence of sub-ethnic communities within the people of Azerbaijan. I believe that they go back not to economic zoning adopted in Soviet times but rather to the borders of late medieval Turkic khanates that existed in the second half of the 18th and the early 19th century.[16] It is not surprising that analysts tend to mix economic zoning with historical and ethnographical zones, as in Azerbaijan economic, historical, and natural geographical areas largely correspond with each other.[17]

The choice of contrasting features, or »diacritical« features according to Barth, is dictated by historical chance and is entirely arbitrary. For instance, the Rus-

13 Magomet Mamakaev, *Chechenskii rod v period ego razlozheniia* (Groznyi: Checheno-ingushskoe knizhnoe izdatel'stvo, 1973), p. 28. *Taip* is a Chechen tribal organization or clan, self-identified through descent from a common ancestor and geographic location.

14 Mämmäd agha Şiräli oghlu Şiräliyev, *Azärbaycan dilinin dialektoloji atlası* (Baku: Elm, 1990).

15 Vagif Guseĭnov, »Aliev posle Alieva: nasledovanie vlasti kak sposob ee uderzhaniia«, at: http://www.ng.ru/ideas/2004–03–19/10_aliev.html

16 Abbasov, *Azerbaidzhantsy*, op. cit (note 12), p. 45; see also Fuad Aliev, *Azerbaidzhansko-russkie otnosheniia (XV-XIX vv.)* (Baku: Elm, 1985).

17 Abbasov, *Azerbaidzhantsy*, op. cit (note 12), p. 41.

Figure 9.1: A map of the economic partitioning of Azerbaijan.

sian language and urban mentality function as a basis of identity and solidarity among the Baku sub-ethnic group; in case of the Nakhichevaners, it is the experience of living at the edge of the Turkic world and in collision with Christian peoples (Armenians, Georgians) as well as the specificity of their economic activity in their rather sparse environment; with the Borchali sub-ethnic group, it is their experience of coexistence with Georgians; with the Karabakhers, it is belonging to the area where the modern Azerbaijani culture originated.

The preservation and even strengthening of internal boundaries and disintegration of the Azerbaijani people, which occurred in the past decade, were largely caused by two factors: the collapse of the USSR and the emergence of »shadow« states. How did this come about?

Panarin notes that with the disappearance of the USSR as a single state, the harmony of three potential levels of evolutionary dynamics of humankind – global, supra-ethnic and ethnic – was disrupted. The USSR, by promoting the traditions of the Era of Enlightenment, had linked its destiny with the second level; after all, the Era of Enlightenment was an era when large single nations were formed by re-melting contiguous ethnic groups and subcultures into major

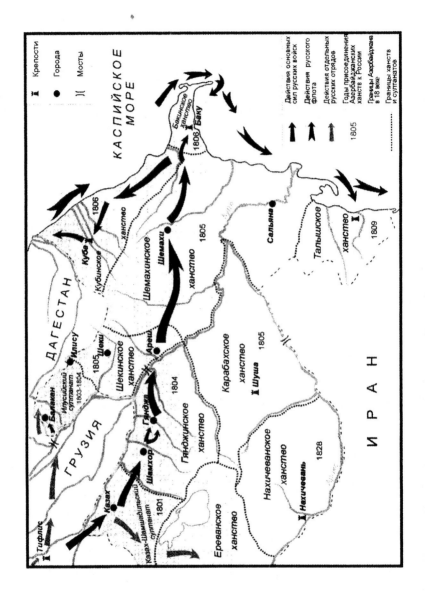

Figure 9.2: Historical map of Azerbaijan (1805), Source: Todua 2001 (see note 48).

socio-economic communities acquiring a large integrated economic, political-legal, and information-education space.[18]

The supra-ethnic level within the Soviet Union was embodied in the phenomenon of a »new historical community, the Soviet nation« that existed not only as état-nation but also as regular poly-ethnic nation – the Soviet nation.[19] Ethnic groups that constituted the Soviet nation shared a number of social and anthropological features that can be defined by the term »*sovetskost'*«, or »sovietness«. It has to be noted, though, that sovietness has acquired an ethnic character: for example, Kazakhs from the same *juz* (confederation of tribes), but living either in the former USSR or in China, which means they are separated by political and cultural borders, differ from each other dramatically.[20]

Within the Soviet nation there was an active consolidation of the Azerbaijani ethnic group with neighboring and closely related ethnic groups and subcultures.[21] Being part of it was possible because in the framework of the »Soviet nation« the Azerbaijanis were »contrasted« with other major ethnic groups (Russians, Georgians, Armenians, Uzbeks, etc.). Thus, the »Soviet nation«, being real and abstract at the same time, served as kind of reference group that facilitated the consolidation of ethnic groups that inhabited the USSR. Yet, with the destruction of the second level, its role was passed on to the third level – the ethnic one. As a result, the level of ethnicity became referential and abstract. Just as support for the second level used to consolidate ethnic groups, support for the third level resulted in the fact that within the Azerbaijani ethnic group, subethnic boundaries and »contrapositions« began to grow stronger because, with the creation of the nation state, the »contrapositions« to other ethnic groups in the former Soviet Union disappeared and »contrapositions« began within the

---

18   Aleksandr Panarin, *Iskushenie globalizmom* (Moscow: Eksmo, 2003), p. 76.

19   Sergei Cheshko, *Raspad Sovetskogo Soiuza: etnopoliticheskii analiz* (Moscow: Nauka, 1996), p. 141.

20   Edward Schatz, *Modern Clan Politics: The Power of »Blood« in Kazakhstan and Beyond* (Seattle & London: University of Washington Press, 2004), p. 152: »Even where subethnic divisions were significant for villagers, they were not necessarily the dominant division. In rural Taldy-Qorghan region, the most salient cleavage cross-cut umbrella clan lines. On the one hand were Kazakhs from the Younger and Elder Umbrella Clans who remained in the area continuously under Soviet rule. On the other hand were those Kazakhs from the Middle and Elder Umbrella Clans who fled to China in the late 1920s, returning to their original villages in the 1950s and 1960s. The main cleavage was between ›Sovietized‹ Kazakhs and ›Hanified‹.«

21   Abbasov, *Azerbaidzhantsy*, op. cit (note 12), p. 45; Rasim Musabekov, »Stanovlenie azerbaidzhanskogo gosudarstva i etnicheskie men'shinstva«, in: *Azerbaidzhan i Rossiia: obshchestva i gosudarstva*, ed. by Dmitrii Furman (Moscow: Letnii sad, 2001), pp. 337–362; Arif Yunusov, »Etnoiazykovaia situatsiia i problemy natsional'nykh men'shinstv v postsovetskom Azerbaidzhane«, in: Minoritetsile natsionale shi relatsii interetnice: traditsia europeane shi experientsa noilor democratsii pentru Moldova (Iashi: Universitatea de Stat din Moldova, 2002), pp. 183–202.

same ethnic group. This, in my view, revealed the close connection between supra-ethnic and sub-ethnic levels of identity.

The process of disintegration of the ethnic group of Azerbaijanis was largely facilitated by the actions of Azerbaijani elites. The policy of the first democratic government – led by the National Front of Azerbaijan (NFA) – was one of quick rapprochement with Turkey. Pan-Turkist slogans (»Only a Turk can be a friend to a Turk«), and the adoption of the language law in late December 1992, in which the Azerbaijani language was renamed Turkic, at the same time led to the disintegration of two communities: first, the Azerbaijanis as a single ethnic group, and secondly, the Azerbaijanis as a civic community of all people living in Azerbaijan regardless of their ethnic origin. For example, representatives of such a sub-ethnic community as the one of Baku, whose primary language was Russian, felt their difference acutely compared to other sub-ethnic groups of Azerbaijanis.

In regards to the Azerbaijanis as a community of all residents of the country: prior to the adoption of the language law, many representatives of Muslim peoples, including the Tats, Talyshs, Kurds, and Lezgins, especially those living in the regions with a predominantly Azerbaijani population, considered themselves »Azerbaijanis« and were registered as such during Soviet censuses. The adoption of the language law pushed the minorities out of the Azerbaijani community. The then extremely sluggish process of ethnic self-identification of national minorities was given a powerful boost.[22] The ill-considered human resource policy of the NFA government also played a role.[23] For example, the majority in the first democratically elected government (14 ministers) were Gazakhers,[24] coming from Gazakh, Agstafa, Tovuz, and Shamkir, all of which are districts of Azerbaijan located in the territory of the former Gazakh-Shamshaddil sultanate. The population of these districts is considered to be a separate sub-ethnic group of Azerbaijanis.[25]

The »godfathers« of the »shadow« state in Azerbaijan have largely strengthened processes of ethnic disintegration launched by the collapse of the USSR. This was a result of creating clientele networks that consisted of solidarity groups based on sub-ethnic identities. Accordingly, a growing number of people in Azerbaijani society had to resort to their respective sub-ethnic communities as the most appropriate instrument for the realization of their socio-economic and

22   Yunusov, »Etnoiazykovaia situatsiia«, op. cit. (note 21), in particular p. 198.

23   Stanislav Cherniavskii, *Novyi put' Azerbaidzhana* (Moscow: Azer-Media & Kniga i Biznes, 2002), pp. 92–94.

24   Author's interview with Hafiz Hajiev, 28.04.05. Author's interview with »Insider« 16.03.05; see also Färämäz Novruzoghlu, »AXC – anormal doghulan uşaq. Millätin üzünü qara etdilär!!!«, in: *Xural* 080 (2005), p. 8–9 for the list of names and sub-ethnic affiliation.

25   Abbasov, *Azerbaidzhantsy*, op. cit (note 12), p. 44.

political goals. Participating in the competition for economic resources, professional status and political representation became possible mainly within the framework of strategic groups employing sub-ethnicity as a mechanism of political mobilization as well as a guarantee of loyalty and social control. The liquidation of Soviet institutions such as the Komsomol, trade unions, cooperatives, the Party, creative unions, etc. that used to be the primary channels enabling one to meet one's economic and political needs, finished the job. Thus, Azerbaijanis as an ethnic group have disintegrated into several sub-ethnic components and as a supra-ethnic community into »Turks« and »non-Turks«.

Having this understanding of the processes in mind, I disagree with the pessimistic assessment of R. Badalov who, when stating the fact that Azerbaijanis, like some other peoples of the Soviet Union, were »created« during the Soviet time, wrote: »political and cultural developments during the post-Soviet period enable one to say that they actually constructed a »chimerical ethnic group« in analogy with the »Soviet nation« whose viability could not endure the test of time«.[26]

Emergence of the Yeraz

In 1993, as in neighboring Georgia, independent Azerbaijan was led by the former Communist Party leader, Heydar Aliev. He, his spouse-to-be, and numerous relatives and in-laws were born either in Armenia or in the Autonomous Republic of Nakhichevan within Azerbaijan. At that time, Azerbaijan was on the brink of civil war and there was no trace of a civil society or a functional political system.[27] In such circumstances, there was only one support left to Aliev – his »own« people: relatives, in-laws, fellow countrymen, friends, and former colleagues.

Within the ruling camarilla, key positions were held by the representatives of the Nakhichevan sub-ethnic group who, however, had no allies in other regions of the country to secure effective control by the newly established central government. To avoid a situation where he could turn from the president of the whole country into a »mayor« controlling only the capital city of Baku, Aliev had to bring to power other Azerbaijani politicians in addition to those who themselves, or whose relatives, originated from Armenia – the so-called »Er-

26   Rakhman Badalov, »Baku: gorod i strana«, in: *Azerbaidzhan i Rossiia: obshchestva i gosudarstva*, ed. by Dmitrii Furman (Moscow: Letnii sad, 2001), pp. 256–279, in particular p. 271.
27   For details, see Thomas Goltz, *Azerbaijan Diary. A Rogue Reporter's Adventures in an Oil-Rich, War-Torn, Post-Soviet Republic* (New York & London: Sharpe, 1998).

menistaners« or »Yeraz« (a detailed explanation of these terms see below). In doing so, Heydar Aliev managed to kill two birds with one stone: firstly, he freed himself from being excessively influenced by the Nakhichevaners and somewhat balanced their position in the pyramid of power by introducing »aliens« into it; secondly, he acquired numerous potential allies throughout the country. This is due to the fact that during the 20th century Azerbaijanis originating from Armenia were settling not only in Baku and the Apsheron Peninsula but also in other regions of Azerbaijan, including Nakhichevan. This group include both the refugees/re-settlers of the three waves of migration (1918–1920, 1948–1952 and 1988–1990) and their descendants.

The question that emerges from this is: how many are they, generally? Some Yeraz politicians claimed that the number of individuals who could be reckoned Ermenistaners (three waves of emigration since 1918 plus their descendents) was around three million. I believe these numbers certainly belong to the domain of political mythology. Another, more plausible figure is offered by the Azerbaijani historian and sociologist A. Mamedov:

Considering more or less credible data on the number of Azerbaijanis deported from Armenia after the Second World War and in 1988–1989, the minimal number of this regional community can be estimated at 500,000 people (taking population growth into account). Another several hundred thousand people, apparently, are direct descendents of those who emigrated from Armenia to Azerbaijan individually between these two mass deportations throughout the entire Soviet period. This totals to approximately 10 percent of the electorate spread throughout the entire territory of the country.«[28]

Heydar Aliev and his Ermenistani associates could not count on automatic support and solidarity since until the early 1990s neither in Armenia nor in Azerbaijan immigrants and refugees from Armenia did form any consolidated community or group with a clear self-ascription and self-identification. As my interviews show, the Azerbaijanis from Armenia, in the course of resettling into Azerbaijan, soon got completely assimilated to the local environment in Azerbaijan, adopting not only the way of life but even dialectical features of one or another Azerbaijani sub-ethnic group among which they settled:

In Ganja (second largest city of the country – B. S.) in my childhood there was a corner that since the nineteen twenties had been known as Yeni Iravan – the new Erivan. Native Armenians lived there (Azerbaijanis – B.S.) – those who fled or moved voluntarily, unable to endure nationalistic pressure (from Armenians – B. S.). Almost until our days they called themselves Ganjiners and spoke Azeri with a characteristic Ganja accent. My (female) cousins had (in Azerbaijan – B.S.) a father, originally coming from Armenia, and

---

28   Mamedov, »Vliianie regionalizma, op. cit. (note 12), p. 8.

a mother from Ganja. They would have cut the throat of anyone who had spoken ill of our Ganja.[29]

Azerbaijanis originating from Armenia only preserved the memory of their native land, a kind of localism:

In Ganja the word ›Yeraz‹ never existed: they said, such and such *(Azerbaijani originating from Armenia – B. S.)* is göyçalı from the Göyçä mahal (Göyçä is the Azerbaijani toponym of the Lake Sevan in the territory of Armenia) or Iravanly. This is certainly a social phenomenon, and had the regional clan mechanism not been formed, these people would have never recalled they came from Armenia.[30]

Aliev and his Yeraz supporters undertook a number of targeted efforts and measures to consolidate Azerbaijanis originating from Armenia into a special sub-ethnic group with a self-identification different from that of the rest of Azerbaijanis. This is a rather paradoxical policy, for it is in total contradiction with the logic of the post-Soviet nation-building. And there is no analogy to it in the entire post-Soviet space where political leaders and elites strive to build a nation state, giving specific attention to the consolidation of titular ethnic groups.[31] Before turning to the policy of designing a particular sub-ethnic group out of Azerbaijanis originating from Armenia, a few words should be said about prerequisites that made such a design possible.

Instrumentalizing Tragic History

Azerbaijanis originating from Armenia are like Nakhichevaners, the so-called Üç-Turks, that is, Turks living on the edge (üç), at the margins of the Turkic world.[32] Due to historical circumstances (life on the edge of the Turkic and generally Muslim world, surrounded by Christians, primarily Armenians), the Nakhichevaners and Azerbaijanis from Armenia are distinguished by their heightened political activism and social mobility, as well as by a high degree of solidarity among »their own«.[33]

Aliev and the elites that supported him tried to single out Azerbaijanis from

---

29   Author's interview with Toghrul Juvarly, 05.05.2005.
30   Ibid.
31   See Oliver Roy, *The New Central Asia. The Creation of Nations* (London & New York: I. B. Tauris, 2000).
32   About the term »üç« see Andrei Kononov, *Rodoslovnaia Turkmen* (Moscow & Leningrad: Nauka, 1958), p. 91.
33   Arif Yunusov, »Azerbaidzhan v postsovetskii period: problemy i vozmozhnye puti razvitiia«, in: *Severnyi Kavkaz-Zakavkaz'e: Problemy stabil'nosti i perspektivy razvitiia. Materialy mezh-*

Armenia and turn them into a special sub-ethnic community, based on social, psychological, and other particular characteristics. Due to their tragic history, Armenian Azerbaijanis are certainly »different« (Azerbaijanis). Therefore, when designing them as a sub-ethnic group, the central authority paid specific attention to the actualization, or more precisely to the »invention«, of their historical memory and collective experience.

With financial support from the Azerbaijani government and economic elites, articles, brochures, and books appeared since 1992 in which attempts were made to link the self-identification of Azerbaijanis originally coming from Armenia with the permanent loss of their native land. The beginning of this process was marked by the resettlement of Armenians from the Ottoman Empire in the territory of the former Erivan khanate that was carried out by the Russian authorities in the second half of the 19th century.[34] The ultimate loss befell the Azerbaijanis in the late 20th century during the conflict between Armenia and Azerbaijan over Nagornyi Karabakh when about 186,000 Azerbaijanis were driven out of the territory of modern Armenia.[35]

Azerbaijani historians engaged by the authorities had no difficulty in recalling the memory of expatriation for between these two extreme events, history had not been particularly merciful to Azerbaijanis in Armenia either. During the civil war, particularly in 1918–20, the ancestors of the Ermenistaners were subjected to brutal persecution, harassment, and mass murder committed by Armenian gangs that had already employed »scorched earth« tactics.[36]

Azerbaijanis were subjected to mass displacement from their native land in Armenia during the Soviet time from 1948 until 1952, as well. Sticking to the Soviet government resolutions, dated 23 December 1947 and 10 March 1948, »On the Resettlement of Collective Farmers and Other Azerbaijani Population from the Armenian SSR to the Kura-Arax Depression of the Azerbaijani SSR«, it was planned to resettle 100,000 collective farmers and other people »on a voluntary basis« to enable the settlement of Armenians from overseas on the vacated land.

After the death of Stalin, the said resolutions were radically revised. Officially, Azerbaijan received around 67,000 displaced Azerbaijanis – while the total number of people banished from the land of their fathers exceeded 150,000.

dunarodnoi konferentsii, 24–26.10.1997, ed. by Aleksandr Iskandarian & Ol'ga Vorkunova (Moscow: Kompaniia Grif-F, 1997), pp. 144–165, in particular p. 159.

34   For detailed description of resettlement processes see Khajar Verdieva & Rauf Gusein-zade, »_Rodoslovnaia« armian i ikh migratsiia na Kavkaz s Balkan_ (Baku: Elm, 2003).

35   Arif Yunusov, »Pogromy v Armenii v 1988–1989 gg.«, in: _Ekspress-Khronika_ 9 (1991); Arif Yunusov, »Armiano-azerbaidzhanskii konflikt: demograficheskie i migratsionye aspekty«, at: http://www.ca-c.org/journal/16–1998/st_10_junusov.shtml; Sabir Asadov, _Istoricheskaia geografiia zapadnogo Azerbaidzhana_, (Baku: Azerbaidzhan, 1998), in particular p. 90.

36   Asadov, _Istoricheskaia geografiia_, op. cit. (note 36), p. 65.

Despite all obstacles, around 40–45 percent of Azerbaijani re-settlers, who survived (every third of them perished), returned within five years (1948–1953) to their native ground in Armenia.[37] Although Azerbaijani scholars link the deportation of Azerbaijanis in 1948–1952 with the clout of A. Mikoian in the Soviet government, I suppose that it was part of a strategy aimed at reducing the influence of Muslim peoples in the Caucasus that was pursued in the Soviet Union during the post-war period. All deported peoples – the Karachay, Chechens, Ingush, Balkars, Meskhetian Turks, Kurds – were Muslim. The Soviet government, therefore, was continuing the policy of the Russian Empire to »pacify« the Caucasus through the expulsion and deportation of the Muslim population being seen as not especially loyal the Center: St. Petersburg and later Moscow. The idea of the »betrayal by Muslim peoples« during the war against Germany was very popular among Soviet leaders.[38]

During the »liberal« Brezhnev period, daily life of Azerbaijanis in Armenia was accompanied by discrimination and numerous restrictions. It manifested itself primarily in the mass closure of higher education institutions, technical vocational schools, and media outlets that used the Azerbaijani language, unofficial bans on employment, dismissals from administrative and Communist Party positions, etc.[39] The Armenians in Azerbaijan were unlike Azerbaijanis in Armenia a highly privileged ethnic minority. The final ousting of Azerbaijanis from Armenia occurred in 1988–1991. District leaders and some senior officials in the Council of Ministers of Armenia organized their banishment.[40]

Self-Ascription and Ascription by Others

A rather telltale picture in the context of creating a specific sub-ethnic identity of Armenian Azerbaijanis also emerges from the analysis of self-ascription and externally given names of Azerbaijanis originating in Armenia. One of the local self-referential terms is Iravanlı, pointing to their »historical homeland«, the Erivan khanate. This self-referential term is sometimes mistranslated as »resident of/from Yerevan«, while the correct version is »resident of/from the Erivan khanate«. For instance, the earlier mentioned name of the city quarter ›Yenı Iravan‹ in Ganja is translated as ›New Erivan‹. The other self-referential term, »Ermänistanlı«, was created already after 1992 from the word »Ermänistan«

---

37 Asadov, *Istoricheskaia geografiia*, op. cit. (note 36), p. 85.
38 Boris Vasil'ev, *Refleks samozapugivaniia*, at: http://islam.ru/pressclub/vslux/vasiliev.
39 Asadov, *Istoricheskaia geografiia*, op. cit. (note 36), p. 86–87.
40 For details, see Yunusov, »Pogromy v Armenii«, op. cit. (note 36).

(»Armenia« in Azerbaijani language) and can be translated into Russian as »Ermenistaner« [of/from Ermenistan – Armenia].

Regarding the externally given name (nickname) »Yeraz«, an abbreviation of »Yerevani Azerbaijanis«, it did not have the negative and pejorative connotation that it has now. In Azerbaijan the name Yeraz had always been given to all people from Armenia, regardless of the city or village they came from. Until 1988–98 this nickname only indicated the geographical origin of these Azerbaijanis. Only after the mass exodus of Armenian Azerbaijanis did the nickname »Yeraz« acquire the new semi-contemptuous connotation.[41]

Some observers see the explanation of this phenomenon in the collision of urban and rural mind-sets, which the central authority took advantage of, setting Armenia-originating Azerbaijanis off against those from Baku and the Apsheron peninsula. One cannot but agree that the most prominent feature of Ermenistaners is their agrarian mentality. The conflict between the agrarian and urban mentalities was one of the system-building factors for »creating« Ermenistaners. The latter were actually rejected by Azerbaijani society because of their mentality. To exemplify this, I will quote from an article entitled *Dukhovnoe prostranstvo* [Spiritual Space], authored by Ali Bagirov, Medical Doctor (sic!):

»Thanks« to the Perestroishchiks [engineers of Perestroika], we have been flooded by a huge influx of people from Western Azerbaijan–Armenia who were born and brought up in that environment. Their ancestors have lived there for centuries. And, naturally, they have their own notion of honor and dignity, moral and ethical code, and behavior stereotypes... While those who left us were primarily urban dwellers *[the Baku Armenians – B. S.]* – skilled specialists, part of the elite- those who arrived were farmers, cattle-breeders – rural people bringing in their lifestyle and spiritual baggage.«[42]

However, it would be inappropriate to say that the agrarian mentality is a characteristic of every single Ermenistaner. Among them there is a thin stratum of urban *intelligentsiia* originating from the city of Erivan (later named Yerevan). Their descendents are represented in the political establishment of the country. To give some examples: Eldar Namazov, former advisor to President Heydar Aliev, whose family, according to him, used to own large areas of land in the former khanate of Erivan and represented the elite of the city;[43] Dilyara Seyid-zade, former Head of President Aliev's secretariat and, according to some reports, El-

---

41 Irada Guseinova, »Bezhentsy, ikh polozhenie i rol' v sovremennnom azerbaidzhanskom obshchestve«, in: *Azerbaidzhan i Rossiia: obshchestva i gosudarstva*, ed. by Dmitrii Furman (Moscow: Letnii sad, 2001), pp. 323–336, in particular p. 324.

42 Ali Bagirov, »Dukhovnoe prostranstvo«, in: *Novoe vremia* 55 (2004), p. 11.

43 Thomas de Waal, *Black Garden. Armenia and Azerbaijan through Peace and War* (New York & London: New York University Press, 2003), p.80–81.

dar Namazov's aunt; and Zarifa Alieva, the mother of the incumbent President Ilham Aliev. They all belong to the Erevani Azerbaijani *intelligentsiia*.

Some other authors« believe that a long residency in the Armenian milieu and having being a suppressed minority there, has turned Ermenistaners into a community that is significantly different from Azerbaijanis in Azerbaijan. The older and the first generations of resettled Ermenistaners mastered the Armenian language and often could communicate in Armenian as fluently as Armenians from Baku communicate in the Azerbaijani language.[44]

Despite contradictory and sometimes hostile relationships with Armenians, Azerbaijanis in Armenia have adopted many of their characteritics, including their mental frame. The medical doctor Bagirov, whom I quoted earlier, wrote:

They grew up among people who were jealous, embittered, vengeful, treacherous – in a word, »long-suffering«. Clearly, they could not but absorb many of the things they observed.[45]

I, certainly, do not accept these emotional clichés. They, however, indicate that Azerbaijanis from Armenia brought to Azerbaijan their entire life experience gained in Armenia.

Among these peculiarities of mentality some observers note a high degree of consolidation, heightened aggression towards their surrounding, organizational skills, strong willpower, high efficiency, etc.[46] Considering everything that had happened to them, Azerbaijanis from Armenia are always alert and ready to fight; they surely do not want to again go through the loss of everything accumulated by previous generations. Their goal is to augment whatever there is.

The Azerbaijanis never existed in Armenia as a consolidated sub-ethnic group. In the Armenian environment they were the suppressed Azerbaijani minority. Having found themselves in qualitatively different surroundings in Azerbaijan, the Armenian Azerbaijanis, with massive »support« from the Azerbaijani government, consolidated themselves into a community with a clear-cut structure, hierarchy, and solidarity only during the post-Soviet period. In other words – and this is paradoxical – the Azerbaijanis from Armenia have preserved and consolidated the mentality of a ethno-religious minority in what appears to be their native Azerbaijani environment. Even today, they function as an »ethno-religious minority«.

A kind of social inertia had its effect here: having left Armenia, Armenian Azerbaijanis could not abandon their black and white vision of the surrounding world, the habit of dividing the world into »own« and »alien«. A major role here

---

44   Guseinova, »Bezhentsy«, op. cit. (note 43), p. 324; also author's interview with Arif Yunusov, 03.02.2004.

45   Bagirov, »Dukhovnoe prostranstvo«, op. cit. (note 44), p. 11.

46   Zurab Todua, *Azerbaidzhanskii pas'ians* (Moscow: KON-Liga Press, 2001), p.121.

was played by the conviction that Azerbaijanis from Armenia are »true« Azerbaijanis, for, living among Armenians, they were able to preserve their language
and traditions unlike Azerbaijanis from Baku who mostly shifted to the Russian
language and adopted »russophone« culture.

The problem of the relationships of Azerbaijanis from Armenia with the remaining section of Azerbaijani society can be formulated in a different plane.
What is it that dominates the mentality of the Yeraz – the »Yerevanian«, that
is the Armenian or Azerbaijani cultural element? In many respects, Azerbaijani
Armenians were assimilated into the local environment. Following their banishment Azerbaijani society received »in return« the Azerbaijanis who, in terms of
mentality, turned out to be more Armenian than the Armenians of Azerbaijan
themselves. Often, during my interviews, I was to hear that »our« Armenians
were better than Ermenistaners![47]

Moreover, the »replacement« of one element with another also occurred on
the functional plane: not only did Armenian Azerbaijanis, move into apartments
and houses that once belonged to Azerbaijani Armenians but they also occupied
their professional and social niche. For instance, in Ganja Ermenistaners occupied positions in the prosecutor's office, police, and other governmental agencies
that, in keeping with unspoken tradition, used to be filled by Armenians.[48] Thus
the integrity of Azerbaijani society was restored.

Ermenistaners are, like Nakhichevaners, not a homogeneous sub-ethnic community. They comprise assimilated Kurds (Kurdish substratum) as well. Hence,
Ermenistaners differ from other Azerbaijanis in their folklore, musical culture,
and even rituals (a significant number of Ermenistaners are Sunni Muslims),
which sometimes causes conflicts with the local Shia Muslim population. A crucial »diacritical feature«, for example, is that some Sunni Ermenistaners celebrate
their weddings during the holy month of Muharram in which most Azerbaijanis as Shia Muslims commemorate the Battle of Karbala (680) during which
Prophet Muhammad's grandson Husayn ibn Ali was killed by the forces of Yazid
I, the Umayyad Caliph.[49]

The representatives of the Ermenistani elite initiate regularly various ritualistic events and use these events to strengthen the community's identity. A case
in point is the implementation of special sections in cemeteries and even special
cemeteries to bury »their own« apart from other Azerbaijanis (for example in
Qovsanı, a village on the outskirts of Baku).[50] Affiliation with Ermenistaners is
also confirmed in financial terms. Ermenistani politicians have a »black pool«

---

47   Author's interview with non-Ermenistani residents of Ganja, 24.04.2004.
48   Author's interview with »Insider«, 27.03.2004.
49   Author's interview with non-Ermenistani residents of Ganja, 24.04.2004.
50   Author's interview with Mehman Aliev, 11.02.2004.

(*obshchak* [colloquial Russian for »shared cash pool«]) and its resources are used to address its various political and economic objectives.[51]

Strengthening Diacritical Features – Strengthening Boundaries?

As the Azerbaijanis originating in Armenia and Azerbaijanis of Azerbaijan constitute virtually one ethnic group, the central authority and elites in every way possible tried to emphasize the »diacritical features« of Ermenistaners. These include history, geography, genealogical information, rural mentality, and the belonging of a certain section of Ermenistaners to Sunni Islam. History, rural mentality, and belonging to Sunni Islam have been briefly addressed earlier. Thus, how are geography and genealogical information being used to create the Ermenistani sub-ethnic identity?

By using the press and other measures, the authorities and cultural elites try to inculcate into Ermenistaners that the latter fall into 10 subgroups whose supposedly localist identity is traced back to the boundaries of nine (9) *uezd* [districts] (*mahal*) of a number of provinces within the former Russian Empire: Derelegez, Yeni Bayazid, Iravan, Echmiadzin, Shoragel, Gümri of the Irevan Province, Dilijan and Zangezur districts of the Ganja Province, Lori-Pambek district of the Tiflis Province. As a separate group, they distinguish between, as was mentioned, those who originated from the city of Erivan, which was not a part of the Irevan Province, as well as their descendents. The attempt to divide Ermenistaners has not been incidental either: the sub-ethnic community being created has also the capacity for self-development. On the contrary, the Azerbaijani authorities, for fear of loosing control over the process and following the logic of »*divide et impera*«, are preparing ground in advance for potential disintegration of yet unformed sub-ethnic group into localized components.

After the abolition of provinces during Soviet times, they were divided into districts that became part of Armenia. Every Ermenistaner nowadays is informally forced to know exactly the place of birth or the place of birth of his/her ancestors (more precisely the district and the name of village). Geographical knowledge of this kind is literally imposed on them by the authorities, by the system of relationships, by informal networks, and by the elite. Genealogical information about people originating from these areas, which is continuously updated, is »stored« in oral form by the so-called *aqsaqqals* [white beards] or informal leaders of the Ermenistani community. Presently, however, attempts

---

51   Author's interview with »Insider«, 19.03.2004.

are being made to secure genealogical information in printed form, using it for the purposes of strengthening sub-ethnic self-identification as well.[52] Each of the custodians of genealogical information looks after his own district [*rayon*], which no longer exists in reality but is represented by people originating from it and their descendants living in different parts of Azerbaijan. In this sense, Ermenistaners are the »purest« example of a community that is being »re-created« continuously by the imagination of a certain number of people.

Now and again it comes to the point of being an oddity: Ermenistaners born in the territory of Azerbaijan are somehow considered to have been born in the very same village in the territory of contemporary Armenia where their father or grandfather was born. However, when their curriculum vitae is presented, only the date of birth is indicated while the place in Azerbaijan, where they were actually born, is irrelevant and not specified. For example, the Qasimov family comprises three generations (grandfather, son, and grandson).[53] Eylas Iman oğlu Qasimov, the grandfather, was born in 1924 in the village of Böyük Vedi.[54] All his life he worked for the agencies of internal affairs in Soviet Azerbaijan. Presently, he resides in the town of Imişli in Azerbaijan. He has four sons: Eyvaz, Arif, Maarif, and Aydın; and two daughters, Nailä and Töhfä. His first born Eyvaz was born in the same village as his father, but it is not known where the other three sons were born, or rather, it *is* known that they were born in Azerbaijan, but not known exactly where for the place of their birth was not specified, only the dates of birth. One of the grandsons, Rövşän, was honored by being included in the Collection; apparently, because he, like his grandfather, works for the police. It features his photograph and a short biography saying that he was born in 1977 (again, no place of birth!) and is presently serving in the police with the rank of lieutenant.

Summary

It is still hard to assess in how far the authorities and cultural elites in Azerbaijan have advanced in the »creation«, »imagination«, as well imposition of a sub-ethnic identity upon Azerbaijanis originating from Armenia, although one

---

52 For details, see the cv collection of prominent Ermenistaners, Äziz Äläkbärli, *Qärbi Azärbaycan. I cild. Vedibasar mahalı (Vedi vä Qarabaghlar rayonları)* (Bakı: Aghridagh, 2003); Äziz Äläkbärli, *Qärbi Azärbaycan. II cild. Zängibasar, Gärnibasar vä Qirxbulaq mahalları* (Bakı: Aghridagh, 2002); see also Asadov, *Istoricheskaia geografiia*, op. cit. (note 36), pp. 488–523.

53 Äläkbärli, *Qärbi Azärbaycan*, opt. cit. (note 54), p. 257.

54 In the Vedi (now Ararat) District, the former uezd Irevan, the Irevan Province on the territory of contemporary Armenia. – B.S.

occasionally comes across situations in which the nickname »Yeraz« and the name »Ermenistaner« become self-referential terms (self-ascriptions).

Although Ermenistaners have found themselves in Azerbaijan through the course of historical events that go back to the Russian conquest in the Caucasus, their emergence (and being an »imagined«) as a sub-ethnic identity is not a result of »natural« historical development, but is mostly the product of the creation and invention of traditions as described by B. Anderson and E. Hobsbawm. The situation described above is different in that it is *a sub-ethnic group, not a nation*, that is being subjected to »imagination« and »invention«. As a sub-ethnic group, Ermenistaners are being created in the context of strategic groups vying for power and associated resources and privileges.

Although Ermenistaners represent a sub-ethnic group that is imagined and invented, there are reasons to believe that they are capable of developing independently. In this case, they should be able to preserve themselves within the Azerbaijani people long after the disappearance of the conditions and agents (authorities and cultural elites), which tried to create the them.

The Staging of Politics and the »Folklorization« of Political Discourse

Ashot Voskanian

The Republic of Armenia, which had already applied for membership in the Council of Europe on the sixteenth day of its independence,[1] needed ten years to establish itself as a full member of this European organization in Strasbourg in 2001. This political positioning was no coincidence. The European tradition had always played a significant role in Armenia, even if it was understood more in the classical sense of European nation-statehood and traditional »education«.[2] The past years in Armenia have been marked by the acceleration of European processes of integration. There have been considerable achievements in legislation and in the development of institutions.[3] Approaching the contemporary Europe of codified value systems and legal complexes that encompass almost all dimensions of social life is a goal being consciously pursued in Armenia.

Politics addresses the »European-oriented« transformation of societal institutions. Yet its forms of discourse remain constrained within a universal language of modernization that »detaches modernity from its modern European origins« and stylizes it »into a temporally and geographically neutralized model of societal development processes par excellence«.[4] The Weberian conception of societal modernization as a disenchantment of the world accompanying a comprehensive rationalization is thus left by the wayside. The latter was, as is well-known, not just related to relations of production, political structures and so on, but rather, as Jürgen Habermas has insistently emphasized, anticipated a parallel transformation in the *Lebenswelt* (every day life and social environment), that

---

1 The independence of the Third Republic was proclaimed on 9/23/91 after the referendum of 9/21/91.

2 Cf.: Boghos Levon Zekiyan, *The Armenian Way to Modernity: Armenian Identity between Tradition and Innovation, Specificity and Universality* (Venice: Supernova, 1997).

3 For an assessment of this situation see: *European Neighborhood Policy. Country Report. Armenia (Commission Staff Working Paper, COM /2005/ 72 final)*, in: http://europa.eu.int/comm/world/enp/pdf/country/armenia_cr_0503.pdf. *February 25, 2006* as well as Ashot Voskanian (Ed.), *Armenia on the way to Europe* (Yerevan: Antares, 2005).

4 Jürgen Habermas, *Der philosophische Diskurs der Moderne* (Frankfurt/M.: Suhrkamp, 1988), p. 12.

is, of cultural patterns of behavior, social orders, and structures of individuality, interpreted from the internal perspective of a participant.[5]

If these aspects of the rationalization of the worldview are missing from the modernization procedures, a tense dialogue between the European and the traditional is also missing from politics. Both forms of discourse co-exist indifferent to one another as different »language games«, or else they simply oscillate disjointedly in the spontaneous shifts within individual political subjects who appeal to diverse values in diverse contexts. However, when the confrontation only proceeds implicitly, there will be no synthesis, no resolution. Rather, both discourses only tend to transform their counterparts into their own structural moments and thus disarm them.

One of the possible defensive measures of the native tradition is the purely formal recognition and rhetorical use of the newly permeated discourse of modernization: In doing so, this one can create (sometimes unintentionally) a »safe distance« that retains the traditional notions untouched. Yet proceeding formally with the universally understood neo-European forms of discourse does not mean that one uses them unfeelingly, or »cooly«. On the contrary, in emotionalizing »Europeanness« to the maximum, one puts it into question: the Europeanization slogans, felt purely emotionally, can be either recognized or repudiated – but they are not subject to rational discussion. This immunity to criticism of the »emotionally European« arrays it in the series of traditional *Lebenswelt* elements of national politics; attributes the same status to each constituent of this mixture; and, removes the whole from any demand for some sort of rational verification. What remains, then, of a discourse the essence of which has to be molded by »rationality«?

To the extent that European integration constitutes itself as the convergence in understanding of nations, it is hermeneutic in its very essence. Yet a critical identification of the mythologizing forms of discourse is no less a part of the task of understanding than respectful attention for what is particular about the collective or targeted emotional promotion of EU-Europe. The discourse of modernity must be able to assert itself in a rationalizing encounter with old received ideas and new political »staging«. Only in this way will the European discourse of integration become reflexive and self-critical and able to be substantially received and appropriated by the political subjects of a country of transformation.[6]

5   Jürgen Habermas, *Theorie des kommunikativen Handelns,* Vol. 2 (Frankfurt/M.: Suhrkamp, 1982), p. 209 ff.

6   Just how fruitful this sort of attitude can be shown by works such as Edward W. Said, *Orientalism* (London: Penguin Books, 1978), long a classic in the field, as well as recent publications such as: Werner Stegmaier (Ed.), *Europa-Philosophie* (Berlin, New York: W. der Gruyter, 2000); Dušan I. Bjelic & Obrad Savic (eds.), *Balkan as Metaphor. Between Globalization and Fragmentation* (Camb., Mass., London: The MIT Press, 2002).

What I am concerned with is the deconstruction of the immanent folkloristic nature of national politics and their return to the universalistic standards. This self-elucidation of the political through the concepts of European ethnology, its inner de-colonization and secularization, i.e. the self-critique and self-opening of national politics, I would like to characterize with reference to Kierkegaard as an overcoming of the demonical.[7]

In this article I will concentrate on phenomena in Armenian politics that at a first glance seem quite marginal. But in transformation societies, these marginal phenomena play a significant role and sometimes come to occupy a dominant position in political processes. They produce countless stagings connected not only to the media side of politics but also directly affecting its core. This phenomenon, which can be traced back to the specifics of societal and cultural developments in Armenia, will be called here the »folklorization« of politics.

I will focus on the following two points. First, traditional Armenian political projects will be presented, which with reference to Lyotard I have brought under the title of »grand narratives«.[8] These projects, which have long been part of the Armenian *Lebenswelt* repertoire, cannot without fundamental transformation be harmonized with the project of European integration that has for the most part been handled in its globalized, universalistic form in the Republic (without direct connection to the cultural impact of European modernity). In the circumstances, where discussions of the public realm are absent, both projects (the traditional as well as the European) have shrunk to icons symbolically hinted at that one tries to »folkloristically« stage rather than to rationally discuss. This renunciation of rationally guided, critical discourse, which I will hereafter characterize as »muteness«, opens a certain leeway for countless »stagings«.

The second section will present several concrete stagings of the political in Armenia. In contrast to the grand narratives, they tend much more towards the mythological patterns oriented around the originating and founding act. They present a symbiosis of folkloristic and performative elements and arise at that critical juncture where the pre- and post-modern collide. This multifarious and heterogeneous »folklorization« of the political fulfills an important function: it takes its transparency from political discourse, in order to »generate particular

---

7　Cf.: Sören Kierkegaard, *Die Krankheit zum Tode. Furcht und Zittern. Die Wiederholung. Der Begriff der Angst* (Cologne, Olten: Jakob Hegner, 1956), pp. 584–630.

8　The »grand narratives« are certain narratives whose goal it is »to legitimate institutions, social and political practices, legislations, ethics and ways of thinking. Yet in contrast to myths they do not seek legitimacy in an original founding act but rather in a future to be cashed out, that is, in an idea still to be realized.« Jean-Francois Lyotard, »Randbemerkungen zu den Erzählungen«, in: *Postmoderne und Dekonstruktion*, ed. by Peter Engelmann (Stuttgart: Reclam. Lyotard, 1990), pp. 49–53, in particular p. 49.

social loyalties whose sense and justification are no longer amendable to critical questioning«.[9]

The Grand Narratives

I would like to consider the most important historically produced political projects in Armenia – its »grand narratives« in term of conditions of possibility. This involves three fundamental questions: How is national existence or national survival possible? How is national liberation possible? How is the national future or the progressive societal development of Armenia possible?

The Project of Existence

This is depicted in the famous novel by Khatch'atur Abovyan. The work is called »Wounds of Armenia, lament of a patriot« and is considered path-breaking for the new Armenian literature – not only because it for the first time suggests a transition from *Grabar* (old Armenian) to the new Armenian language, but also because this transition is conceived consciously as a program, explicitly characterized in the text of the novel as »overcoming of muteness«. The book's foreword begins with a metaphor: the son of Croesus, king of Lydia, had found the ability to speak after twenty mute years in the moment that his father's life was in danger. His cry »Against whom do you raise your sword? Do you not know Croesus, the great king of Lydia?« halted the sword-stroke of the Persian mercenary and saved his father's life. The author, the foreword claims, a son of Armenians, similarly needs a language that would overcome the muteness of the nation and restore the dignity and grandeur of an ancient people.[10] That language, as Abovyan sees it, is composed of at least three elements: a new vocabulary and grammar, a new style (he wants to become a minnesinger, since the people only listen to them) and political self-awareness.

The most renowned *Leitmotif* of Armenian political thought stems from this novel: »There is no salvation for Armenia without Russia«.[11] Yet the main idea of this work cannot be reduced to an apology for Russia. The author is concerned with invoking Armenia to a struggle fighting at the side of the Russian

---

9   Wolfgang Kaschuba, »Geschichtspolitik und Identitätspolitik. Nationale und ethnische Diskurse im Vergleich«, in: *Inszenierungen des Nationalen: Geschichte, Kultur und die Politik der Identitäten am Ende des 20. Jahrhunderts*, ed. by Binder, Kaschuba & Niedermüller (Cologne, Weimar & Vienna: Böhlau, 2001), pp. 19–42, in particular p. 32.

10 Khach'atur Abovyan, *Verk' Hayastani* (Yerevan: Sovetakan groï, 1984), pp. 5–11.

11 Abovyan, *Verk' Hayastani*, op.cit. (note 10), p. 71.

protector by no longer acting as an object of manipulation by external forces and once more taking up an active role in history. Here one should note: in a purely personal sense Abovyan was no Russophile (he had studied at a German University in the Estonian city of Dorpat (Tartu), married a German and wrote his first ethnographical articles in German). Yet in Dorpat (which was situated anyway within the Russian empire) Abovyan finally realized that Europe, just as it is geographically, is culturally too far removed from his homeland. He only reflected back as the reality of the epoch, the repercussions of concrete historical events. In 1828 the Iranian part of Armenia was conclusively brought under Russian sovereignty and thereby in a sense truly liberated from the purely Asian (too often: barbarian) conditions. It is precisely in this sense that the presence of Russia in Armenia is seen as the single guarantee of survival, hence: as the condition of the possibility of national existence. The novel was completed in 1841 and published in 1858. Thus it represented not so much a direct »call to action« as a subsequent enlightenment and national awakening.

The Project of Liberation

The beginning of the next project is connected with the activity of the revolutionary democrat Mikael Nalbandyan. Originally it brought together elements of social and national liberation (an idea of Michail Bakunin's about the pan-Slavic uprising in the three empires: the Ottoman Empire, Russia and Austro-Hungary, in which other Christian, non-Slavic peoples also had to participate).[12] The divergence of the social and the national elements can be easily seen in the legacy of Nalbandyan.[13] In his renowned article where he argues for agrarian reform, he assessed the situation of Armenian peasants in the Ottoman Empire as being catastrophic and pointed to the urgency of solving the problems in those areas. Thus his work broached the topic of the liberation of western Armenia, which was to be realized with Russian support. A written memorandum about this was presented to the Russian consul in Constantinople.[14]

Later the idea of national liberation won the upper hand for good and the idea of social revolution was pushed into the background. The concept was continued and developed by traditional Armenian parties – the social-democratic »Hench'akyan«, Armenian Revolutionary Federation »Dashnakts'utyun« and the precursor parties to the liberal »Ramkavar-Azatakan«. All three argued for the liberation of »West Armenia«. The Russian part (Russian Armenia) was in fact

---

12   See Leo, *T'urkahay heïap'okhutyan gaïap'arabanutyune*, Vol. 1 (Yerevan: Shaïik, 1994), pp. 5–27 (esp. 21–23); cf.: Mikael Nalbandyan, *Yerker* (Yerevan: Sovetakan groï, 1985), p. 485ff.

13   Leo, *T'urkahay heïap'okhutyan gaïap'arabanutyune*, op.cit. (note 12), p. 16.

14   See Karen A. Simonyan, *Azatutyan Aspetn u Nahatake* (Yerevan: Edit Print, 2004), pp. 408–409.

perceived as being free. The conviction that the liberation of Armenia was only possible with Russian support had been markedly strengthened in the time of war. After the catastrophe of the Great Genocide[15] the two concepts fused together: Russia was permanently established in the self-consciousness of Armenians as the condition for the possibility of national liberation; as a protector that guaranteed the survival of the Armenian people within its realm of sovereignty; and as the means of securing the hope for a liberation of the western areas (Turkish Armenia).

The Project of the Future

The Bolsheviks contrasted the internationalist idea of social liberation with presocialist nationalism. Just how painful was this overcoming of the »traditional« national in Armenia can be seen in the work of Yehgishe Ch'arents', who transformed the social and cultural controversies into an existential dilemma and reflected them back poetically. In 1927 Ch'arents' produced a brilliant deconstruction and ideological critique of misty national mythology in the novel »Land of Nairi«, the structure of which shows clear parallels to the »Wounds of Armenia«.[16] Here he showed how dangerous a poetic mythologem (*Nairi* as spiritual home – a concept put forward by Vahan Teriyan) could be when someone tries to realize it as a political project.[17]

In the political discourse of his time this project was shaped by the renowned words of the revolutionary army commander Gay (Hayk Bezheshkyan): »The fate of Armenia will be decided in Samara«. With these words the purely national liberation project was replaced by an internationalist Bolshevist endeavor that brought together the guarantee of existence and the prospects for the future. National liberation was reinterpreted as a social liberation, the project »West Armenia« was bracketed off and made taboo. Paradoxically, this future project also belongs to the same *Russian* paradigm. Thus Russia was also seen as the condi-

---

15   The literature on the genocide of the Armenians in the Ottoman Empire is vast. See: Vahakn N. Dadrian, *The History of the Armenian Genocide* (Oxford: Berghahn Books, 1995), Wolfgang Gust, *Der Völkermord an den Armeniern* (Munich, Vienna: Hanser, 1993), Taner Akçam, *Armenien und der Völkermord* (Hamburg: Hamburger Ed., 1996). As a practical guidebook, Gunnar Heinsohn's, *Lexikon der Völkermorde* (Hamburg: Rowohlt, 1998), can be recommended, where one can also find a commendable bibliography. Websites include: www.armenian-genocide.org/, www.armenocide.net/. See also: Ashot Voskanian, »Die Versöhnung als politische Aufgabe. Eine Herausforderung für Europa«, in *ADK. Armenisch-Deutsche Korrespondenz* No. 2 (2001), pp. 34–37.

16   Yegishe Ch'arents', »Yerkir Nairi« in *Yerkeri zhoïovatsu 4 hatorov*, Vol. 4, ed. by Yegishe Ch'arents' (Yerevan: Sovetakan groï, 1987). In the later works of the poet (»The book of paths«, 1933) this same question is further radicalized.

17   Compare with G. Scholem's warning to never confuse Jewish messianism with the political Zionist project.

tion for the possibility of a national future. The opposition of the national and the international lasted until the mid-sixties (the symbolic border was crossed in 1965). Afterwards the national idea was taken up in Soviet ideology,[18] thus finally merging the three projects. With this step, Russia emerges as the condition for the possibility of the existence, liberation and future of Armenia.

The assessment of Russia as the condition for the possibility of the existence, liberation and future of Armenia was determined by the concrete political realities of the 19th century. Today's Russia has fundamentally transformed its foreign policy. It can no more (if ever it was really so) be interpreted as a ground for the existence of Armenian national projects. No wonder, that with the dissolution of the Soviet Union, the traditional project was countered by the idea of European integration. The former, however, was not completely replaced by the European project and was not abandoned. The fierce debates in the first years of independence produced a standstill in the Armenian public realm that persisted for a long time. In purely formal terms one could have spoken of a societal consensus that assimilates both projects. In fact, however, it is clear that the projects cannot be unified; they can only »co-exist«. It is just this all-neutralizing co-existence of both projects that comprises the specific character of political discourse in Armenia. The more one discusses the possibility of an unproblematic reconciliation of the national and the European, the thicker the silence becomes about the essence of the matter. Those who see the European project as the unequivocal alternative to the traditional have long since stylized demonstrative silence as the sole possible political gesture. The Others find themselves on the detour of a decorative rhetoric in which the most important point of Europeanization, the question »if the traditional political project of Armenia can be harmonized with the premises of European modernity«, has no space. In a situation in which both grand political projects (the traditional and the European) are in fact »preserved«, Armenian political consciousness has fallen into exactly that muteness that Abovyan wanted to lead it out of in the middle of the 19th century.

---

18   On 4/24/1965 (on the 50th anniversary of the genocide) hundreds of thousands demonstrated in the streets of Yerevan for recognition of the Great Genocide of 1915. The persecution of the activists by the KGB lasted around two years. In 1968 the Genocide Monument was built in Yerevan and officially inaugurated by the first secretary of the Communist Party of Armenia.

Folklorization of Politics

The political muteness of society, the silent preservation of the essential political projects or the ironic distance to them, has led to a »folklorization« of the political. I use this term to characterize the unreserved utilization and media multiplication of the heterogeneous *Lebenswelt* repertoire: from ethnically disposed narratives of legitimization, myths and folk-festivals to every day notions that oust the rational forms of discourse from politics and render political events immune to questioning. Typically they appear in the form of mediated staging. I would like to illustrate this »folklorization« of politics with several examples. In the following, three cases of political staging are described that indicate such marginalizing tendencies in the field of the political: 1) The feast in Sardarabad after the second »Armenian diaspora« conference (9/24/1999); 2) The round dance *shurch par* around the Aragats mountain (5/28/2005); 3) The TV phenomenon »Tigran Karapetovitch«.

Magical Invocation of Fate

Large conferences and conventions always conclude with a banquet or feast; this is nothing out of the ordinary. The Sardarabad feast of 24.09. 1999 was also in accord with the tradition,[19] and yet had several conspicuously new features that provide interesting ethnographic insights. First, the scale of the feast should be mentioned. The thousands of participants were transported to a region about 30 km from Yerevan, flawlessly waited upon and richly entertained. This was no easy task, given the circumstances of post-war Armenia[20] at the time. A man who at that time combined in his person the authority of two of the most important institutions (the army and the government) stood at the center of this endeavor: the victorious former minister of defense, who a few months earlier (after his »Justice« coalition had won a distinct parliamentary majority) had been elected prime minister.

What proved to have a mythological character in this context was firstly the complacent dynamics of the »fairy-tale hero«[21] who succeeded on a particular day and place in guaranteeing the presence of everything that the traditional national consciousness symbolically calls »Armenianess«. The numerous guests

---

19   »Armenia – Diaspora« conferences are regularly organized by the state; the Sardarabad feasts have been celebrated since 1986.

20   The acute armed phase of the Karabakh conflict lasted until 1994.

21   The minister was honored as a kind of Armenian warlord and typically called »Sparapet«. The term stems from the Middle Ages and can be translated as »princely military commander« (*Stratege* in the antique sense of the word). This title is used metaphorically today with a certain symbolic pathos.

from all areas of the republic, from Nagorno-Karabakh and from practically all diaspora communities were there, including representatives of significant Armenian political and cultural associations and charitable organizations and celebrities of the Armenian heritage from all over the world. The political elite was represented by both state presidents (from Armenia and Arts'akh[22]), the two church leaders (deputies of Armenian *Catholicos* and of the *Catholicos* of Cilicia) and the Primas of the Arts'akh diocese, two prime ministers, two speakers of parliament, two foreign ministers and others. Thus one can say without exaggeration that the structure of the guest list for this feast very accurately represented the structure of »Armenianness« as it had been formed in the collective vision of the nation for decades.

The second mythological element related to the sacral topography of the feast, which in essence reflected the sacral topography of the site. The Sardarabad memorial commemorates the decisive battle of 1918, which in Armenian historical consciousness is seen as the contemporary analog to the Battle of Vartanantz.[23] In those early days of May the regular troops of the first Armenian Republic, including the National Guard and spontaneous volunteers from all strata of society, halted the advance of the Turkish troops towards Yerevan and secured the physical existence of its population. On 28.05. 1918, Kemalist Turkey recognized Armenia as an independent state.

The battle occurred in a part of the Ararat valley between the »holy« mountains of Ararat and Aragats. Both mountain masses loom directly up out of the valley without any gradual transition and form a typical »heroic landscape« whose expressivity was further emphasized with the construction of a complex of monuments.[24] Visitors to the memorial come through the *Bull gate* to the *Bell tower*, reach the *Eagle Avenue* on the left alongside the central square with the great curved wall held to be the focal point of the monument. On one side of the wall flying horses are depicted tearing apart snake-like dragons. In order to see the rear, realistic depiction of the battle, the visitor has to pass under the arch in the wall. Here one has reached the vantage point from which the entire historical site of the battle can be seen in all its glory. The landscape suddenly opens up before the visitor, floating in the air, and thus seems unlimited. The flashing reflections of sunlight from the Arax River do not limit the broad span of the landscape. That the current closed Armenian-Turkish border becomes visible here tends to make the ongoing presence of danger more palpably felt: the

---

22   The Armenian term for Nagorny-Karabakh.

23   The legendary Battle of Vartanantz (451 CE) is considered the high-point of armed resistance against the Persians (the religious war of the Vartanid dynasty) and the most important event in Armenian history in terms of the formation of Armenian identity.

24   The monument was set up in 1968 for the fiftieth anniversary of the battle. Since then the 28th of May is celebrated each year as the day of the Sardarabad victory.

river indicates the immediate proximity of the »enemy«. The silhouettes of both mountains in the north and south complete the picture.

Against the backdrop of this natural, historical and cultural scenery, the politician staged his mythological happening. He had a podium for the political elite situated directly against the wall, the numerous feast tables set up on the battle field in the form of an enormous half-circle and a stage set up next to them. This was essentially the topography of the feast. The prime minister himself left no room for doubt that the whole thing was no contingent action of state protocol but rather a consciously organized political staging. In his address opening the feast he presented his concept as follows: in the past several centuries of its long history Armenia suffered painful losses and defeats culminating in the catastrophe of the Great Genocide of 1915. With the Sardarabad victory and the founding of the first independent republic in the year 1918, the formative character of the Battle of Vartanantz for Armenian identity was repeated and the wheel of history had come full-circle. Thus began an era of victories: The end of the twentieth century was marked by the new historical victory of the Arts'akhians and the regaining of independence. With this third Vartanantz, Armenia had entered the third millennium of its Christian history. All signifying Armenianness had gathered in its center – on the ground of the holy Sardarabad field, soaked in the blood of heroes – in order to receive the blessing of the holy mountains and step peacefully together in to the future under the original sign of victory.

The event of 24.09. 1999 cannot be characterized as a PR-event. There was no advertising and the mass media did not take part in the event. No particular echo was felt in the days afterwards in Yerevan. This was lucky for the organizer, since the societal reaction to this »banquet in the times of plague« would certainly have been negative. I would characterize the feast as more of a magical event, as a collective invocation of fate, which suggests clear allusions to the classic fundamental mythologem of the festival. Simply listing to the characteristics of the mythical feast makes the parallel clear.[25] A festival begins with a situation in which the cosmic organization of the world is subject to chaos. The situation can only be saved by a miracle equivalent to the miracle of the first creation. One has to precisely reproduce the precedent that existed »in the beginning« of the cosmos. (Every festival recalls the memory of the genesis). The reproduction of what once occurred is only possible through a precise definition of its spatio-temporal center; that is, one has to locate the time and place where the ordering

---

25   In the next paragraph I rely on the article by Vladimir N. Toporov, »Prazdnik«, in: *Mify narodov mira. Enciklopedia*, Vol. 2 (Moscow: Sovetskaja Enciklopedia, 1988), pp. 329–331, p. 330.

creation first occurred. The parts of the dismembered sacrifice, identified with the elements of the lost cosmos, are re-assembled and given a new unity.

However, the question remains as to what extent the *sparapet* was aware of this mythological constellation. In my opinion he was concerned with his own, purely personal mythologizing and simply modernized the ancient archetypal pattern to the minutest detail. Conceptually, his idea of the nation as »resolute and lonely« one was given clear expression. It was subjectively a completely conscious staging of what the organizer saw as his own triumph, as a convergence of personal fate and the destiny of the people. However, the question arises: how could this success story be further developed after such a *crescendo*, such a *nonplus ultra*? Exactly one month later, on October 27th, 1999, the Prime Minister Vazgen Sargsian and seven other statesmen were murdered in the parliament building in one of the most brutal assassinations in the history of the modern Armenian state.

PR-actions and Presentation of Power

In contrast to the Sardarabad feast, the round dance *shurch par* around Mount Aragats, despite a certain coquetry with religious symbolism on the part of organizers, should be seen as a purely profane event. The topic of the sacred came up in a side-discussion of the question as to whether it was pagan to honor a natural phenomenon, rather than the Lord God, by dancing around a mountain. The ultimate verdict came from the clergy and referred to the lamp hanging over Aragats in heaven in which the tears of St. Gregory Illuminator burn forever instead of oil. With this, the event was shown to be faithfully Christian and the religious problem was solved.

The worldly motives were defined as follows: The Armenian people wished to demonstrate their internal unity and commitment to further struggle as symbolized by the dance around the holy mountain. In order to publicize this unity to the whole outside world, the event was to be documented by aerial photos and entered into the Guinness Book of World Records as the largest round dance in the world. This required an uninterrupted ring of at least 130,000 dancing people, who were to gather around the mountain on May 28th.[26] The arguments of those who opposed the unity dance that it was a waste of money in a land where almost 40% of people lived in poverty were rejected with the justification that this was a private matter that in no way would burden the state budget. Then how can the »hungry people«, the opposition countered, be united with *those* who were capable of financing such an event using private means? Further reproaches against the attorney general, who was considered the main organizer of

---

26   The holiday celebrating the First Republic and the Victory of Sardarabad.

the round dance in his private capacity, were that the dance was merely a further presentation of the power of this man who was on the point of strengthening his own national organization »Nig-Aparan« by mobilizing broad sectors of the population and transforming it into a political party. The population itself remained oddly even-tempered and didn't intervene in the political conflicts. The idea of a unity dance was thus seen generally positively. It was not associated with concrete political personalities and seen more as a rare chance to take an amusing trip for free and at the same time demonstrate the emotional unity of the nation. Why not?

Instead of 130,000, allegedly around 200,000 people took part in the dance. Everything ran smoothly and was copiously propagated through national TV. Yet no aerial photos were shown. Due to a lack of organization the human chain was not entirely closed at all points. There was no more talk about the Guinness Book of World Records.

Disqualification of the »People's Representatives« and the »Presentation of the People«

Tigran Karapetovich' Karapetyan (hereafter referred to as »TKK«) founded the channel ALM (Alternative Information Source) in Yerevan in 2001. The first televised appearances of this elderly Armenian, who had accumulated his formidable wealth somewhere in Russia and now after many years living in Russian surroundings faced distinct difficulties speaking Armenian, came across strangely. The programs of the first few years consisted of long analyses by the owner, usually in Russian, who always appeared personally on the screen in order to discuss a bizarre set of foreign and domestic policy issues. His reasoning – sometimes in a *petit bourgeois* and even »primitive« style, sometimes cynically provocative, perspicacious, or simply dumb – were nonetheless different from the banal official propaganda that one normally received from other channels. The whole work of the channel was organized as a one-man show. Lack of direct communication in the studio was replaced by interactive contact with the audience. In the course of the program TKK answered numerous calls from viewers, whose greeting »good day, Tigran Karapetovitch'« made him famous under this traditionally Russian title in the Armenian public realm. His schoolmasterly responses were at times amicable and benevolent, at times belligerent and purposefully insulting. Since his virtual antagonists never had the chance to continue the conversation live, the calls were gradually omitted, which led to a homogenization and consolidation of the ALM-audience.

Two other matters contributed to a further politicization of the ALM endeavor: the »acquiring« by TKK of a political party (the People's Party of Armenia) that for years had existed only on paper, and the organization by the

ALM of weekly TV debates with current politicians, largely from the opposition. Both of these points remain important today. The opposition politicians, who gladly appeared in the ALM studio due to a lack of TV alternatives, were treated as whipping boys by TKK. The reproaches came in cookie-cutter form: All politicians, those governing as well as those in the opposition, are corrupt, avaricious and power-hungry, they never think of the good of the people and are obsessed with power. The natural goal of every politician, to take power by legal means, was continually »exposed« by TKK as hunger for power. The attempts to explicate the metaphorical and emotional questions of the host and resolve them rationally are marked as the tricks of »a freemason«. The deathblow comes with the question »what concrete things have you personally done for the good of the people?« Answers such as »politicians aren't there to personally solve the concrete everyday problems of individual people« are indignantly and contemptuously condemned. Only very few (if any) succeed in demonstrating to the TKK audience the real relevance of their political activity to the good of simple people. Here it is not only politicians but also *the political* as such that is held under suspicion and wholly disqualified.

TKK contrasts traditional politics with its practical and direct relation to the people. As the chairperson of the »People's Party«, which he has built up and strengthened in the last few years,[27] the media giant visits all regions of the republic with his charitable missions, which always culminate in a folk-festival with eating, drinking, expressions of gratitude from the provincial elite and toasts to the well-being of TKK. There is lots of singing and dancing, and the most »talented« children and youth are rewarded with gifts. The celebrations are typically capped by a collective folk-dance with TKK taking part. In particular cases Tigran Karapetovitch' blesses the gathering by personally singing.[28] Every event of this sort is extensively filmed by ALM and broadcast throughout the country. The ALM music program emerged in close connection with these shows and presents its audience with a series of »young talents« almost every day. The lay artists between the ages of 5 and 25 and without any musical training sing everything that they and their relatives consider music for hours on end. Here as well »the best« are richly praised and rewarded with TKK's personal participation. Despite the loud indignation of the »intelligentsia«, who find that TKK steps all over all extant musical standards and would like to erase all professionalism from society, the program continues to run unhindered in the liberal democratic circumstances of Armenia and retains a formidable number of loyal followers.

In this way the quasi-political activity of TKK encounters the classical representative model of politics, in which politicians and political parties indirectly

---

27 The attempt by this party to move into parliament in 2003 failed, however.
28 A comparison with the famous Russian political clown Zhirinovsky seems appropriate here.

represent the people. For »representation« means an »arbitrary principle of attribution« that creates an »enlightened« relationship between the world of words and the world of things through »intervention of ordering and allocating procedures.«[29] It is this position of »enlightened« politics, understood as the holding of real people at a distance, that TKK resolutely disclaims on the basis of a pre-deliberative intuition.

The magnate, who has distinctly improved his Armenian (he uses urban lingo) in the last years and now presents himself as an »urban guy (k'aïak'i tïa) from the rail way station district«, seeks to found his activity in the opaque and raw fundament of the political: in the people themselves. His successful method is simple: he suspends the professional discourse of politics and wants to talk about the people and to the people, in the language of the people. Through the renunciation of every possible meta-discourse, political representation transforms itself into a simple presentation. This essentially post-modern procedure claims to be a direct presentation of what the people truly are. In fact it shows us no everyday reality – only a costumed staging where everything revolves around the pop star Tigran Karapetovitch'. Yet besides the destructive impulses inherent in this consciously cynical stance towards politics, it is impossible not to recognize the positive effects of healthy common sense in this political para phenomenon. TKK's media entrepreneurship, quite apart from its pragmatic goals, shows concrete people: with their popular notions about what is beautiful and distinguished, with the Barbie clothing their children wear, with their cheap or not so cheap jewelry. It is not the world in which they usually live, but rather the world they would have wished for themselves. It is this ideal of life oriented more towards international kitsch than »ethnic roots«, that most offends the viewers' sensibilities. Yet this segment of the population also belongs to »our« reality, and, after all, should be accounted for in the political process. Ordinary people want to have a place in politics. One would have to guarantee this in some different way – not necessarily in the way that TKK does. Traditional politics as well as the new projects of »representational politics« will not count for very much without considering these people.

Instead of a conclusion, a question needs to be raised. What do the three cases presented above have in common? In fact they embody different ways of replacing rational political discourse with emotionally colored *Lebenswelt* realities. Each of these stagings, whether the legitimization of current politics through a founding myth, the camouflaging of one's own political goals through a re-activation of the emotional »we« identity via mass-events, or the destruction of public political discourse through a quasi-folksy »sole legitimate« simple

---

29   See: Manfred Frank, *Was ist Neostrukturalismus?* (Frankfurt/M.: Suhrkamp, 1984), p. 151.

language, display tendencies that could be further illustrated through other examples.

In light of the simultaneous pre- and post-modern invasion, both forms of modern political discourse (the traditional and the new) lose their official stage. The idea of European modernity is debased to a superficially globalized modernizing procedure that is, incidentally, very much compatible with the exoticism of the ethnic tradition. The use of iconic symbols from both discourses taken out of their contexts plays a specific role in this. The scraps torn out of the regular fabric of discourse now reappear in manifold arbitrary combinations in order to conceal the political vacuum and veil the perverse conditions of »actually existing« social orders.[30] If one wants to reestablish the earnestness of the political, one should limit the benumbing noise of folkloristic garrulousness.

Translated by Karsten Schoellner

---

30   These sort of icons were defined as a »fractal (or viral, radiant) stage of value« by Baudrillard. This »value radiates in all directions, occupying all interstices, without reference to anything whatsoever, by virtue of pure contiguity [...] Properly speaking there is now no law of value, merely a sort of *epidemic of value,* a sort of general metastasis of value, a haphazard proliferation and dispersal of value.« Jean Baudrillard, *The Transparency of Evil* (London, N.Y.: Verso, 1993), p. 5.

Afterword: Representations of the National on the Fringes of Europe

Jörg Baberowski

Representations are manifestations of knowledge. Whenever something is expressed, it manifests itself in symbolic representations. We would not be able to communicate, nor would we understand anything, were we not surrounded by symbolic forms or representations. They allow us to disclose the world that we live in. What we call identity is actually an accomplishment of the practices of representations that show us and others what and who we are. Only those who can identify themselves and others have an identity. But we can relate to human expressions only against the background of situational contexts. We are always part of a symbolic world before we understand ourselves and others. That is the reason why something remains at first misunderstood, if it is not from the world of the known and the familiar. One could also say that representations are culturally variable forms of symbolic disclosure of the world that are only accessible to those who live in the culture the representations arise from. Only in their own cultures humans can develop their selves and have them recognized by their people. In speaking, that which has been said develops a life of its own and it becomes part of a general language shared by all listeners. What has been said »speaks« and thus makes itself comprehensible within a culture. That is why we familiarize ourselves with the world through traditional representations. We want to discover new worlds, but at the same time, we like to keep our world stable. Thus, we depend on our representations to make the unknown known. We transform the alien world into our world – and we are once again within the familiar.

Communication between human beings is only possible where a comprehensive context of understanding exists. If a mutual framework of orientation is missing, this may result in misunderstandings and a breakdown of communication. Herein lies the tension inherent in intercultural communication. Nevertheless, each culture depends on other cultures so as to find reassurance of its representations – and this makes it possible for a culture to observe and transform itself and to resolve through understanding what appeared to be alien. For other cultures simply represent different relations of meaning and as such they are accessible to human understanding. It is true that such understanding does not always occur, but it is feasible because we know that we live within the mode of understanding. Therein lies the importance of symbolic representations for understanding phenomena that we call culture.[1] And that is the subject of the present work; it speaks of the national representations of the Soviet empire's successor states and how the fringes of Europe – the Baltic and Southern Caucasian states – symbolically try to bring themselves into the center of Europe.

The end of the Soviet Union at the beginning of the 1990s also brought an end to imperial legitimations. When it came to legitimizing their nations, the elites in the former Soviet republics looked to Europe. In the meantime, some of the former Soviet republics have become part of the institutional European order: be it as members of the European Union, of NATO or of the Council of Europe. But they had to work hard for that kind of acceptance by subjugating themselves to the interpretive predominance of the Western European elites. What could be said and represented had to be expressed through the notions and images of the hegemonic power of interpretation. For in the hegemonic understanding of the West, the open European fringes belonged to an East that was defined as non-European. The East can only gain acceptance if it silences the East within itself and recognizes the West's dominant forms of representation. According to this dictate of acceptance, the West is a representation of open society, of the constitutional state founded on the rule of law and civil society, of the nation of citizens and of the equality of different people, whereas the East represents the past, tradition, and cultural ethno-nationalism.

The East is a synonym for backwardness. At times, even Soviet intellectuals who imagined themselves to be in Europe thought this way. When the Russian writer Andrei Bitov traveled through Armenia in 1968, he wrote an account of his journey which was also published in full length in German in 2002. In his book, Bitov describes Armenia as a country that represents nothing but the past. To him, Armenia seems like a distant reality, a life turned into tradition. It is the mourning over the loss of the old that lets Armenia appear as a country inhabited by old and wise people living in the past.[2] However, there is no room for Bitov's romanticism in speaking of Europe. In this context, the exotic does not represent a place for mourning over the loss since it is only known as »backwards«.

Those who talk of Europe in Western Europe are usually situated within the mode of self-evidence, »the taken-for-granted«, and not within the mode of self-description. Everyone is convinced that violence, heroes, and communities of descent or fate do not exist any longer in Europe. Why do we have to believe this? Because different interpretations of events are suspected of not being

---

1   See Oswald Schwemmer, »Die Macht der Symbole«, in: *Aus Politik und Zeitgeschichte* 20 (2006), pp. 7–14.

2   Andrej Bitow, *Armenische Lektionen. Eine Reise aus Russland* (Frankfurt am Main: Suhrkamp, 2002).

European – and that is why the elites in the eastern European countries are constantly working on meeting such expectations. They create new images of their own countries, they rewrite history and »discover« that the republics they live in have in reality always been associated with the West of Europe and not with Russia. Historiography is the discipline of legitimation. Although this was also the case before 1991, history is nowadays in the service of national elites who are looking to substantiate their belief that their country has always been European. Outwardly, the post-Soviet states are being »relabeled«, they receive a new image that gains them recognition in Europe and secures them a place in the nation-hierarchy of free market democracies. Inwardly, these ideas have a homogenizing effect by aligning the history of their own country with Europe and remodeling it in such a way that no trace is left of Russia and the empire.

A society of citizens and a civil society can only be established if school lessons are used at the right time to teach the schoolchildren what they do not know yet, as Artur Mkrtychian argues in his contribution. However, this striving for a European impregnation of one's nation doesn't take into account the native culture of those inhabitants who are yet to be convinced of the value of everything European. It is a refutation of history and of people's personal experiences and their experiences of the empire. In this way reconciliation between Europe and »its« East will not be successful.

The elites in the former Soviet republics speak of a new Europe that they want to be part of, but they can only do so under the terms of those who decide what is considered European and what not. Nevertheless, they can not detach themselves from the imperial past that forces them to speak about the present in a different manner to that expected of them by hegemonic European discourse. There are, however, creative ways out of these constraints. The imported European terms can for instance be reinterpreted in the local horizons of comprehension. Nations are changed into families, human rights into rights of males and the elders and democracy is changed into the rule of clans and families. This is the case in the republics of the Southern Caucasus as is highlighted in the contributions of Hrach Bayadan and Florian Muehlfried in this volume.

However, a conflict of ideas occurs where new states represent themselves as cultural nations (*Kulturnationen*) and communities of descent. Such strategies of demarcation and exclusion conflict with the decreed rhetoric of Europe. Those states that violate the discourse are punished with banishment to the »backward« East. But how can the small nations at the Eastern and Southeastern fringes of Europe possibly escape this dilemma? Their representations take place in the mode of history. It is a history of self-assertion that is narrated in the post-Soviet republics, a history of modernization and Europeanization that ends as an act of secession. For only those that left the empire behind and separated themselves from it could make it to Europe – as we see in the case of the cities of Narva and Ivangorod, situated on opposite sides of the Estonian-Russian border. Their official history claims now that the inhabitants of both cities did not know each other, that they belonged to different nations and have different pasts (Olga Brednikova). A Europe that can picture life only as an act of integration has no notion of what it means to become independent. »Everything comes down to the numbers«, says Andrei Bitov.

We are many. We do not have to offer proof to anybody, and why should we, that we exist. Everyone else except us knows that. That is how it is. What is beautiful and honorable and arouses admiration in a small country cannot be transferred to the same extent and with the same logic to a big country.[3]

That is exactly the case here. In the Baltic republics, history has to be narrated as a struggle against suppression, occupation and terror so as to show that the nation consists of victims and heroes. In these representations, Communists are seen as collaborators because the Soviet empire is defined as an occupying power, whereas Estonian soldiers who served in the SS and the *Wehrmacht* are represented as freedom fighters.

In the understanding of the hegemonic model of interpretation, such representations contradict the convention that only such memories may be made public that can claim a place in the European canon. However, those who are part of different traditions and speak of the past will have reasons for judging differently. Do we not know from our own experience that »European« was once understood as a rejection of the Germans? Those who remember the stories about freedom told in Poland and France a few decades ago know that this freedom was always also represented as resistance against the hegemony of the Germans.[4]

All of the post-Soviet nations are confronted with the difficulties that arise from the conflict between cultural nationalism and an open society. Memory gains authority only when it can bring itself into accord with history as it was lived and experienced. That is why the terror that brought an end to national independence lies at the center of the Baltic republic's national representations. It is under these terms that Estonian soldiers who served in the SS and the *Wehrmacht* are seen as resistance fighters.

The empire, in the meantime, has been erased from every possible past, and where it is occasionally mentioned, it appears as a demon. The experiences of occupation have inscribed themselves to such an extent into the people's memories that the Tsarist Empire can only be presented as the enemy. Where the nation-

---

3   Bitow, *Armenische Lektionen*, op.cit. (note 2), p. 179.
4   See Jan Behrends, *Die erfundene Freundschaft. Propaganda für die Sowjetunion in Polen und in der DDR* (Cologne: Böhlau, 2006).

state manifests itself as a refutation of the empire, it denies the imperial identities the right to public representation. The experiences of Russians and Jews whose homeland (*Heimat*) was the empire were excluded from the sponsored national memories. In public memory, the life worlds are nationalized and minorities are marginalized. This is the consequence of the cultural nationalization of multi-ethnic empires.

Nearly all stories about the nation and its heroes told in the post-Soviet republics are attempts to erase the empire from the collective memory or to demonize it. But these stories reveal more about the legacy of the empire than one might think. For what appears in various forms as national representation is instantly understood by everyone in the spaces of the collapsed empire.

Nowhere is the legacy of the empire more visible than in Central Asia and the Southern Caucasus, where the national is combined with Soviet staging to create something new. The official memory is no refutation but a continuous re-writing of Soviet possibilities – for it was the Communist leadership in Moscow that allowed the Armenians in 1965 to erect a memorial site in commemoration of the genocide in 1915. The memorial site was opened in 1967. It resembled in style the Soviet sites for heroes that were set up all over the Soviet Union during the 1960s in commemoration of the Second World War. With the opening of the Armenian memorial site, the central state tried to link the memory of the genocide to a Soviet history and ritualize the commemoration in a Soviet mode. But it provided Armenian nationalists with a site that told of the singularity of the Armenian victimized nation and allowed for local Communists to gain national legitimation by referring to the genocide. Such compromises between center and periphery were possible where nationalism was not suspected of turning into separatism. The aggressions of Armenian nationalism were directed at a state beyond the Soviet border, not at the empire and its strategies of homogenization. Therefore, even during Stalin's time, the Armenian Communists could dismiss all attempts of the central state to de-nationalize their history and literature as happened in the Ukraine.

After 1991, the post-Soviet governments and national movements in Armenia could follow Soviet experience. The memorial site in commemoration of the genocide remained the central meeting place for the national movement after 1991. No one would have thought of building another site to mourn the loss. Instead, new meanings were attached to the Soviet monuments, and the genocide was talked of in such a language that also made it possible for the Armenian diaspora to find its place in the ritual of commemoration. While in the Baltic republics the Soviet memorial sites, especially the war memorials, were seen as an impertinence and provocation by the occupying power, in the Southern Caucasian republics they can apparently be easily combined with different sorts of national discourses of memory (see the contributions of Tsypylma Darieva and Maike Lehmann).[5]

In all of the post-Soviet republics, the elites speak of nations, and they only speak of the empire when recalling the suffering of their nations. However, these tales of woe are usually variations of Soviet narrative traditions. In the Soviet multi-ethnic empire that had redesigned itself since the early 1920s as a nation-state, every subject had to belong to a nation. Some nations had their own republic and capital. Those nations that did not have their own republic were entitled to the status of a national minority. For each nation there existed a national language, a national history and a national territory that belonged only to that particular nation and to no other. The Bolsheviks nationalized the empire, they assigned their subjects to advanced and backward, friendly and hostile nations, and gave them different rights and privileges. Socialism was a modernization project that materialized itself in nations. One could also say that the Bolsheviks sovietized nations. And since the subjects' places within Soviet society also depended on their nationality, stereotypes of cultural nationalism inscribed themselves into Soviet daily life. It was the signum of Stalinist socialism that it spoke of cultural homogenization, but insisted upon the cultural and ethnic differences of its subjects. Thus, in the end, the imagined enemies of the Bolshevik order were also assigned to ethnic collectives. Enemies were visible, one could recognize them by their language and physiognomy and one could, if one participated in the discrimination against them, obtain privileges.[6]

The Stalinist deportations and stigmatizations left profound traces in the societies of the Soviet Union. Hence, ethnocentrism, the belief that one's own nation is singular and superior to other nations, and xenophobia are part of the legacy of the Bolsheviks' experiment. The Europeans of the Old Europe were thought to have left all of this behind – and that is why they reject ethnocentrism and the cultural formation of nations. But how can Estonians, Latvians, Armenians or Chechens stop being what they are if their national peculiarity expresses itself in being stigmatized victims? This kind of ethnocentrism will not simply vanish all of a sudden from people's lives in the post-Soviet republics with their arrival in Europe.

In Armenia, Azerbaijan, Estonia, Latvia and Lithuania, the nationalist move-

---

5   See also Arnold Bartetzky, Marina Dmitrieva & Stefan Troebst (eds.), *Neue Staaten – neue Bilder? Visuelle Kultur im Dienst staatlicher Selbstdarstellung in Zentral- und Osteuropa seit 1918* (Cologne: Böhlau, 2005).

6   See for an overview: Jörg Baberowski, »Stalinismus und Nation. Die Sowjetunion als Vielvölkerreich 1917–1953«, in: *Zeitschrift für Geschichtswissenschaft* 3 (2006), pp. 199–213; Ronald G. Suny & Terry Martin (eds.), *A State of Nations. Empire and Nation-Making in the Age of Lenin and Stalin* (Oxford: Oxford University Press, 2001); Terry Martin, *The Affirmative Action Empire. Nations and Nationalism in the Soviet Union, 1923–1939* (Ithaca: Cornell University Press, 2001).

ments merged with the democratic movements. The national movement that fought for the independence of Nagorno-Karabakh from Azerbaijan was the beginning of the end of Soviet dictatorship, as Harutyun Marutyan argues in his contribution. It turned subjects into citizens and mobilized the nation in a democratic direction. War and violence, says Harutyun Marutyan, confirmed national certainties both in Azerbaijan and Armenia and led people to organize themselves politically. In the Baltic republics, democratic self-affirmation also appeared in the national mode. The continuation of Soviet ethnocentrism is in this case a representation of the people's will and democracy. However, no one in the Europe of the Western Europeans wants this kind of democracy – which results in the new Europe being a Europe with a West and an East.

It is at this point that historians and anthropologists get involved to tell us about the diversity of representations and their roots and thus contribute to the understanding of what is not understood, an understanding which is needed more than ever in the new Europe. For the European project will only be successful if it manages to live with differences in such a way that all forms of life are legitimate. The realization that integration of the new is not possible under the terms of the old Europe constitutes a precondition for the success of the European project. How different stories about the fringe of Europe can arise from a diversity of perspectives is what the contributions in this volume show. For even in academic disciplines, there is no unambiguity. Grounded in »thick description«, anthropologists tell us of the meaning that people attach to their actions and they lead us into fields of encounters and contexts of understanding within which these actions take place.[7] Historians search for causes – and from time to time, they tend to forget that they are the ones who give their stories a beginning and a corresponding end. Anthropologists do not speak of a beginning and an end and rarely of origins. They talk of events and phenomena and they describe those in such a way that one understands how human beings act in different situations. It is above all Tsypylma Darieva's contribution that lets the readers understand how the commemoration of the genocide in Armenia has changed in the process of cultural practice. No interpretation of texts can accomplish what a thick description of cultural practices of human beings can achieve.

However, we will be able to gain a better understanding of such practices and their meanings if we know in which traditions the people we are describing are grounded, to which history they belong, and which tales they have been told in the past. Humanity's expressions are always bound to a particular space and locality. And we need historians who locate this space, who tell us under which

---

7   Martin Fuchs & Eberhard Berg, »Phänomenologie der Differenz. Reflexionsstufen ethno-graphischer Repräsentation«, in: *Kultur, soziale Praxis, Text. Die Krise der ethnographischen Repräsentation*, ed. by Martin Fuchs & Eberhard Berg (Frankfurt am Main: Suhrkamp, 1999), 3rd Edition, pp. 11–108.

constraints people have to live and what this has to do with their past. That is what, above all, Maike Lehmann and David Feest speak of in their contributions, letting the thick descriptions appear in a different light. One understands the practices of memory in Estonia much better if one understands that not only Stalinist terror, but also the destruction of the Estonian nation preceding the German occupation. We find out that life existed before the memory and that this memory could not be imagined or presented without it.

Historians and anthropologists gain their perspectives through the interests of the present. Therefore, their perspectives are various. What matters is that one identifies the place from which one speaks about oneself so that it becomes clear why something is considered right while something else is considered wrong. That is also one aspect that the book reveals to its readers, for it also lets those speak who write about their subject as if they were one with the people that they describe. History is a discipline of legitimation and a medium of self-ascertainment – at least that is how it still seems in some of the contributions of Armenian historians and anthropologists in this volume. It is within this challenging context of anthropology and history, self-description and external description, that we should rethink nation, nationalism and their representations. The contributions in this volume have shown that the final word on this matter has not yet been spoken.

Translated by Franziska Exeler

Notes on the Contributors

Levon Abrahamian received his Ph.D. degree in social anthropology from the Institute of Ethnography (presently Institute of Ethnology and Anthropology) in Moscow in 1978. Currently he heads the Department of Contemporary Anthropological Studies at the Institute of Archaeology & Ethnography, National Academy of Sciences of Armenia, and also teaches special courses in social anthropology at the Yerevan State University. Among his recent publications are »Armenian Folk Arts, Culture, and Identity« (co-editor – Nancy Sweezy, 2001) and »Armenian Identity in a Changing World«, 2006.

Jörg Baberowski is Professor of East European History at the Humboldt University Berlin. His research focuses on the history of political violence and statehood in communist Russia and the Caucasus. His recent publications include »Der Feind ist überall. Stalinismus im Kaukasus«, 2003; »Der Sinn der Geschichte. Geschichtstheorien von Hegel bis Foucault« 2005; »Ordnung durch Terror. Gewaltexzesse im nationalsozialistischen und stalinistischen Imperium« (in cooperation with Anselm Döring-Manteuffel, 2006).

Hrach Bayadyan is a cultural critic and teaches cultural studies at the Yerevan State University. His research focuses on the social and cultural implications of information and communication technologies. He has written on the relationship between culture and technology and on the post-Soviet media. His recent publications include: »Culture and Technology«, 2003; »Development and Dissemination of Information and Communication Technologies in Armenia«, 2005.

Olga Brednikova is a senior research fellow at the Centre for Independent Social Research in St.Petersburg. Her research interests focus on ethnicity and economy, migration and borderlands studies in postsocialist societies. Her many writings include »›Caucasians‹ in St. Petersburg: Life in Tension«, Anthropology & Archeology of Eurasia, 2003; »›Schmutziges‹ Dorf und ›vermüllte‹ Stadt«, Berliner Debatte Initial, 2004.

Karsten Brüggemann has studied History and Slavic Literature in Hamburg and Leningrad. Currently he is a lecturer at the Narva College of Tartu University in Narva/Estonia and a post doc research fellow at the Nordost-Institut, Lüneburg/Germany. His research project is focused on Russian Baltic discourses in the 19th and 20th centuries. His publications include »Die Gründung der Republik Estland und das Eine und Unteilbare Russland«; »Die Petrograder Front des Russischen Bürgerkriegs 1918-1920«, 2002 and »Von Sieg zu Sieg, von Krieg zu Krieg. Motive des sowjetischen Mythos im Massenlied der 1930er Jahre«, 2002.

Tsypylma Darieva received her PhD in Anthropology at the Humboldt University in Berlin in 2002 and recently was a fellow at the Max-Planck Institute for Social Anthropology, Halle (Germany). Currently she is a postdoctoral research fellow at the Collaborative Research Centre »Changing Representations of Social Order«, Humboldt University Berlin. Her research interests are focused on migration, transnationalism, memory and media in Eurasia. She is the author of »Russkij Berlin. Migranten und Medien in Berlin und London«, 2004; »Recruiting for the Nation. Transnational Migrants in Germany and Kazakhstan«, 2005.

Dace Dzenovka is social anthropologist and is currently completing her PhD thesis at the University of California, Berkeley. Her interests in research are subject formation and difference, liberalism and multiculturalism, postsocialism and governmentality. Her most recent publication is on »Remaking the Nation of Latvia: Anthropological Perspectives on Nation-Branding«, in Place Branding, 1(2) 2005.

David Feest completed his PhD thesis in Eastern European History on the sovietization of Estonian villages in 2003 and has been awarded the Epstein Prize in 2006. Currently he is a postdoctoral research fellow and the coordinator of the Collaborative Research Centre (*SFB 640*) »Changing Representations of Social Order«, Humboldt University Berlin. He has conducted research focused on nation building processes, the history of terror, violence and statehood in Tsarist Russia. His recent articles include »Terror und Gewalt auf dem estnischen Dorf«, in: Osteuropa 6 (2000); »Neo-korenizacija in den baltischen Sowjetrepubliken? Die Kommunistische Partei Estlands nach dem Zweiten Weltkrieg«, 2006.

Wolfgang Kaschuba is Professor of European Ethnology and Director of the Institute for European Ethnology at the Humboldt University in Berlin since 1994. He has published numerous papers and conducted extensive research focused on national and ethnic identities, urban studies, the history of knowledge and science, and everyday life and culture in European modernity. His most recent books include »Die Überwindung der Distanz. Zeit und Raum in der europäischen Moderne« (2005) and »Einführung in die Europäische Ethnologie«, 1999, 2. edition 2003.

Maike Lehmann studied history and philosophy at the Eberhard-Karls Univeristy (Tübingen) and at the University College London. Currently she is a fellow at the Collaborative Research Centre »Changing Representations of Social Order«, Humboldt University Berlin. Her research focuses on negotiation of national identities under Soviet power in Armenia. A recent publication is »The Sacred Lands of our Motherland! – Memory, Myth and Landscape in Popular Representations of Armenian Identity«, 2006.

Harutyun Marutyan is Senior Researcher at the Department of Contemporary Anthropological Studies of the Institute of Archaeology and Ethnography at the National Academy of Sciences, Armenia. He received his PhD in Cultural Anthropology at the Institute of Ethnography in Moscow in 1984. He has been an IREX/RSEP and a Fulbright research fellow in 1998 at the University of Michigan, Ann Arbor, and in 2003-2004 at the MIT, Cambridge, USA. His recent publications include »The Interior of the Armenian National Dwellings (Second Half of the XIX - Beginning of the XX century«, 1989 (in Russian); »Stories on Poverty«, 2001.

Artur Mkrtychian recieved his PhD in Sociology at the Yerevan State University in 1998 and currently holds the chair of sociology at the Yerevan State University. He was a fellow at the University of Bielefeld and the Humboldt University Berlin. His main research interests are transformation, migration and ethnopolitical conflicts. He has published many articles, among them »Die Globalisierung ethnopolitischer Konflikte«, 2003. He is a co-editor of the »Armenia: A Human Rights Perspective for Peace and Democracy«, 2005.

Florian Mühlfried currently works as a post doc fellow at the Max Planck Institute for Social Anthropology in Halle, Germany. After having defended his PhD thesis on »Post-Soviet Feasting – The Georgian Banquet in Transition« (published in German in 2006), Mühlfried lectured Social Anthropology at the Tbilisi State University in Georgia supported by a grant from the Academic Fellowship Program of the Open Society Foundation Europe.

Bahodir Sidikov studied oriental languages, history and geography at the St. Petersburg State University, Russia. He received his PhD at the Martin-Luther University Halle-Wittenberg (Institute of Oriental Studies) in 2003. He was a research fellow at the Free University Berlin Osteuropa-Institut and is currently a research fellow at the Institute of Oriental Studies in Halle, Germany. He is the author of »Eine unermessliche Region. Deutsche Bilder und Zerrbilder von Mittelasien 1852–1914«, as well as several articles on Central Asia and the Caucasus.

Asta Vonderau studied European Ethnology and Scandinavian Studies at the University of Vilnius, University of Copenhagen and Humboldt University Berlin. Currently she is a PhD Student at the Department of European Ethnology Humboldt University Berlin and a scholarship holder of the Heinrich Böll foundation researching the lifestyles and consumer identities of the ›new elites‹ in Lithuania. She is the author of »Geographie Sozialer Beziehungen. Ortserfahrungen in der mobilen Welt«, 2003.

Ashot Voskanian received his PhD in Philosophy in 1983 at the Yerevan State University. Former Ambassador of the Republic of Armenia in Germany, he is currently Adviser to the Foreign Minister of Armenia on issues of European integration, and a co-operation partner at the Department for European Ethnology, Humboldt University Berlin, SFB 640. He has published numerous articles and edited the volume »Armenia on the Way to Europe«, 2005.

Index of Geographical and Political Names

List of Figures

Social Science

Stefani Scherer, Reinhard Pollak, Gunnar Otte, Markus Gangl (Hg.)
FROM ORIGIN TO DESTINATION
Trends and Mechanisms in Social Stratification Research
2007 · 323 p. · ISBN 978-3-593-38411-5

Johannes Harnischfeger
DEMOCRATIZATION AND ISLAMIC LAW
The Sharia Conflict in Nigeria
2007 · 260 p. · ISBN 978-3-593-38256-2

Helmut Willke
SMART GOVERNANCE
Governing the Global Knowledge Society
2007 · 206 p. · ISBN 978-3-593-38253-1

Michael Dauderstädt, Arne Schildberg (eds.)
DEAD ENDS OF TRANSITION
Rentier Economies and Protectorate
2006 · 249 p. · ISBN 978-3-593-38154-1

Magdalena Nowicka
**TRANSNATIONAL PROFESSIONALS
AND THEIR COSMOPOLITAN UNIVERSES**
2006 · 280 p. · ISBN 978-3-593-38155-8

Sonja Puntscher Riekmann, Monika Mokre, Michael Latzer (eds.)
THE STATE OF EUROPE
Transformations of Statehood from a European Perspective
2004 · 358 p. · ISBN 978-3-593-37632-5

campus
Frankfurt · New York